A volume
in
THE DOCUMENTARY HISTORY
of
WESTERN CIVILIZATION

THE LONG GENERATION

Germany from Empire to Ruin, 1913–1945

The
Long
Generation

Germany from Empire to Ruin,
1913–1945

edited by

HENRY CORD MEYER

WALKER AND COMPANY
New York

First published in the United States of America
in 1973 by the Walker Publishing Company, Inc.

Published simultaneously in Canada by Fitzhenry &
Whiteside, Limited, Toronto.

Library of Congress Catalog Card Number: 72-95796

ISBN: 0-8027-2054-4

Printed in the United States of America

Volumes in this series are published in association
with Harper & Row, Publishers, Inc., from
whom paperback editions are available in Harper
Torchbooks.

For Hank, Chris, and Jane:
"There is within us a basic human substance which changes less than is sometimes imagined."

Anatole France

Acknowledgments

I am particularly indebted to Mrs. Agnes F. Petersen of the Hoover Institution, Stanford, California, for consultations and assistance with bibliographical details. My colleague, Professor Jon S. Jacobson, was ever-helpful in scanning material and text.

Valuable translation assistance was given by Evelyn Champagne, Gunter Mende, George Harlow Mills, and John T. Walker.

Finally, I appreciate the painstaking typing of Mrs. Mary Stechow, Mrs. Betty Beth, and Miss Dee Gerald.

Villa Serbelloni
Bellagio, Italy
October 1972

Contents

Introduction

"I AM leading you towards wonderful times!" Boasting and exuberant, William II, by God's grace king of Prussia and emperor of Germany, gave this message to the German people at the opening of the twentieth century. Some years later, in the celebrations of the twenty-fifth anniversary of his reign, that spirit was dampened by public awareness of internal tensions and deteriorating foreign relationships. Yet Germany was then, indeed, riding a crest of power and prosperity.

Sixty-five million citizens of the Reich thronged a dozen of the largest cities of Europe, worked in the most modern industrial plants of the Western world or tilled the land with intensive agriculture. From the birch forests of East Prussia to the vineyards of the Rhine valley, from the rusticity of the Bavarian Alps to the maritime industry of Bremen and Hamburg, a network of railroads, canals, and telegraphs integrated the historic regions of Germany into a pulsating national and economic enterprise. But industrialization had not produced national and cultural uniformity. Regional traditions were deeply rooted and still influential in the presence of the relatively recent ties of national enthusiasm and political unification. Religious differences and attitudes dating from the Reformation were the strongest bastion of tradition. Northern, central, and eastern Germany were preponderantly Protestant; western and southern Germany were strongholds of Catholicism. Diversity in unity was explicit in the persistence of local dialects and customs alongside the use of high German and expressions of national patriotism. Only in the next fifty years would mechanical standardization, Nazi ideological conformity, and the disasters of war distort and partially destroy this many-splendored pattern of the old and the new.

Several groups of minorities, however, were not included in the German variation of the arrogant European nationalism of that era. Most numerous were the Poles of Prussia, a million of them wedged between Brandenburg and East Prussia and a thorn in the

Prussian-German side for several generations. Forty years after the Franco-Prussian War, half a million French in Alsace-Lorraine still thwarted efforts to digest them into imperial Germany. In Schleswig-Holstein thousands lived in irritation over severance from their fellow Danes. Each of these peoples remained generally in a cohesive group in their particular border area. A fourth minority, by contrast, was spread throughout the middle-class urban culture of the Reich. These were the half-million Jews, descendants of forbears released from the restraints of their ghettos barely a century before. From their point of view they had accomplished a remarkable feat of integration. Their influence far outranked their limited numbers in enterprise, the professions, and cultural creativity. And yet barriers persisted; they were not fully equal citizens. The aristocracy and higher ranks of the military were closed to them; the imperial bureaucracy offered only limited opportunities; and almost everywhere in German society they sensed latent, if not open, anti-Semitism. Minority problems would continue to haunt the German scene. The Poles, French, and Danes would separate in 1918 to join their larger national groups. The tensions they had raised in German minds and behavior would be transferred to another minority, the millions of Germans living outside the redrawn borders of the Reich in 1919. The people of the Jewish minority left within Germany would become hostages to fanaticism and fate. Only after 1945 would most Germans of *Mitteleuropa* finally be living together, without troublesome minority problems, in a shattered and internally divided community.

The burgeoning German economy aroused wonder and envy. Production of coal, iron, and other heavy industrial materials increased steadily in quantity and value; from 1902 onward the Reich was the greatest steel producer in Europe. Lighter industry, electrical products, and consumer goods grew even more rapidly during the prewar decade. Scientific research and technological innovation improved the quality and desirability of German products. The Reich led the world in dyes, pharmaceuticals, and other sophisticated items of industrial chemistry. In 1913 Professor Fritz Haber perfected a process for extracting nitrogen from the air, thus liberating German armaments from dependence on imports of nitrates from overseas and giving further impetus to development of the synthetics industry. Germany's world trade almost doubled between 1900 and 1914. Her merchant marine ran a close race with

England, from fleets of freighters to giant liners competing for speed records and the profitable passenger trade of the North Atlantic. By 1914 Berlin was the world's third largest capital investor: twenty-three billion marks were placed abroad, notably in North and South America, Austria-Hungary, Africa, Turkey, and Russia. The German colonial empire, not yet a generation old, gave promise of great future wealth, particularly in Africa. Like a great heart, the German economy pulsed in the center of Europe, importing a full third of Reich requirements for food and fodder as well as the strategic raw materials it lacked, and exporting a rich diversity of finished goods and services. From this process Germany derived much of her confidence, strength, and power.

In contrast to her sophisticated economic relationships with the wider world, Germany's stance in power politics showed barefaced militarism in the saddle of affairs. Rooted in Prussian and conservative traditions, the spirit and authority of the greatest European army enjoyed unquestioned prestige and privilege among the German people. More recently Germany had added a powerful navy and was building a fleet of impressive Zeppelins. Obviously all the European nations contributed to the rising fever of competitive armaments, but Germany was particularly visible in the race. She had the unfavorable identity of being both the youngest and most vigorous of the great powers. Her position in the heart of Europe placed extra defensive demands upon her that were resolved by creating aggressive military plans which inevitably became known to her neighbors. Finally, the rapid construction and technological superiority of the high seas fleet gave ominous promise of yet more to come from German scientific and industrial genius in the service of militarism.

To preserve this combination of economic interdependence with her neighbors and military independence from them, would have required a cautious and astute foreign policy. Unfortunately for Germany and for Europe, both were lacking in the reign of William II. Caution was hardly the tone in the aggressive and tactless poses of the emperor, while his three most important civilian advisers on foreign policy contributed only to a succession of brilliant miscalculations (Holstein), clever failures (Bülow), and inept crisis management (Bethmann-Hollweg). From a position of real independence and significant influence at the turn of the century, Germany had slipped by 1914 to isolation in middle

Europe, dominating and yet depending upon the uncertain strength and policies of the tension-ridden Hapsburg monarchy. The Germans, and particularly William II, increasingly interpreted this isolation as the result of aggressive policies of "encirclement" by Britain, France, and Russia. Decision making in Berlin became in turn apprehensive and nervous, boastfully confident in periodic illusions of military strength or fatefully resigned to a test of arms in context of unflinching loyalty to Vienna. This condition was obscured from view by the affluence and cultural vitality of the empire and by impressive parades of its military strength. Yet, by the summer of 1914 Germany had virtually no options open and would fall prey to exaggerated international antagonisms, psychological panic of its leadership, and the relentless demands of pre-planned military timetables.

What influence did the German parliament and political parties have upon the great decisions of internal and foreign policy? At first glance Germany looked like a properly functioning constitutional monarchy. But appearances deceived. The Bismarckian parliamentary structure of 1871 was still intact: a relatively powerless Reichstag, an upper house dominated by ultraconservative Prussia, and executive authority concentrated in the king-emperor and his agencies. While other states of the German Empire were slowly democratizing regional government, Prussia held to its reactionary three-class voting system and throttled all German political modernization. The Reich had no responsible cabinet system; chancellors came and went at pleasure of the crown. Yet, the Reichstag was composed of modern political parties that tried to exercise a full range of parliamentary functions. The three conservative parties generally held together on major issues. The powerful Catholic Center party combined a broader social spectrum with defense of church interests, and the Social Democrats by 1912 had become the single largest party in the Reich. Year by year, in local, state, and national elections, these parties faithfully mirrored the changing political and sociological patterns of Germany; yet they could not translate the strength and character of their numbers into significant parliamentary action. On two crucial issues, in 1908 and 1913, the Reichstag voted no confidence in the government, but no changes were made. By 1914 there was broad criticism of Reichstag impotence and delays in Prussian electoral reform, and the Reich was on the verge of a fundamental constitutional crisis.

Imperial Germany probably had an apt symbol in William II. He vacillated between efforts to be a popular, quasi-parliamentary monarch and emphatic public reaffirmations of his divine-right status. His forced, rather than forceful, personality was equally at home on the bridge of a battleship or in the saddle with his Prussian cavalry regiment. He accepted praise from an impenetrable circle of admirers for German technological accomplishments as though they were his own work. The strong materialistic industrialism of his era was suffused with an aura of dynastic romanticism. Germany and her emperor alternately posed and threatened in their foreign relationships, confusing rank opportunism with statesmanship. Both combined qualities of the hard-working, youthful extrovert with a sense of historic Prussian German political destiny and cultural superiority. Both were confident of their immediate accomplishments, insensitive to many of the reactions they aroused in Europe, and prone to instability in crises.

Thus Germany entered upon the fateful days of June–July 1914. The larger factors contributing to the war were common to all nations: imperialistic and political rivalries, arrogant nationalism increasingly whipped up by an irresponsible popular press, a vigorous armaments race expressing convictions that certain matters of honor could be resolved only by war, and patterns of entangling alliance commitments supported by elaborate plans for rapid mobilization. Germany made three particular contributions to the crisis. First, she pressed Austria to crush Serbia and win a brief, local war. Second, when Vienna's actions raised the promise of a general European conflict, Germany's civilian leadership erred about, seeking some political solution that would not produce a loss of prestige. Third, increasingly the German military pressed for action lest Berlin lose the advantage of the Schlieffen Plan. In a few days the civilians were pushed aside, other European arms responded to the violation of Belgium, and a shaken Kaiser proclaimed from his palace balcony: "I no longer recognize any political parties, only Germans!"

The First World War was a major turning point in German history. Quite contrary to expectations, the worldwide imperial network of commerce and communications was abruptly shattered. The impressive military planning failed: the great armies bogged down in trenches, and the vaunted navy held to the protection of its harbors. By Christmas of 1914 Germany was blockaded and isolated with her weak Viennese ally in middle Europe. The ingenuity of German science filled some of the pressing needs, but generally belts were drawn tighter and controls increased. From 1915 onward Germany accelerated toward a totalitarian war system: the needs of civilians and traditional habits of a peacetime economy were ruthlessly altered and subjugated to the demands of the military fronts.

Initially the working classes stood with other Germans to wage what appeared as a struggle of self-defense and national survival. But as the demands of the conflict and its losses grew to staggering proportions, certain questions became insistent: What were the aims of the war? Who ruled Germany and to what end? How could the mounting death and privation be ended? In various ways these questions were raised in the Reichstag, discussed in the press and expressed in political activity. Conservatives and much of the bourgeoisie supported the Kaiser and military high command as the only way to victory or survival of traditional Germany. The Social Democrats split into a perturbed majority and a more radical Leninist minority. The winter of 1917–1918 brought both triumph and despair to the Reich: Russia was beaten, and all efforts were concentrated on an early knockout blow in the west before the Americans arrived; but it was the worst winter ever on the home front with starvation, strikes, and war-weary agitation for peace. By summer the great offensive had failed, and in early autumn Berlin's Bulgarian ally collapsed, opening the way for invasion of the exhausted and disintegrating Austro-Hungarian monarchy. Knowing that they were beaten, the generals called for immediate peace.

Revolution was at the door, strange and abortive though it would be. William II had lost all spirit and placed full reliance upon the military, especially Generals von Hindenburg and Ludendorff, who had dictated all major decisions in the later years of the war regardless of the Reichstag and ineffective civilian chancellors. Now the generals thrust full responsibility upon the civilians, who were unprepared for the abrupt transition and were to be held accountable for the way they ended Germany's role in the most destructive war of history. A moderate aristocrat, Prince Max of Baden, wrestled briefly with circumstance: workers' unrest grew in the cities; Woodrow Wilson vowed he would negotiate only with a republic; and mutiny broke out in the rusting German navy. Faced with civil war at home and imminent invasion from abroad, William II abdicated and fled to Holland. The Reich was at the mercy of events.

Thereupon followed three months of chaos. The moderate Socialists proclaimed a republic, but their power was precarious. Competing groups of radicals captured control of various areas of the nation or sectors of German society, at times drawing support from Moscow. Local councils of workers and soldiers vied for power with emerging democratic institutions. In the meanwhile a hastily gathered delegation concluded an armistice with the enemy, and the masses of German armies abroad began streaming home. Tensions and rivalries increased between the moderate Socialists and more radical groups, notably the Independent Socialists. The former feared a coup like the Leninist revolution in Russia, and the latter suspected "betrayal of the revolution" by the moderates. With left-wing evolutionary socialism facing a possible dictatorship of the proletariat, Chancellor Friedrich Ebert of the interim government tried to assure continuity and public order by seeking support from the demobilizing army command. The Independents and other radicals took to the streets in the Spartacist revolt of January 1919. The army supported the government in a bloody suppression of the uprising. Further flurries of revolt would occur in Germany, but the major threat was contained. On January 19, millions of Germans voted by universal suffrage to send some four hundred delegates to frame a new constitution for the Reich.

While the Constituent Assembly was building the structure of a new republic at Weimar, the victorious Allies prepared their peace terms for imposition upon the Germans. The conditions were very severe. The loss of Alsace-Lorraine was a sharp blow to German pride, but the frontiers of the new state of Poland caused constant and massive irritation. The Polish Corridor separated East Prussia from the Reich. Danzig was cut off as a so-called free city, and over a million Germans became subjects of Warsaw. The military and naval power of the Reich was drastically reduced and placed under Allied control, allegedly as a first step toward general European disarmament. Germany lost her colonial empire, her merchant marine, and overseas capital investment; and she was saddled with a huge reparations debt that would require two generations for payment. Once the strongest state on the continent, Germany was reduced to a third-rate power.

The effects of the Versailles Treaty, and reactions to it, were complicated and far-reaching. First, there was a sense of infuriating humiliation. In addition to all of their losses, the Germans were required to acknowledge sole responsibility for starting the war (Article 231). Second, there was a sense of betrayal: idealists and opponents of Prussian autocracy who had embraced Wilson's Fourteen Points were outraged; conservatives and nationalists were strengthened in their hostility, cynicism, and bitterness. Third, the real and lasting sting of the treaty lay in its economic clauses: the Reich was crushed as a commercial competitor in world markets, and its potential recovery was hobbled by the reparations schedules. Thus the nascent German Republic came to life as an economic cripple and with the psychologically deforming birth scar of the Versailles treaty. Yet Germany remained intact, with great potential, and surrounded by small, vulnerable states and the weakened nations of France and Russia.

In less than a year the Germans had taken three massive psychological blows: the rapid breakdown of their apparently victorious armies, the unanticipated collapse of the autocratic empire, and an unexpectedly punitive peace settlement. Any government that had to deal with these events and their resulting problems was bound to have difficulties. The delegates at Weimar considered rejecting the treaty and resuming a hopeless struggle, but saner counsel prevailed —to be vilified by the opponents of the republic. Conservatives, the military hierarchy, and nationalists could never accept the basic ideas or actions of the Weimar Republic. They considered it an institutionalization of treason, radical social change, appeasement of Germany's enemies, and of corrupting Jewish influences. The Socialists and Communists could never rid themselves of the tainted myth (later popularized by the Nazis) that they had stabbed the hard-fighting, loyal army and navy in the back. As "Marxists" they were further accused of seeking the final overthrow of all fine, traditional German values. Catholics and Democrats were added as collaborators in the Allied looting of the German economy. And the Jews were seen as leaders in all of these activities. As of 1919 these warped attitudes were already outspokenly evident; the Nazis would make them pervasive in Germany by 1933.

The new government of Germany was a blend of innovation and tradition. The Weimar constitution combined democracy and parliamentary government with a high degree of centralization. The historic German states remained as instruments of regional government, but Berlin established supremacy clearly over them. Prussia lost its preponderant prewar role, though still the largest state and now in republican hands it had major influence. The Reichstag was the focus of political activity, its members elected by universal suffrage, men and women, in proportional representation. Executive authority was vested in a powerful president elected by popular vote; the emergency powers given to this office were to prove fateful between 1930 and 1933. Though the political structure was new, some of its basic procedures continued on virtually unchanged from prewar times. The overdeveloped party structures and ideologies continued to overshadow individuals and impede the necessary pragmatism of political maneuver and compromise. Law and the legal system carried over without significant change. Most important of all, the personalities, procedures, and attitudes of the broad imperial bureaucracy continued into the republic with hardly a ripple of adjustment. If there was something of a new blood in the body politic, it would not flow easily through these old veins.

Instability was a constant threat to the Weimar Republic in its early years. The voters split into six major parties and other national or regional splinter groups. After every election a coalition cabinet had to be constructed; often the government rested on tenuous political compromise not even representing a majority of the Reichstag membership and hostage to votes of no confidence. Successive chancellors and ministers had to tread cautiously; forthright personalities or policies had a low survival rate. The inherent political instability was heightened by outbreaks of unrest. Tension was rife all along the eastern borders of the Reich. Germans now had strong emotional sympathies with *their* minorities in the new, postwar victor states of central Europe. Demobilized war veterans joined regional groups of Germans as volunteers or mercenaries in various Free Corps units that fought against communism in the Baltic states, against the Lithuanians in Memel, and against the Poles in East Prussia and Upper Silesia. When those ventures were over, many of these activists trekked back into the Reich, ready fuel for other political fires. Groups of them participated in the Kapp *putsch* of 1920, an abortive conservative coup that caused the government to flee, but was broken by resolute Socialist strikes. There was growing unrest in the Ruhr over reparations deliveries; in

1923 the French occupied the industrial basin to guarantee the flow of goods. Politically motivated murders took hundreds of lives, notably those of Erzberger and Rathenau, both prominent political leaders who had signed the armistice. During 1923 there were Communist uprisings in Saxony, French-sponsored separatist conspiracies in the Rhineland, and the Hitler *putsch* in Munich. Free Corps patriots and nihilists participated in all these events as supporters or opponents and became the nucleus of the budding storm troopers. Could democracy survive in Germany?

The German economy deteriorated disastrously. The victors found it difficult enough to reconvert to normal production; the even more regimented war economy of the Reich had to readjust to a postwar era that was neither peaceful nor normal. The Allied economic blockade continued in full force until the treaty was signed in mid-1919, while German material reserves were conveyed to the victors under the immediate terms of the armistice. The mark, one of the world's strongest currencies in 1914, had little international validity because German commerce was destroyed and her treasury burdened with a multibillion internal war debt. Unemployment mounted as the soldiers returned and the nation sagged into a subsistence economy. The full sum of reparations was finally calculated in 1920; for the next two years payments were met by some earnings from exports and exhaustion of the last acceptable financial reserves. Accelerating inflation indicated the pace of deterioration, while international speculation on the mark speeded its declining value. During 1923, when the government sent the printing presses whirling, partially to support widespread workers' resistance against the French occupation of the Ruhr, the mark declined precipitously from day to day, finally from hour to hour, reaching an ultimate absurd quotation of a trillion to a dollar. This financial debacle affected everyone materially and psychologically, but it was felt most by the broad middle classes who lost their savings and bore emotional scars for decades to come. Later, in the era of the Great Depression when the Nazis promised financial stability, they garnered tens of thousands of votes on that issue alone.

Allied dismay over the collapse of the German economy and reparations opened a way out of the disaster. Major officials of the German government had been in consistent negotiation with the Allies about German payments. The victors now relaxed their pressure in the Ruhr and upon Berlin. A new rentenmark was created that was tied to inherent values of real estate and anticipated co-operation from abroad. The support came in form of the Dawes Plan of 1924, which eased reparations and provided an international loan of $200 million in gold to bolster fiscal stability. Given a strictly balanced budget, proverbial German industriousness, and new international support, the rentenmark was converted to a reichsmark, and the economy began to recover.

The Reich moved from relaxation of economic tensions to the wider horizons of foreign affairs. The postwar re-establishment of political ties with nations abroad had been slow and halting. Even the dramatic rapprochement with Russia in 1922 was evidence that misery loved company, rather than a significant improvement of Germany's status. With encouragement from the British envoy in Berlin, the German foreign minister, Gustav Stresemann, under-took negotiations with London and Paris to stabilize Berlin's west-ern frontiers. At issue were two problems: the anxious Franco-Belgian search for security from renewed German aggression and the German desire to end the humiliating Allied occupation of the Rhineland. Careful diplomatic negotiations bore fruit in the Treaty of Locarno (October 1925) by which Germany, France, and Bel-gium affirmed the inviolability of their frontiers and the demilitari-zation of the Rhineland. Britain and Italy became guarantors of this stabilization. Franco-Belgian troops evacuated several occupied areas, and controls over German armaments were relaxed. When a hitch developed in Germany's acceptance into the League of Nations, she signed another pact with Russia (Treaty of Berlin, 1926), which mutually improved economic opportunities and in-ternational political flexibility. Finally, in September of 1926, Ber-lin entered the League of Nations and ended her postwar isolation.

Internally the Weimar Republic continued its efforts to foster democracy in the traditional Prussian-German milieu. The death of Socialist President Ebert in early 1925 evoked a broad popular recognition of his services to the republic, but the choice of his successor sent a wave of apprehension over Europe. Elections for the new president produced seven candidates and no clear major-ity. Thereupon the nationalists and conservatives got their candi-dates to withdraw in favor of the aged and retired General von Hindenburg. The continuing effect of his wartime influence as a symbol of Teutonic strength and patriotism carried him to a small plurality over the Catholic and Socialist compromise candidate. Much to the surprise of his backers, Hindenburg subsequently carried out his duties with meticulous loyalty to the precepts of the Weimar constitution—he became a problem only when senility overtook him in the early 1930s. In the later 1920s Stresemann was the political star of successive minority coalition cabinets. Democratically though these men functioned, under their aegis Weimar Germany took on a more traditional and national tone. Yet, with a number of states and cities in left-wing democratic hands, it appeared that Germany was completing a successful transition to responsible self-government.

One significant sector, however, did not respond to these changes: the German army and its supporters. The treaty had limited the Reich to an army of one hundred thousand men serving twelve-year periods. These limitations were meant to inhibit the rebirth of militarism; in fact, they provided a tightly-knit elite cadre for future expansion. Under General Hans von Seeckt the new Reichswehr perpetuated the strong traditions of the Prussian-German military and combined them with ultramodern concepts of strategy and weaponry. The Allies had forbidden Germany the use of offensive weapons like planes and tanks, but cooperative arrangements were soon made with Russia; Berlin offered technological aid for the Red Army and enjoyed the remoteness of the Russian steppes for experimentation and practise. The partial democratization of German life hardly affected these circles and their adherents. They maintained an obedient but inherently hostile neutrality toward the Weimar regime. Thus they lived tolerably in the aura of Hindenburg's aristocratic conservatism and Stresemann's mildly internationalist foreign policy successes. Given continued propitious circumstances, they might have been slowly digested into a republican state.

Between 1925 and 1929, the Locarno era, the Weimar Republic blossomed forth in new confidence, prosperity, and cultural achievement. Men and women visibly reconstructed their shattered lives materially and psychologically. Unemployment diminished rapidly. Factories and transportation worn out by the war were rebuilt, enlarged, and modernized. Foreign trade improved spectacularly, carried by a merchant marine rebuilt virtually from scratch. The quality of German goods and services again became an international byword. Renovation and innovation for home use were as significant as the new international influence of the Reich. Municipalities large and small, often governed by the Socialists, gave their people better lives through publicly owned utilities, modernized mass housing, expanded educational opportunities, and new recreational facilities. The remarkable recovery expressed itself in dramatic technological accomplishments: twin ocean liners that made two new speed records on the North Atlantic and the "Graf Zeppelin," which opened the era of transoceanic air travel. Germany had produced her second economic miracle of the twentieth century.

Even more impressive and of greater lasting influence in the western world were the cultural achievements of the Weimar Republic. Walter Gropius and Mies van der Rohe led the Bauhaus movement with its innovation in architecture and city planning. German literature offered a wide spectrum: from the humanism of Thomas Mann and the naturalism of Heinrich Mann to the experimental theater of Georg Kaiser and Max Reinhardt. Expressionism and abstraction were major trends in painting, sculpture, and music. Albert Einstein led the vanguard of those who gathered Nobel Prizes recognizing the flourishing of theoretical science. Freedom and great diversity marked the culture of Weimar Germany that thrived amidst the broad continuity of traditional forms and values from the prewar empire and the noisy superficialities of the Flapper era imported from America.

Seen in the context of their immediate times, the accomplishments of the Weimar regime appeared both remarkable and promising. In August of 1929 a qualified observer wrote:

The German Republic has triumphed, but its struggle was real. The indifference and open suspicion to which the young German Republic was treated is one of the amazing facts of modern history. In an age confronted with war breakdowns, the disillusions of war settlements, with the loss of faith in democracy and the jubilant denial of liberty and personal rights, the German experiment had to show its vitality by asserting itself against opposition and crouching hostility. Through the blistering blasts of Bolshevism, through the degradation of treaty and reparations, through the ferocity of Fascism, German democracy stood as the strongest bulwark of free representative government on the European continent. Today, when its enemies have receded into the background, the Republic stands firm, tolerant, superior, ready to pull the country out from the last soft spots of the war mire.[1]

But this optimism did not discern the continuing, latent antidemocratic forces in the Reich, nor could it perceive the dimensions of economic and social deterioration that would soon mortally weaken the Weimar state.

The postwar prosperity of the western world that ended so swiftly in 1930 was based on several economic illusions, one of which was that the Reich would annually pump several billion marks worth of reparations into its monetary circulatory system. The illusion persisted and thrived as long as Berlin received ample credits and loans from her former enemies. The crash of the American financial markets in 1929 marked the end of this deceptive phenomenon; lending ceased, and short-term loans were rapidly recalled. In the spring of 1931 several major banks in central Europe collapsed, triggering a host of business failures in the Reich. Unemployment jumped from less than a million in July 1929 to three million by December 1930; six months later it was five and a half million, reaching a plateau of six million for 1932. German agriculture could not compete with the ruinous low prices of central Europe as peasant and landlord alike were threatened with bankruptcy. In this pre-Keynesian era all governments tried to solve these problems with deflationary policies, seeking balanced budgets at any cost. German government expenditures and salaries were cut and reserves consumed to meet the ever-rising costs of relief; by mid-1932 the Reich social security system faced exhaustion. The psychological impact of these experiences was the more acute in Germany because they occurred so abruptly after the miraculous improvements of the later 1920s and reinforced the despairs of the postwar collapse and inflation. All of the precarious political gains and tenuous ideological hopes of the Weimar Republic were jeopardized by these disasters of the Great Depression.

By March 1930 the first political effects were evident: the coalition of Weimar moderates foundered on the refusal of the Socialists to accept fiscal retrenchment with its accompanying reduction of unemployment benefits. For the next two years a technically competent but politically unimaginative Centrist, Heinrich Brü-

1. Elmer Luehr, *The New German Republic: The Reich in Transition* (New York, 1929), p. 427.

ning, headed a minority cabinet; he was backed by the emergency powers of President Hindenburg under Article 48 of the Weimar constitution when the Reichstag failed to support him. The constructive role of that legislature degenerated as ideological extremism expressed itself in elections and in a general assault upon the values and integrity of the republic. In September 1930 the Nazis vaulted from twelve to one hundred seven seats in the Reichstag and the Communists increased from fifty-four to seventy-seven; these gains were at the expense of moderate right-wing parties and the Socialists. As the economic crisis intensified, the character of political action deteriorated. The last year of the republic saw two presidential elections, two Reichstag contests, and much regional balloting. These contests exhausted the German electorate, many of whom were easily discouraged by the continuing personal involvement and inefficiencies of the democratic process. Irresponsible demagoguery flourished, intrigue began to envelope Hindenburg and his advisers, and the German Socialists contributed their share to the tragedy of European labor by directing the strength and focus of their loyalties to their party and its programs, rather than the viability of the Weimar Republic.

Chancellor Brüning fought his battle to maintain the Weimar regime on three fronts. He tried to stabilize and improve the disintegrating economy by measures at home and abroad. He fought off the rising internal attacks on democratic capitalism and the structure of the republic pressed by both the Nazis and the Communists. And he negotiated with the Allies for tangible economic and foreign policy successes to give the Weimar Republic renewed strength and respect in face of its enemies within.

In the summer of 1929 Germany had signed the Young Plan, a new reparations schedule that gave the Reich more favorable annual terms but prolonged the payments to 1988. An outburst of renewed national indignation followed, which the emerging Nazis skillfully exploited to their benefit and against the government. So great was the furor by 1930, now further abetted by economic distress, that the republic got little popular credit for Stresemann's last success, the final Allied evacuation of the occupied Rhineland. Now Brüning was fully engaged in his trio of struggles. He tried to score on all three fronts by negotiating a customs alliance with Austria. But his hopes for economic relief, a blow against the Nazis, and a success for the republic were all lost when France vehemently opposed the plan and caused its nullification. Indeed, French monetary policies then precipitated the financial disasters of mid-1931. Berlin sought and obtained relief from reparations through the Hoover Moratorium, but the immediate psychological benefits were dissipated by delays in Paris. Brüning had another opportunity for success with the Disarmament Conference of 1932 if he could bring Germany closer to parity of forces with the victors of 1918. He was on the verge of that achievement in May 1932 when a nationalist cabal persuaded the aging Hindenburg to drop his chancellor. Lackluster though he was, Brüning was one of the major figures of the Weimar era, a good German of integrity and ability who earned the respect of statesmen abroad and led his nation through the worst times of the Great Depression. With his dismissal the republic was in mortal danger.

Thereupon followed eight months of confusion and change. Political events occurred in the context of a perceptible new spirit: a national conservative resurgence that re-emphasized prewar traditions and reinforced undemocratic attitudes. The monarchical aura of von Hindenburg was strengthened by the visibility of aristocrats like von Papen and generals like von Schleicher. The old imperial colors reappeared beside those of the republic. But the incipient national resurgence was a broad and disorganized movement, bathed in nostalgia of a happier conservative past and without effective organization or leadership.

In this hazy political atmosphere the Weimar Republic expired. Intrigue at the presidential palace affected the senile Hindenburg as he tried to fulfill his constitutional responsibilities. All parties carried on frenzied political activity, while extremist shock troops fought in the streets, drawing greater fanaticism from the blood of their martyrs. Chancellor von Papen dismissed the state government of Prussia, still controlled by the Socialists, and a bulwark of the Weimar state collapsed. With the elections of July 1932 the Nazis doubled their strength of 1930 and emerged as the largest party. Now the game sharpened: Nazis and Communists in the Reichstag immobilized the legislative process; Hitler, von Papen, and von Schleicher vied to gain control of the Weimar executive functions; Centrists and Socialists struggled with their adherents to maintain their support for the republic and resist the appeals of nationalism and extremism. With the exception of a few politically activized officers, the German army remained aloof and watchful.

Von Schleicher toppled von Papen, who then thought he could negotiate from strength with the Nazis because they had lost significantly in the elections of November 1932. On January 30, 1933, Hindenburg gave his assent to a coalition cabinet composed of three Nazis and eight aristocrats, with Hitler as chancellor and von Papen as vice-chancellor. "It is not my fault," said the Führer later, "if these men took me for a simpleton and found afterwards that it was they who had been fooled."[2]

What was the appeal of the National Socialists that accounts for the mushrooming of their voter strength from less than a million in 1928 to seventeen million in 1933?

First, they vocalized the persisting German indignation over the Treaty of Versailles more effectively than any other party. Their message cut across class lines, regional differences, and age groups. Nazi damnation of the *Diktat* focused on three major issues: demand for equality of treatment (*Gleichberechtigung*) in armaments, economic relationships, and international intercourse; sweeping rejection of the war guilt clause and the rationale of reparations derived from it; support and aid for disadvantaged German minorities, notably in Austria and Poland.

Second, the Nazis conducted an unrelenting campaign against the alleged corruption and immorality of the Weimar "system." They rejected the statistical egalitarianism and inefficiencies of democracy as hypocritical and incompatible with the true German spirit. More than that, they singled out Catholics, Jews, and "Marxists" (Communists or Socialists) as groups that were unscrupulously using the republic to suppress the people for ulterior personal or group advantage. They further condemned capitalists and aristocrats for manipulating the Weimar regime to perpetuate control of industry and agriculture, reducing peasants and workers to insecure wage slaves. The inner contradictions of their accusations were resolved by the allegation of a Jewish conspiracy that was manipulating all these groups to its ultimate advantage.

Third, the Nazis compelled attention and attracted support by their confrontation and activism. In these tactics they had a strong psychological advantage over the Communists: they argued that the Reds advocated class struggle to destroy Germany and make

2. Hermann Rauschning, *The Voice of Destruction* (New York, 1940), p. 380.

her subservient to Moscow, while they—the brown shirts—fought to maintain German national integrity and independence. They castigated the Socialists for their harmful strikes against the nation for restricted group advantage. Thus Nazi extremist outbreaks posed as activity for the nation against the "interests," for the community against selfish individualism. And they ennobled these actions by consecration of the blood shed by their martyrs in the struggle for a better Germany.

Fourth, the National Socialists held high their vision of a New Germany. Later, as of 1945, death camps, destruction, and total disillusionment had quite destroyed the sense and evidence of earlier appeals to greatness; yet there was a vigorous ingredient of idealism and party ritualism had an irresistible appeal for many commitment and enthusiasm especially from the inexperienced German youth. Much of this idealism was expressed through a mystic concept of a powerful nation reborn in a disciplined Aryan race. The precepts of the new society were expressed in attractive slogans such as, "Group welfare has priority over individual desire" (*Gemeinnutz geht vor Eigennutz*). Nazi socialism was a curious mixture of communal egalitarianism and elitism, of appeals to self-subjection to the group, and of individual achievement in service of the nation. These ideals had a more powerful impact than Marxist materialism because they were innately self-fulfilling —until the panorama of human degradation in the later Nazi era became evident.

Fifth, there was the extraordinary personality of Adolf Hitler. Like few other men in history, he had a subtle, primitive awareness of ways to induce support of individuals and great masses to his views. More than a demagogue, he was almost a religious figure, compelling attention to his message and way of life. These qualities strongly influenced the youth and the women. The combination of idealism and party ritualism had an irresistable appeal for many German young people, and Hitler ruthlessly exploited the generation gap. Women were given legal equality by the German Republic, yet essentially remained the unnoticed *Hausfrauen* they had been before. No doubt some of them were infatuated with *der schöne Adolf*, but his general appeal to them was more fundamental. While their actual status was hardly altered, he gave them dramatic recognition in the context of race, the nation, and service to the community. Obviously, some of the youth and many women were repelled by the Führer, but no other German personality in his time influenced so many of them.

Finally, all of these appeals were intensified by the consummate skill of the Nazi propaganda apparatus. Joseph Goebbels demonstrated a demonic mastery of the communications media. By 1932 a nationwide Nazi press network carried their blaring headlines into every community. During the three national election campaigns of that year, Goebbels and his experts perfected their use of radio for maximum impact, and soon these techniques could be applied to the entire German film industry. Photographers and commentators followed Hitler's cross-country journeys by black Mercedes or silver Junkers aircraft. Historic sites were dramatized and Nazified by the Führer's presence. Crowds were gathered and manipulated in local meetings, regional rallies, and the culminating spectacle of the huge annual *Parteitag* held in Nuremberg. It was impressive political theater that had a profound mass psychological impact.

Given these appeals and devices, it was a wonder that only 44 percent of the German electorate voted for Hitler in the last free election of the republic, especially in light of the propagandistic dramatization of the Reichstag fire and ensuing intimidation of the voters. Hitler and von Papen continued their coalition basing their government on 52 percent of the voters. For a few months it appeared that the Brown Shirts could be assimilated into the national resurgence of traditional conservatism.

These expectations were short lived. With adroit political maneuvering Hitler persuaded a constitutionally necessary two-thirds of the Reichstag to suspend the Weimar constitution for four years in order to speed economic recovery. These powers were then used in every way to destroy the structure and functions of the republic. Individualism and dissent were systematically reduced in every walk of life, first by coaxing and appeals to national loyalty or economic advantage, then by veiled threats escalating into bald terror. Labor, the professions, and all other social organizations were rapidly "synchronized" into Nazi formats; resistance was sporadic but ineffective. The concentration camps filled. In July 1933 the last political parties disbanded, and the Reichstag became Germany's most prestigious male choir. Hitler used the Reich-Vatican Concordat of July 1933 with devastating effect, immobilizing Catholic opposition at home and giving an impression abroad of "recognition" by the papacy. The army and the churches remained aloof, very uncertain factors for the Nazis. By June 1934 the two had worked out a *modus vivendi*. When rumblings developed in various sectors of the Nazi movement over Hitler's "compromising" of Nazi-Socialist ideals, the Führer crushed dissent with the infamous Blood Purge. In August 1934 President Hindenburg died and was laid to rest with Wagnerian pomp in the memorial celebrating his great victories of 1914. With him was buried the last vestige of the Weimar Republic, as Hitler transferred the executive power of Germany to his person as Führer and Chancellor.

Nazi successes in foreign affairs were equally dramatic or fortuitous. Initially Hitler played the responsible statesman in earnest search of peace. The strengthening sinews of German rearmament were concealed in measures for economic recovery. Reparations were settled for a tiny closing sum that was never paid. In October 1933 the Reich emphasized its new personality by stalking out of the League of Nations. In January 1934 all was smiles again as Hitler signed a ten-year nonaggression and friendship pact with Poland. That summer Viennese Nazis, encouraged by Berlin, killed Chancellor Dollfuss in an abortive coup; the Reich fumed over Austrian Catholic fascist repression. In March 1935 Germany blossomed forth with a new air force, an enlarged army and an arsenal of weapons forbidden by the Versailles treaty. Hitler followed with a magnificent speech for international peace and reconciliation. By June London signed a naval pact with Berlin granting equality in submarines. Throughout 1935–1936 Hitler quietly supported Mussolini in his Ethiopian war conducted in the face of European opposition. The Duce rewarded the Führer by standing aside as Germany tore up the Locarno treaties and reoccupied the demilitarized Rhineland. In 1937 the two Fascists, already supporting Franco in the Spanish Civil War, established their axis that was soon broadened into a tripartite agreement with Japan. Hitler had torn the heart out of the Treaty of Versailles and re-established Germany's equality before the world with a vengeance.

On the home front the changes in materiel and spirit were astounding. All the resources of the state were focused upon reemployment; the first hundred kilometers of *Autobahn* were quite literally built by hand to absorb a maximum of manpower. The Nazis sponsored an outpouring of social concern for the needy; everyone was mobilized for the propagandistically effective *Win-*

terhilfe. A national labor service absorbed the energies of the youth, indoctrinated them ideologically, and gave them paramilitary training. Anticipating the 1936 Olympic Games, there was a nationwide explosion of competitive sports. Art, architecture, music, theater, and film flourished in a conservative milieu, purged of Jewish and "degenerate" influences and progressively prostituted to Nazi ideological or personal ends. A recreational organization, *Kraft durch Freude* (Strength through Joy), pressed into every corner of life to fill leisure time, provide vacation travel, and convey more indoctrination. Economically and psychologically, in material goods and popular culture, Germany came vividly alive in the shadow of the swastika.

"Give me four years' time," Hitler had cried in the election campaign of 1933, "and you will not recognize Germany." And so, indeed, it was. As of 1938 a majority of Germans had not had it so good since the empire, and a significant minority had never had it so bad. The factories hummed, new streamlined trains ran punctually, and the prototype of the peoples' car, the *Volkswagen*, was ready. But freedom—the freedom to dissent, to be an individual, or even to starve—was gone. Several hundred thousand men populated a national network of concentration camps and detention centers, successors to thousands already murdered there. The infamous Nuremberg Laws of 1935 were the first step toward the "final solution" of the alleged Jewish Problem. The Reich legal code was systematically revised to fit a *Herrenvolk*, a master race. Everywhere the multifaceted Nazi bureaucracy spread and thickened, distributing more affluence and demanding more of every German's integrity and obedience.

It was difficult for many Germans to see through the evidences of returning prosperity and dismantling of the Versailles treaty to the heart of National Socialist evil. When the Nazis were initially weakest, they took on the protective coloring of the national resurgence that was "saving" Germany from Bolshevism, restoring her honor, and putting the nation back to work. They immobilized most of their political opponents by their obvious achievements while they less noticeably prepared the chains and used the terror that would later characterize their society. The greater number of their political prisoners prior to 1939 were not Jews but the potential membership of their opposition. In this way the political and intellectual leadership of the Weimar era was nullified, forced to immigrate, or left huddling in silenced resistance. With Germany thus divided between the enthusiastic, the befuddled, the terrorized, and the imprisoned, real opposition developed only gradually and precariously among a handful of opponents with a comparable intensity of ideological persuasion—Socialists, Catholic and Protestant churchmen, and nationalist conservatives of deep moral conviction. Some of them would try to seize power in July 1944 with abortive and disastrous results.

Late in 1937 Hitler decided that the coincidence of Nazi military and economic rearmament with the short-term weakness of Britain and France dictated that he must move within the next five years to complete his grasp for European domination. As opportunities arose, he used them. The top military command was replaced with men more attuned to his impulsive decisions. Austria fell to Nazi occupation in March 1938, and Czechoslovakia began to feel the full weight of Nazi psychological pressure. Thanks to help from Anglo-French appeasement, Italian aid and Polish connivance, Czechoslovakia was partitioned at Munich. In short order Hitler then renounced his pact with Poland, occupied Bohemia, and nullified his naval treaty with Britain. Throughout the summer of 1939, he waged a tense psychological campaign, culminating in the totally unexpected Nazi-Soviet nonaggression pact. A week later World War II was under way.

Unlike 1914, the Germans did not enter this conflict with jubilation; many now wondered illogically if this war was really necessary. Poland was easily beaten, but then? Their doubts were largely dispelled by the smashing defeat of France and isolation of Britain. Now the last scores were settled, and Hitler was at the absolute peak of his popularity. The euphoria persisted through the winter of 1940–1941, as U-boat packs contested control of the North Atlantic and General Rommel drove into Egypt. The invasion of Russia opened the climactic phase of the war; by December the Germans had surrounded Leningrad and were at the gates of Moscow, but they had not achieved victory. It was really the beginning of the end.

Meanwhile the New Order was established in eastern Europe and Russia. While the regular army fought on the peripheries of the distended *Grossdeutsches Reich*, the black-uniformed elite storm troopers of the SS transformed the occupied areas. Their leader, Heinrich Himmler, had developed the concentration camp system for the Reich, the spirit and functions of which now marked the subjugation of tens of millions of *Untermenschen* (sub-humans). Most Germans were slow to realize that the practices of the distant occupation administrations would become the structure of a new state within a state that would subjugate them as well. It began with Himmler's formation of SS combat units parallel to the army, air force, and navy but responsible only to him. Millions of war prisoners were largely placed in agriculture under his security surveillance; to these were soon added several million labor deportees for industry. The character and spirit of Reich government began to change as Hitler, ever more neurotic in the face of mounting military defeats, reviling the army and vilifying established administration, gave Himmler widening areas of jurisdiction. Under these auspices six million Jews were exterminated, and all of Europe was terrorized. Had the Reich won the war, the Germans as well as the vanquished peoples would have entered a "Stalinist phase" of the National Socialist revolution.

The SS control of Germany intensified comparably with her rising military losses and the mounting destruction of her cities by air attack. As the Nazi leadership cried for ever-greater sacrifice and more commitment to the cause, the portents of collapse appeared: weariness, bewildered anger, psychological confusion, escapism—and for some, belated wisdom and awareness of the paths the Germans had taken.

What of the future? In the western nations important German political refugees from the Weimar era had small influence in Allied planning for a post-Nazi Germany. In mid-1943 Russia produced a Free Germany National Committee consisting of German Communist emigrés with a sprinkling of officers captured at Stalingrad; this was the seed of the later Soviet-controlled East German government. At home a German resistance movement formed precariously among a tiny group of conservatives and officers. On July 20, 1944, they bombed Hitler's military headquarters and set out to imprison all major Nazis, while proclaiming an interim conservative national government for Germany. The Führer, however, escaped death and by evening the first plotters were being killed. Subsequently five thousand victims went to Nazi gallows and firing squads, a fair cross-section of the conservative and military circles who had helped Hitler rise to power in 1932–1933 by their acts of commission and omission.

In the last year of the war the Germans experienced a veritable
Wagnerian "Twilight of the Gods," as their cities sank in flames,
their military fronts collapsed, and hordes of refugees streamed out
of eastern Europe in front of, and engulfed by, the advancing
Soviet armies. At long last the oppressed peoples rose—the long-
suffering Russians, Poles, Yugoslavs, and Czechs—to wreak their
vengeance on German soldiers and civilians, innocent and guilty
alike. In the spring of 1945 the extermination camps in Poland were
discovered, and the emaciated remnants of their inmates rescued.
Late in the climactic battle for Berlin, Hitler and Goebbels committed suicide in a bunker under the ruins of the ornate Reich
chancellory. When the firing ceased on May 8, 1945, the German
nation appeared to be destroyed forever.

No period of German history offers a greater abundance and
variety of documentation than the long generation that spans the
two great wars of this century. Any book-length selection of
materials for the period will inevitably have restrictions and show
major gaps in its presentation. These limitations can be partially
overcome by a presentation somewhat focused and interpreted
within the moving stream of changing political, economic, and
psychological circumstances. The selections in this volume were
compiled to illuminate three major and continuing characteristics
of the German historical experience in the twentieth century.
    First of these is the unusual importance of youth in Germany
from the culmination of the empire in 1913 to the collapse of 1945.
More than in other nations of the western world, the German
youth movement was a clearly identifiable sociological and psychological phenomenon. The prologue to these readings gives an historical summary and sociological evaluation of the active identity of
German youth with its changing times: from the neoromantic
critics of heavy Wilhelmian materialism, through joyous devotion
and self-sacrifice to Nazi ideals and objectives, to the shattered
generation surviving in the ruins of postwar Germany. The theme
reappears in disgruntled protests against the early republic, in the
viciously and tragically effective Nazi propaganda impact on the
younger generation, and in the unbelievable experiences of a young
Jew passing from childhood to early maturity under the terror of
the Third Reich. The last two selections return to the opening emphasis, conveying the appeals of a convinced Communist and a

liberated Democrat as they seek to convey the lessons of the past and renewed idealism to youth in a divided Germany. Thus was born the "sceptical generation" of the 1950s and early 1960s, now succeeded by a new generation with a vigorously active cutting edge.

A second major theme is the persistence of conservative attitudes and influences. The book opens with the aristocratic pomp and circumstance of the Kaiser's twenty-fifth jubilee. All through the Weimar Republic and the Nazi era German conservatives tried to move from a weakening power structure, based on nineteenth-century patterns, to stronger and more effective twentieth-century expressions of influence. They suffered disaster in their efforts to capture and command the vigor of National Socialism in order to make it a vehicle for their own modernization. Their confession of failure appeared in the proclamation prepared by ex-Mayor Goerdeler and General Beck for the abortive conservative revolt of 1944. To this very day the essence of these strains continues in the Christian Democratic Union, the conservative party of the western German Federal Republic.

The third major theme is the persistent German search for psychological security, combined with broadly recognized political and cultural self-expression in the context of a world of power politics. Kaiser William II appears to personify the materially powerful but psychologically defensive German drive for "a place in the sun." German reactions to the injustices of Versailles and the inadequacies of the Weimar Republic were the more vehement because of this insecure search for identity. Hitler provided a compelling vision, but his initial thrust to restore German freedom culminated in the enslavement of Europe, including the many duped Germans who first gave him their support. Even today this German search is not ended. It is only suspended, as the eastern German Democratic Republic strains to construct a new totalitarian identity and the western Germans (together with those in West Berlin) wrestle with problems of democratic disintegration while seeking some kind of reunification of Germans in the divided nation.

The problems and reactions of Germans in the first half of the twentieth century can be seen in an instructive relationship to major questions with which we Americans are wrestling in the 1970s. A significant minority of our youth abjures our affluent materialism while seeking some better kind of society for the future. American conservatives are not caught up in the same net of circumstances that the Germans were, but they also struggle with various political alternatives and devices as they try to transfer their power from a simplistically perceived past to a socially more complicated future. And finally, Americans as a nation, shaken by the East Asian adventure and resulting world censure of the 1960s, are embarking on a renewed search for identity and psychological security. History never repeats itself, and the differences between Germany and America are probably greater than the similarities. Yet, broadly and sensitively perceived, the mistakes and misfortunes of the Germans can give us propadeutical insight into the issues of our own times.

Prologue

THE CONFLICT of generations is a constant social happening in the ongoing history of mankind. It has always been most readily evident in the family where youthful inexperience, vigor, and desire for experimentation conflict with the maturity, stability, and cynicism of the older generation. The preindustrial Western world developed social restraints and rituals to control the youth, while absorbing them into its established ways with a tolerable measure of generational friction. Social stratification and economic insecurity further limited the opportunities for social expression of youthful idealism. The industrial revolution, however, undermined traditional European social patterns and restraints; at the same time it hastened the emergence of a broad middle class. This combination of changing social structures with burgeoning bourgeois affluence broadened and accentuated the generation gap from the family into the larger society and transformed youthful idealism into modern political activism.

The German youth movement has a unique place in recent history. After 1918 many nations sprouted youth organizations, both democratic and totalitarian. Only in Germany (and a generation earlier) did a self-conscious youth movement emerge that was closely tied to nineteenth-century cultural, national, and psychological sources. German romanticism supplied a context of myth and intuitive idealism. Nationalism, just recently consummated in dramatic political unification, continued as an aggressive ingredient of popular idealism. Psychologically the Germans swung between expressions of individualism and a search for group relationship. By 1900 these romantic, national, and psychological attitudes combined with increasing wealth and quickening social change to foster expressions of generational conflict seldom perceived before.

Young German men and women were openly hostile to the philistine Wilhelmian establishment. They skipped the traces of authority and social convention. They condemned industry for

befouling the romantic German landscape. They decried materialism for corrupting the idealism of youth. And some of them
readily found the causes of defilement and degeneration in the un-
German Jew. The flower of this generation was destroyed in the
First World War. Its romanticism, readiness for self-sacrifice, and
accentuated psychological instability lived on into the struggles of
the Weimar era, where it was ultimately prostituted to National
Socialism and then destroyed by it.

1. German Youth from Confidence to Skepticism

SOURCE: Helmut Schelsky, *Die Skeptische Generation; eine Sozi-
ologie der deutschen Jugend* (Düsseldorf: Eugen Diederichs
Verlag, 1957), pp. 58–63, 65–75, 77–80, 82–85. Reprinted by
permission. Translation by the editor.

The German youth movement at the turn of the century grew out
of the disillusionment of the younger generation with the adult
world. The values and institutions, prejudices, and traditions of the
established, upper-middle class world appeared to be shabby and
trite in context of the increasingly complex and powerful modern
social structure. The older generation, sensing the insecurity of its
status, responded either with permissiveness devoid of principle or
form, or with rigidity and an excessive insistence on the values of a
changing, yet restrictive social system that cherished petty bourgeois and romantic patriotic values. Youth often found that these
social values and customs produced hypocrisy. They felt that
it was morally and socially dishonest to insist on values and attitudes
which had become meaningless and were being ignored silently—
or rather, blatantly—in business, politics, and public life. So they set
out in a search for virtue and freedom, in contrast to the world of
business and civil service careers with its false morality and its
petty private deceitfulness. It was an affirmation of aesthetic idealism in protest against the social corruption or impotence of the
adult world.

There was also an obvious revulsion against "civilization," a protest against the most offensive structures and symbols of the modern technical and industrial world. The young bourgeoisie which
gave birth to this youth movement did not choose the factories and
industrial world of labor as its negative symbols, for these were too

far removed from their own experience, but focused instead on the modern city with its traffic, asphalt, and bourgeois comfort. They went tramping in a kind of social protest against modern civilization of the metropolis. Hans Breuer, editor of the *Zupfgeigenhansl* [a collection of songs for guitar music] wrote in 1910: "the metropolis despoils youth, corrupts their drives, estranges them increasingly from a natural, harmonious way of life. A new ideal arose out of the great sea of urban housing: 'redeem yourself, take a hiking staff, go outside the city and seek the human identity which you have lost, your plain, simple, and natural self.' Youth now had a new gospel that could be personally discovered. The goal was recognized and the march began." It led into the country, into the forests, into the past, into a realm of youth. "From grey city walls, we set out into the world!"

This generation of youth desired to overcome its sense of impotence, uncertainty, and loathing for the modern world with its rigid society, mechanization, complexity, and artificiality. Eduard Spranger, who wrote his *Psychology of Youth* about this generation . . . identified the protest as a "tension between the structure of associations maintaining the cultural establishment and the very simple, undifferentiated structure of the youthful soul." Youth [he found] longed for a more simple, natural, and harmonious spiritual environment because it lacked behavioral sophistication. That yearning produced a striving for psychological security, a need to re-establish some congruity of values, to find a new environment and a personal mode of living. It became the basic concern of the youth movement to fulfill these needs. But the youth did not just wish for these things; it was "setting out" toward these goals. It desired to achieve by its own efforts these things which home and society could not supply. The movement was an attempt of the youth "to organize their lives by self-determination, with the responsibility to themselves for their inner veracity."

How did they propose to attain this desired behavioral security? How was it achieved, at least for that one [prewar] generation? . . .

In terms of social and ideal models, the youth movement exhibited the whole pattern of concepts commonly referred to as the "romanticism" of that generation: their love for the past and for national traditions, their love of nature by sentimental experience and their yearning for a "simple life." This imaginative world was a reaction against the artificiality and complexity of modern civilization, a return to simple ways of living in Rousseauean primitiveness by reversion to a glorified and idyllically reconstructed past. Rejecting factory wares and mass production, the urban-bourgeois youth valued things hand-made and rural, substituted folk dancing and campfires for dancing lessons, movies, and pubs. The ideals of pure and honest living were not found in the real world developing around them, but rather in one that vanished before their very eyes. Still, some essence of this other world was incorporated in a genuine rebirth: they elevated images of the past which transcended an antiquarian preservation of history to absolute and eternal validity.

Though we may explain this romanticizing as a negative protest against the modern world, we must not ignore the progressive content of this intellectual attitude. It was more than dissent, it was also a movement of ethical emancipation which sought to educate the individual. The essence of this endeavor lay in its demands for freedom; initially these were demands for the emancipation of young people from the traditional stratifications of the patriarchal-authoritarian family, from the castelike isolationism and established antithetical role of the sexes; and from everything that bourgeois propriety expected in behavior from its offspring. However, it was also a demand for unity, simplicity, truth, and autonomy of the individual; it rejected social bonds for new ties of friendship and active youth community; it meant surrender to an ideal of life which was felt as a moral and even ascetic demand upon itself. . . . Thus, the youth movement—despite all its longing for a sense of community, or precisely *because* of it—was fundamentally concerned with the ideal freedom of the individual. . . .

The prewar youth movement developed no social or political program, no doctrine to engage the modern world theoretically or pragmatically by penetration, clarification, and change. Such an involvement would have meant descending from that rarified realm of idealism and personal verve which they set up against the stolidity of the practical business of living and the workaday world of their protests. Therefore, Nietzsche was the philosopher of the youth movement, not Marx; Stephan George was their poet, not Hauptmann. There was certainly concern for the "future of the people" in the basic impulses of this movement; but wherever issues of the social future were raised, they remained in the context of general ethical demands, buried in the uncertainty of ambiguities.

And yet this prewar generation of the youth movement brought about one of the most impressive social innovations in recent history. In opposition to decadent bourgeois society, they set up a closed world of intimate, small-group social patterns. It was a socially independent world of youth groups and clubs, which provided their members with norms and assurances of a "spirit of youth" for all situations. The clubs provided friendships and conformity within small, like-minded circles, related to a hierarchy and leadership by older members that was enthusiastically and spontaneously accepted. Common ideals and security fulfilled the social needs which they demanded from the outside world; here was the social environment which allowed youth to live in the pure idealism which had been instilled in them by their bourgeois families but which was no longer a reality there. These new kinds of associations were seen by youth as the restoration of a pristine social environment necessary for man, as a social rebirth within the degenerating modern world. . . . The first phase of the German youth movement and its search for behavioral security were intimately related to the relative peace, stability, and easy affluence of the prewar bourgeois world.

The sociological bases for the behavior of the prewar youth disappeared in the bloodbaths of World War I and in the subsequent political, social, and economic chaos and distress of the twenties. Indeed, the organized youth movement actually did not mature until the twenties, when it experienced its greatest expansion; this was the great period of federations, which saw the amalgamation of smaller youth groups into larger associations yet without loss of their individual character. Their modes of operation were influenced by elites of youth and of youth welfare that did not directly belong to the federated youth movement or necessarily stem from it. In this second phase of the youth movement a stronger political interest became evident in many of the federations. It tried to deal in its own way with the pressing political and social problems of the time: in nationalistic endeavors along the German borderlands, in the voluntary labor service of the Free Germans, in the agricultural corps of the "Artamans," etc. Now an unstable German society, shaken by war and changing rapidly in the postwar period, provided a context for the youth movement very different from the era of its origin. Its relationship to contemporary society became ever more obvious and pressing, demanding of youth a different sense of social relevance and action. Outside of the organized youth movement, new behavior patterns, affected by new circumstances, developed in the entire younger generation. This youth felt other needs and sought other ways of fulfillment, no longer responding to the earlier precepts of individual ethical idealism and small-group autonomy. Here was a new generation of political activism. . . . The new "political youth" were members of groups founded either after the beginning of the twenties or rejuvenated by the new spirit of the period. Emerging in close connection with the political action groups or tendencies of the adult world, they were frequently only off-shoots from adult organizations and showed a marked trend toward mass organization. Despite antagonistic political aims and efforts . . . which frequently led to severe struggles among themselves, this generation of youth demonstrated a uniform behavior pattern. It included young men and women from parties or political "movements" from the Left to the Right and from so-called *Wehrverbände* [military associations], the trade unions, etc. . . . As we know, this trend of the twenties culminated in the Hitler Youth of the Third Reich, in a state monopoly controlling the one surviving political youth association. . . .

The rift between the prewar (ethical) and postwar (political) generations apparently originated with the German working class youth. After World War I, a large part of the organized working class youth joined the youth movement federation and accepted its principles. Yet, the proletarian youth movement differed from the middle-class movement: though it also rejected bourgeois society, it did not oppose the principles of its own adult generation because the working class was itself antagonistic to the prevailing social system. Labor youth thus largely accepted the political convictions of their parents; they also were socialists. Nevertheless, this solidarity was interlaced with the basic values of the broader youth movement; many of the labor youth of that period also espoused ideals of individualism, freedom, and independent small-group living. Another portion of the labor youth, however, in greater identification with the adult generation of its own class, reached other conclusions, held other goals as more important, and sought other forms of organization. They aspired to become a part of the workers' political organization intimately tied to current political practice and confrontation. Thus they welcomed political mass organization as a form of social action. . . .

What were the social structures in which these "political types" organized? Let us take the example of the Communist youth. At the Third Congress of the Communist International, which met in Moscow in 1921, the "unified guidelines for youth organizations were prepared and their implementation subsequently undertaken by the Second World Congress of the Communist Youth International, which convened soon after, again in Moscow. The formation of the youth organizations was centrally controlled and the jurisdictions of its cells, local groups, districts, etc., were carefully delineated, right up to the Central Committee of the Youth International. Representatives were sent from each of these institutions to the corresponding units of the party, and the chairman of the Central Committee also received a seat and vote on the Central Committee of the Communist International. It was the duty of these youth delegates to take the decisions of the party and carry them out in their own organizations. At the same time factory youth cells were established, . . . which fostered greater solidarity of the comrades, bringing greater pressure and having more significant propaganda effect on the other workers in the factory. Definite party activity in agitation, teaching, or whatever, was required from each cell member, thus, forging a close and effective link with the party. A community of purpose and action was transformed into a well-organized army. . . ."

These features of the political labor youth were also evident in the political youth of the bourgeoisie. Comparable relationships developed between the general bourgeois youth movement and the youth organizations or military associations of the bourgeois Right and Center. The bourgeois political youth was similarly characterized by simple thought patterns focused upon action. It associated with the same kind of highly organized mass organizations which agitated and propagandized, worked for "pressure" and "action," and culminated in mass demonstrations and rallies. Here again the need of youth to join adult political organizations coincided with adult needs to organize youth in this way. The bourgeois political youth tended more obviously towards militarism, but the Communist youth had no aversion to weapons and entered the "struggle" just as robustly as its opponents did. . . .

Reliable statistics on the numbers of youth organized in the several kinds of associations are difficult to obtain and, where they exist, they are based on very divergent estimates. . . . In 1931, the largest federations included in the ethical youth movement were the German Boy Scout Federation and the German *Freischar* (Free Troop) with memberships at 12,000 each. By contrast, the political associations numbered: Young *Stahlhelm* (16 to 23-year-olds), 100,000; Young Banner (Youths in the Reichbanner Black-Red-Gold, 14 to 25-year-olds), 705,000; Hitler Youth, 20,300; Bismarck League (German National Peoples Party), 40,000; Hindenburg League (German Peoples Party), 12,000; Windthorst Leagues (Center Party), 10,000; Communist Youth Association, 18,768; Red Youth Front (Youth division of the Red Front Veteran League, 16 to 20-year-olds) 22,500; and so on. Unfortunately, for the Socialist labor youth, only statistics of rallies were reported, between 20,000 and 40,000.

What kinds of attitudes affected the pattern of this postwar generation of political youth? They grew out of disillusionment with the liberties earlier won from the disintegrating bourgeois world. The individual, once freed from traditional ties and attitudes, became a creature of his drives and impulses. The new social freedoms led to a succession of crises and emergencies, which made social justice appear as an illusion. The new German state was an unstable structure. War, revolution, social chaos, economic insecurity, poverty, and unemployment were the most evident phenomena of the new society. They threatened every individual at the roots of his existence, created a widespread feeling of crisis and insecurity and aroused a basic feeling of disillusionment. With unusual intensity, these social circumstances demanded a new sense of responsibility. People were politicized in their search for stability, social peace, and order.

To these general social needs were added the typical pressures upon youth to achieve behavioral stability in the process of overcoming their own immaturity. More fully than ever before, this generation of youth was prepared to take responsibility for the whole of society; it wrestled with the disorderly modern world, to replan and remodel the existing society. Youth sought to transform the social reality of public life, the economy, politics, and culture. These efforts coincided with those of the adults; youth worked in adult spheres of behavior and hence did not retire into their own independent world. Despite this coalition with the older generation, they did not feel a part of it. The reforms and the methods of the adults were too much like compromises for them, too experimental, too slow and hesitant. Only in the most radical and total upheaval did they envision the achievement of a final stabilization, a harmonious order for the world. It seemed to them that only they, the youth, had the real strength to achieve where the adults had failed. Thus, the most radical and revolutionary convictions were most typical for this generation.

They saw themselves as a vanguard of the future, not by waiting while they matured in their own world of youth, but in a more radical assault on the adult world itself. This time they wanted to attain their desired behavioral security in a direct and rapid transformation of the realities of industrial society. They had learned that their own insecurity originated not only in archaic bourgeois social structures, in restrictions of the family and the stale air of plush furniture, but in the recent crises and problems of the modern times: in the political, economic, and intellectual tensions of the modern society; in the social maldistribution of power and in world politics. They felt that as youth they had personal responsibility for these things; they were prepared and strove to assume responsibility themselves for creating a better world, a new sense of social security and order.

How did they expect to achieve these objectives? Here we must distinguish between two levels: the world of imagination and the realities of social change.

On the level of social idealism and dedication to social goals, these youth found fulfillment in demanding social planning and advocating intellectual concepts of a society fundamentally transformed by a new set of political principles. These principles were totally contradictory. There were many different -isms, each one claiming and establishing belief in a social world that would eventually be harmonized and ordered by systematic management: communism, nationalism, socialism, conservatism, etc., or the combination of ideas which would become most persistent as National Socialism. . . .

From their ideological faith and from the rigid certainty of their concepts for the total planning and ordering of society, sprang the totalitarianism and exclusiveness with which each of these groups defended its own position as the only truly right one. In the politics of the twenties almost all parties, not just those consciously striving for dictatorship, tended toward ideological totalitarianism. Naturally, this trend was especially pronounced in the political youth which was placed in the ideological and agitatorial ante-chamber of practical politics. . . . Quite apart from adult philosophical totalitarianism, the youth of itself had an innate tendency toward simplistic ideological conformity. This was not a monopoly of the Hitler Youth; it more or less characterized all political youth of the twenties and the beginning of the thirties.

On the level of political reality, the postwar generation differed fundamentally in attitude and organization from the earlier youth movement by virtue of contrasting relationships to modern industrial and bureaucratic society, to kinds of organization, and to types of political activity. The attitude was positive; it affirmed and used the devices of technology. Youth did not go tramping in young idealism; it took to wheels where it could. The affirmation of motorization in every form culminated in the creation of motorized units in youth organizations. The drive for para-military training was founded on an eagerness to master weapons as a modern technique. An even more important contrast to the prewar youth movement was the idealization of labor and craftsmanship. The socialist youth of the twenties fostered cooperation with factory labor; in the union youth organizations they worked toward political and social ends and also for more effective job training. Later the Hitler Youth engaged in very intensive political activity to foster job training, which culminated in the annual "Reich Occupational Competition." The Nazi Youth leader, Baldur von Schirach, proclaimed: "The symbol of the Federations was the trip; the symbol of the Hitler Youth is Occupational Competition,"—which was a half truth, because the "symbol of Hitler Youth" that paralleled "traveling," was the youth rally. . . .

The young men and women of this era sought identification with the great political organizations that corresponded to ideological systems of planning and order. The climax of this youthful experience was indeed no longer the evening campfire on the forest meadow or a gathering on the mountain top; it came in the rallies of youth or party celebrations, or with May Day demonstrations of solidarity and readiness to take control of society as a unified and disciplined power. The tasks of party agitation and propaganda which these organizations frequently assumed and the many auxiliary services which the affiliated adult political organization expected of them were carried out enthusiastically by the youth. Thus they felt themselves as part of the same concrete and practical political reality of the day in which they desired to participate. . . .

This second phase of the search of modern German youth for behavioral security was thus dominated by disciplined and standardized mass organizations that drew strength from the faithful devotion of individuals to ideology and supplied one-sided, pseudo-personal, small-group relationships.

In West Germany [of 1955] such a mass pattern of youthful behavior was as much a thing of the past as the earlier ethical movement. It had vanished as a structure for behavioral security and thus also as a goal of youthful aspirations. . . .

In addition [to the fact that the Hitler Youth system carried the seeds of its own social destruction], there was also the effect of the last war and the postwar period on the behavior of the third youth generation [in modern German history]. These events eliminated the conditions that produced the political pattern of the second youth generation, notably the optimistic expectation that the entire society would experience social planning and organization, the need to believe in "ideas" or ideologies, and the hope of creating harmonious and beneficial social conditions by revolutionary change. Several preconditions for the elder patterns have vanished, among them being the relative freedom of youth from their own oppressive daily worries. [Before World War I] the youth considered those emergencies and crises which they saw as primarily the concern of society which, though it touched and unsettled their personal and private lives, did not fundamentally affect them. They could still maintain their private and personal lives from remnants of bourgeois wealth or benefits of petty-bourgeois thrift. The postwar political youth was much closer to experiencing social insecurity than was the prewar ethical youth movement, but they transferred the problems of their personal lives and search for security to the level of general historical and political events. It was then a personal decision whether to participate or not. They did not have the agonizing experiences which the Nazi war and its postwar era inflicted upon all our population, including the youth. From these events developed another new pattern of social behavior for today's youth. . . .

The behavior of our youth today [1955] stems from our disintegration and from rejection of the previous political pattern. The processes of removing politics and ideology from the youthful consciousness are predominantly a result of the last war and the postwar period. They occurred partly as a result of political propaganda and re-education by the occupation powers and our new German political leadership. Much more important, however, were the effects of the social and political realities that affected the youth during this period. . . . These experiences of the war and its consequences were hardly suited to the inherent nature of youth; they not only shook youthful readiness to identify with given political systems, such as National Socialism or nationalism, but they cut the very roots of political belief and ideological activity that characterized the whole pattern of the political generation. These days one often hears adults cry, "We need new ideas for youth!" There is widespread disappointment over the lack of "idealism" in the present younger generation. This attitude ignores the fact that many ideas are circulating, but that youth simply is not influenced by them because they lack a willingness to believe—a condition that follows from the crises of political events of the twenties and thirties. Their search for behavioral security takes other paths. The effect of social crises on the behavior of individuals has passed a certain psychological threshold; they no longer lead to political and ideological solutions or activism because everyone, especially the youth, is utterly convinced of the individual's lack of power to plan in the face of massive political and social forces.

[Since these words were written nearly two decades ago, a fourth generation of German youth has arrived on the scene. In West Germany it lives amid the electronic, motorized, and winged affluence of the "economic miracle." Many individuals of this new generation continue the political skepticism and protective noncommitment of their private lives that characterized the post-Nazi youth. An important minority, however, especially in the universities, stands on the barricades of neo-Marxian (but not Communist) social activism and finds resonance in comparable movements of France, Japan, and America. In East Germany the young

are enrolled and indoctrinated in the so-called Free German Youth
—a behavioral re-run of the *Hitler Jugend*, but with different
colors and slogans. Still, they are a growing source of worry to
their leaders, for some of them respond to the spirit of Wood-
stock and appear to threaten the Communist establishment.]

I

The German Empire in Peace and War, 1913–1918

In little more than five years the German Empire plunged from the climax of Emperor William's Silver Jubilee of 1913 to the brink of revolution in 1918. Many Germans attributed the decline to military exhaustion and internal subversion, but the great issues of 1918 were already evident before the war began. In his proclamation of June 19, 1913, the Kaiser expressed the conservative authoritarianism and pompous self-consciousness so characteristic of his reign. German Socialists were hardly impressed by his rule and distrusted his judgment. Even some of the more deferential commentators worried about his reactionary or incompetent civilian advisers and saw the need for reform. These problems were only intensified by the war.

By 1913 Germany was virtually locked into her alliance with the shaky Hapsburg monarchy and in potential confrontation with the Triple Entente. Arrogant nationalism escalated into virulent antagonism between Germans and the other "races" of Europe. The Kaiser's attitudes expressed these feelings and they contributed to the precariousness of his decisions in late July of 1914.

The outbreak of the war intensified national enthusiasm, giving many Germans a sense of exhilaration and release. Socialist Philipp Scheidemann recorded most vividly the passions of the day and the conflicts of interest, values, and loyalties they caused. As the armies began to march against the enemy, it appeared briefly that internal disagreements were overshadowed by higher unity. But soon the quarrels reappeared, now intensified by the strains of war. In those hard years the Germans experienced very complicated psychological changes that illuminate their subsequent relationships to revolution, democracy, and dictatorship.

2. The Kaiser's Proclamation of Gratitude in Contemplation of His Silver Jubilee

SOURCE: *Schulthess europäischer Geschichtskalender* (1913), LIV: 263. Translation by the editor.

I thank the Lord that I may look back with satisfaction upon the past twenty-five years of serious endeavor, upon the great achievements which they have brought to the fatherland in all fields of intellectual, social, and economic life, and upon the unprecedented growth in the strength of our people and our national wealth. The German realm, founded on the unity of the Germanic peoples and their princes as conceived by Kaiser William the Great [1858–1888], has developed into a well-protected and friendly community for its inhabitants. It makes me particularly happy that this could happen under the beneficent rays of a sun of peace whose strength successfully dispels every cloud on the horizon. It has fulfilled one of my fondest wishes. On this, my day of honor, I have received full measure of love and loyal affection from all sides. Once again, the illustrious German Princes and the Free Cities have displayed gratifying friendship and affirmed the solidity of the bonds of German unity by their personal presentation of friendly felicitations. By delegations and thousands of letters, telegrams and artistic communications, from all regions of the fatherland, from the colonies and from all parts of the globe, the German people have conveyed their loyal felicitations to me. In city and country alike the day has been celebrated with joyous enthusiasm. An unusually fervent patriotic attitude was demonstrated.

But the attentions and honors given me have not been limited to felicitations and addresses. When festive joy is heartfelt it presses for expression through thanksgiving. Despite other great demands upon them, various provinces, counties, cities, communities, and organizations have established charitable foundations in my name to assuage the distress of the needy, sick, and miserable, and to foster diverse measures for the common good. It is my special joy that the Christian missions doing blessed work in our colonies and the needy war veterans have also been gratefully remembered on this great occasion. And so the Silver Jubilee of my reign has become the source of a stream of blessings for the German nation and for coming generations. Cheered and moved by the enthusiasm with which my Day of Honor has been celebrated as a national festival, I wish to express my warmest thanks to every individual who thought of me with such friendship and who contributed to increase the festive joy. And further, I shall most willingly apply all my strength for the well-being of the German People as long as God permits. May He give His blessing to my work and efforts and always preserve the precious fatherland in His gracious keeping.

To the Imperial Chancellor: please bring this writ to immediate public attention.

The New Palace, June 19, 1913.

(Signed) William, I[mperator] R[ex]

3. Socialist Reaction to the Silver Jubilee

The *Vorwärts*, the official newspaper of the German Social Democratic movement, was founded at Leipzig in 1876 by Wilhelm Liebknecht and re-established at Berlin in 1891. Subjected to harassment and censorship in the first decades of the empire, it survived and triumphed to become the major news and editorial spokesman for prewar German left-wing democracy.

SOURCE: *Vorwärts*, June 16, 1913, p. 1. Translation by the editor.

WE AND WILLIAM

We are *not* joining the celebration!

We shrug our shoulders and stand apathetically aside as a foaming torrent of ceremonial speeches, articles, and hurrahs flood the country. We know how much abysmal hypocrisy is being uttered in this rattling noise-making and how the staunchest monarchists discuss the emperor intimately among themselves—if all the cases of *lèse majesté* occurring in these circles were known, the state prosecutors would have to install night shifts. And we know that as soon as the intoxication has vanished tomorrow, the glum headaches will return and many a patriot will curse as he digs into his well-filled wallet to pay his share of the special defense levy. But today they are screaming hurrah, today the champagne corks are popping, today the colors black-white-red are flying high.

So be it! We Social Democrats, as a basically republican party, would appear ludicrous if we joined in celebrating a monarchical jubilee. The East Elbian [Junker] celebrants are particularly amazed and indignant about the fact that we are republicans and will remain so. With outraged cries these gentlemen denounce our "lack of patriotism" because we watch the mechanical opening and closing of jaws—hurrah! hurrah!—with a quiet smile. But any boy in knee pants today knows that the monarchists alone do not constitute the fatherland. . . .

Though we reject monarchy in principle, our attitude toward different monarchs can vary. There are rulers whom even a republican can praise for not succumbing to absolutist tendencies and for being exemplary first citizens of their nations. William II belongs to the other category. Not that we express feelings of hatred for the German Kaiser, as our beerhall-prosecutors would assume—forbear! forbear! Even though his words and deeds have done more for our cause than he intended, we should be objective enough to view him as a product of circumstances. If proletarians are so judged, the same method should be applicable to those who move in the allegedly highest spheres of humanity. Considering the tribe of Byzantine parasites who press upon him in every place and at every hour; noting that his view of reality is constantly blurred by clouds of incense, massed flags, and garlands; observing that "his people" always meet him wearing cutaways and top hats—even when he visited the Krupp factories they presented him with a selected group of workers fattened up for the occasion—it is hardly his fault if the world shapes up differently in his head than in most others. There is hardly a more telling example than the Kaiser's amazed reaction when Chancellor Bülow in November 1908 conveyed to him, on behalf of the Reichstag, the sense of vibrant dissatisfaction in the nation and he countered: "What do you mean? Everyone is cheering for me! . . ."

The contradictions in William II are not primarily a result of his personality; they reflect the circumstances of our times. This member of the Hohenzollern dynasty occupies his throne in an age when aristocratic hypocrites, the bourgeoisie, and the working classes are joined in conflict with each other; and each of the three classes is powerful in its way. It will not do for the Monarch to stand with one of these classes against the others. Instead, he has to balance and shift between them, so that he does not give the one too much and the other too little. Thus, on occasion William II gives the hypocrites their fill of sweets; on another, he harvests bourgeois praise for his advancement of technology and especially his *Weltpolitik;* and he honestly appears to believe that he has done more for the workers than anyone else. His position between the classes is the basis for the well-known fluctuations of the Wilhelmian era, even though these actions may bear the particular coloring of his personal temperament.

William II was almost always sharply defensive in his dealings with the Social Democrats. True, he once said "My Social Democrats are not so bad"; but more typical for his innermost convictions were such expressions as "unpatriotic journeymen" and "a bunch of rabble not worth calling Germans." We harbor no grudge against him for these expressions; inherently they correct themselves. Twenty-five years ago he proclaimed proudly and confidently, "Social Democracy is a temporary phenomenon; just let me deal with it and I shall soon close it out!" And today, at his jubilee? *Four and a quarter million* Social Democratic votes, a hundred and ten Social Democrats in the Reichstag—not in spite of, but partially thanks to William II! His friendships and enmities have produced tragic unforeseen consequences. He once assured 300 million Mohammedans of his friendship, called Abdul Hamid his friend and offered his protection to Abdul Aziz of Morocco. The two Abduls are long since toppled from their thrones and the world of Islam is crumbling. But the "temporary phenomenon" of Social Democracy, against which William II vowed a powerful crusade. . . . : it grows, flowers, and prospers. It has red cheeks, stout muscles, and looks like eternal life itself. And for him most awkward of all, every one of the Kaiser's controversial speeches has brought us thousands of new members. The lightning that Jupiter sent to strike our heads has only illuminated the presence of countless new ones.

Therefore, with thankful hearts, we *do* join the celebration! Millions, many millions of "temporary phenomena" salute the ruler today with their cry: *Long live the Republic!*

4. Liberal-Bourgeois Commentary on the Reign of William II

The *Berliner Tageblatt* was founded in 1871 by Rudolf Mosse, an enterprising German-Jewish advertiser and publisher. In competition with the staid middle-class *Vossische Zeitung*, it became one of the leading liberal newspapers of prewar Europe. Its accurate news service and penetrating editorials made it required reading in foreign offices the world over. This editorial was written by Paul L. Michaelis, a skilled political commentator and author of several plays and novels.

SOURCE: *Berliner Tageblatt*, June 15, 1913, p. 1. Translation by the editor.

THE KAISER'S SILVER JUBILEE

A quarter of a century has passed since William II took the imperial scepter from the weary hands of his noble father. The young Kaiser assumed his high and difficult duties with burning eagerness, a quick mind, and a multitude of interests. We have observed his development, and all the idiosyncrasies and obscurities of his character have been revealed in the course of time. Not only the German people have continuously observed this official representative of the recently united empire. The whole civilized world, even those areas where civilization is barely emerging, have had to deal with the personality of William II. Since he is unusually versatile, his contemporaries have judged him from very different points of view. Thus it must be said that his image and popularity vacillate, torn between partisan hatred and praise. It would be premature to assess the Kaiser's eventual place in history, for he is still in the prime of life. Perhaps his vital, energetic pace has lessened slightly; but it is far from exhaustion. It may yet produce some surprises for this generation. But in general we have already come to know the Kaiser in these twenty-five years, and we can recognize his merits without exaggerating his successes and achievements by flattery. . . .

The dominant trait of William II is his strong consciousness of sovereignty. His emphasis on divine right, that he did not receive the crown from mortal hands, is another expression of his self-assured concept of sovereignty which also derives from religious convictions. He is not insensible to the difficulties that result from the assertion of a ruler's absolute will in the context of modern life. Occasionally William II has spoken of his "fearful responsibility to the creator alone" from which a prince cannot be absolved by man or official, by a house of representatives or a people. Still, this concept is based on the fact that in the Kaiser's view "his course is the right one," that he must carry out his predetermined policies despite opposition, and that the people must submit to his sovereign insights. Repeatedly the Kaiser has proclaimed that he desires to lead his people of Brandenburg to "glorious times," and he has rejected the "malcontents" and "pessimists" of the country by demanding full confidence in his leadership. . . .

Harsh reality has, nevertheless, considerably shaken divine right. Precisely those circles whom the Kaiser designated as the "nobles of the nation," those who constantly supported the king's absolutism, are the very ones which most successfully opposed the goals of William II. They were early in revolt against the commercial treaties of Caprivi, which the Kaiser saw as an "act of deliverance" in times of economic distress. On the surface, their differences were set aside, but essentially the Junkers did not yield an inch. They set up a Landholders League against the Kaiser's government and twice they rejected the Mittelland Canal. What good did it do to put some of those who opposed the canal on half-pay? They soon advanced again and today they make Prussian economic policy just as they enacted the high protective agricultural tariff of 1902. Together with the Junkers and agrarians, the Catholic Center Party became the focus of power. . . . Today a blue-black coalition rules in Prussia without restriction and it would find no resistance in the German Empire if the last elections had not produced a slight nudge to the left.

It was hardly different with the Social Democrats. Once William II thought he could "deal with them alone." One must admit that his initial activity in social politics was promising. Old age pensions and disability insurance were enacted at the outset of his reign, as a "patriotic achievement," in the Kaiser's own words. William II realized the social objectives of his grandfather in regulating social welfare legislation based on international agreement. We know how much resistance he had to overcome from Prince Bismarck in this matter. . . . And in the course of the last decades considerable social legislation was enacted. But the Kaiser's attitude toward the Social Democrats changed very quickly. Earlier he had rejected the power politics recommended by Bismarck, because he did not want to begin his government with conflict and because he would not have it said of him that he was starting out by shooting his subjects. But as Social Democracy grew stronger and stronger, the Kaiser called the people to fight against the parties of revolution and for religion, tradition, and order. That was already in September of 1894. Count Caprivi hesitated to submit to these impulses of the Kaiser. He was replaced by Prince Hohenlohe who, in December of the same year, came up with the draft of an antisubversion bill. But an emergency law against a political party cannot be enacted twice. The antisubversion bill failed in the German Parliament and in the following years similar attempts failed in restricting the right of assembly in Prussia. In 1899 the penitentiary bill was also defeated and finally, a year later, the greatest part of the [repressive] *lex Heinze*. Since then it has been calm, and even Herr von Bethmann-Hollweg has declared that he wishes to pass no emergency laws. In the meantime the Social Democratic party has grown to more than four million voters and has become the strongest party in Parliament. Could they have already reached their peak? Who knows! At least, they have grown continuously in the last twenty-five years.

The German citizenry has had to foot the bill. It has always been loyal. It has patiently borne the constantly growing burdens for the army and the navy and has had to be content with the crumbs from someone else's table. From time to time the German people have been comforted with lofty words, without finding true recognition of their vital interests. Yet, the German people have asserted themselves. The eminent economic and ethical fitness of the tradesmen, the intellectuals, the merchants, and the industrialists have broken through the limitations that were artificially imposed. And even now the German citizenry is ready to sacrifice for "the glory of the Empire." But one cannot hide the fact that there is a limit even for the German citizen beyond which he can no longer sacrifice himself. For twenty-five long years the German people have been neglected. Now they are demanding reform. They are demanding release from bureaucratic pressures, demanding that schools be freed from clerical domination, demanding justice and fairness in taxation; and, finally, they are demanding reform of the

Prussian three-class voting system, which is a hindrance to the healthy development of the Prussian Monarchy. Five years ago the King promised modernization of the Prussian suffrage. Only a sophist would insist that this promise has already been fulfilled, merely because the Prussian government has presented a useless draft which was rejected by the Prussian Chamber. We know of no wish more urgent on the occasion of the Kaiser's jubilee and no demand which expresses the vital interests of the Prussian people more completely than the introduction of direct, equal, and universal suffrage in Prussia.

As in domestic politics, so also in the field of world politics, not all the golden dreams of the Wilhelmian era have materialized. Here, too, well-intended wish collided at times with stubborn reality. One only needs to remember the Krüger Telegram, the Kaiser's trips to Jerusalem and Tangiers, Kiaochow and the crusade against China, the Herero wars [in southwest Africa], and the entanglement in Morocco, in order to appreciate how many fine intentions have fallen by the way. Especially at this moment, when political change in the Balkans is raising German armament costs to unprecedented heights, there is certainly no cause for an optimistic view of the world. And whoever holds to the fine slogan "Germany ahead in the world!" is in practice already satisfied if we can merely maintain our rank among the nations. There is one thing about the era of William II that does deserve praise: it has kept the German Empire in undisturbed peace for a quarter of a century, at times under very difficult circumstances. Moreover, William II personally deserves the largest part of the credit. He has proved a strong support, perhaps the strongest, for European peace. Not only the German people, but also foreigners unbiased by foolish prejudices, know that under William II this way of peace will be continued as long as it coincides with the honor and vital interests of the Empire. This is surely the ultimate reason for the growing population, the increase of economic power, and the cultural progress of these twenty-five years.

At times we have boasted of our successes too loudly and occasionally we have sought praise before it was due. Festivals and celebrations of all kinds have been plentiful and perhaps too extravagant, as even the most loyal citizen could agree. Fortunately, the German people had not yet forgotten how to work. So even we can enjoy today's festivities. Not that we approve of everything that has been said and done in the last quarter of a century, and not that the German people could have the least reason for being self-satisfied, but because we are convinced that William II has the best and most honest intentions and is not a commonplace personality, even if the truth often does not penetrate the walls surrounding him. The Kaiser is the living representative of German unity. May he become more and more clearly aware that the most secure foundation for unity rests in the freedom of his people.

5. Selected Documents on Prewar German Foreign Policy

Prewar imperial foreign policy documents are available by the tens of thousands. The four selections below indicate that even two years before the July Crisis of 1914, German decisionmakers had precious little flexibility for political adjustment, and that the Kaiser had no temperament for sophisticated negotiation or diplomatic maneuver.

a. Report of Foreign Minister Alfred von Kiderlen-Wächter to the Foreign Affairs Committee of the German Bundesrat, November 28, 1912

SOURCE: *Verhandlungen des Bundesrats des Deutschen Reiches*, reprinted in Ernst Jäckh, *Kiderlen-Wächter, der Staatsmann und Mensch* . . . (Stuttgart, 1924), II: 193, 194–195, 197–198. Translation by the editor.

Let me make a few introductory comments to my discussion of developments in the Balkans, . . . based on our diplomatic instructions and incoming reports.

We have traditionally formulated our policy in terms of the most feasible preservation of a viable Turkish state, as indicated by our sizeable economic interests in that Empire. Yet, given this pro-Turkish policy, we have always carefully avoided political entanglement in the affairs of Turkey. . . . As regards our attitude to contemporary Balkan troubles, I would like to emphasize that we (like any calm and objectively thinking statesman) have long since anticipated the eventual separation of these European provinces from Turkey and their absorption by the Balkan states. We have only bent our efforts to delay this development as long as possible, so that it might occur without a general Balkan struggle and especially without armed conflict among the great powers. . . .

Here is the situation created by the present [Balkan] war: Turkey will lose her European provinces either now or at a later peace conference. Our interest for the immediate future is to make certain that Turkey (if restricted to Asia Minor and Constantinople) survives as a viable political and economic entity. This interest coincides with that of our ally [Austria-Hungary], and we know from repeated assurances that it also coincides with the interests of England and France. All the powers are agreed that the partition of European Turkey can be left to the Balkan states; they will have to face, and resolve among themselves, whatever difficulties arise from this new situation. It is also the clearly stated view of all the great powers that the ultimate peace settlement affects their various interests so intimately that it must not become a *fait accompli* without their concurrence.

First of all, the powers have a common concern to support the interests of their creditors who hold mortgages based on collateral in European Turkey. This concern has been forcefully expressed to each of the Balkan states by a united action of the accredited ministers of those nations participating in the funding of the Turkish public debt. Nor can the great powers, especially those bordering the Mediterranean, remain unconcerned by the fate of the Aegean Islands. If Turkey is to remain a viable nation those islands immediately adjacent to her coasts in Asia Minor cannot pass into the sovereign control of another power. Finally, all of the great powers have considerable interest in the stability of the Straits of Constantinople. . . .

Generally speaking we are but secondarily involved in the present crisis. Thus we have restrained ourselves publicly wherever possible; yet without attracting public attention we have attained considerable success as a mediator dealing with proposals and counterproposals. Our ally, Austria-Hungary, and secondarily also Italy, have very basic interests at stake. We have thus given Vienna broad diplomatic support and we will continue to do so in the future. We leave to our ally any ultimate assertion of its claims. But if Austria-Hungary were attacked by Russia in process of asserting [Hapsburg] vital interests (which it must do to preserve its great-power status in face of internal Slavic usurpation), then in preservation of our most essential interests we would have to utilize all our power in observance of our alliance obligations. It is often said that Germany need not fight for the Albanian or Adriatic interests of Austria, or even for the harbor of Durazzo. But that is not the issue. The purpose of our alliance is to maintain the great-power status of the mid-European Monarchy at our side, so that we might not some day (as Prince Bismarck put it) find ourselves nose-to-nose with Russia and with France at our back. If Austria must ever fight for her position as a great power, no matter for what reason, we must stand at her side, in order that we will not afterwards have to fight alone. This fact has not prevented us, and will not prevent us in the future, from bringing all our influence to bear in reducing international conflicts. We are limited only by the fact that we cannot expect our ally to suffer humiliation. We wish to avoid conflict as long as that can be done with honor; if that is impossible, we shall look into the eyes of war with calm and determination.

b. The German Ambassador in London, Prince von Lichnowsky, to the Imperial Chancellor von Bethmann-Hollweg, December 3, 1912

SOURCE: Germany. Auswärtiges Amt. *Die grosse Politik der europäischen Kabinette, 1871–1914* (Berlin, 1926), XXXIX: 119–123. Translation by the editor.

No. 1130

London, December 3, 1912

Lord Haldane called on me today to discuss the political situation. During our lengthy conversation, he repeatedly stressed the need to settle our differences in the Near Eastern crisis, since the results of a military conflict in which one or more of the great powers became involved could not be foreseen. England is absolutely peaceful, he said, and no one there wants war, especially for economic reasons. But it is hardly likely that Great Britain could look on passively,[1] were all Europe to be thrown into chaos by an Austrian invasion of Serbia if Belgrade did not voluntarily evacuate the occupied Adriatic coast.

Marginal comments written by Kaiser William II:
1. no one expects it; they'll aid the Gauls

I responded that I did not want to ask him whether that was saying that England would take sides against us.[2] He replied that this was certainly not the inevitable, but the possible consequence of a war between the two continental alliances. The roots of English policy as he expressed it, lay in the feeling which is widely held here that the balance of power ought to be maintained to a certain extent.[3] Thus, England would not under any circumstances be able to tolerate a défeat of the French,[4] which he foresees with some certainty, being a great admirer of our armed forces and our military institutions. England could and would not accept the fact of a united continental coalition under the leadership of a single power.[5]

Thus, should Germany be drawn into the dispute by Austria and hence into war with France, pressures would arise in England which no government could resist and which might have inestimable consequences.[6] The theory of the balance of power is an axiom of British foreign policy[7] and has led to their association with France and Russia. He assured me that England desires the best relations with Germany,[8] and the acceptance of Your Excellency's and Herr von Kiderlen's statements in the Reichstag, as well as my recent speech at the banquet of the Royal Society, could only prove to me the correctness of this view.[9] Further, no one here would want to wage war with us so long as no European entanglements[10] develop. However, the consequences of a European war are so totally unforeseeable that he could not guarantee anything in that event.[11]

Lord Haldane mentioned the policy of Sir E. Grey and his proposal. As you know, he is a close friend of the Foreign Secretary who even occasionally lives with him. He confirmed that Sir Edward has the hope, given the opportunity, of acting in a mediatory role and avoids giving the appearance of favoring the Entente

2. of course
3. it'll change!
4. but they'll have to
5. that's really a hidden threat or challenge!
6. right; we've already estimated them
7. balance of power is nonsense! And will make England our permanent enemy
8. absolutely useless with such assumptions!
9. all is nonsense! will have no significant results
10. they will occur
11. neither could I!

in this crisis.[12] Lord Haldane is of the opinion that the lively preliminary discussions will force the Russians and Austrians to present concrete proposals, which has not hitherto occurred. He supported the selection of London as the most appropriate city. But in the meantime, everything must be avoided which would stiffen the alliances.[13] Instead, they should turn into "gelatine" as much as possible.[14]

c. Memorandum of Kaiser William II to Foreign Minister von Kiderlen-Wächter, December 5, 1912

SOURCE: Germany. Auswärtiges Amt. *Die grosse Politik der europäischen Kabinette, 1871–1914* (Berlin, 1926), XXXIX: 123–125. Translation by the editor.

[To] His Excellency von Kiderlen, Foreign Office, Berlin

[no place, no date]

Haldane's conversation with Lichnowsky, which I read this morning, removes all the veils of uncertainty. England, out of envy and hatred for Germany, will definitely espouse France and Russia against us. The ultimate struggle for existence which the Teutons in Europe (Austria, Germany) will have to wage against Slavs (Russia) who are supported by Neo-Latins (Gauls), finds the Anglo-Saxons siding with the Slavs. Reason: envy, fear of our becoming too powerful! This constitutes desirable clarification which must henceforth be the basis of our policy. We must make a military treaty with Bulgaria and Turkey as well as with Rumania. We must also conclude such a treaty with Japan. Any power which is available is good enough to help us. It is a matter of Germany's being or not being. Young Stolberg, who came through Sofia in the autumn and visited [King] Ferdinand, shortly before the [Balkan] war, told [Prince] Adalbert yesterday during a fox-hunt in Primkenau that the King had said to him: "We shall soon

12. but he still is an ally of the Gallo-Slavs against the Teutons!
13. nonsense!
14. because England is too cowardly in this case to leave France and Russia openly in the lurch, and is too jealous of us and hates us; therefore, other powers should not be allowed to defend their interests with the sword, for then she will go against us despite all assurances, despite Marschall and Lichnowsky. What a nation of shopkeepers! They call that a policy of peace! Balance of power! The final conflict between the Slavs and Teutons will find the Anglo-Saxons on the side of the Slavs and Gauls.

have a war in which it will scarcely be possible for Germany to maintain peace. If she wishes to maintain her alliance, she will have to join and become entangled."

William I[mperator] R[ex]

d. Imperial Chancellor von Bethmann-Hollweg to the Ambassador in London, Prince von Lichnowsky, June 16, 1914

SOURCE: Germany. Auswärtiges Amt. *Die grosse Politik der europäischen Kabinette, 1871–1914* (Berlin, 1926), XXXIX: 626–630. Translation by the editor.

Highly confidential

Berlin, June 16, 1914

It will not have escaped your Excellency that the article in "Birschewija Wjedomosti," which is known to stem from the [Russian] Minister of War, General Suchomlinow, caused a considerable stir in Germany. As a matter of fact, probably no officially inspired article has ever revealed the warlike tendencies of the Russian military faction as recklessly as this press statement does. It is probably written too clumsily to strengthen French chauvinism permanently. On the other hand, one cannot fail to note its considerable repercussion on German public opinion.

Hitherto only the most extreme Pan-Germans and militarists insisted that Russia was deliberately scheming to attack us, but now calmer politicians are also beginning to incline to that view. The first result is a demand for renewed, immediate, extensive strengthening of the Army. As things are now, this will produce competition with the navy, which refuses to be shortchanged when anything is done for the army. I mention *very confidentially* that since His Majesty the Kaiser is already quite set in these views, I fear that the summer and autumn will see a fresh outburst of armaments fever.

Although the uncertainty of conditions in Russia makes it hard to discover the real aims of Russian policy with any precision, and although, disposed as we are politically, we must consider that Russia, more than all the Great European Powers, is prepared to run the risk of a great warlike adventure, nevertheless I still do not think that Russia is planning to make war on us soon. She wishes rather—and we cannot reproach her—to be secured with more extensive military armaments than during the last troubles in the Balkans, presuming a new outbreak there. A European conflagration—if there is to be one—will be determined entirely by the attitudes of Germany and England. If we act together as joint guarantors of peace in Europe (in doing so we are hampered neither by the engagements of the Triple Alliance nor of the Triple Entente, *so far as we pursue that aim from the start according to a jointly conceived plan*), war may be averted. Otherwise any minor conflict of interests between Russia and Austria-Hungary may kindle the war-torch.

It is obvious that more violent agitation by German chauvinists and armament fanatics will hamper such Anglo-German cooperation quite as much as any secret pressure from French and Russian chauvinism upon the British Cabinet. Germany will never be able to give up growth of her army in relation to the growth of her population. There is no thought of extending the Naval Law; but within the limits of that Law the commissioning of extra cruisers for foreign service, the arming and manning of battleships, etc., will demand ever-increasing expenditures. Yet it does make a great difference whether such measures come forward as the result of gradual and quiet development or are undertaken in panic under pressure from public opinion that is excited and full of war fears.

It is very gratifying that Sir Edward Grey firmly denied in the House of Commons those rumors of an English-Russian naval agreement and that his denial was emphasized in the *Westminster Gazette*. Had these rumors had substance, even if only to the extent that the English and Russian navies planned cooperation in a future war against Germany (similar to the agreements which England made with France at the time of the Morocco crisis), it would have highly agitated Russian and French chauvinism, and public opinion here would have reacted in justified alarm that would have stimulated a "navy scare" and renewed poisoning of our slowly improving relations with England. In the context of the nervous tension which Europe has experienced in the last few years, the further consequences would have been unforeseeable. In any case, the idea of a common English-German effort to foster peace would have been fatefully endangered from the very beginning by threats of emerging complications.

I most respectfully bid Your Excellency to express my special gratitude to Sir Edward Grey for his open and straightforward declarations and with it to express in an informal and cautious manner those general observations which I mentioned above.

I await with particular interest your report on the reception you encounter with Sir Edward Grey.

Von Bethmann-Hollweg

6. A Socialist Records the Coming of the War

Philipp Scheidemann, who in 1918 was to proclaim the German republic from a balcony of the Kaiser's palace in Berlin, became a Socialist in the 1880s and worked his way up through the party. In 1912 he was elected vice-president of the Reichstag. His vividly written memoirs portray the emotions of the crisis in 1914 and record the failure of international socialism to prevent the outbreak of war.

SOURCE: Philipp Scheidemann, *The Making of New Germany. The Memoirs of Philipp Scheidemann* (New York: Meredith Press, 1929), I: 201–204, 208, 211–216. Copyright 1929 by Meredith Press. Reprinted by permission.

CRITICAL DAYS

At express speed I had returned to Berlin. Everywhere where a word could be heard the conversation was of war and rumors of war. There was only one topic of conversation—war. The supporters of war seemed to be in a great majority. Were these pugnacious fellows, young and old, bereft of their senses? Were they so ignorant of the horrors of war? I only heard voices advocating peace in the circle of my own Party friends, apart from the few Social Democratic newspapers. Yet the vast majority of the people were opposed to war, without a doubt. Vast crowds of demonstrators paraded "Unter den Linden." Schoolboys and students were there in their thousands; their bearded seniors, with their Iron Crosses of 1870–71 on their breasts, were there too in huge numbers.

Treitschke and Bernhardi (to say nothing of the National Liberal beer-swilling heroes) seemed to have multiplied a thousandfold. Patriotic demonstrations had an intoxicating effect and excited the war-mongers to excess. "A call like the voice of thunder." Cheers! "In triumph we will smite France to the ground." "All hail to thee in victor's crown." Cheers! Hurrah!

The counterdemonstrations immediately organized by the Berlin Social Democrats were imposing, and certainly more disciplined than the Jingo processions, but could not outdo the shouts of the fire-eaters. "Good luck to him who cares for truth and right. Stand firmly round the flag." "Long live peace!" "Socialists, close up your ranks." The Socialist International cheer. The patriots were sometimes silenced by the Proletarians; then they came out on top again. This choral contest, "Unter den Linden," went on for days.

"It is the hour we yearned for—our friends know that," so the Pan-German papers shouted, that had for years been shouting for war. The *Post*, conducted by von Stumm, the Independent Conservative leader and big Industrial, had thus moaned in all its columns in 1900, at the fortieth celebration of the Franco-German War: "Another forty years of peace would be a national misfortune for Germany." Now these firebrands saw the seeds they had planted ripening. Perhaps in the heads of many who had been called upon to make every effort to keep the peace Bernhardi's words, that "the preservation of peace can and never shall be the aim of politics," had done mischief. These words are infernally like the secret instructions given by Baron von Holstein to the German delegates to the first Peace Conference at The Hague:

"For the State there is no higher aim than the preservation of its own interests; among the Great Powers these will not necessarily coincide with the maintenance of peace, but rather with the hostile policy of enemies and rivals."

The Executive of the S.P.D. wished in any case to do what it could to ward off the horror. On 28th July, it summoned by telegram a general meeting with the Committee of Control, whose members lived in various parts of the Empire. Though the Executive was badly "hauled" (this is what we called it among ourselves in jest) by the Royal and Imperial (K.K.) representatives, as per usual, we came through the meeting very well. We were speechless when we were actually congratulated on our efforts. We had never experienced anything like this. But the meeting did not close without a word of blame. A member of the K.K. complained that "Comrade Ebert, one of the chairmen of the Party, has not even returned from his leave of absence. It will create a painful impression in Leipzig, and must not occur again."

On 28th–29th July, 1914, the International Socialist Bureau met in Brussels. Among those present were Jaurès (France), Troelstra (Holland), Vandervelde (Belgium), Keir Hardie (England), Marjorie (Italy), Haase, etc. The Bureau took a serious view of the imminence of war, and exhorted the workers in every country to agitate.

For September, 1914, an International Socialist Conference was arranged in Vienna, to be followed by a Social Democratic Congress in Würzburg. Owing to the outbreak of War both congresses were declared off.

Bethmann-Hollweg warned our Press, through his henchman Wahnschaffe, Assistant Secretary of State, a clever and honest man devoted to his master, to be very careful, for if war did come, a "state of siege" (martial law) would be proclaimed, and it would be a very grave matter for the Press.

The Executive within a few days launched a manifesto, sent a circular letter to the Press, and published an "extra special" edition of the *Vorwärts*. We were working at high pressure.

The Executive published the following manifesto on 25th July:

"The territory of the Balkans is streaming with the blood of thousands of slaughtered men; the ruins of devastated towns and sacked villages are smoking; starving men without work are wandering from place to place, and widowed women and orphan children; and the unbridled fury of Austrian Imperialism is preparing to bring death and destruction on all Europe. . . . No German soldier's blood must be spilt to gratify the murderous intentions of the Austrian tyrant. Comrades, we call upon you to express at once by mass meetings the unshakable desire of the class-conscious Proletariate for peace. . . ."

Ebert had been spending some weeks of his leave on the island of Rügen. He could not, and clearly would not, believe in the terrible earnestness of events. In a letter dated 27th July he wrote to the Executive that they could not have a second "Bâle" over again—*i.e.*, the last International Socialist Conference. On the other hand, a manifesto by the International Socialistic Bureau seemed to him likely to do good. He did not know that members of the International Socialistic Bureau were already on their way to Brussels. "I earnestly ask you to inform me speedily. Naturally I am quite prepared to return at once. We are very comfortable here. But as things are, one cannot be easy, as I told you." Pastor Felden, in his book on Ebert, reports a conversation between Ebert and his wife, from which it is perfectly clear that Ebert alone of all his colleagues did not return to Berlin, because he thought the outbreak of war impossible. "The ultimatum is a warning gun. The Executive think otherwise. In Berlin they look too much on the black side. I said that in reply to their last letter in which they asked me to return. . . . Frau Ebert was doubtful, he was sure; it's nonsense; there will be no war."

The Ebert family had been for a walk; when they came back they found a telegram urgently begging the Chairman to return. His family had never before seen him in such an excited condition. . . .

On July 31st, 1914, a meeting of the joint Executives of the Party and Section took place, at which Haase and Ledebour agitated for the rejection of the War Credits. I was opposed to any definite motion. In any case I made up my mind to consult with more intimate friends, whose view I thought I knew perfectly, before the meeting started. The only definite motion at the meeting was to the effect that Hermann Müller should be sent to Paris via Brussels at once to consult our French colleagues. It would have a great effect in the whole world if identical motions could be brought before the Reichstag and the Chamber of Deputies.

Müller started off the same day, although a "state of war" had been declared. Next morning, 1st August, the news reached us of the murder of our friend Jean Jaurès. We were all dumbfounded by the terrible announcement. I could scarcely accept the duty of drafting a telegram of condolence. I telegraphed to the *Humanité* in Paris:

"Deeply moved we read the terrible news that our Jaurès, both yours and ours, is no longer among the living. No more serious loss could have happened to all of us at this grave time. The German Proletariate bows its head before the genius of this great champion and bitterly deplores that this man can no longer be where he was—a man who fought all his life for an understanding between France and Germany. His work will be unforgettable in the history of International Socialism and human progress."

As we learned after the War, this telegram never reached Paris. On the evening of this black day the awful tension was over that had distracted millions and trillions—whether they were men of peace or war. Mobilization! Here was the cruel truth that banished all doubts; now the wholesale slaughter would begin.

FOR OR AGAINST THE WAR CREDITS

On 2d August the Executives of the Party and the Section of the Reichstag met together in the Party committee room. The Reichstag was to meet on 4th August to pass the War Credits—that had been told us officially. Haase and Ledebour advocated their rejection, all the others their adoption. Unanimity was impossible, abstention likewise, for a Party of our strength could not think of abstaining from voting in this critical hour for the Fatherland. At this time I felt Bebel's absence more than ever before; he had such a keen sense for reality. Haase, as the Party leader, dissented—in my opinion, in a most unreasonable way. The wise Fischer became so agitated that his nerves failed him during his speech and he began to cry. Haase and Ledebour were not to be won over; but I had afterwards an impression that they were quite pleased to be in a minority. It was arranged that we should meet again at nine in the office of the *Vorwärts*, and then make a declaration—for or against. No matter who secured the majority, we had to work in common at getting out a statement of some sort. At 5 P.M. David, Fischer, Molkenbuhr, Schöplin, Wels, Südekum, and I met in Goehre's garden in Zehlendorf, and there drafted a statement, after a discussion of several hours. At 9 P.M. another argument with Haase and Ledebour at the *Vorwärts*. Neither had made a formal statement in writing, but only a few rough notes.

We parted about midnight. I spent a sleepless night. Should we succeed in getting a majority for acceptance in the Section or not? In the course of the day a message from the Chancellor, Bethmann-Hollweg, came to my house, inviting me to talk things over on 3d August at 12 noon.

On 3d August the Section met at 10 A.M., received a few reports, and then adjourned till Haase and I returned from our interview with the Chancellor. . . . At first we talked quite freely, without sitting down, over the motions to be carried along with the War Credits. The Chancellor then read the speech he made next day in the Reichstag; here and there he put in some more or less confidential remarks. The nearer he got to the end, the more agitated he became; he did not know what to do with his long arms, and sometimes hit the table with both his fists. His voice sounded quite hollow when he said, "My conscience is clear."

[Reichstag President] Kämpf thanked the Chancellor for what he had said, and Bethmann-Hollweg at once asked to withdraw, as he had a great deal to do. Delbrück [State Secretary] was then questioned about Italy's attitude; Bethmann-Hollweg had said nothing about it. This well-informed man pretended to know nothing. From Italy we went on to the agenda, and discussed the best way of presenting the draft proposals at the full sitting of the Reichstag. As the gentlemen talked as if the unanimous acceptance of all measures, including the votes of credit, was an absolute certainty, Haase and I reminded them that our Section had not finally made up its mind. Haase, by the tone he adopted in the conversation, would have led no one to suppose that he was not in favour of the credits. That made me angry, because before going down to the House he had declared, right up to the last minute, that he would do his utmost to vote against the Bill. I said this to him on the way from the House to the Restaurant Zollernhof, where we dined together, and his answer was: "I have always maintained that the Section has not yet made its decision." Haase's procedure, quite apart from his acting on principle, angered me immensely. It was agreed that Kämpf should make a short speech after the Chancellor, and announce the welcome fact that the votes of credit would be passed unanimously. Even the members who objected on principle to war had given their assent. Haase swallowed all this, while I referred to the Section's not having yet given its decision, and asked President Kämpf to frame with us his reply in accordance with what the Section should decide. All were agreed to that.

We declined to entertain the request that no one should speak after Kämpf, for our decision, no matter what it might be, must be justified by us in all circumstances. After a rather long discussion we finally arrived at this conclusion: the wording of our statement should be submitted to the other Party leaders at 9 P.M., so that they could make amendments. On that Haase solemnly declared that there was no necessity for it. In no circumstances should our statement be aimed at any party, but should in general terms decline all responsibility for a policy that, in our opinion, might lead to war. In its form it should be suitable and worthy of the occasion.

MÜLLER'S REPORT FROM PARIS

The Section met at once after dinner under my chairmanship. The discussion was extremely bitter, and in the course of it Müller arrived from Paris. Surprised by the declaration of War, he had had considerable trouble in recrossing the frontier. He reported as follows: he had been well and kindly received, as usual, by our French colleagues, but unfortunately no understanding had been reached. Pierre Renaudel had given the clearest statement of the attitude of our French colleagues at the meeting:

"The position of the French and German democrat is not the same. The French Socialists were fully informed of diplomatic proceedings by their Government in due course; in Germany this was not the case. If France, whose people and Government desired peace, were attacked by Germany, their French colleagues would be forced to vote for the War Budget, because measures for self-defence had to be taken by France, if attacked. Thus situated, the French democrat could not abstain from voting. The German democrat was in a different position, if Germany were the aggressor. They could perhaps vote against the War Credits."

After one of the French comrades had stated that Germany would be generally considered guilty for the outbreak of war, Müller replied:

"German Socialists are in the habit of speaking the truth in the most pointed way to their Government. We have latterly reproached our Government most bitterly in the public Press because they did not take sufficient care to inform the country before sending off the ultimatum to Serbia. But this is a thing that cannot be altered, and, as matters now stand, the greatest danger is threatened from Russia. . . . Yet it is the general opinion in all Party circles in Germany that Russia would be the guilty party if it now came to war, and that France is in a position to stop war if she will put the requisite pressure on St. Petersburg for preserving peace."

It was very soon clear to our friend Hermann Müller, in the course of his conversation with the French Socialists, that the French would vote for the War Credits. Identical declarations both in the Reichstag and the Chamber of Deputies were now out of the question. After Müller's report the Reichstag Section continued to discuss the War Credits, with the result that only fourteen members voted against passing the War Credits. That a few members abstained from voting, as was stated later, is absolutely discredited.

7. The Psychological Impact of World War I upon Germany

The years of the Weimar Republic were fraught with recrimination over the reasons for Germany's military and political breakdown in the autumn of 1918. The quarrels became so vicious and politically disruptive that the Weimar Constituent Assembly set up a commission in 1919 to investigate the causes of the German collapse. Its final work was not completed until 1928. The following analysis was made by Joseph Joos, a prominent official of the Catholic trade unions, a Reichstag deputy for the Catholic Center party between 1919 and 1933, and inmate of Dachau concentration camp, 1941–1945. This report was included in the official records of the investigating committee. But it was all to little practical avail in the longer run. The four words of the Nazi slogan, "Stab-in-the-back!" were politically more effective than seven volumes of official documents and expert testimony.

SOURCE: R. H. Lutz, ed., *The Causes of the German Collapse of 1918* (Stanford, California: Stanford University Press, 1934), pp. 270–276. Reprinted by permission.

SPEECH MADE BY DEPUTY JOOS (CENTER PARTY) AT THE MEETING OF 12TH OCTOBER 1927

The remarks which I have to make refer to the psychological causes of our collapse. In what I have to say I am not following political periodicals but make use of the observations I made and the experience I gained in the country. . . .

One opinion, with regard to the collapse, may be expressed more or less as follows: *Before* the war everything was in order in Germany; we were a united people in 1914; then followed the evils, the great loss of human life, the blockade, and so on; these brought in their train discontent and bad feeling; unscrupulous agitation hastened the collapse and caused the revolution. I consider this opinion to be wrong and also unhistorical. It leads to an *over*estimate of the state of affairs before or at the beginning of the war and to an *under*estimate of certain occurrences. In that case one does not see things aright. One must then assume that a state of error existed, and Dr. Philipp is also compelled to assume that. In reality, the German people before the war was permeated by great breaches in its inner and mental constitution, not only in what concerns its form of government. By these breaches I mean the process of disintegration in town and country with regard to traditional customs and to the feeling of nationality, the uncertainty of the national instinct, the tension between capital and labor, and the lack of human relations, that is to say of solidarity, in all groups of the population. What we endeavored to do at that time by means of instruction in constitutional matters and the work of popular education was in no way suited to bring about a substantial improvement. We entered the war with the people in an inner mental frame of mind which in itself gave rise to anxiety. The next question was what effect the war would have on this popular frame of mind. Dr. Philipp has paid no attention to this inner mental frame of mind of our people before the war, but begins his remarks with the outbreak of war. He differentiates quite correctly between the collapse and the revolutionary movement, but the differentiation is not always consistent and, in many places, not regularly carried out. The appreciation of the one against the other is blurred, but I follow his summary: "The responsibility for the origin of the German collapse and the course it took is, however, borne not only by the unchangeable and fatal forces which almost arbitrarily determined and explained the behavior of the German people but also by those disintegrating forces which intentionally worked for the collapse."

One may agree with this and say that such revolutionary forces certainly existed which also worked to bring about certain actions and were also in touch with foreign countries. It also appears to me to be proved that, at least up to a certain phase, not only mental influences came from abroad but also material support for the men who worked for the outbreak of the revolution. But we are not dealing with that, and the question is and remains: which of these various factors, which worked unchangeably and fatally and intentionally revolutionized the others, had the greatest effect, that is to say, what is the order of precedence of these factors in the entire process. Volumes of evidence, speeches, and revolutionary expressions can be collected; for me they are no proof, and, even objectively, they have no power of conviction. Revolutionary speeches could ensnare the listeners only if the ground was prepared beforehand. ["*Quite so!*"] They cannot simply eat their way into a smooth marble wall. Dr. Philipp speaks of pacifists on principle who may well have been there during the war. Perhaps he is thinking of the people who now found peace societies. [*Chairman Dr. Philipp: "Like Quidde!"*] These people were very quiet and unimportant here, as in other countries, during the war. I may remind you in this connection of Romain Rolland's book, *Clerambault*. The pacifists were huddled together and sought for a watchword which, in the end, was perhaps "then in God's name war for the sake of peace." But they did not know what to do with themselves during the war and withdrew altogether.

I also follow the sentence in which Dr. Philipp says: "There was no absolute necessity to break off the war suddenly; anyone who has been hungry for years can go on being hungry for three months longer." That is just the salient point. A state of affairs had arisen within them which said: "We cannot do more and we do not *want* to do any more." That was the end of the business. It was not a final success gained by the revolutionaries but the end of the process which was taking place in the minds of thinking men.

We must therefore penetrate somewhat more deeply into these connections in our national psychology. Dr. Philipp speaks of nerves, and I also constantly hear it said that they had lost their nerve; yes, but that is no final explanation. That was certainly also the case and runs alongside, but it does not penetrate to the spot where the final decisions are made. We shall get nearer it if we think of the disillusionment which constantly increased among those who had never prepared themselves for a war in this form and of this kind and who cherished the primitive hope that it would all be over in a few months. Dr. Philipp's conclusions in this respect appear very interesting to me. He enumerates a large number of symptoms, including war weariness, feeble desire to fight, and artificial inflation; he speaks of atrophy of the ethically national enthusiasm and of a loss of mental balance.

Dr. Philipp, you get nearest the matter when you speak of the war as a mental revolutionary. I do not say war *as such*. I cannot do that because I have only experience of *this* war. I do not know whether or not every war has this revolutionary effect, but *this* war undoubtedly had it. War is a revolutionary in itself, especially *this* war, and my opinion is that this war, in the form in which it had to be waged, destroyed of itself in the interior of the country the primitive manner of thinking of our population in town and country, disintegrated the consciousness of the inevitable connection between things among the people and thus prepared the way for the collapse. By "primitive manner of thinking" I mean what is peculiar to the people. Vast masses of the people live on primitive and direct ideas. This is also their great strength; for purposeful thinking merely aimed at advantage is not their way. It is for this reason that they have the power, which the so-called differentiated man no longer possesses, of really believing in things and of sacrificing themselves for ideals. This fundamental stock, this power in our people, has been corroded by the war and men have been reduced to a state of mental conflict. The war was regarded as a war of *defense*, and it was therefore a holy and a just war for the masses of the population. But at the moment people began to speak of *conquests*, of the urge toward expansion and the lust for domination, those who had started on the assumption of a holy war found themselves at variance with themselves and this conflict developed within them. Admittedly, the military said to them: We now need guarantees in order not to be involved in a fresh war. But these are reflections which do not appeal to such people and the most they saw was that something different was being made out of the war.

And now we come to war economics! How important was the women's work during the war and the equalization of wages. Skilled and unskilled workmen, the young and the old, all were reduced to the same level. I ask you to consider what a revolution was caused by these necessary measures in the manner of thinking and the judgment of the masses. In the third place I consider the stimulus to production which had to be given. We were a nation in distress and the population felt this to be so. But they saw that, in order to carry on the war, the producers of war material had to be stimulated in order that they might make the greatest possible war profits. They therefore appeared to the people as profit-makers. The farmers declined to make deliveries. The reasons given by Dr. Philipp are plausible, even psychologically comprehensible. But the *effect* remains the same nevertheless, and the effect among the people was that they said to themselves: "It is no longer a question of ideals but of business; ideals are stupid." And a feeling of hypocrisy pervaded our public life as early as the second year of the war. The "privileging of those who paid the highest prices," as

Dr. Philipp calls it in one passage, was one of these revolutionary facts which occurred every day. The standing in queues by those who could not obtain food otherwise caused the mental breakdown of the people. I do not consider it quite exact when you say in one passage: "This example, offered by the people who could afford to buy this and that while the others could not do so, provided 'water for the mills of the revolutionary agitators.'" That is merely secondary; what I wished to point out is that something gave way *in the people themselves,* quite independently of the agitators who worked upon them. The war rationalized, sobered, and impoverished our people's manner of thinking and caused its internal breakdown.

Those who wish to observe these effects on our national psychology and how they reacted on our children during the war and also after the war should read Heinrich Kautz's book, *Im Schatten der Schlote.* This teacher in a people's school in the coal area describes how the child of the war became the child of the revolution, and he observes the souls of these children during the war. It seemed to him from the observation which he made that the type of war child he saw must become a revolution child. One passage in his book runs as follows: "What a hatred of the rich who had a good time everywhere, who could buy everything they wanted with dirty paper money, who never waited for hours in the freezing cold outside the food stores, who got everything by roundabout means, and whose external appearance alone was a passport for everything."

You can imagine what effect such things had. We underestimated that. Our colleague, Lambach, has made a footnote in one place where he modified something with regard to the feelings which he described at that time. He says: "But I did not wish to say that what the people assert is *true.* The point is not whether it *is true* but whether it was believed to be true and thus what its effects were."

I read in one passage how the *longing for peace* developed into a great moral force and became one of the factors of power and allies of the revolutionaries. I can quite imagine that a longing for peace *and* a will to war can exist by side, but only so long as the war has a *meaning* in the thoughts of the people, and here again I am faced by a fact which became clear to me during the war. It was not the sacrifice of blood and treasure nor was it hunger which was the decisive factor. It is possible to perform superhuman services and even more, as we did in the war; but it can *only* be done so long as there is an answer to the question: *wherefore and for what purpose. If the war loses its meaning*, the masses can make no further sacrifices. This state of affairs came about in our case. I saw it growing up during the war. The clear idea of defense and the Fatherland which obtained in 1914 faded into the background and in their minds the meaning of the war was obliterated by hundreds of impressions. All that ran parallel to the efforts of the revolutionary defeatists and wet-blankets.

We now come to the civil powers and the General Staffs of the Armies. Well, what those above wished may have sounded passably well, but what it led to among the people was bad, and Dr. Philipp says in one passage that it was a fatal disaster that during the World War the civil authorities and the General Staffs often ruled side by side in accordance with completely different principles and thus helped on the disintegrating forces in the German people in an undreamt-of fashion. That is true. Teacher Kautz expresses that as follows:

"Whether it was the food card or the passport, the purchase ticket or the certificate of poverty, the transfer of a wounded soldier to a hospital at home or the application made for the grant of leave to her husband by a sick mother, or the admission of a soldier's child into a home or the choice of the children who were to be given a holiday in the country—the disdain of the fighting man and his family was only too easily expressed in all these matters; at least this was the indisputable impression among the common people, who personally had no inclination at all to accept with understanding or to excuse official dilatoriness and fussiness."

In publishing my periodical I have had to do with the censorship and not only with military censors. In Germany the military censors were more sensible than their civil colleagues. In our case the latter was the Chief Burgomaster of our town. It was absolutely impossible to convince him that I must explain what was wrong with the food order. He forbade every discussion of any kind and even quite practical proposals and details. One day he forbade us to publish an article about the Pope, I believe because it had to do with the peace resolution. The article merely gave the Pope the credit for his efforts in the cause of world peace without making any reference to policy. Imagine what kind of impression it made when the title was left: "Pope. . . ." and underneath a blank space with the remark, "Forbidden by the local censorship."

I regarded that as a sign of increasing estrangement from the people on the part of the officials. The old system was not consciously regarded with hostility in the sense that everyone consciously wanted to be done with the cast out old system on the day when the revolution came. But the old system had become so *indifferent* to so many people owing to so many causes, and that is what first made later developments possible.

I should like to make one more remark with regard to *electoral reform* in Prussia. I made the following observation in this connection: The average man, who was everywhere undervalued, disdained, and slighted and yet called upon to render the same services in the field and at home, suddenly ceased to accept this and regarded electoral reform in Prussia simply as the expression of the appreciation of the plain man; and this desire for self-assertion which forced its way out was quite natural. It is always painful to me when I meet with Conservatives who have not understood that with regard to those times. If a man can no longer assert himself either in public or in his work or in social life, his wishes are forced in another direction and he takes refuge in politics, and then he wishes to be respected in that sphere. That has been overlooked. The movement was encouraged among us by the kind of opposition offered to it and I am fulfilling a historical duty when I remind you that we in western Germany came into a serious conflict with our own spiritual leaders with regard to this question, because the then Cardinal Archbishop of Cologne, von Hartmann, did not actually issue a prohibition to the great workmen's associations regarding the discussion of the suffrage, but he did not wish it and recalled the priest who was chairman of our association on account of this matter. That first really fostered the idea that everything that was Conservative did not wish to grant the people rights. This haggling about the suffrage and about progress really did a great deal of harm in the country. Among the troops at the front it was different in part, but in the country it was an acute question. What would have been necessary during the second half of the war was not the prohibition of this and that but solely a practical example of unselfishness, given by those at the head of affairs. The nameless made enough sacrifices; they suffered from hunger and privations and gave their sons for the sake of the war and the national future. But it was those with big names that the people wished to see, the authorities and the officials. In this connection I am entirely in agreement with what Dr. Philipp says in one place:

"It appears to me most improbable that the bourgeoisie, which was completely broken down morally, would have pulled itself together and taken its place firmly at the side of the opponents of the revolution. For the major part of it the passable personal security and the protection of its goods and chattels under the new democratic republic guaranteed by the alliance between Ebert and Groener was preferable to the October monarchy which was controlled by parliament and which would probably first have to be restored by sanguinary fighting."

What he says about the bourgeoisie is the truth, and it is because this power was no longer there that not only could no power be transferred from this bourgeoisie to the masses of the population but, on the contrary, that this bourgeoisie also destroyed the forces which were still available in the people. That provided the basis for the events which occurred.

II

Revolution, Constitution, and
Peace Treaty, 1918–1919

WHEN OPPORTUNITIES for major reform suddenly appeared in the autumn of 1918, they caught most Germans quite unprepared, for they were diverted by worries about the decline of the Reich as a great power. Even the great majority of Social Democratic politicians were not ready to deal with the abrupt changes they encountered. The men of Prince Max von Baden's interim regime were concentrating on negotiating Germany out of the war when the naval mutinies and sporadic urban uprisings broke out in early November. Once the armistice was signed and the Kaiser had fled to Holland in order to prevent civil war in Germany, the revolution was virtually up for grabs. For the next two months parliamentary groups, soviets of soldiers and sailors, and workers groups maneuvered for control in Berlin. Simultaneously a Communist regime briefly seized power in Munich. In early January of 1919 the ultraleft (supported by Soviet Russian influence and funds) attempted a coup comparable to the Russian October Revolution. This "Spartacist revolt" was suppressed by the less radical Socialists with support from the demobilizing army.

Now Germans turned to formulate a new kind of government. At long sessions of the Constituent Assembly in Weimar (February–July 1919) delegates from all German political parties hammered out a new constitution that tried to combine the best of Anglo-Saxon and Continental democratic ideals and practices. In the midst of these labors and hopes the Germans were brought up sharply by power political realities; they were called to Versailles and forced to accept a peace treaty virtually dictated by their wrathful opponents.

Incomprehensible military defeat, unanticipated revolutionary uprising, and an unexpectedly harsh peace treaty: these were psychological experiences, the reverberations of which would disturb the German political and social environment for years to come.

8. A Memoir of the Revolution and the Spartacist Revolt

Theodor Wolff, a talented nephew of newspaper dynast Rudolf Mosse, was appointed editor of the *Berliner Tageblatt* in 1907 and held the reins until the paper was confiscated by the Nazis in 1933. He became the best-known political and cultural commentator of Germany in the era when the *Tageblatt* was one of the staunchest supporters of the Weimar republic.

SOURCE: Theodor Wolff, *Through Two Decades* (London: William Heinemann Ltd., 1936), pp. 115–120, 123–132, 134–147, 149–151, 153–157. Reprinted by permission of William Heinemann Ltd. and Allert de Lange N.V.

All other revolutions had their specific costume. The great French Revolution had its own, proclaiming the victory of the Third Estate over the Court party and the aristocrats; it was cut to the pattern of the youthful enthusiasm of Camille Desmoulins, of the powerful will of Danton, of the affected puritanism of Robespierre's dictatorship. The German Revolution of 1848 had a gorgeous gallery of characteristic costumes, a wealth of exquisite fancy in the external presentation of personality. Friedrich Hecker and Gustav Struve, the Baden leader, with their blouses and braided jackets, their broad-brimmed hats with feathers stuck saucily in them, and cavalry-sabres buckled at their side, were unmistakable captains of rather romantic fighters for freedom. . . . In November 1918 the only dress was the worn and shabby coat of the little man; nobody was in search of the picturesque, and where, indeed, could it have been found amid the grey destitution of that day? That Revolution could not have a costume, and nobody seemed to feel the need of one. After the four years of war there was no creative energy left, not enough even for a rebel's necktie, and while the other revolutions had their particular postures, their physical and intellectual attitudes, that of 1789 the Roman tradition and that of 1848 the gesture of the fighter at the barricades and the rebel volunteer, the revolution of 1918 had no such element. Too much of tragic reality had been lived through for any interest to be left in following the tragic models. Fifteen years later other men, with more time and inclination for such inventions, fitted themselves and their followers into interesting uniforms. That November of 1918 was no season for new fashions.

Nor did there beat, except rarely, any fervently revolutionary hearts in the tired frames beneath that November drabness. No literature had prepared men's minds for the Republic, no Freiligrath, no Herwegh had shaken the thrones of princes by the might of the poet's pen, and the prose of the most radical critics had been least concerned of all with constitutional forms. Apart from Rosa Luxemburg there was no strong revolutionary figure. The feeble and fidgety Liebknecht, whom nothing but self-sacrificing loyalty prevented that remarkable woman from abandoning, was a poor substitute for a tribune. The Social Democratic leaders were like a stage-player who has always filled the decorous part of the old father in Schiller's *Kabale und Liebe* and suddenly has to play the fiery young Ferdinand. They were compelled to do the work of the Revolution because it was a proletarian movement, and because they could not permit immature rebels and Bolshevistic Spartacists to snatch the working classes from them, and to produce a chaos at the thought of which their elderly souls, used to the orderliness and reasonableness and discipline of trade union officialdom, were filled with horror.

Some of these Social Democratic leaders became Ministers. The imperial system had never allowed them the slightest opportunity to study the part, and yet they developed into statesmanly personalities, perhaps too statesmanly, and showed more talent for government than many of their predecessors under the old régime. Ebert, Otto Braun, and Severing had not been to universities, had not sat at examinations, had not advanced from post to post in the public service; but they would have made an excellent showing in any modern state, any democratic republic or liberal parliamentary monarchy. They came into office in the midst of the endless confusion of defeat, they had to bring the nation out of the deluge on to firm soil, they had to find their way through unending difficulties, vexations, and dangers such as no rulers had ever faced before. . . .

They felt the task that had fallen to them to be a burdensome one; they and the German Social Democracy had had no longing for the day of revolt; August Bebel had regarded the monarchy as an entirely tolerable form of state; the Republic had been regarded as Utopian, their ambition had not reached so far. The ill-considered decisions of July 1914 had shown only too convincingly the immense dangers of a conduct of the state that was free of all control and all possibility of control; and from then on I was one of those who demanded a parliamentary system. Until then the destiny of the nation had depended on the ideas and the sudden impulses of a single individual. He had settled these things with a few deferential subordinates, themselves revelling in the sense of their high importance and wisdom, and neither the nation nor its representatives had been allowed the slightest knowledge of what was going on behind the palace walls. That could never be allowed again. But as the German Socialists made progress in the parliamentary field they inevitably sacrificed more and more of their revolutionary enthusiasm. So it was in every country. Everywhere the revolutionary energies relaxed amid the smoothly working routine of ordinary parliamentary business. The German Social Democrats, like their comrades in England and France, had long been content with "evolution," and, indeed, "gradualism."

No, they were not prepared, they crossed the Rubicon with reluctance. There might be something of exaltation in waking up famous one morning like Byron, but it was less pleasant to find oneself in the morning supreme commander of the Revolution after going to bed as a member of the respectable middle class. Especially if one were convinced that the Revolution was a particularly stupid affair. It was impossible that politicians of the Left parties, if they still had their wits about them and could weigh pros and cons, should desire the fall of the monarchy at that moment or have any eagerness to come into power themselves in those November days, either alone or even as leaders in a coalition. They had had no part in the diplomacy that preceded the war, and no influence over the conduct of the war; they had no share in the responsibility for the military defeats; and were they now to conclude this peace, which was only to be attained under fearfully hard and perhaps absolutely ruinous conditions? Were they to do this service to their reactionary opponents? Were they themselves to face the tragic struggle and the inevitable humiliations, while those others kept out of the way, laughing up their sleeve, looked on from a comfortable distance, and awaited the hour of their return to power? That was contrary to all political sense, as well as to all logic and justice. It would have been a thousand times wiser for them to leave it to the Empire with its parties and partisans and its generals to face the terrible liabilities of the peace negotiations, not to put their own signature to the treaty, not to let that disastrous shadow fall across the path of a newly created Republic, not to begin the new chapter of history with that page. After that peace William II would plainly be unable to remain Emperor, and meanwhile there would have been time to consider the organization of the State. . . .

It was learnt on October 31 that William II had gone secretly that morning, without informing Prince Max's Government, to G.H.Q. He was suspicious, there was something sinister now about Berlin, men were slinking about like menacing ghosts; in his own entourage every face was strained and anxious; there was an atmosphere and a reticence that suggested a hospital. He was afraid that this Prince Max and his accomplices would carry the scandal too far, that in the end they might want him to abdicate, and in this place there was nobody left to rely on, one was surrounded here with treason. The only safety was with the army, which would fight and die for its Emperor; he must get there as quickly as possible, without the loss of another hour.

There was enormous excitement in governmental and political quarters at the news of the flight—for that was the only name given to this departure. The Cabinet met at once, and it was decided to induce the Kaiser to return; the High Command was rung up, but in vain. William II was not to be tempted back; he kept silent and stayed where he was, sheltering behind the broad backs of the soldiers. The Berliners told one another that he had placed himself under the protection of the reactionary generals and was going to march the troops against the people; thus something of the nature of real revolutionary excitement gradually developed. When William II left the royal apartments so quietly, the door closed behind him, and he had locked himself out.

On the following morning everyone was talking of coming disturbances, and households made provision as well as they could against expected strikes. In the afternoon Herr Wahnschaffe, Secretary of State and Head of the Chancellery, asked me to go to see him, and sent me his official car—a necessary facility at a time when there were few opportunities of transport. . . .

He came straight to the point, telling me, as, of course, I had expected, that he wanted to discuss the question of the Kaiser. In Munich, he said, there was great excitement; the Premier, Herr von Lerchenfeld, was extremely nervous; demonstrations were being held again everywhere that evening. The rumor that the Kaiser intended to carry out a military coup had been widely spread in Munich, even more than elsewhere, but there was not a word of truth in it. The Kaiser had gone to Headquarters only in connection with military questions and was returning shortly. I suggested that there was no absolute necessity to trust these assurances, and Herr Wahnschaffe, by his manner and cautious replies, betrayed a like incredulity. But could I not telephone, he asked, to my Munich correspondent, the Social Democrat Auer, who was to take the chair at the demonstrations, and authorize him to state that all the rumors of coups were regarded in Berlin as wildly fanciful? If the rumors in Munich were not combated, there would be paving stones flying about before the evening was over, and irreparable harm might be done.

I did as he asked, and telephoned from his room there and then to Munich; but I felt sure that he had only made use of this cock-and-bull story as an opening for the conversation, for the Government had plenty of representatives in Munich who could have spread the official assurances with more authority.

He went on at once to a general discussion of the problem. He accepted the view that the Kaiser's abdication was inevitable, but was anxious to show consideration for him and to give him time to get used to the idea; he was also anxious about the preservation of the unity of the Reich. I replied that what he had just told me about Bavaria showed plainly that the unity of the country would be much more likely to be endangered by a refusal to abdicate.

He went on to say that really the Kaiser was not quite getting justice. It was true enough that William II had a great deal to answer for and had made some bad mistakes; but he had had no desire for the war, and he, Wahnschaffe, had heard the Kaiser talk about it with genuine grief. All I could say in reply to that was that it was all true enough, but unhappily the situation was not to be controlled by sentimentalities. The only thing that could be done now was to try to postpone the formal renunciation of the throne until the conclusion of peace, and the ill-advised departure had added to the difficulties in that respect among others. Herr Wahnschaffe nodded gloomily, and although he said nothing it was evident that his judgment of things did not differ greatly from mine. . . .

Immediately after this conversation there came the first news of the naval rising at Kiel. On the following day the complete victory of the revolutionaries was reported. On November 6 there came the same news, or very much the same, from Hamburg, Lübeck, Geestemünde, Schwerin, and many other places in the country; already Soldiers' Councils were in control everywhere, and the flood had come close to Berlin. Any discussion about the choice of "a better opportunity" had become empty and ridiculous.

I did not look on at the Revolution of November 9 from its points of departure or its centers, but only from the margin of events. But did not Stendhal describe the Battle of Waterloo by giving merely scraps of incident, the smoke of the guns, a fleeing cavalry squadron, episodes of a moment's duration, the distant offshoots of the actual engagements; and is not his picture rightly regarded as incomparable and placed by all who have a knowledge of art high above the "complete" battle pictures? . . . All this I have mentioned by way of apology for the scrappiness of the entries which I made at the time in my diary and reproduce here.

November 8. There is feverish tension. Will the Kaiser abdicate, or will he try to put up any resistance? Yesterday afternoon the Social Democrats resolved to withdraw from the Government if there is no abdication; thus, if the Kaiser refuses, or even hesitates too long, the present Cabinet will disappear, and probably, even if only momentarily, the workers will achieve unity. Their leaders will then be simply carried along. Every minute some acquaintance or complete stranger is ringing me up and declaring that William has already abdicated or has refused to, or is on his way with an army against Berlin. News is coming in from all over the country of the progress of the revolution. All the people who made such a show of their loyalty to the Kaiser, and were so proud of their decorations, are lying low; not one is moving a finger in defence of the monarchy. Everywhere the soldiers are quitting the barracks. In Berlin the railway stations are occupied by troops, and there is still a double guard outside the Palace, the Ministry of War, and other public buildings; externally everything is as usual. In the men's heads, under the helmets, there is probably a whirl of ideas: this is the last time on guard, tomorrow, or tonight, the free life will begin. Among the civilians many are frightened and apprehensive, hiding their money, providing themselves with the little acetylene lamps with their horrible stink, so as to have light whatever happens; some of the people I know who have villas in Grunewald or on the banks of the Havel are shutting them up, feeling too isolated and unprotected there, and coming back to town. They are all afraid of the Spartacists, and their one hope now is in the Social Democracy, which they know is sensible and will not smash everything up at once. At 1 P.M., still no reply from the Kaiser. The Social Democratic party executive, which is so keenly anxious for a good-will settlement, is still ready to have patience and is extending its ultimatum period. . . .

November 9 . . . At about a quarter to one the message came off the paper's morse machines that the Kaiser had abdicated. As I wrote my leader the news of the latest happenings were brought in hot succession, second by second, into my room. The red flag had been hoisted over the *Vorwärts* building. The Kaiser Alexander Regiment had gone over to the Revolution; the soldiers had rushed out of the barrack gates and fraternized with the shouting crowd outside; men shook their hands ·with emotion, women and girls stuck flowers in their uniforms and embraced them. Similar reports came in one after another about all the other regiments. The sentries and military posts and machine guns which a few hours before had provided the appearance of a plan of defence have suddenly disappeared, and with them the broad-shouldered policemen, pillars and symbols of the imperial order and stern custodians of the Kaiser's subjects. Liebknecht, restless and excited, has made a speech to his supporters from the balcony of the Palace, and the choice of this rostrum was no doubt intended to give the people to understand that now he is the new master and no one else. Members of my staff came in and told me that the officers are being stripped of their cockades and gold lace—needlessly, and in an ugly spirit—that the trams have stopped, that the revolutionaries have taken possession of the official Wolff News Agency, and that the red flag is now waving over the Brandenburg Gate.

Ulrich Rauscher, full of life as always, and Dr. Kurt Hiller had been waiting for me for some time at the office, in the mistaken hope of learning some special news from me, or perhaps just feeling the need to unburden their minds. . . . The three of us set out westwards about four along the Leipzigerstrasse. Endless processions of soldiers and workers were passing without a break along the road; or rather it was a single interminable procession that marched past us, going eastwards. . . .

Most of the workers were of middle age, with grave bearded faces. They had not had the army training in fatigues, but they had the trade unionists' corporate spirit, and marched conscientiously in order. Some of them were shouldering rifles which had been handed to them from some store. The soldiers' rifles were dangling across their backs, they had pushed their caps askew, they were cheeky and jolly, smoking furiously and waving to the girls. Everybody in the procession had a red badge in the button-hole or on the breast; the marshals of the procession, marching alongside with rifles slung over their shoulders, were distinguished by red armlets. In the midst of the slowly marching throng great red flags were being carried, and it was astonishing that at a time of shortage and requisitioning of all fabrics there was so much still left of this red cloth. Alongside the procession the motor cars of the Revolution rushed past, evidently on important business, for otherwise why such haste? Army lorries passed by with the red flag; they bore soldiers and red-ribboned civilians, crouching, sitting, kneeling or standing alongside machine guns, all in some fighting attitude and ready to fire, although there was no sign of any enemy about. There were also elegant smaller cars, with five or six soldiers in them, similarly ready to fire, going to and fro across the city on patrol duty. I said to myself that this is the thing that distinguishes modern wars and revolutions from those of the past: at the outbreak of every war and in every revolution the cars are taken at once from their owners as the very first thing, and every fight for power or freedom begins with the pride and joy of the new speed merchants in their attack on the record. . . .

At 7 P.M. I went back to the office. The trams were not running. Such other diminishing transport as the war had still left us had now been stopped entirely, and along the dark and desolate embankments, faintly lit here and there by the few electric lamps still in use, there went the same motor cars with armed guards ready to shoot, even more ominous now, with the almost complete darkness, than in the afternoon. The few pedestrians were hurrying home, as careful as Lot himself not to look behind them. But around the Potsdamer Platz there waited a packed crowd of interested onlookers, just as amenable to the control of the occasional armed marshals (simple civilians) as they have always been to the police. As I reached the Charlottenstrasse crossing in the Leipzigerstrasse there began a furious rattling of shots. The sound was so loud and sharp that the shots might have been striking the walls of the neighboring houses. A young man who was in no hurry told me that the machine guns had been turned on the Marstall, the royal mews, from the windows of which royalist officers and cadets had been shooting at the revolutionaries. That sounds hardly credible: the officers and cadets are scarcely likely to have entrenched themselves in the middle of the city in so untenable a fortress, and to have begun from there a heroic but insane bombardment. Possibly excited imaginations had made a dauntless garrison of officers out of a forgotten stable-boy and the porter. At other spots too this peaceful and bloodless revolution is being decorated with a little romanticism. . . .

November 10. The shooting went on in the Potsdamer Platz throughout the night, and I still have no idea of the reasons for this battle and its strategic significance. Probably it was not a battle at all, as there was no enemy. The total impotence of the monarchists with, to put it mildly, the complete absence of any inclination to resist, the abandonment of the old régime by all its supporters and privileged protectors without lifting a finger in its defence, has been so astonishing to the revolutionaries that they simply do not know what to make of it. They still think, as they did yesterday at the royal mews, that some opponent ready to fight to the last is hiding somewhere, and that an attack is being planned from some ambush. Thus last night they seem to have believed that royalist regiments were marching in from Potsdam. That still leaves unexplained the wild shooting that could be heard far around until the morning. . . .

This morning I went out with my wife and children; they were determined to see what a revolution is like. Except for occasional intervals, the air was filled with the crackling noise of mysterious fighting, and the motor patrols were incessantly going to and fro. There was an enormous red flag over the Admiralty. In Unter den Linden there was a crowd of many thousands of people, hoping to find something to see, and manifestly attracted by the firing, the sound of which came from the direction of the Palace. A great deal of history has passed through the "Linden," and among other recollections there would come back to those who stood there the picture of the great funeral procession that had slowly followed the coffin of old William I to the vault, amid the roll of drums; at its head, matchless in the majestic gravity of his aloofness, strode the old Emperor's grandson. The Brandenburg Gate had then been hung with long streamers of black bunting: now red flags waved from it in the November wind. . . .

November 11. In the afternoon I went with Otto Nuschke, editor of the *Volkszeitung*, to the Chancellor's palace, where we were to discuss the coup of Adolf Hoffmann and the Independents with Scheidemann and other "Commissars of the People"—the members of the improvised Socialist Government have considered this the proper title for the moment. The same well-drilled, noiseless old attendants who had opened and closed the doors here in the time of William II, took us to the room on the ground floor which had been Bethmann's anteroom. The first to join us was Herr Kurt Baake, formerly on the staff of *Vorwärts*, now Head of the Chancellery: he bore all the outward signs of doing very well indeed. Then Scheidemann came in, bothered and nervous. While we were reporting the case he shook his head now and again to show his disapproval. Before Scheidemann actually said anything, Kurt Baake interposed softly, simply oozing wisdom: he could only advise giving way and accepting things as they were. Rather astonished at this, I asked Scheidemann:

"Is that what you think too?"

He threw up his arms in perplexity:

"Yes, the Independents now have the power; I have no soldiers, what can I do?"

I pointed out that after all, at yesterday's meeting of representatives of the Workers' and Soldiers' Councils in the Busch Circus, the soldiers voted with the Majority Socialists; but the argument failed to move him; he merely repeated: "I have no soldiers," and gazed into the distance, evidently looking for the soldiers.

Landsberg came in: a very clever lawyer, representing the Majority Socialists, with Ebert and Scheidemann, in the Provisional Government: the other three members represent Hugo Haase's radical wing. We put the matter to him.

"Yes," he said, "we are in an impossible situation. Haase is much stronger than we are. If things go on like this we shall have no alternative but to resign."

At that moment a grey-haired attendant announced, in the same tone in which he used to announce Ambassadors:

"The Supreme Soldiers' Council."

It was obviously an unwelcome announcement, and there was general agitation and perplexity. Landsberg said under his breath: "More trouble!" Scheidemann jumped up in annoyance—"That lot again!" We quietly departed. The impression given by the scene was almost that the executioner and his men were at the door. . . .

During the days that followed I had many discussions and conferences and a great deal of trouble and vexation in connexion with the founding of the [new Democratic] party. I had to negotiate with men not all of whom were to my liking, and in between these meetings, and in the moments between my other activities, I wrote the manifesto to voters with democratic sympathies. On November 14 there came to a conference in my office, with several of his friends, Dr. Hjalmar Schacht, who was then the Managing Director of the National Bank and the leader of a group who called themselves "Young Liberals." This group, most of them elderly, had formed themselves into a sort of Brigade of Youth of the gouty National Liberals, to give the impression that a new branch was growing out of that withered old trunk. Schacht and his friends wanted to join us and then, no doubt to bring in with them their old party family. They did not at all want, of course, to go so far as the manifesto required, and give allegiance to the Republic; they were only prepared to countenance it. However, after a rather heated debate they made up their minds to become Republicans, and gave us their signatures.

It very soon proved that we had no need to fear a shortage of adherents; far from it—the danger was that the new party would prove all too attractive. Herr Fischbeck, the Prussian Minister of Commerce, told me that even Stinnes, von Borsig, and some other big industrialists of their kidney, had "seen light" and would like to join us, and at times it cost us a good deal of trouble to extricate ourselves from unexpected embraces of this sort. When the manifesto appeared on November 16 it included the pretty blunt phrase: "We are adopting as our basis the principle of republicanism." It was received with the warmest approval, but the comment was made, not entirely without justice, that among the signatories there were rather too many big capitalists. All the time I felt rather like old Noah facing a vast crowd pushing to get into the Ark, and compelled to keep on saying: "Sorry, full up."

At a later time I was often reproached for not having permitted Stresemann to sail in the Democratic ark. When Stresemann had really "seen light" and had become a Chancellor hotly attacked by the Nationalists, the omniscient declared that we had made a terrible mistake in turning him away instead of warmly welcoming him and making him leader of the party. But there was no magic mirror in November 1918 to show the Stresemann of 1925; all we could see was the Stresemann who during the war had been an annexationist and a follower of Tirpitz, and who had declared that there was no need to be afraid of America because the Americans had no ships and could not cross the ocean. Even if the magic mirror had shown me the Stresemann of the future, it would have availed nothing and I could have done no differently, for a majority of the voters on whom we counted would have been guided by things as they were, and would have refused to vote for a party whose list included a candidate with such blunders in his record. For all that, it was painful to have to reject him, and a painful memory later, during the period when I stood near to him as a politician and a friend, and watched him until the last, suffering severely from grave ill-health and from the malignity of his enemies.

On November 18 he had come unannounced to one of our meetings, which we were holding in the residence of the President of the Reichstag. With him were several of his National Liberal party colleagues in the Prussian Parliament, including Friedberg, Lucas, and Weber; and a number of "Progressives" had also come uninvited and unwanted, since their names also would bring us no strength. Professor Alfred Weber, who at my desire had taken the chair in the foundation committee, rose at once and said that he was instructed to refuse all cooperation with members of the old parties who did not unreservedly accept the new programme, or were compromised by their past policy. We were overwhelmed, he said, with adherents, and almost everyone who came to us warned us: "No compromise with the old discredited parties!" Alfred Weber was a man of strong feelings and delivered this verdict in very biting terms. Half a dozen times he told the intruders to their faces that they were compromised. There was a heated dispute and tempers were thoroughly roused. During the whole scene Stresmann sat silently in his place. I brought the unpleasant wrangling to an end by proposing an adjournment; I assumed that Stresemann and his friends would themselves consider it advisable to go away in the interval. This they did; when we resumed the sitting their places were empty.

The Provisional Government worked well and honestly to establish order, to calm the population, and to provide food for the hungry, and the walls of buildings were covered with endless proclamations in warning and appeal and promise. In the administrative offices of the Guards and in other official buildings I found young men, soldiers, and civilians, who had seated themselves on the abandoned office chairs, cheerfully taking up their new responsibilities and working zealously and optimistically, but without experience, in the effort to satisfy a public that was continually crying for help and levelling complaints and accusations. But the Spartacists also were very active, working under Russian instructors; they were able to count on the hatred of the Independents for the Majority Socialists and on the support of Eichhorn, who was supposed to be President of Police, a man of the lower middle class, filled with the fury of the small shopkeeper turned Jacobin. Their task was easy, for at the time the people were asking only for words from them and for bread from their opponents. The rifles that had been brought back from the field to be kept at home, or sold for a few pence to any who wanted them, were constantly to be heard, and many more waited in their corners for a signal for use on a greater scale. Many buildings, including the newspaper offices that might be honored with an attack, were provided with guards, and Noske, who as Minister of War and Commander in Chief was organizing defence, offered me for the *Tageblatt* building a hundred of his "absolutely loyal and reliable" sailors. I said a hundred would be too many, a dozen would do, and twelve bright and lively young fellows were installed and billeted on us.

Kurt Eisner, Prime Minister of the Bavarian Republic, came to Berlin on November 22 for a conference of all the Republican heads of governments. On the following morning he telephoned to me that he would be pleased to see me. I was not well acquainted with him, had not met him for twenty years; I went with a little curiosity in the afternoon to the Bavarian Embassy, where he was staying. On the steps I was met by a young student, with his tie out of place and nothing particularly elegant about him, though this did not prevent him from being perhaps more intelligent than not a few of the magnificent young attachés of the past. He told me that Eisner was ready to see me at once, and took me upstairs without further ceremony into a little room. Here Eisner, with a regular revolutionary's beard and long gray hair, wearing a black coat and gray trousers too short for him, was standing dictating to a young man who worked with glowing zeal at a typewriter. Three other young men, probably students from Munich, formed a group round the master, who greeted me with a wave of the hand and, without allowing himself to be interrupted by the visit, continued dictating in some such words as this:

"The Bavarian Prime Minister enters a protest against the attitude of ex-Field Marshal von Hindenburg."

He spoke in resonant tones, a little theatrically and obviously very pleased to have one more listener; with a further thunderous phrase he closed his protest against some action of Hindenburg's. Then we sat down at a table on which some cups with the remains of the afternoon coffee and a few cigarette ends added their contribution to the local color, and he began to tell me of his Munich revolution. "Our revolution was really fine. There was no bloodshed, and it was a splendid fight: we all came out into the street and stormed the barracks." After adding detail to this historic picture with the gusto of the literary æsthete, he began to abuse the Berlin Government: it could not be trusted and was disliked abroad, especially by Clemenceau. All this differed from my own view, and as we could not agree he came back once more in the end to:

"You should have seen our revolution in Munich!"

In December the situation grew worse. On the evening of the 23d Professor Eberstadt telephoned to me that sailors had made an assault on the University. They had done more than that. After a dispute on questions of pay they had dragged the commandant out of the garrison building in Unter den Linden and locked him up with his adjutant in the Royal Mews. There and in the Palace they had put up barricades. After that they forced their way into the Chancellery, and for an hour held Ebert and Landsberg prisoners. Then troops loyal to the Government came on the scene and the sailors withdrew.

On the following days the Palace was besieged by Government troops, and there was a tremendous bombardment. On New Year's eve, when my wife and I were celebrating "Sylvester"—seeing the old year out—with Max Reinhardt and other friends in the restaurant under the Deutsches Theater, the harsh sounds of the shooting close at hand broke into the melodious Italian songs which Moissi was singing to us to the accompaniment of a guitar. On Sunday, January 5, 1919, the Spartacist revolt broke out in full force. My diary records what I saw and experienced:

Sunday, January 5. I was rung up about 5 P.M. from the *Berliner Tageblatt* office by the secretary in the editorial department. He told me that about a thousand armed Spartacists had drawn up in front of the building and were evidently determined to force their way in. I asked: "Are you alone?" He was alone, but fortunately not nervously inclined.

"And what are our twelve loyal sailors doing?"

"The loyal sailors went over at once to the besiegers."

I asked him to leave the building by a door at the back; I should be there as soon as possible to see what was going on. Then I set out.

There was a lot of firing, but it was impossible to say where. It was completely dark by the time I reached the crossing of Leipzigerstrasse and Charlottenstrasse. It was six o'clock, and once more the street lamps were unlit. But when I could see Schützenstrasse from Charlottenstrasse there were flickering in the wind at three or four places in front of the *Tageblatt* building the smoky red flames of an *auto da fé*. Where it crosses the Markgrafenstrasse the Schützenstrasse (on which one side of the building fronts) was blocked by lines of Spartacist volunteers, and the whole area round the *Tageblatt* building was invested. I saw no way of getting through, and could only guess that the low and not very vigorous flames were consuming the leaflets containing my manifesto for the elections to the National Assembly. . . .

The fires in Schützenstrasse had gone out, but there was a smell everywhere of burnt paper. The line of sentries opened to let Petty Officer Müller and his comrades go through; they were regarded as friends. I was also allowed to go through, being so well protected and accordingly unsuspect.

The courtyard of the building is surrounded by the machine rooms, stores, and boiler house. Here, there loomed out of the darkness a crowd of armed figures. They were standing about or sitting on the great rolls of newsprint with their legs dangling and their rifles across their knees. Some were in uniform, some in poor civilian clothing, but in the gloom it all had the attraction of a night camp scene such as we may see on the stage—a scene arranged this time by a producer of no great distinction. I went up the stairs leading from the courtyard to the upper stories of the main building, and came to the long composing room, now dark, deserted, and cold. From there into the editorial rooms. In the corridor someone brushed past me.

"Where are the leaders?" I asked. "There must surely be someone in command?"

He pointed to one of the rooms—a room belonging normally to one of the subeditors for home affairs. I opened the door and found in the little room three men, busily smoking and a little astonished at the arrival of a visitor. They looked at us without moving. Petty Officer Müller greeted them, politely introduced me, and then disappeared, considering that his mission was ended. He could not have shown more decency or good manners if he had been a gentleman brought up at the English Court.

To start as well as possible I cheerfully apologized for our unpreparedness for receiving guests. But there were plenty of ash trays —the gentlemen were evidently keen smokers. The three were of very dissimilar appearance and of different social classes. . . .

"Are you staying long with us?" I asked [one of the men].

He replied with a friendly smile:

"But you surely know what is the situation in Berlin, and how things stand?"

No, I knew absolutely nothing; I had not been able to find out on my strolls between this building and the Royal Mews.

"We have all the important strategic points in our hands," he said. "All the railway stations have been occupied, and most of the public buildings; tomorrow morning Liebknecht will take over the government; resistance would be useless."

He said all this with modesty, but in an unmistakable tone of triumph—the tone of a man confident in his cause and thus with no reason for any tasteless crowing over the defeated adversary.

"And of course the Liebknecht Government is going to last. Well, are you going to settle here for all eternity and throw us out?"

"No," he said soothingly, and as if it was for him to decide, "when the Liebknecht Government has been formed you will be able to bring out your paper again—of course with a different policy, the Liebknecht policy, obviously."

"You are not very likely to live to see that, though I wish you long life—really, you have got the wrong end of the stick there."

He laughed with a good-natured superiority, and of course incredulously. The conversation continued for some time with such pleasantries, and I learned a little more about the alleged complete conquest of Berlin. I learned also that the *Vorwärts* building had been occupied as well as ours. Our building is a splendid "strategic point": the whole neighborhood as far as Dönhoffplatz can be swept from it by machineguns. To be a strategic point is very fine, but has its disadvantages. . . .

The Spartacists had won only a few unimportant points, and on the following morning were still not masters of Berlin. During the night the masses who had remained loyal to the Majority Socialists were given the alarm, and in the morning they marched out of the factories and came from every quarter in endless processions to the Wilhelmstrasse, blocking access to it from all the neighboring streets by their own numbers, and surrounding the Chancellor's palace on all sides. Our compositors and machine men, and the technical and commercial staffs, were greatly annoyed at being turned out of their workplace, and collected together in the Dönhoffplatz; in a restaurant close by we contrived some placards bravely demanding "Liberty of the Press!" and at the head of our battalion we marched to our common objective. In the Wilhelmstrasse officials of the trade unions squeezed in among the crowd and summoned the ex-combatants to the Vossstrasse, where they were handed rifles.

I went to the Chancellor's palace. Scheidemann, perspiring in spite of the winter cold, was standing at an open window, already hoarse with the exertions of a fiery address to the crowd. I found Ebert, calm or at all events without any visible signs of nervousness. Noske was driving to and fro in the city, collecting auxiliaries, and already exhibiting the extraordinary lack of knowledge of human nature, and of foresight, with which he was later to make possible the Kapp *putsch* and to deliver the Republic into the hands of its enemies. It was, indeed, not the White Guards who saved the Republic at this moment. That was done by the workers, whose massed assembly prevented the perplexed and irresolute Liebknecht from occupying the governmental quarter.

There was, nevertheless, a week's fighting over our splendid "strategic point." In the *Tageblatt* building the ringleaders with whom I had talked were very soon replaced by a personality of greater weight. Machine-guns were placed at the windows, and protected by piled books from the library. Troops loyal to the Government fired from the roofs of the opposite houses and from the tower of the Jerusalem Church. The walls of the building were splashed all over with bullet-marks. Crowds that had learned to appreciate fine points of strategy during the years of war watched the course of the struggle from a safe distance. Leaders of partisan bands formed from unemployed ex-soldiers offered to storm the building, almost always in return for a stipulated fee. The most serious offer came from the "Reichstag regiment"; its commander, a banker's son, was also the only one among these leaders of mercenaries who was not merely out to do business; he asked only that his men should be rewarded. Another leader, a strapping fellow in officer's uniform, with a row of revolvers and hand grenades round his waist, was merely an ex-sergeant major, but he was unexcelled at braggadocio. The strategic problem offered no field for such talents as he boasted.

Then General von Lüttwitz's [Free Corps] brigade marched into Berlin, bombarded the *Vorwärts* building with heavy guns, pulled out its garrison of Spartacists, took them to a neighboring courtyard, and there shot the whole of them, old men and boys with the rest, with senseless brutality. The defenders of our building were given a military ultimatum, expiring at midnight. I had been negotiating with the garrison for some days through women intermediaries. If they voluntarily abandoned their fortress I would help those who brought about that result to escape; I had secured permission for this. We were anxious to prevent our machinery from being bombarded, and a couple of thousand of men thus put out of work. These were trying hours; we knew that there were wild men in the building who were intent on showing fight. But shortly before midnight the defenders all got away, over the roofs or by other means.

At once the commanders of the volunteer parties began to report to me, one after another, that they had just stormed the building, and the pompous officer who was really only a sergeant major insisted on dragging me from home next morning to lead me into the realm his heroism and his men's irrepressible dash had reconquered for me. He turned up early in the morning with half a dozen of these ironsides, in an armored car they had borrowed from somewhere, warriors every inch of them, and the "liberators" won admiration and refreshment and reward all along the street. I had, willy-nilly, to drive through the city with them, and none of the spectators dreamed that it was a mere carnival procession.

The recaptured building was in a dreadful condition inside. Many cupboards had been broken open, books torn to pieces lay about everywhere, the floor was littered with rubbish, there was endless dirt and a horrible stench. Masses of documents lay on the tables, and the writing on some of the papers showed that the occupying force had included a Russian element. But most of these documents were draft love-letters and sketches and verses— material for a whole collection of *erotica*.

This German Revolution had two special characteristics. Considering the times, it was more or less intelligible that in England, when Charles I was led to the scaffold, the king's adherents maintained a horrified silence, and that in France only the Swiss made a heroic stand on behalf of Louis XVI and Marie Antoinette. But the Hohenzollern monarchy rested on so many apparently indestructible pillars, and not only on the vast organization but on the far-famed loyalty incessantly celebrated in songs, speeches, and schoolbooks. And now the appointed guardians of this monarchy, its proud paladins and its parasites alike, scattered and disappeared, without a blow, into a safe seclusion. Yet this revolution—and this was its other unique feature—was so well-behaved, so good-natured, to a degree only to be found in a few figures in some of the old English novels. It might have inscribed its banners with the slogan: "Love your enemies more than yourselves!" It was not pretty to tear off the badges of officers who refused to do it for themselves, but at least there was no ill-treatment—perhaps because there was not sufficient resistance. No one was kidnapped, imprisoned, beaten, or murdered, on account of his political opinions, and those men who were stood against the wall and shot were only poor proletarian youngsters, mowed down by White Guards. A respectable and simple class of men marched in, without any instinct of cruelty, any desire for vengeance, with the inborn respect for freedom and for the lives of others that protects civilized men from the misuse of their own freedom. No one had sadist lusts, or replied with a shrug of contempt when human rights and human dignity were mentioned.

This Revolution had its idealist officer with the bushy eyebrows and the childlike purity of heart; and its fine sailors with their boyish delight in the great event—which ended in a courtyard with shots fired with perfect aim by a military squad. Of course there were various other figures, cranks or adventurers. But they were merely incidental, and even where they played a leading part it cannot be said that they were the most characteristic element. In the composite picture they yield place to another type—the small man, tired and hungry, with the jacket too short for him and the rifle slung from a strap that dug into his shoulder, who was my escort that night—the unassuming, down-trodden, disappointed, or cheated man of the rank and file, cannon fodder for the nation's wars and the national industries, patient beast of burden for every expedition, eternal victim, *poire*, as the French call him, and dupe of all history, promised everything for the morrow and denied everything in his own day. Earlier revolutions had borne the stamp of a Mirabeau or Danton or Cromwell. The character of the upheaval which fifteen years later made an end of the Republic is conveyed by the names of other men, without whom that upheaval would never have come. The Revolution of November 1918 was the revolution of the unnamed man, and if a name must be given, it was the Dupe's Revolution.

9. Politics and Democracy in the Making of the Weimar Constitution

Dr. Arnold Brecht was appointed to a rural Prussian judgeship in 1910, when he was twenty-six. In 1918–1919 he was an official in the ministry of economics and the chancellory. By 1928 he had risen to minister of finance for the state of Prussia, the position he held until dismissed by the Nazis in 1933. His long life has given him an unusual opportunity to evaluate German democracy in light of the failures of Weimar, the disruptions of National Socialism, and awareness of the structure and experiences of parliamentary government in West Germany since 1949.

SOURCE: Selections from Arnold Brecht, *The Political Education of Arnold Brecht: An Autobiography 1884–1970* (Copyright © 1970 by Princeton University Press), pp. 147–159. Reprinted by permission of Princeton University Press.

POLITICAL EDUCATION THROUGH THE ACT OF VOTING

The elections for the National Assembly on January 19, 1919 included not only women among the voters for the first time, but also the twenty, twenty-one, twenty-two, twenty-three, and twenty-four-year-olds who had not thus far had a vote. For the first time they were held according to the system of proportional representation (P.R.). A certain number of votes cast within the whole of Germany (or in one of the large regions) for any one party, secured that party one seat each; no party therefore lost votes merely on the ground that its candidates were outvoted locally.

This time, in contrast to my views in 1912, I was in no doubt as to whom I should vote for. Owing to the conditions which I had experienced during war and revolution, I was resolved to cast my vote for the Social Democrats, officially known as the "Social Democratic Party of Germany." I did not become a party member however. According to my political views, which I still hold today, government officials, at least senior ones, ought not to take an active part in the actual business of party politics, ought not to canvass for any one party publicly, nor write or speak against other parties that stay within the basic principles of the constitution. They ought to avoid giving any impression in public of making their judgments and decisions out of party-political reasons. . . .

This was not the only reason why I failed to enlist in the Social Democratic party. There were also differences between my opinions and official party doctrine. I was not able to agree without reservations with the official party's deep mooring in the doctrines of Marx and Engels, which was tighter than it is today. I recognized the great importance of Marx and Engels and their scientific contributions. But the assertion that it is possible to make long-term forecasts about the future and the course of history has always seemed to me to be a survival of outdated scientific thinking of the nineteenth century. Many forecasts had already proved to be false. To generalize experiences of only three economic systems (slavery, feudalism, and capitalism in its early stages) and to declare them in advance to be valid for all following systems is methodologically untenable. To disparage all value judgments except one's own, and to regard other people's values as mere ideological superstructures over their class interests, while claiming for one's own absolute truth, seemed to me to be rather naïve. Nor was I able to feel or preach "class hatred."

What drove me as a voter to the Social Democrats despite my reservations was that old urge for justice which had guided me from childhood and now attracted me to the simple workers whose principal spokesmen seemed to me to be the Social Democrats. It was my feeling for equality, nourished by the awareness that all human beings are, despite all their differences, equal in one, the essential point: every day and every hour they can and must make the choice between good and evil. . . .

I was especially pleased by the fact that the Social Democrats were less encumbered by bourgeois prejudices and more inclined to reform than the other parties. I was thoroughly oriented toward reform. I believed in the possibility of improvements. I wanted reforms in every sphere, but realistic reforms only, the consequences of which had been carefully thought through.

In many respects I was close also to the newly formed German Democratic Party. Over the course of the years many of their leaders became my friends. But I was more attracted to the workers than to the lower middle class who were the principal supporters of the Democratic Party in Germany apart from the numerically small intellectual elite that headed the party. The lower middle class had a strongly marked class-consciousness. Why stop halfway? I also mistrusted—as in fact many members of this party did—the belief in the completely free interplay of forces in the economic sphere. I felt that a considerable degree of planning was necessary because of Germany's economic and political situation at the time. . . .

What pleased me about the Zentrum, a party consisting almost ninety percent of members of the Catholic minority, was its fusion of all classes and its respect for transcendental values. I was politically as close to its left wing as to the Social Democrats and the Democrats. But the predominance of the Catholic element was alien to me, a North German Protestant and grandson of a pastor, without my having any hostile feelings on this account.

Many of my friends voted for the German People's Party (*Deutsche Volkspartei*), the substitute for the National Liberals of the imperial era. Most of the senior ministerial officials voted for this party (if not for the German Nationals, the conservative Right). But its indecisiveness in acknowledging the democratic republic, its arrogance toward the Social Democrats, to whose resistance to Bolshevism it owed its very existence, and its only slightly camouflaged love of power-politics and jingoistic patriotism deterred me. Some of their leaders, including Stresemann and von Kardorff, with whom I later had friendly relationships, gradually cast off this dross, but for this very reason they were faced with serious internal conflicts within their own party.

To get back to the elections of January, 1919. It appeared that the Socialists of varying shades, even together, had no absolute majority. Of the 421 seats the Social-Democrats gained 163, the Independents 22, totalling 185. They were thus 26 short of an absolute majority (211). The prospect of reorganizing Germany on Socialist lines had thus disappeared. The prospects for a *democratic* regime, however, were good. The German Democratic Party, formed of the remains of former Liberal groups and of new men, held 75 seats, and the Zentrum, which was honestly prepared to work on a republican democratic basis, 91. Together with the Social Democrats this made a total of 329 of the 421 seats, that is, more than three quarters (78 percent). These three parties together formed the so-called Weimar Coalition, created the so-called Weimar Constitution, and they would, had they kept the majority —a prospect which at first all observants reckoned with—have been able not only to create a democratic constitution but also to see it carried through. . . .

The increase in Socialist votes from 1912 to 1919 was not as violent as had been hoped for or feared. Every fourth German had voted Social Democrat as far back as 1898, and every third in 1912.

Now the combined Socialist votes had become considerably higher than a third, but not yet one half. Thus a coalition government between Socialist and non-Socialist parties had to be formed; no cabinet could be confirmed, no law passed, without at least one of the non-Socialist parties agreeing. . . .

While matters in Weimar proceeded comparatively calmly, in other parts of Germany bitter unrest flared up. In Munich Premier Eisner, an Independent Social Democrat, was assassinated. The ensuing dictatorial regime of a council-type government reached its climax in the murder of anti-Socialist hostages (April 29), but then, after military intervention, came to a bloody end on May 2. In Berlin, Ebert was able to control the excesses of a general strike (March 3-9) by enforcing martial law with transference of executive power to Noske. Noske dissolved the remains of the Marine Division and of the Republican Soldiers' Guard, which had to some extent joined the revolt. He issued an order, which was militarily effective but highly objectionable in terms of human rights and due process of law, to the effect that anyone who was found carrying weapons and fighting against government troops was to be shot immediately. The volunteer corps, roused on account of losses in their own ranks, took advantage of this decree. There were over 1,000 dead. On March 11, for example, 31 sailors were shot without investigation. The lesson from these experiences was drawn too late—that such summary orders to shoot were not to be given.

At the end of March a revolt on the Ruhr followed. Only with great difficulty—after much shooting and ill-treatment from both sides—did Carl Severing, as appointed Reich Commissioner, succeed in suppressing it with the assistance of General Watter and his troops. Then came a general strike in Braunschweig under the leadership of Eichhorn, the former Berlin chief of police (April 19). All this showed only too clearly how important it was to pass the new national constitution as soon as possible, but also what difficult conditions were to be taken into account.

DEMOCRACY AND CONSTITUTION

What is democracy? Opinions on this have changed in the course of history. That democracy has something to do with rule by the people is expressed in the term itself, but not how this rule is to be realized. The word admits of many interpretations: from the exercise of all governmental powers—legislation, administration, and justice—by the entire nation (or its adult males), united in a people's assembly, as in ancient Athens, down to the carrying out of the supposed will of the people by a dictatorial government, as in the Soviet Union. The modern concept of democracy in western countries combines three principles: the protection of human or basic rights, the independence of the courts of law, and the maxim that all *other* matters are decided or controlled by the majority on the basis of general elections, in such a way that the people, by making free use of their right to vote, can determine and change (either at any time or periodically within reasonable periods of time) both the membership of the legislative assembly and (directly or indirectly) the holders of the highest executive offices. No scientific argument can compel anyone to use the word "democracy" in just this sense. But when I got on here to speak of democracy, I mean democracy in the modern western sense that I have just outlined.

In the older western democracies the term "democracy" conjures up the image of a state in which human dignity is respected and human rights are assured—the happy image of freedom from tyrannical despotism. This is also the primary connotation of the term in Germany today, with the people looking back to the Hitler regime and sidewise to present-day Communism. But in 1919, when the Weimar Constitution was being written, things were different. Human rights had on the whole been protected in Germany before the war, not through the Constitution itself, but by virtue of national laws which, once passed, could be modified only with the Reichstag's consent (see Chapter 12). Rights could be temporarily suspended by proclaiming martial law, but until 1914 this had happened only seldom and then only in narrow geographical and time limits. When martial law became a permanent condition during the war, the Reichstag promptly issued (with the consent of the Bundesrat!) the excellent Protective Custody Act of 1916, which set down the rights of those in custody and protected them from complete arbitrariness. The really new thing in Germany at that time was not, therefore, the principle of respect for human dignity—old Kantian spiritual heritage—nor basic rights, although they were considerably extended. There had been general elections, free and secret, for over forty years, at least for the

Reichstag. What was fundamentally new, because it had previously been absent, was the maxim that the people were to determine not only the legislators but also the highest executive officials, and the release of parliamentary legislation from any veto by princes, whether in a federal council, or by the monarch's right of veto.

In the Germany of 1919, therefore, the word "democracy" did not call the glory of freedom and human rights before the eye, but the far less fascinating picture of parties fighting for executive power and of frequent government crises, connected, in relation to foreign countries, not with freedom but with lack of it, to a degree which had not been known in Germany since the time of Napoleon.

Only those who were deeply filled with the *total* idea of democracy and the value of personal responsibility, and who were aware of the causal connection between the former undemocratic conditions and the outbreak of the war and its loss, were immune to the deceptive impression that the distinguished aristocratic methods of government in the imperial era had been something better than the contemporary loud and often vulgar struggle among the parties, and that the miserable situation of Germany after the war was causally connected with her new democratic form of government.

The men who formed the new national government shared the belief in the superiority of democracy. The new Minister of the Interior, Dr. Hugo Preuss, had already been appointed head of that department as early as November 15, the seventh day of the revolution, and had been instructed to prepare the draft of a democratic constitution. He was at that time one of the few, if not the only, professor of constitutional law firmly grounded in democracy and entirely familiar with its principles and history. He had for this reason never held a chair at a German university (also because he was a Jew), but taught at a business school in Berlin.

His principal task—setting down article by article the parliamentary system of democracy and the basic rights of men—seemed to him and to us at that time relatively simple. It was more difficult to reorganize the relationship between the federal government and the state governments, and to redraw Germany's political map. Preuss proposed to abolish the smaller states, with the exception of the three Hansa towns, and to combine several Prussian provinces, and also some Prussian and non-Prussian areas, within larger units.

Bavaria, Wurttemberg, and Baden were scarcely to be altered, except that the Rhenish Palatinate was to be joined to the Rhineland. Berlin was, like each of the Hansa towns, to form a separate state. Since Preuss published his plan before the Treaty of Versailles, he included Austria. It was to form a single state within Germany. Vienna was to be an independent unit like Berlin.

The problem of territorial reorganization proved too difficult for the Assembly to solve in due time; it was referred to subsequent special legislation. But otherwise the Constitution was completed and passed by the end of July. Taken as a whole the Weimar Constitution, as it is generally called, was a venerable document from the democratic viewpoint, evidence of the idealistic desires which inspired its originators. But too little experience, a lack—not only in Germany, but in the whole world—of a really advanced political theory, and finally the confidence in the continuance of democratic majorities and in the democratic reliability of elected presidents, led to some fateful errors in important details. For even though the principles of modern democracy in the West (basic rights, independent courts, in other matters free decision of the majority) are the same in all western democratic states, the forms in which they are realized are different, and the fate of the individual democracies depends to a considerable degree upon this.

A few words here about the mistakes. *First:* the majority was to decide. This principle appears to be simple and unambiguous. But different methods of polling give rise to different majorities. In order to be particularly democratic, proportional representation was prescribed for all legislative bodies, and this requirement was even set down in the Constitution itself, so that it could be changed only by a two-thirds majority. For—thus it seemed at that time to many and even seems so today—what could be more just or more equitable?

Proportional representation is indeed entitled to be considered the best democratic method for the election of the constitutive assembly, since it assures all sections of the population a proportional share in the setup of the constitution. But that it be the best thing also for the recurrent parliamentary ballots is not nearly so certain. One might just as well argue that it would be most just if each governmental cabinet consisted of members proportionally selected from all parties, including the radicals on both sides. This conclusion is rarely drawn, because it is obviously incompatible with the functions of the cabinet. Proportional representation often deprives the people of that very cooperation in fundamental decisions that general elections were supposed to grant them. They are compelled to elect candidates who represent special interests or philosophies instead of persons seeking the necessary balance between different interests and philosophies. The voter cannot even decide upon the person; the party bureaucracy does that for him. Thus under the system of proportional representation the independent political thinking of the individual citizen atrophies. Far from being induced to seek for union, integration, compromise, he is in fact cunningly prevented from doing so. He can at best leave such constructive decisions to his party. Proportional representation encourages the breakdown into many, or at least more than two, parties. In this way a small group, which holds the pivotal power between large parties, often influences the decisions in a degree quite out of proportion to its size, as for example the small party of the Gauche radicale did in France between 1924 and 1932, and in Germany during the Weimar Republic sometimes the Bavarian People's Party, sometimes the Economic Party, and after the Second World War, especially, the Free Democrats. This may in individual cases be good or bad, but it refutes the alleged mathematical justice of proportional representation. The worst defect: proportional representation throws the doors of parliament wide open for antidemocratic radical groups. The lowered voting age of twenty contributed to increasing the number of votes cast for radical parties.

In vain, Friedrich Naumann warned of the dangers of proportional representation in the constitutional committee of the National Assembly. The selfish interest of the parties and their bureaucratic machines in proportional representation is so great that after the Second World War every parliamentary country on the Continent of Europe introduced or retained proportional representation, if with some modifications, as in the Federal Republic of Germany. In 1945 I advised the U.S. occupational authorities to support P.R. in the elections for a National Assembly only on the condition that the parliamentary elections later be held according to the Anglo-American majority system. Unfortunately the official adviser of the military government at that time happened to have little knowledge of this question; he cherished the illusion that P.R. was something unequivocally good.

Second. In the Weimar period P.R. played an especially fateful part through the indirect influence it had upon the nomination of candidates in presidential elections. The president was to be elected not, as in France at that time, by the two legislative houses, but as in America, by general elections. This was considered the more democratic method. Even Max Weber, misunderstanding the differences, strongly advocated this procedure. In the United States, where practically the entire nation stands behind its federal constitution and where the method of legislative elections secures the two-party system, the selection of the president by national elections has worked well. However, where the constitution is attacked by strong parties on the left and on the right, as was the case in Germany, and P.R. keeps parliament split into many conflicting parties, so that no one party is in a position to carry its own candidate, then it can easily happen that in presidential elections outsiders are nominated, who enjoy great popularity but who are laymen in politics and without inner ties to parliamentary democracy. Thus popular opponents of democracy can come to power.

Third. Article 48 gave extended authority to the president in times of crises. It was hoped that four factors would guarantee democratic control: the power to issue emergency decrees was to reside in a president elected by the people rather than a prince; each decree required for its validity countersignature by a constitutional chancellor or minister, who was responsible to the Reichstag and could be dismissed by it; the Reichstag was entitled by simple majority to enforce repeal of any emergency decree; finally, statutory law could regulate details such as protective custody and the length of time for which rights might be suspended.

Had these guarantees gained real significance, presidential emergency powers might indeed have been kept under democratic control. Their dictatorial abuse was made possible, however, by the broad power given the president to appoint and dismiss a chancellor. According to the wording of the Constitution he was able to dismiss the chancellor at any time, even though no motion of censure had been passed against him; and he could appoint as chancellor anyone, irrespective of his chances to receive a vote of confidence, and could then have him countersign a decree dissolving the Reichstag, and emergency decrees, before there was a new Reichstag to pass a vote of censure. The power to suspend basic laws could thus fall into the hands of a person not controlled by parliament. This was the more dangerous because the statutory law which might have provided some protection against abuse did not come into being; the parties had failed to reach agreement on it.

These mistakes affected only a few lines in the long text of the Weimar Constitution. The influence they had on the fate of the first German Republic, however, proved great. Had the rights of the president been more prudently defined, then in 1932 Hindenburg would neither have been able to discharge Brüning nor to appoint Papen; nor to dissolve the Reichstag with Papen's—from the democratic standpoint worthless—signature; nor to remove the Prussian ministers; nor finally, in February, 1933, entirely to suspend the constitutional protection of human rights. Had the voting system made it possible, as in England, in the United States, and at that time in France, to keep extremist candidates away from parliament by locally outvoting them, then the National Socialists and the Communists would never have had the large Reichstag representation which gave their movements such impetus. If the president had been elected by a joint session of Reichstag and Reichsrat or by other indirect methods, Hindenburg would never have become Ebert's successor in 1925 and so would not have been able to play the disastrous role he did in 1932 and 1933.

All this can be easily shown now and its significance realized, because we know now that the prodemocratic parties in Germany soon lost their majority. But when the Constitution was written there were still those overwhelming majorities in parliament for democracy, and the thought that these majorities might be lost was far from the minds of most observers. The makers of the Constitution should not be too strongly criticized for having left these loopholes, *which became dangerous only with the loss of prodemocratic majorities.* I could deny all responsibility on my own part on the ground that I took no part in the drafting. But I doubt that, had I participated, I would have recognized these errors and their full significance. Only the observation of their practical effects has made me, like many others, a "constitutional expert," and the study of other constitutions has increased my insight *ex post.* At that time I was no constitutional expert. There was no such thing in Germany as political science. Nor did foreign experts in political science draw the attention of the Germans to these errors and dangers.

Other sources of danger were much more obvious at the time. The postponement of territorial reorganization placed tremendous obstacles in the way of a healthy development of German democracy. So did the constitutional guarantee of lifelong tenure for all former officials in office. . . .

In retrospect it is perhaps possible to say that due to those technical defects of the Weimar Constitution the battle for democracy, like the World War on the Marne, was half-lost for Germany as it had hardly begun. At the time this was far from certain. Democracy had strong battalions of electors behind it. As long as that was the case there was little to fear.

10. The Trauma of Versailles

When the victorious Allies met at Versailles in late 1918 to reorganize Europe and its worldwide dependencies, they faced issues far more complicated than those at the last comparable peace settlement at Vienna a century before. Above all, they sought to avoid quarrelling among themselves in the presence of their foe, lest defeated Germany maneuver into positions of advantage as France had done in 1814–1815. The Germans were, therefore, not admitted to the peace table until a full treaty was agreed upon among the Allies for presentation to the enemy. The Germans had little information about these deliberations except for some leaks of fact and a steady flow of rumors. They thought they had an agreement to end the war on the basis of Wilson's First Point: open covenants openly arrived at. When they were finally summoned to Versailles in early May, they resented their treatment and were aghast to find that the terms of the draft treaty exceeded the worst rumors in severity.

The following documents indicate the mood of the German negotiators at Versailles, the spirit of their counterproposals, and the depths of German antagonism when the emerging Weimar Republic was forced to accept the "Diktat."

a. Letters of Dr. Walter Simons, Delegate to the Versailles Conference, to His Wife

SOURCE: Alma Luckau, *The German Delegation at the Paris Peace Conference* (New York, 1941), pp. 117–120. Translation by the author. Reprinted by permission of the Carnegie Endowment for International Peace.

Versailles
May 7, 1919

In ten minutes the automobiles are coming to take us to the session at the Trianon Palace Hotel, where we shall hear the conditions of peace of our enemies, which, in one way or another, will decide the future of Germany for generations to come. Last night until half past two we were trying to decide what the attitude of the German delegation should be, without at all knowing what the attitude of our opponents would call forth from us. Until noon today more impassioned debates were taking place in the council of the "Olympians." May Count Brockdorff-Rantzau [chief of the German delegation] keep his dignity and his self-command in spite of everything. . . .

Versailles
May 10, 1919

Of all the hundreds of things which I have a great desire to tell you, I shall speak of only one, the afternoon session of May 7. The six delegates, five secretaries—Haniel, Stockhammern, Lersner, Rödiger, and I—and some German journalists were driven through the park to the Hotel Trianon, at the entrance of which a number of camera men were waiting for us. The French liaison officer, Colonel Henry, and a number of civilian and military functionaries received us and accompanied us to the hall of the session between solid ranks of representatives of all the states that were at war with us. It was interesting to me to observe the varying expressions on the faces of our "conquerers." The French showed either exaggerated hatred or marked, but possibly assumed, spirit of chivalry, the British haughty withdrawal. One Japanese evinced an intense, I might almost say a scientific curiosity. The hall of the session was arranged so that a great rectangle of tables stood in the center. When we entered we were facing Clemenceau, the President of the Conference. To his right sat Wilson and Lansing, to his left were Lloyd George and Bonar Law. On our left the nearest of our opponents were the French and the Italians, and on our right the Japanese. The table at which sat the six German delegates formed one of the two small ends of the rectangle, opposite Clemenceau. In the center the interpreters were seated; and behind the table of the delegates were the secretaries, in seats somewhat higher. Since my place was in the middle of the German secretaries, I was directly opposite Clemenceau, and had a good view of the whole assembly. Clemenceau, who has perhaps lived the most extraordinary life that fate could give to any mortal, makes a strangely bourgeois impression, in spite of his untamable expression. He wore gray gloves over his short, thick hands, and he did not remove them during the session. When we had taken our seats, he rose and spoke his introductory words in short staccato sentences which he threw out as if in a concentrated anger and disdain, and which from the very outset, for the Germans, made any reply quite futile. When Count Brockdorff-Rantzau remained seated while he gave his answer, this caused a general sensation. But he had told me beforehand that he would remain seated. In a diagram of the hall of the session which appeared in the French newspapers, the German table had already been designated as "banc des accusés." The Count therefore had heard, in spirit, the words, "the prisoner will stand up," and it was for that reason he kept his seat. He spoke with a voice that was remarkably calm, precise, and curt; he had our interpreters translate every sentence in turn into both French and English, the French proving to be not very good, and the English excellent. One must give Clemenceau credit for curbing his temper sufficiently to keep him from interrupting Rantzau's speech; but his face became red with anger. Wilson listened attentively, and the English translation, spoken with great passion, obviously made its impression upon him, although not a favorable one. The British feigned boredom and indifference. Lloyd George laughed and Bonar Law yawned. Most of the other delegates paid close attention, which can perhaps be attributed to the fact that they had difficulty in understanding one of the three languages spoken. After a brief half-hour Clemenceau closed the session just as laconically and sharply as he had opened it. Again, on the way to the door, we had to run the gauntlet. Rantzau lighted a cigarette, which caused a sensation. Meanwhile twice as many camera men had gathered at the door as before, and the moving-picture cameras were still clicking as we drove away.

I cannot very well tell you what went on in me in that half hour; the predominant feeling was that of a great unreality. Outside of the big window at my right there was a wonderful cherry tree in bloom, and it seemed to me the only reality when compared with the performance in the hall. This cherry tree and its kind will still be blooming, when the states whose representatives gathered here exist no longer.

The treaty which our enemies have laid before us is, in so far as the French dictated it, a monument of pathological fear and pathological hatred; and in so far as the Anglo-Saxons dictated it, it is the work of a capitalistic policy of the cleverest and most brutal kind. Its shamelessness does not lie in treading down a brave opponent, but in the fact that from beginning to end all these humiliating conditions are made to look like a just punishment, while in truth there is in them neither shame, nor any respect for the conception of justice.

b. Speech of Count Brockdorff-Rantzau on May 7, 1919, at the Trianon Palace Hotel, Versailles

SOURCE: Alma Luckau, *The German Delegation at the Paris Peace Conference*, pp. 220 223. Translation by the author.

Gentlemen, we are deeply impressed with the great mission that has brought us here to give to the world forthwith a lasting peace. We are under no illusions as to the extent of our defeat and the degree of our powerlessness. We know that the strength of the German arms is broken. We know the intensity of the hatred which meets us, and we have heard the victor's passionate demand that as the vanquished we shall be made to pay, and as the guilty we shall be punished.

The demand is made that we shall acknowledge that we alone are guilty of having caused the war. Such a confession in my mouth would be a lie. We are far from seeking to escape from any responsibility for this World War, and for its having been waged as it has. The attitude of the former German government at the Hague Peace Conferences, its actions and its omissions in the tragic twelve days of July may have contributed to the catastrophe, but we with all emphasis deny that the people of Germany, who were convinced that they were waging a war of defense, should be burdened with the sole guilt of that war.

Nobody would wish to contend that the catastrophe goes back merely to the fateful moment when the successor to the throne of Austria-Hungary fell a victim to murderous hands. In the past fifty years the imperialism of all European states has constantly poisoned the international situation. The policy of retaliation, the policy of expansion, and a disregard of the right of national self-determination have played their part in that illness of Europe which came to its crisis in the World War. The Russian mobilization made it impossible for statesmen to find a remedy, and threw the final decision into the hands of military power.

Public opinion in every enemy country is echoing the crimes Germany is said to have committed in the war. Here, too, we are ready to admit that unjust things have been done. We have not come here to diminish the responsibility of the men who have waged the war politically and economically, and to deny that breaches of the law of nations have been committed. We repeat the declaration which was made in the German Reichstag at the beginning of the war: injustice has been done to Belgium and we shall make reparations.

But in the manner of waging war, Germany was not the only one that erred. Every European nation knows of deeds and of individuals which the best of their people remember only with regret. I do not want to reply to reproaches with reproaches, but, if we alone are asked to do penance, one should remember the Armistice. Six weeks went by before we obtained an armistice, and six months before we came to know your conditions of peace. Crimes in war may not be excusable, but they are committed in the struggle for victory, when we think only of maintaining our national existence, and are in such passion as makes the conscience of peoples blunt. The hundreds of thousands of noncombatants who have perished since November 11, because of the blockade, were destroyed coolly and deliberately after our opponents had won a certain and assured victory. Remember that, when you speak of guilt and atonement.

The measure of guilt of all those who have taken part can be established only by an impartial inquiry, a neutral commission before which all the principals in the tragedy are allowed to speak, and to which all archives are open. We have asked for such an inquiry and we ask for it once more.

At this conference, where we alone and without our allies are facing our many opponents, we are not without protection. You yourself have brought us an ally: that justice which was guaranteed us in the agreement as to what should be the principles governing the treaty of peace. In the days between October 5 and November 5, 1918, the Allied and Associated governments swore that there would be no peace of violence, and inscribed on their knightly banners a peace of justice. On October 5 the German government proposed that the basis of peace should be the principles set forth by the President of the United States of America, and on November 5 their Secretary of State, Mr. Lansing, declared that the Allied and Associated Powers had accepted this basis, with two definite reservations. The principles of President Wilson thus became binding for both parties to the war, for you as well as for us, and also for our former allies.

Certain of the foregoing principles call upon us to make heavy national and economic sacrifices. But by such a treaty, the sacred and fundamental rights of all peoples would be protected. The conscience of the world would be behind it, and no nation that violated it would go unpunished.

Upon that basis you will find us ready to examine the preliminary peace which you have submitted to us, with the firm intention of joining with you in rebuilding that which has been destroyed, in making good whatever wrong has been committed, above all the injustice to Belgium, and in showing mankind new goals of political and social progress. Considering the confusing number of problems which arise, we ought, as soon as possible, to have the principal problems examined by special commissions of experts, on the basis of the treaty which you have submitted to us. Our principal problem will be to restore the broken strength of all the nations which took part in the war, and do it by providing international protection for the welfare, health, and freedom of the working classes.

I believe we should then proceed to restore those parts of Belgium and Northern France which have been occupied by us and which have been destroyed by the war. We have taken upon ourselves the solemn obligation to do so, and we are resolved to execute it to the extent which has been agreed upon between us. In this we are dependent upon the cooperation of our former opponents. We cannot accomplish it without the technical and financial participation of the victor nations, and they could accomplish it only with our cooperation. Impoverished Europe must desire to bring about this reconstruction as successfully, but at the same time at as little cost as possible. Such a project could be carried through only by means of a clear and businesslike understanding as to the best methods to be employed. To continue to have this done by German prisoners of war would be the worst of methods. Unquestionably such work can be done cheaply. But it would cost the world dear if hatred and despair should overcome the German people, forced to think of their sons, brothers, and fathers still held prisoners, and languishing as if in penal servitude. We cannot arrive at a lasting peace without an immediate solution of this problem, a problem which has already been postponed too long.

Experts on both sides will have to give thought as to how the German people can best meet the financial obligations called for by such reparations, without collapsing under the weight of their burden. A financial breakdown would take from those who have a right to reparations the advantages which are theirs by right, and would throw into irreparable disorder the whole European economic system. The victors as well as the vanquished must guard themselves against this menacing danger and its incalculable consequences. There is only one means of removing it: belief without reservation in the economic and social solidarity of all nations, and in a free and all-comprising League of Nations.

Gentlemen, the sublime idea of deriving from the most terrible catastrophe in history the greatest of forward movements in the development of mankind, by means of the League of Nations, has been put forth and will make its way. But only by opening the gates of the League of Nations to all who are of good will can the goal be attained, and only by doing so will it be that those who have died in this war shall not have died in vain.

In their hearts, the German people will resign themselves to their hard lot if the bases of the peace, as mutually agreed upon, are not destroyed. A peace which cannot be defended before the world as a peace of justice would always evoke new resistance. No one could sign it with a clear conscience, for it could not be carried out. No one could venture to guarantee its execution, though this obligation is implied in the signing of the treaty.

We shall, with every good intention, study the document submitted to us, in the hope that our meeting may finally result in something that can be signed by all of us.

c. Covering Letter to the German Counterproposals of May 29, 1919

SOURCE: Alma Luckau, *The German Delegation at the Paris Peace Conference*, pp. 302–306. Translation by the author.

Mr. President:

I have the honor to address to you, herewith, the observations of the German Delegation with regard to the proposed Peace Treaty. We came to Versailles, expecting to receive propositions of Peace on the proclaimed basis. We had the firm desire to do all we possibly could, to accomplish obligations accepted by us. We expected the Peace of Right which had been promised to us. We were grieved when we read this document to see what conditions victorious might demanded of us. The more we entered the spirit of that Treaty, the more we were convinced of the impossibility of carrying it out. The demands of that Treaty are beyond the strength of the German people.

It is demanded that we renounce, with a view to the reconstitution of Poland, a territory which is indisputably German, that we renounce Eastern Prussia, entirely German, German parts of Pomerania, Danzig, a city which is essentially German, a former Hanseatic city which we must allow to be constituted into a free State under the sovereignty of Poland. We must accept that Eastern Prussia be cut off the political body of which she is a part, that she be condemned to decay, and bereaved of her northern extremity, essentially German. We must renounce, in favor of Poland and Czechoslovakia, Upper Silesia, in spite of the narrow political bond which has kept it united to Germany for over 750 years, in spite of the German life which fills it and though it constitutes the very basis of industry in the whole of Eastern Germany. Districts where the German element is in majority must be given to Belgium, without sufficient guarantees in favor of the independence of a plebiscite which shall only be made after they are given away. The country of the Saar, essentially German, must be separated from our Empire, and its reunion to France must be prepared, though we do not owe France any populations but only coal.

During 15 years, the Rhine territory must be occupied and the Allies will keep after 15 years, the facility of refusing to retrocede this country; during this period they will be free to do all that may cause the economic and moral ties to slacken between that country and the motherland, and finally warp the mind of the population.

A Germany, thus partitioned and weakened, must, though the payment of war expenditures has expressly been given up, declare herself ready to bear the weight of all the expenditures of her adversaries, which amount to twice the national and individual wealth of Germany. The adversaries, even now, going beyond the basis agreed to, demand the reparation of the damage supported by the civil population, reparations for which Germany must also answer in the name of her Allies. The sum to be paid is to be settled and ulteriorly modified and increased in a unilateral manner by the adversaries. The limit will be indicated by the capacity of payment of the German people, the degrees contemplated do not depend on the conditions of its existence but solely on the possibility in which it will find itself to satisfy the demands of its enemies by its work. The German people would thus be condemned to a perpetual slavery.

In spite of these exorbitant demands, the reconstruction of our economic life is, at the same time, made impossible. We must give our merchant fleet, give up all foreign property. We must transfer to the adversaries our property rights over all German enterprises in foreign lands even in our Allies' countries. Even after the conclusion of Peace the enemy states will have the right to confiscate the totality of German wealth. No German businessman, in the countries of these States, will be sheltered against such war measures. We must give up the whole of our colonies, German missionaries will not even have the right to exercise their profession. Therefore it is our very existence, from a political, economic, and moral point of view, which we must renounce.

Even at home we must sacrifice our right of self-determination. The International Commission on Reparations has received a dictatorial power even over our whole national life, in the realm of economy and culture, its rights being much in excess of those ever possessed, over the territory of the Empire, by the Emperor, the Bundesrat and the Reichstag together.

This Commission has full power over the economy of the State, the communities and the individuals. Education and Public Health are absolutely under its control. It can maintain the whole German people in intellectual slavery; it can, with a view to raising the

payments to which she is obliged, fetter the work of social provision in favor of the German workers.

In other realms also, the sovereignty of Germany is suppressed.
The principal waterways are subject to an international administration; Germany is compelled to build, on her territories, the canals
and railways requested by the adversaries, to give her assent to
treaties, the tenor of which is unknown to her and which shall be
concluded by her adversaries with the new Eastern States, even
beyond her frontiers. The German people is excluded from the
League of Nations, to which the work in common of the world is
entrusted.

Thus, a whole nation must sign her own proscription, more than
that, her condemnation to death.

Germany knows that she must consent to sacrifices, in order to
obtain peace. She knows that, in conformity with a convention, she
has promised these sacrifices; she is ready to go to the extreme limit
of what is possible.

1. Germany offers to anticipate all other nations, by her own
disarmament, to show that she wants to help create the new era of
Peace of Right. She sacrifices obligatory military service and reduces her army to 100,000 men, abstraction being made for transi-
tory measures. She even renounces the warships that her enemies
still wish to leave to her. But this with the understanding that she
will be immediately admitted with the same right as the other
states, into the League of Nations and that a true League of Nations will be formed, including all the Nations, animated by good
will, even the enemies of today. This League will have the sentiment of responsibility before Humanity, as foundation, and will
have a power of coercion, sufficiently strong and worthy of
confidence, to protect the frontiers of its members.

2. As far as territorial questions are concerned, Germany takes
rank, without restrictions, on the ground of Wilson's program. She
renounces her rights of sovereignty over Alsace-Lorraine, but desires a free plebiscite. She gives to Poland the greater part of
Posnania, the territories indisputably inhabited by Poles and the
capital of Posen. She is ready to insure to the Poles by the cession
of free ports at Danzig, Koenigsberg and Memel, by a chart governing navigation on the Vistula and by special treaties regarding
railways, free and certain access to the sea without international
guarantees. Germany is ready to insure the economic supply of

France in coal, especially from the Saar coal field, until restoration of the French mines. The parts of Schleswig which have a Danish majority will be given to Denmark after a plebiscite. Germany requests that the right of self-determination be also respected in favor of the Germans of Austria and Bohemia.

She is ready to put all her colonies under the administration in common of the League of Nations, if she is recognized as mandatory for the latter.

3. Germany is ready to make the payments incumbent upon her according to the peace program agreed upon, up to the maximum sum of 100 billion marks gold, of which 20 billion marks gold are to be paid by May 1, 1926, the other 80 billion marks gold in annual sums without interest. These sums are in principle to represent a percentage fixed according to the revenue of the Empire and the German States. The quota will approach the former budget of peace times. For the first ten years, it shall not exceed a billion marks gold. The German taxpayer shall not be taxed less than the most highly taxed taxpayer among those represented on the Commission of Reparations.

Germany supposes from this that she will not have to make other territorial sacrifices than those heretofore cited, and that she will be permitted all liberty of movement at home and abroad.

4. Germany is ready to put all her economic force at the service of reconstruction. She desires to collaborate by her work in the reconstruction of the ravaged districts of Belgium and the North of France. For the deficit in the production of the mines destroyed in the North of France she will furnish as high as 20 million tons of coal for the first five years, 8 million tons a year for the next five years. Germany will facilitate other deliveries of coal to France, Belgium, Italy, and Luxemburg.

Moreover, Germany is ready to furnish important quantities of benzol, coal tar, sulphuric ammonia and dye-stuffs, and pharmaceutical products.

5. Finally, Germany offers to put her entire merchant tonnage at the disposal of the world's commerce, to put at the disposal of the enemy a part of the cargoes, which shall be put to her credit toward the damages to be repaired, and for a term of years to construct for them in German yards a tonnage whose figure exceeds their demands.

6. To replace the river boats destroyed in Belgium and the North of France, Germany offers her own river fleet.

7. Germany thinks that she sees an appropriate means of rapidly fulfilling her obligations in the way of reparation, by according industrial participation, especially in the coal mines, to insure the delivery of coal.

8. In accord with the wish of organized laborers the world over, Germany desires to see the laborers of every country free and equal in their rights. She wishes to see them insured, by the Peace Treaty, in their right to participate, by their own decisions, in social politics and social insurance.

9. The German Delegation reiterates its demand for a neutral examination of the responsibility for the war and crimes committed during the war. An impartial commission should have the right to examine under its own responsibility the archives of all the belligerent countries and of all the principal participants.

Only the assurance that the question of guilt will be examined without prejudice can give to the hostile countries the state of mind necessary to the constitution of the League of Nations.

These are only the most important propositions that we have to make. As to the other great sacrifices and details, the Delegation refers to the enclosed memorandum and its supplement.

The time limit given us for the drawing up of this memorandum was so short that it was impossible to exhaust all the questions. A fruitful and useful discussion could take place only by means of oral conversations. This peace is to be the greatest treaty of history. It is without precedent to carry on such vast negotiations by means of written notes only. The sentiment of nations that have made such enormous sacrifices requires that their fate be decided by a public and unrestricted exchange of ideas, after the principle: "Public Peace Treaties," which have been drawn up publicly; and henceforth there must be no international conventions of any sort, but diplomacy must always operate publicly and under the eyes of the world.

Germany must sign the treaty that has been presented to her and must carry out its conditions. Even in her misfortune, right is too sacred to her for her to stoop to accept conditions that she can not promise to fulfil. It is true that in the course of the last centuries the peace treaties of the great powers have always proclaimed the right of might. But each one of these treaties is one of the causes that has started or prolonged the world war. Wherever in the course of this war the conqueror has spoken to the conquered, as at Brest-Litovsk or at Bucharest, the affirmations of power were only the germs of future discord. The lofty aims which our enemies have been the first to give to their way of conducting the war, require a treaty in a different spirit. Only the collaboration of all nations, the common labor of all arms and brains, can create a durable peace. We are under no illusions as to the depth of the hatred and bitterness which are the fruits of this war; and nevertheless the forces working for harmony in humanity are today stronger than ever. The historic task of the Peace Conference at Versailles is to bring about this harmony.

Brockdorff-Rantzau

d. Unconditional Acceptance of the Treaty of Versailles: German Note of June 23, 1919

SOURCE: Alma Luckau, *The German Delegation at the Paris Peace Conference*, p. 482. Translation by the author.

Sir,

The Minister of Foreign Affairs has requested me to submit the following note to Your Excellency:

The government of the German Republic is overwhelmed to learn from the last communication of the Allied and Associated Powers that the Allies are resolved to enforce, with all the power at their command, the acceptance even of those provisions in the treaty which, without having any material significance, are designed to deprive the German people of their honor. The honor of the German people cannot be injured by an act of violence. The German people, after their terrible sufferings during these last years, are wholly without the means of defending their honor against the outside world. Yielding to overpowering might, the government of the German Republic declares itself ready to accept and to sign the peace treaty imposed by the Allied and Associated governments. But in so doing, the government of the German Republic in no wise abandons its conviction that these conditions of peace represent injustice without example.

[Signed] von Haniel

e. Appeal of the German Government to the German People,
June 24, 1919

SOURCE: Alma Luckau, *The German Delegation at the Paris Peace Conference*, pp. 496–497. Translation by the author.

The government of the Reich, with the consent of the National Assembly, has decided to sign the treaty of peace. We do so with heavy hearts, under the pressure of the most unrelenting power, and with only one thought: to save our defenseless people from having to make further sacrifices and endure added pains of hunger.

Peace has been concluded. Now guard and preserve it.

The first demand is that you fulfill the conditions of the treaty. You must bend every effort to fulfill it. It must be carried out, so far as it can be carried out. We shall never forget those who are to be severed from us. They are flesh of our flesh. Wherever it can be done, we shall take their part as if it were our own. They will be torn from the Reich, but they will not be torn from our hearts.

The second demand is work. We shall be able to carry the burdens of this war only if no hand is idle. To every unfulfilled obligation our opponents can respond with invasion, occupation, and blockade. He who works defends his native soil.

The third demand is faithfulness to the call of duty. Even as we have remained at our posts, at whatever cost to our self-respect, each and everyone of us should do the same. The soldier, whether he be officer or private, the public servant, everyone, must be steadfast in his duty for the sake of the general good, even in this worst day of all. We are compelled to hand over our fellow Germans to foreign tribunals. That is something which we opposed to the last. We know full well how bitter a thing this is for our brave soldiers. But if officer and man alike do not give their full support to the present government, not merely hundreds, but millions of our compatriots will be delivered over to terror, to armed occupation, to annexation. Germany must retain the power to live. If we have no order within, we shall have no work. Without work we cannot meet the conditions of the treaty. If we fail in that, there will be not peace, but a renewal of the war.

If we do not all help, our having signed the treaty will be worthless. We shall then have no ameliorations, no revisions, and no final removal of the gigantic burden. What we leave undone today may cost our children years of servitude. Both government and people must set to work forthwith. There must be no delay and no one must stand aside. There is only one way out of the darkness of this treaty: the preservation of Reich and people through unity and work.

Help us, men and women, to attain that.

The President of the Republic, Ebert
The Government of the Reich

Bauer	Robert Schmitt
Erzberger	Dr. Bell
Hermann Müller	Giesberts
Dr. David	Noske
Dr. Mayer	Schlicke
Wissell	

III

The Consolidation of the
Weimar Regime, 1920–1929

As of 1920 Germany had attained a kind of outward stability: the newly formed government was at work, and it had to accept a severely diminished role for Germany in European affairs. Internally, however, dissatisfaction and disruption were seldom absent. Democracy and its servants were hostages to activism; between 1919 and 1922 nearly four hundred men were assassinated, mostly by right-wing elements. Others were killed fighting in the Free Corps and various ideological bands or became victims of those paramilitary groups in German cities or frontiers of friction with the Slavic world. Antirepublicanism thrived in this intimidating atmosphere. More immediately, every German was frightened and dismayed by the vast and apparently uncontrollable inflation. Material and moral values decayed in the face of speculation and corruption. Though internal stability returned by 1925, these disruptive political and economic experiences left their mark in continuing psychological insecurity.

German history between 1925 and 1929 is like the slow revelation of a political and economic miracle. Much of the credit goes to Gustav Stresemann, who worked within a more relaxed international atmosphere to return Germany to international political normalcy. He overshadowed, but did not exceed, the political effectiveness of the lesser-known men in Berlin who learned how to develop political democracy into a working system. They were, of course, greatly aided by Germany's dramatic economic revival. It was a tragedy for much of mankind that their efforts had just begun to take root when the necessary productive soil for their enterprise was eroded and swept away by the Great Depression.

11. Conditions for Conversion to National Socialism

Professor Theodore Abel, a Columbia University sociologist, visited Germany in the summer of 1933 and was struck by the willingness of most people he encountered to discuss the circumstances that had led them to become members of the Nazi movement. He subsequently announced a prize contest to induce those of Hitler's followers who had joined the party before 1933, to tell what circumstances during the pre-Nazi era had caused them to seek out National Socialism. He received nearly seven hundred autobiographies and a wealth of material for his study. The following four excerpted selections from his work indicate conditions and attitudes in different walks of life during the early 1920s.

SOURCE: Theodore Abel, *Why Hitler Came into Power* (Englewood Cliffs, N.J.: Prentice-Hall, 1938), pp. 44–47, 247–248, 254–257, 278–281. Autobiography of the School Teacher is excerpted from original Abel files now in the Hoover Institution. Translation by the editor. Copyright © 1938, renewed 1966. Reprinted by permission of Prentice-Hall, Inc., Englewood Cliffs, New Jersey.

a. A Man from the Free Corps

Completely disconcerted, a bourgeois generation faced the new world of 1918. It had managed during the war, adapting itself to all the unaccustomed limitations, suffering bitter need in the belief that some time, after peace was made, it would be able to continue down the broad, comfortable avenue it had traveled before. Now it found itself confused and frightened, in an arid meadow. In place of the imposing goal, they were confronted by unknown apparitions. An entire bourgeois generation stood and waited, in the hope that some time these spectres must disappear, and the broad open road must once again open before it.

There was a gaping abyss between fathers and sons. We soldiers of the front had never known the fabulous comfortable road; nor did we feel any longing for it. Fighting had become our life purpose and goal; any battle, any sacrifice for the might and glory of our country. The new state of affairs, to be sure, was a surprise to us. But we couldn't sit on the side lines, like people in a trance. Somehow we had to take a hand in affairs, one way or another.

There were those of the Marxist school among us. Like the rest of us, they had done their duty in the field. Now as red flags waved and processions marched, the mottoes and ideals of their fathers came back to them. They entered the soldiers' councils, spoke, organized, and tried to erect the free workman's state, dreamt of by Marx and Engels, LaSalle and Bebel. They fought with idealism and enthusiasm, until they finally fell back into the life of parasites, lolled comfortably in easily conquered arm chairs, and made good living their goal. Others turned away in disgust and roamed from leader to leader, from party to party, only to meet everywhere the spirit of Jewish materialism that their courageous soldiers' hearts could not accept.

And there were the rest of us—nationalists by education and tradition. We knew nothing of politics, yet we felt that therein lay the destiny of Germany. Slowly we came to recognize that we must learn to think in terms of politics if Germany was to live.

In the days of the revolution, discipline predominated. "Don't shoot," commanded the governor of the fortress of Kiel. Though convinced of the necessity of repelling Bolshevism, we didn't shoot. Then the sentries were withdrawn, weapons turned in; defenseless, bound by the command of our superiors, we young officers of the Imperial Marine stood face to face with the mob and its alien leaders. For more than four years death had been a matter of course for us; but we could not understand dishonorable surrender. Nor did we want to. What chance had we to resist?

On foot I made my way in the streaming rain to Neumünster. At least the infantry might undertake the battle aganist the reds. There too I was faced with disappointment. "Discipline! No bloodshed!" On to the office of the commanding general in Altona I went. The same hateful word, "discipline," greeted me there too. In my native city I made a last attempt to contact an anti-Bolshevist troop. The old commander silently laid down a telegram before me: "No resistance!" Already men with red arm bands stood on guard; automobiles flew red flags. Deserters were hoisting red rags on the roofs. Offices and barracks were opened to them without resistance. "Discipline." It was the end.

One must bear these things in mind to understand the course of our lives, to comprehend how two generations became estranged in a few days. In those days our trust in the old leaders, in the old generation, was destroyed, struck dead. We had to take our fate in our own hands.

To feign indifference to the new conditions was impossible. The attempt failed miserably. Disgusted with the red cloths, drunken heroes of liberty, and uniformed bands of thieves, I turned my back on everything. Naturally only Kurland remained now. [Kurland: a historic German name for most of Latvia and Lithuania, in 1919–1920 scene of German and Baltic Free Corps fighting against the Russians.]

Kurland meant to become a soldier again, to be allowed to fight again. It meant forming a decent troop which might one day clear up the mess, and finally it meant making primeval German land German again. So we marched, sang, and fought. But once victory was in our hands, Germany betrayed us. Germany? To us the Berlin of ministries was not Germany. Germany was ourselves, only we—no matter where, no matter under what flag.

Without further thought we surrendered our German citizenship, became Letts, and filled our pockets with the freshly printed rouble notes of the new Latvian Republic. Again we conquered, on the battlefield, only to lose once more at the parley tables. No matter. Under the Russian flag, we remained Germans. Only our uniforms were different; and soon we were fighting without pay. We suffered many privations, but we saw how our depleted group remained steadfast, until retreat was forced upon us by treason and unequal circumstances. We were back again, across the border, where Ebert and Noske ruled. They would see! Kapp was the name of our new leader, our next disappointment. Gritting our teeth we had to leave the conquered ground as our leaders disappeared. We were put to work in Pomerania, to protect the landed estates, to us the strongholds of nationalism. Soldiers were to become farmers. Confidently we set to work, only to realize before long what a world separated us from those "nationalists." At first we only sensed this. Still we did not want to resist these important landowners, whose ancient noble blood we felt we ought to respect. After all, they were *Deutschnational*, just as we were. Like us, they were fanatical opponents of Bolshevism. And yet our emotions were different. They spoke of Germany, but they meant money and privilege. They envisioned us not as free farmers, but as serfs. Unaccustomed as we were to expressing ourselves, we could find no words for our feelings.

Then—it was the summer of 1920—a summons came to us in Pomerania. Cheap paper . . . shabby print . . . slogans. . . . The contents didn't matter to us, but the signature aroused our enthusiasm. We had found what we had been seeking since the end of the war. *Deutsch-sociale Partei* was the name of the organization soliciting our support. It was German, of course . . . German, patriotic, nationalistic . . . that was what we were, and so too were the gentlemen with whom we could not agree. But there was another word that aroused our enthusiasm; the word connected with "German," instead of being coupled with democracy and liberalism as was usually the case. Socialism, enlightenment, the development of the communal spirit. . . . Once more we could respect every German as our brother. We sensed and we knew that if we succeeded in animating these printed words, if we could unite the concepts of nationalism and socialism, we would have a banner under which we could lead the German people to freedom.

b. An Unemployed Bank Clerk

The youth movement and *Wandervögel* were my personal preparatory school for National Socialism. The German youth movement was a training for personality in the best sense, for it taught us independence of action. Blood and soil were the two factors which played the largest part in this training. Love of the homeland and faith in the destiny and preservation of our nation were here for the first time experienced by maturing youths. They gave a meaning to life and turned us away from the superficial teachings of people who thought purely in terms of economics. We turned away from the skatplaying politicians of the beer table; we became rebels, revolutionaries, because we saw our nation in danger. We recognized the poisoning of the German soul in the form of superficial, shallow music, in the form of the trashy literature which could be bought cheaply at any newsstand. On the stage of the German theatre we heard words which were foreign to our nature and our spiritual attitude. Our mind's eye envisioned the breakdown of Rome, Babylon, Nineveh, and the other ancient states. Everywhere one turned one saw Jews. The press, theatre, motion pictures, literature, music—indeed art in every form—technical science, and education were all decisively influenced by them. Was the degeneracy of the abovementioned nations also to seize our people? Never! That must not be.

But the *Wandervögel* could not fulfill this mission of regeneration. The flood of Bolshevism would have passed over it. Our youthful, vital forces, together with the other constructive forces of the nation had first to create a revolutionary movement and gain control of the state in order to accomplish reorganization of our entire national life. A man like Walter Rathenau, who, because he was a Jew, saw everything in a Jewish perspective, was insufferable to us, the youth who were consciously German. Therefore, the first determining factor of our movement was its anti-Semitism. The *"Deutschvölkischer Schutzbund"* was the vanguard of the movement which fought for our national Germany, until the government dissolved the organization and new ways had to be found to meet a new situation. Down in the south we heard of Adolf Hitler, the "Drummer" who was perceiving the same problem with the same emotions as so many other German fellow-countrymen. Prussia was closed to him. In his spirit, which we recognized as right, we began our work in the years 1921 to 1923 in the *"Preussenbund,"* which was under the leadership of Captain Ammon, the "Chief," as we called him. From 1923 until 1924, I put my strength at the disposal of the "Schlageter [Nazi hero] Memorial Association." Our present banner of war, the swatika, was even then our symbol of faith.

When it was made known in 1925 that Adolf Hitler had decided to reestablish the various local Nazi groups (prohibited and dissolved in 1923) on a national scale, then nothing could hold us back. In the extreme northeast, in March to April 1925, the first local group of the Party was formed. When the Leader then proposed the head of the general staff of the World War, Ludendorff, in the presidential election of 1925, we headed the ranks who fought for his candidacy. To be sure we were not understood. But we knew what we were doing. Half a hundred members were able to astonish the whole city: Ludendorff received a thousand votes. We were proud and prepared for further successes. The idea, its strengthening, and above all organization, were the problems that always had to be solved. The National Socialist press at that time was insignificant. The *Völkische Beobachter* in the beginning appeared with only four pages and only as a weekly. Because we were so far removed from its place of publication, Munich, the newspaper always reached our subscribers two days late, and even later, as a daily, it was always out of date. It did not have the needed staff of contributors. Therefore the newspaper offered our citizens nothing. Despite this, our will to build up the battling paper of our movement was stubborn and undaunted. At that time I succeeded in acquiring about a hundred subscribers for the party publication. That was about 1925 or 1926. As a reward, I received from the party organization in Munich both volumes of *Mein Kampf*, with the signature of the Leader, and several photographs of our Leader likewise autographed. Today, after the victory, I look upon these proudly in memory of those hours.

c. A Disillusioned Socialist

My father was a Social Democrat. . . . I saw facts from the inside. Other people did not live in our narrow confines. All of us—parents and children—slept in one room. I saw what happened with wakeful eyes. Others did not see that. I saw—and in my mind's eyes still see—my father standing at the window, breathing on the frost on the window-panes. Those were cold winters that made one's hands freeze. Buildings were untouched and there were no earnings. There was no unemployment relief then. I remember how, at the birth of my youngest brother, my mother was given salt herring and potatoes to eat right after her confinement. I was forced to become acquainted with the contrasts existing not only between different social castes, but also in all classes of society. Even during my school days I felt this bitterly. We went to school barefoot. Though our clothes were clean and whole, the sons of middle-class families appeared with collars and shoes. Only too often I was made to feel that this gave them an advantage, though such superiority was not justified by achievements or capacities. . . .

I had to work from my ninth year on. Today I stop at every bowling alley to watch the pin boy, because I know how badly his back hurts when midnight comes and the bowlers start one game after another, and how parched his throat is after being exposed to dust hour after hour. The teachers were out of luck as far as my homework was concerned. However, a quick perception came to my aid, so that I did not have to work nearly so hard as others who actually appeared with carefully plotted compositions and arithmetic problems, trying to be model boys. I never was a model boy. I received plenty of beatings for my pranks. Up to the time of my confirmation, I was employed by a merchant for whom I acted as house servant; actually, however, I played a lot in the streets. Thanks to this, I did not forget how to laugh while a child. I brooded about it more and more and found the solution as to why my father was such an ardent Social Democrat. I saw with my own eyes that now and then a demand for a raise was justified; and I also saw how bitterly one had to struggle for it. I saw only too often the honest working man being exploited by the supporters of capitalism. I felt most bitter about the way the puffed-up bourgeois passed by the fellow German, who was only a workman with matter of fact gestures. My own view of life and my own observations of life led me to see that the class struggle was not a condition brought about by the working group. The middle class created the prerequisites for it, while on the other side false prophets found it only too easy to drive the wedge so fatefully amid the German people. . . .

I marched through the war, saw battlefields that made cheerfulness die. At the front I observed the phases of the mighty struggle, and as we stood alone beneath the grenade tracks, ragged and dirty, embittered and defiant, with the mask of death under every steel helmet—then only did I begin to understand Germany. Thus the revolution rose out of the craters of the battlefield. We sat in trenches and heard of lost prisoners, and decaying homeland. We heard the shirkers laugh. But we were silent, because we could say nothing, and because there was no one there to whom we could have said anything. We saw the horror approaching, but we were helpless against it. We felt that the Frenchman and the Tommy were not our worst enemies, but that worse, poisonous things were being brewed in the witches' kitchens at home. And when in November 1918 we marched through Lüttich—I was with the Seventy-seventh Reserve Infantry Regiment at the time—under Red flags—my heart seemed to break.

Then we were told that English fleet had approached ours with Red flags waving. *Sancta simplicitas.* I believed it and said to my men: "Now the greatest thing in the history of the world since the life of Christ has happened: soldiers who fought this terrible war are ending it themselves, and the subterfuges of those who heard no whistle of bullets are at an end." I was ashamed when I learned that they had lied to us, ashamed not of myself but of the others, ashamed that they were Germans, just as I have at times since then been ashamed of Germans.

The march home was the bitterest experience I have ever had. . . . I was a broken man, on the point of losing himself, who could no longer find God. I have preserved a picture of those days. So that was how I looked! I cannot recognize myself. Out of fear and courage, out of storm, enthusiasm and defiance, out of blood and dirt, out of hope and misery I returned, still with love in my heart. But when we saw Germany, the ground sank under my feet. We soldiers of the front walked in a thick night, in boundless darkness. We shook hands for the last time and passed others by; they did not know us. . . .

It seemed as if professional soldiers faced nothingness. So I grasped at the least thing that was offered me. I became a gendarme, only for a few months. It was not so very difficult to get a position as a government employee; one was offered me by the community of Pankow. Slowly a new, different life began to unfold itself. I became an assistant city clerk on probation, and married a good German woman. Our first home was in a basement. I received several other offers of positions and perhaps with a different choice of profession I might have led a splendid life. . . .

The inflation took my young wife's heritage, honestly earned savings that had been worked for, inherited from her brother who had fallen in battle. The party mismanagement shot high; it disgusted me. I tried various ways of finding manliness and manly action. Many a circle was open to me, but I found nothing but disappointment everywhere. Bearers of power in the Socialist party courted me. They promised me a tempting future. But when this became the subject of conversation I thought of the fairy tale of world brotherhood and of the lie of the waving red flags on the English battleships, and I saw the sea of flags in Lüttich. I heard the cries of my dead comrades. Gradually passivity became unbearable for me. I was a member of the "Association of Nationally Minded Soldiers." It was prohibited. The *"Jungdo"* tempted me; the leadership could not make me enthusiastic. I became a member of the *Stahlhelm* [major conservative veterans' organization] was soon a local group leader, increased the local group from some forty men to three hundred, became district group leader, and, when I left the *Stahlhelm*, left behind me twelve hundred comrades. . . .

My departure from the *Stahlhelm* was very painful, for I now had to leave my comrades to their own devices. I was not a rebel; therefore I persuaded no one to join me. Many an experience had welded me together with my comrades; again dead men stood between us and before us. The battle of Germany's freedom demanded a tribute of us too. All that, however, I left behind me, because I saw clearly that once again the existence or nonexistence of Germany was at stake, and that there was only one solution: Hitler.

d. A School Teacher

My homeland is in Silesia in the area of the Neisse, close to the borders of the Sudetenland. My ancestors have been German farmers for centuries, ever since the entire Sudetenland was settled by German peasants from Franconia, Bavaria, Hesse, and Thuringia. . . . By dint of very hard work and rigid thrift my parents succeeded in surviving the difficult decades of the 1880s and 1890s and increased the size of their small farm. My father had the constructive notion of maintaining his children on his own land rather than sending them into the city for employment, as many others did. We children vigorously assisted my father, thus replacing some of the necessary girls and farmhands. These were idyllic times in the small, quiet village where we lived together in a genuine folk community. The farmhands still ate with the farmers at the same table, the weddings and funerals involved the whole community, while at the country fairs and other village festivals the rich and poor alike harmoniously danced and celebrated together. . . .

At the age of twenty I passed my teacher's examination and soon received a teaching position in another borderland area. I taught in the district of Rybik (today a part of Poland) from 1908 to 1914, among people who spoke almost exclusively *"wasserpolnisch"* [a Polish dialect of Upper Silesia]. To my great astonishment I found that these "Pollacks" were not Poles at all, but rather proudly considered themselves as Prussians and Germans. . . . [I concluded that] the "Polish question" was artificially incited in Upper

Silesia by Polish clergymen, agents, physicians, and especially pharmacists, who come from the Posen area and Poland. . . . The weak and vacillating position of the central government, particularly on questions involving Germans in the borderlands, caused us much worry. Misunderstanding and neglect of nationality problems in Eastern Germany filled me with apprehension. But in these years I came to realize that we could protect ourselves against the Slavic flood and save ourselves as a nation only if all Germans, regardless of class or religion, and including those living beyond the [eastern] borders of the Reich, would firmly stand together. . . .

During four years of battlefront experience in France, Russia, and Rumania my awareness of a genuine folk community and comradeship was spiritually intensified; and this feeling was the same for all my comrades. I fought in four different regiments from the most varied areas of Germany and everywhere I found the same thing. I saw with astonishment how the profound racial and spiritual qualities of our people were revealed in our simplest sons, how an entire people proved itself in an unparalleled heroic struggle, yet remained inherently both pure and noble. Tragically, our people had incompetent political leadership that tolerated an unprincipled undermining of unity by impure and partially alien social elements.

I was medically discharged in early 1918, and saw with wrath how much the subversives and certain parliamentarians had already been effective. When the Revolution broke out, mostly the alien elements in Upper Silesia captured public attention and skillfully directed the socialistic-bolshevistic wave, which swept through the masses of workers, over into the nationalist-Polish group, and against the German community, whose members were identified as oppressive landowners, civil servants, and employers. . . . The occupation [of Upper Silesia], with its torments and uprising, demonstrated in all clarity for me that in the life of nations, right is only on the side of the stronger, and that a people which disarms itself and tolerates a dishonorable government finds neither mercy nor justice. After the third Polish uprising I was driven out and learned with bitterness that there was neither home nor job for us refugees under a government that showed no understanding of our plight. . . .

My family and many other unfortunate individuals found shelter in a refugee camp and remained without employment for five years. While my attention had up to that point been focused upon Upper Silesia and the situation in the border areas, it was now directed to the entire domestic and foreign situation. . . . I attended political meetings, became a conservative activist and hoped to find the people who would save Germany in the German National Party. Yet nowhere did I find fulfillment. After I gave a speech and succeeded in disrupting a meeting of the Center Party, I was invited by the district chairman of the German National People's Party in Neisse to become politically more involved. I also established contact with *Stahlhelm* circles, but soon I noticed that most of their leaders at that time emphasized monarchistic and reactionary goals, which I rejected because I felt inwardly that somehow socialist ideas must be joined with a national movement. In spite of that conviction, I voted German Nationalist in the subsequent years, because I considered it the strongest party interested in preserving the state. . . .

Some National Socialist propaganda made me aware of the movement and I attended their meetings. Without understanding its goals at first, I sensed the spiritual affinity between the movement and myself and for ideas which gave me inward enlightenment. I still had not come to know the Führer, or his book, and continued to have my doubts. Nevertheless, I joined the Party in 1929. I believe that my experiences in the border areas were decisive in leading me to the NSDAP. . . . Later I read the book of the Führer, heard him speak in person, and became a true believer.

12. From Inflation to Corruption

This selection comes from the pen of a freelance journalist who entered his profession during the Weimar era, spent World War II as a correspondent in Japan and the 1950s writing from Britain. He makes a broad indictment of Germans of all classes and regions for their sins of commission or omission in Germany's road to ruin.

SOURCE: Karl-Heinz Abshagen, *Schuld und Verhängniss. Ein Vierteljahrhundert deutscher Geschichte in Augenzeugenberichten* (Stuttgart: Union Verlag, 1961), pp. 90–103, 105–106, Translation by the editor. Reprinted by permission of the publisher.

There is much talk about inflation in today's world. But what does a generation born after World War I really know about the impact of rampant inflation on a whole nation and on the individual citizen?

Summer, 1923. About 10 o'clock in the morning. Two dozen women gradually gather in front of a small factory in a suburb of Hamburg. They are wives, mothers, perhaps even sisters of men working in the factory. A few landladies or bachelors might also be there. They are waiting for the men's wages to be paid this morning at this hour as on every second workday. The company is now paying its wages three times a week . . . so that the workers can buy what they need without losing too much; the currency is depreciating too quickly to permit them to pocket their money for more than a few hours without suffering loss of value. The wages of most workers in private businesses have long been based on the exchange rate for the American dollar and day by day this rate is rising by leaps and bounds. All the stores close at noon until the new exchange rate is published; when they open again in the afternoon all the prices in marks are usually higher. . . . The women wait at the factory gate until the men hand them the money. They then hurry to the stores to exchange their paper money for groceries or other "capital goods" before noon.

The government money presses cannot keep up with the racing inflation, thus forcing communities and even private businesses to print emergency tokens for payment of their employees. A yellowed newspaper clipping of autumn 1923, . . . illuminates the difficulties of this situation:

> The currency distress is felt most acutely in Berlin because tourism causes an accumulation of diverse monies. You get a bundle of bills the size of a handsome brick. You count and count. The number is correct. Later you discover among them Brandenburg provincial notes, Hallenser and Cologne railroad notes, and a Greifswald grain receipt which no merchant will accept. We now have one hundred and seventy-two different kinds of money with different values for each type. Emergency tokens from large firms and small communes not even included. . . .

The emergency presses have difficulty keeping up with the steadily depreciating value of the currency. The money for payment of two days' wages for twenty or thirty workers must be carried in suitcases or laundry baskets. . . . Pay envelopes disappeared long ago; they could not hold the bundles of thousand mark notes which a simple worker receives for two days' work. For all of this, the workers and employees in commerce and industry are still relatively well off; to a certain extent, though with difficulty, they can still keep pace with depreciation.

The business world has long since adapted itself to the race with the dollar rate. Stores close at noon every day and raise their prices according to the dollar rate. Industry and commerce have found other ways to protect themselves from currency depreciation. Indeed, any but the dimwitted can take advantage of the inflation. Until the very end of the race with the zeros (that is, until the mark has depreciated one trillionfold, a trillion being a one followed by twelve zeros!) the Reichsbank will maintain the fiction that one mark equals another. Of course, this is madness, but there is method in it. The Central Bank of Issue unhesitatingly discounts the industrial and commercial notes offered by private banks. At a time when the value of the mark is falling precipitously, day by day, it continues to pump credit into the economy, traditionally with six month notes later cut to three month issues. Repayment is made at only a fraction of original value. The clever man floats as much paper credit as possible and enlarges his inventory in terms of real goods!

But who shoulders the loss? The immediate answer is: the Reichsbank and the general public. In general that may be true, but it is not the whole truth. There are millions of individual losers, all the people with savings accounts and owners of securities with fixed returns. Stock prices adjust more or less rapidly and completely to the actual value represented by assets of the company. Owners of stock in well-run businesses are thus not affected adversely by currency devaluation. Ownership of property and homes also offers stable value. Owners of government and industrial bonds, of mortgages and trust deeds, are economically deceived along with possessors of savings accounts.

A preponderant majority of the German middle classes of the 1920s were not stockholders. They were accustomed to investing their hard-earned capital in fixed-return securities for their old age. They knew how much interest they could expect year after year. Payment was guaranteed by law on securities of the Reich, federal states, and other governmental entities. Good citizens slept well at night with a naive confidence in the reliability of the government.

It was beyond their comprehension that the state would deprive them, not maliciously but by incompetence of its finance and currency administrators, of their savings and property. When that actually happened, when the savings accounts and government bonds (especially the war bonds thrust upon them with appeals to patriotic duty) dwindled to nothing, their confidence in the value of the currency was also shattered. It was even worse because the middle classes discovered that other people were prospering despite, or even because of, inflation. They probably did not realize that industry was renewing its investments and wholesalers were filling their warehouses while they were impoverished. But they did observe that small and large racketeers and speculators accumulated fortunes in no time. . . .

[One writer] tells of her experiences as a student in high school, trying to earn a little pocket money and save for Christmas by tutoring a younger student:

Inflation was advancing at such a rate that one day a dollar was worth a thousand marks, the next month two thousand, and the next month four thousand.

The end of the year came. I had set a price for my private lessons, which the mother of my pupil increased a bit only after bitter argument, and not at all commensurate with the general increase in prices. By the end of the year, my allowance and all the money I earned were not worth one cup of coffee. You could go to the baker in the morning and buy two rolls for twenty marks, but go there in the afternoon, and the same two rolls were twenty-five marks. The baker didn't know why rolls were more expensive in the afternoon. His customers didn't know how it happened. It had something to do with the Jews. Anti-Semitism was growing apace. "Stock exchange" and "Jews" were closely associated in the minds of the people. When anti-Semitic propaganda said, "It is the Jews," people were ready to believe it. The search for culprits in a situation which no one really understood made those who lost their savings, especially the middle class, easy prey for anti-Semitic propaganda.

I gave up my private lessons, convinced that I could not earn money by honest means. Father began to rail more and more against the Jews. He used to say, "There are two kinds of capital: one is creative, the other is parasitical. Creative capital comes from a working man; parasitical capital is the capital of the Jews."

At mealtimes he spoke increasingly about these things. Mother said something about Shakespeare and "maybe there is something in it." Then Father had a new slogan—"We are the serfs of the Jews." The more he repeated it the more I worried, because until now I had not heard of Jews being parasites. So I decided to face Father. "Your theory is really silly" I said, "—give me one proof of it."

"I can give you the proof," Father replied. "Where did I get the money for my business—from the Jew Holman!" "Father," I said, "it was pure friendship, and you were so happy and so thankful for it." He responded, "But now I have to pay interest to him on the gold value of the mark, while I lose money. If I have to pay him that interest at the beginning of next year at this rate I will have nothing left." "But, Father," I said, "I remember that you said it was the usual way of business to put a gold clause into the contract."

Father was getting impatient. "I looked at it in a different way then," he said; "now I work hard, get up at six o'clock in the morning, come home late, and where does the money go? To the Jew!"

That harried father was no exception. Thousands and thousands, even among the National Socialists, were honest enough to admit that they had met one, perhaps several, "honest" Jews. But even reference to the many "honest" Jews was not enough to turn Germans from their prejudice and anti-Semitic hatred. . . .

Government and state officials were among those hurt by inflation. Governments did their best to adjust salaries to keep up with the rising cost of living; but the legislative apparatus was too clumsy, the bureaucratic organization too rigid, to make these adjustments keep pace with the turbulent depreciation of the currency. On May 24, 1923, a newspaper reported:

> The highest paid official in the Reich, the Chancellor, receives a month's salary of 12 pounds sterling or exactly 240 peacetime marks, figured in stable currency including the May adjustment and his allowance for wife and children.

There was bitter privation in the families of thousands of government officials. As a significant result, the proverbial incorruptibility of officialdom was shattered. Officials would provide "favors" in exchange for money or food. Most often such abuses occurred on the part of authorities who allocated desirable and scarce tangibles, such as housing assignments, ration cards, and purchase permits for the poor. . . .

Public awareness of these abuses increased popular distrust of the government already aroused by the inflationary impoverishment of the middle classes. Burdened by his troubles, the average citizen instinctively contrasted the "good old times" under the Kaiser with the disagreeable aspects of the present, all of which he blamed on the new government and, by extension, on the parliamentary democratic system of the Weimar Republic. One could hardly expect average men and women to realize how much the privations of the first postwar years were the natural results of wartime defeat. They failed to realize that the postwar republican governments had assumed a difficult inheritance and that the Allied powers, who before the Armistice had promised a conciliatory peace if the Germans would convert to democracy, did nothing to help this democratic government get a fair start.

In retrospect, it is difficult to comprehend the inflationary catastrophe of 1919–24, and make a fair assessment of it. One thing is certain, many people and agencies are culpable. Erzberger [a prominent Catholic Reichstag deputy] was not completely wrong in attacking the government of Bethmann-Hollweg . . . for financing so much of the war by loans instead of greater reliance upon taxation. The well-known finance expert in that government, Helfferich, probably used an argument similar to Clemenceau's ("le Boche will pay for everything."). Even the wartime imperial government, like the Pan-Germans, had counted on "reparations" which the defeated enemy would have to pay after the desired victory. . . . Postwar inflation was not solely a German affliction. The expenditure of enormous sums for destruction instead of construction during the war years made most European currencies unstable. . . . The French and Belgian francs, the Austrian and Czechoslovak crowns, to mention but a few, were devalued even more than the English pound, which had been the strongest prewar currency. But only we Germans intensified the madness of currency inflation to a ratio of 1:1,000,000,000,000. Of course, the French occupation of the Ruhr considerably accelerated the last stages of the inflation. In retrospect it remains a mystery that neither government, parliament, nor the bankers had the understanding or expertise to end this madness. One must ask why the directors of the Reichsbank and its president so long perpetrated the fraud of currency devaluation upon the people. They were not revolutionaries, but honorable officials of tradition and experience. How could they continue for years to have facsimiles of their signatures printed on money for which the Reichsbank promised to pay a stated number of marks when they knew full well that the sum promised often was not enough to buy the piece of

paper on which it was printed by the time the note was issued?
. . . One can also ask: could not more understanding and courage
by the legislators have earlier put an end to the inflationary
madness?

A financial disaster of the magnitude we have outlined was
bound to produce a fundamental reassessment of all values in the
social and political structure of Germany. We have already indicated that the middle classes, for centuries the firmest support of
the social and governmental structure, were the hardest hit by
inflation. Hundreds of thousands, even millions of families lost the
greatest part of their wealth or property. These holdings were
modest in the majority of cases, yet they were essential for maintaining a suitable standard of living. The first to suffer were those
of the middle classes whose providers were civil servants and employees or professional men. The entrepreneurs of commerce and
industry were generally able to maintain their positions, though
there were differences. In many cases large industrial companies
actually enlarged and modernized their operations by credits
cheapened by devaluation. The same applied to many large commercial firms, especially retail traders who were able to stock up
their shops and warehouses. Small businessmen in commerce and
manufacture who had no comparable access to credit often fared
worse. Many agricultural owners and farmers paid off their mortgages at favorable rates of exchange, but ultimately they profited
less from the inflation than many businessmen.

Moreover, the return to a stable currency did not in any way
create normal conditions—strangely enough, the change began
directly after the miscarriage of Hitler's beer hall Putsch, by the
appointment of Dr. Hjalmar Schacht as Currency Commissioner
on November 12, 1923. The economy took some time to adjust
itself again to normal currency and credit conditions. In the period
of deflation, following years of rapid currency devaluation, many
large and small companies collapsed. Many a businessman who had
appeared so capable and skilled in repaying his debts at a fraction
of their original value, was no match for conditions which required
figuring with pennies and fractions of percents. The most spectacular example of failure was the giant industrial and commercial
conglomerate built and bought up by Ruhr industrialist Hugo
Stinnes during the inflation years, which was dissolved a few
months after its founder's death early in 1925.

Even before this fundamentally solid though overextended company failed, a whole group of firms which had never had any realistic economic basis were in trouble. Many of the ensuing bankruptcies produced serious, broad political repercussions in addition to their specific economic woes. In December of 1924, the Amexima Company could not meet its financial obligations. Among its prime creditors was the Prussian State Bank, with a claim of approximately 915 million marks. The director of Amexima, a Mr. Julius Barmat, and several members of his family, including his brothers Salomon and Henry, were arrested on suspicion of fraud. Amexima owned a group of German firms taken over during the inflation; they included about forty industrial enterprises bought up at random and with little organic business relationship between them. Even the Prussian Securities Bank had come under Barmat's influence. On December 22, 1925, Ivan Kutisker, the "General Director" of the Breslau banking house, E. von Stein, was arrested as he was just about to leave Germany for Lithuania, apparently to set up an important banking business there. His son Max, who at age nineteen was already the director of an automobile and engine company founded by his father, was also arrested, together with a financial adviser to the board of directors of the Prussian State Bank.

Subsequent investigation revealed that Barmat as well as Kutisker, both of whom were of Russian extraction, had enjoyed the support of a series of political personalities, most of whom belonged to the Social Democratic Party. It transpired that they had repaid these favors with luxurious hospitality and considerable payments of money. A later parliamentary commission of inquiry incriminated, among others, the leader of the SPD faction in the Prussian Diet, the representative Heilmann, and several previous ministers, among them ex-Chancellor Bauer and Dr. Gradnauer, ex-Minister-President of Saxony. Bauer had to resign from the Reichstag when a letter from the Barmat firm revealed exact entries of the sums paid and gifts given to him. The Chief of Police in Berlin, also a Social Democrat, was similarly incriminated. It was especially regrettable that President Ebert, at the urging of party members, but without personal involvement in corruption, had pressed the Foreign Ministry in the summer of 1919 to issue a permanent visa for Barmat, then still living in Holland. Several times the German Embassy in the Hague had warned the Foreign

Ministry that the reputation of Barmat and his firm was not at all favorable in Holland. . . . Thanks to Barmat's close relations with the influential members of the strongest government party, these warnings did not prevent him from building his large enterprise, primarily with credits from the Prussian State Bank. His operation flourished as long as inflation did.

The incrimination of [some] leading members of the Social Democratic Party, and thus of the governing coalition, was a godsend to the rightist parties and their press. The fact that Barmat and Kutisker were both Jewish, made the affair all the more enticing for the racists, the Pan-Germans, and the National Socialists. Kutisker and Barmat had continued techniques of graft and political bribery typical of prewar Russian conditions but not necessarily of Jewry. Various individuals of the Right probably knew this fact (i.e., General Ludendorff, on the basis of his experience in occupied Russia during the first two years of the war), but the opportunity to stimulate the anti-Semitic prejudices of the undiscerning masses was too good to miss. . . .

The scandals of Barmat and Kutisker, and a series of other similar cases, dramatically illuminated the destructive effects of inflation and its impact on the social structure and public morality. . . . It was now apparent that a large number of politicians from parties represented in the government . . . had succumbed to temptation and misused their political influence for personal gain. In considering the reputation for integrity which state and administration had enjoyed under the German monarchy, it is not surprising that large groups of citizens did not explain corruption in terms of postwar disruption and inflation, but blamed the very nature of the democratic parliamentary system. At this time the slogan, "politics is a dirty business," became very popular and fostered the growing estrangement between the republic and a considerable portion of its citizens. It was studiously overlooked that a considerable number of high civil servants from the "good old times" had succumbed to temptation in addition to men of the new era.

The radicals of the right and left primarily benefited from the bitterness aroused by the scandals. Anti-Semitic groups exploited the legal proceedings and the results of the parliamentary inquiry as much as they could for their propaganda. The cases of Barmat and Kutisker were revealed at a time when the National Socialist

Party was weakened after Hitler's abortive Munich Putsch, but later the party still derived propaganda benefit from them.

13. Gustav Stresemann and the Locarno Pact

These selected entries from the diary of Viscount D'Abernon, the British ambassador to Berlin from 1920 to 1926, create a vivid resumé of Germany's re-entry into the European international diplomatic system. D'Abernon was very sympathetic to Stresemann and may have somewhat misunderstood German objectives. He suggests that Stresemann sought European pacification, but the German foreign minister also pressed to reassert Germany's role in Europe. D'Abernon personally took the initiatives that culminated in the Locarno Pact; only gradually did he draw London and the British Foreign Secretary, Austen Chamberlain (elder brother of Neville Chamberlain), along with him.

SOURCE: Edgar Vincent D'Abernon, *An Ambassador of Peace: Pages from the Diary of Viscount D'Abernon* (London: A. P. Watt & Son, 1929–1930), II: 290; III: 11–12, 17–20, 56, 193–194, 203–205, 218, 245–247, 267–268. Reprinted by permission of the publisher and the Estate of Lord D'Abernon.

Berlin, *December* 31, 1923—Thus ends a year of crisis. The dangers from without and within have been such as to threaten the whole future of Germany. A mere recital of the trials will give an indication of how grave the peril, how severe the storm. Though I have lived through the period and have taken an active part in some of the events, I have not always at the moment realized the fatefulness of the position. Looking back, one sees more clearly how near to the precipice this country has been.
In the twelve months from January till now, Germany has lived through the following dangers:
 The Ruhr Invasion.
 The Communists Rising in Saxony and Thuringia.
 The Hitler *Putsch* in Bavaria.
 An unprecedented financial crisis.
 The Separatist Movement in the Rhineland.
 Any one of these, if not overcome, would have brought about fundamental change, either in internal conditions or external rela-

tions. If successful, each and any would have wrecked all hope of general pacification. Political leaders in Germany are not accustomed to receive much public laudation; those who have seen the country through these perils deserve more credit than is likely to be their portion. . . .

My real friendship with Stresemann began in 1921. I had met him before, but we had only exchanged commonplace civilities. In one of the numerous crises which occurred between Berlin and the Western capitals during the years following Versailles, Stresemann —representing at that time an important Parliamentary group— came to the British Embassy with four questions which he wanted answered. These questions were so pungent and precise that I was totally unable to answer them myself, and, indeed, when I promised to telegraph to London to ascertain the views of the British Government, I anticipated receiving from official sources either an evasive reply or a reminder that it was hardly consistent with diplomatic usage to transmit definite points of such a searching nature. It happened, however, that Curzon, who was then at the head of the Foreign Office, was no less ready with pen and tongue than Stresemann, and no less disinclined than he was to seek safety in silence or evasion. So the answer came to these four questions, and from that date Stresemann and I became close friends. Once reassured as to the essential good faith of English policy; once convinced that we were not seeking to hold Germany down in a subordinate position, but to procure Peace in Europe on a durable basis, his whole attitude became one of cordial cooperation. It was part of his frank, buoyant nature to put his entire case forward, to explain his own difficulties, and to relate, without reticence or reserve, the origin of his doubts and hesitation—when, indeed, doubts crossed his mind, for the occasions were rare when he hesitated about anything. . . .

Stresemann began life as a pugnacious student of the full-blooded type, a militant and aggressive Nationalist. During the war he was an advocate of the strongest and most bellicose measures; an opponent of any pledge to restore Belgium, an advocate of submarine warfare and a bitter critic of all negotiations which would, in his opinion, lead to premature Peace. This past gave him a position with the Nationalists (the party from whom opposition to the Peace policy was most to be feared) of an exceptional character. They might detest the measures he proposed; they might consider his concessions dishonorable and dangerous, but they could not attack him with the same vehemence with which they would have attacked similar measures introduced by a Socialist or Catholic minister. His general orientation had been similar to theirs; he had not recanted in principle; he could only be a convert to measures of conciliation from imperative motives of expediency.

Stresemann's relations with his former friends of the Right and Right Center were peculiar and fluctuating. At times he cooperated with them; at times they were his most vehement opponents. While in sympathy with them in being a partisan of the Hohenzollerns, he diverged from them in his readiness to adopt measures he considered politically necessary. Stresemann, in pursuit of his policy, was prepared to cooperate with any party, either with the Nationalists on the one side or the Socialists on the other; he found no consistent support from either; he did not find support even in his own party—the Volkspartei—itself divided into several sections and subsections. So, to gain the necessary majorities for carrying measures that he considered essential, he had to get together casual—almost fortuitous—majorities, enlisted wherever he could find them.

What was his essential policy? To bring about such a moderation of hostility between France and Germany as would permit European pacification. So long as the acute fear of German attack existed in France, so long as Germany was under the menace of armed intervention from France and threatened by a repetition of the Ruhr invasion, any broad policy of European pacification was impossible. Once public opinion in Germany and France was reassured as to the particular danger arising from the other side of the Rhine, everything became easier. There was no more definite objective in Stresemann's mind than the above. The first step was all that he visualized clearly; once that step was taken international politics would settle down and many other things might become possible.

It is called the triumph of Stresemann's career that he achieved not only Locarno but the revision of the Dawes Plan at The Hague. I have always thought Locarno incomparably the more important of the two. Indeed, I have doubted the wisdom of bringing about the revision of Dawes at so early a date, and my doubt has not been removed by the fact that the disputes consequent upon the Young Agreement undoubtedly precipitated the death of

Stresemann. What financial benefit can be compared with the loss to Germany and to Europe of such a man? As to the merit of Locarno, that appears to be incontestable. In 1925, in the course of a few weeks the European barometer passed from "Storm" for "Fair," and while it has since fluctuated at times, it has never receded to the menacing level which was normal up to 1925.

The last years of Stresemann's life were marred by ill health—ill health largely brought about by overwork in the interest of his country and in the interest of Peace. He would, indeed, have broken down many months before the final catastrophe but for his indomitable will and intense nervous vitality. He was, moreover, unusually fortunate in his family life: two sons in the early twenties, both of them good-looking, intelligent and artistic—one of them something of a musical genius; his wife, one of the most charming members of Berlin Society, looking as young as her sons, and maintaining in the family circle an atmosphere of cheerfulness which made the home both stimulating and refreshing. If Stresemann was older than the other three members of the group, he enjoyed life as much as the youngest of them. He relished his own talents, his incisive resonance, his unique capacity for clear thought and clear expression; he was proud to be German, prouder still to be the compatriot of Goethe. Admirably versed in German literature, he could quote with verbal accuracy long passages both of poetry and prose. Indeed, he went beyond the limits of his own language, for he could quote Shakespeare, in German and in English. In addition to literature, he had an intense appreciation of the good things of life; good wine, good music were relished to the full; his capacity for enjoyment was not marred by any hesitations or doubt as to whether the course he happened to be pursuing was right. It was always right—always inevitable. He once said that he never regretted anything he had done—his only regret was for the opportunites of enjoyment which he had foregone or missed. Above all, he enjoyed the success of his own policy, and was rightly proud of the services he had rendered to his country and the high personal position he had attained.

While Stresemann's achievements finally won general approval, it was long before he gained public confidence. Indeed, he was of those for whom it is easier to inspire admiration than to create trust. His capacity for arousing animosity was quite exceptional. Why, it is difficult to say. Perhaps his mind was too rapid to give an impression of solidity—his enunciation too resonant and the phrases too brilliant to suggest reflection or measure.

Of him it may be said, not that he had the qualities of his defects, but that his qualities—clearness, rapidity, and decision—earned him a reputation for defects from which he was entirely free—recklessness, and lack of conviction. With the latter weakness he certainly could not be charged, for he adhered steadfastly to beliefs, when they were not only inconvenient, but damaging.

Comparing Stresemann with other German statesmen of the last half of the nineteenth century and the early years of the twentieth, it should be remembered that Bismarck and Bülow had at their disposal military force and military prestige. With Stresemann these conditions, no less than high rank and social status, were completely lacking. In measuring his achievement, such fundamental differences in basic conditions must be kept in mind. Stresemann may claim to have raised Germany from the position of a stricken and disarmed foe into that of a diplomatic equal, entitled to full consideration as a great Power, and enjoying international guarantee for the protection of her frontiers. To have accomplished this in a few years of power without the support of armed force is a feat worthy of those who have written their names most memorably on the scroll of fame. Stresemann left Germany infinitely stronger than when he took the helm in 1923, and Europe incomparably more peaceful. This achievement is the more remarkable in that Stresemann was not, by temperament, a pacifist; it might indeed be said that pacific results of such magnitude were never before attained by so bellicose a champion.

As one who knew him well through difficult years, who saw him triumph over grave opposition from without and from within, I hold that Germany has never had a wiser or a more courageous adviser. . . .

Berlin, *March* 4, 1924—A conversation with Stresemann today.

He appeared much impressed by the revelations made in the Hitler-Ludendorff trial at Munich. It was clear from what emerged in court that the danger last November had been infinitely greater than the general public realised. He himself had always known that Germany had been within an ace of a serious and successful "putsch" from the Right, but official circles in Berlin had hitherto underrated the danger the country had gone through. It was fairly clear now that Kahr had himself contemplated measures against the Republic not less subversive than the schemes of Hitler and Ludendorff. It was also clear that Kahr had wide assurances of support from Northern Germany. The peril was the more acute in that the Berlin Government had only doubtful means of repression. The men of the Reichswehr were to a large extent partisans of the Right. The officers he considered more trustworthy from the point of view of the Republic than the men, and von Seeckt he considered quite trustworthy, but officers were not much good if the men were solidly opposed to them.

He had always held that the clause of the Treaty of Versailles stipulating that recruits should be engaged for twelve years was a fatal error. It made the Army a caste, a kind of Prætorian guard divorced from and in opposition to the mass of the people. It would have been much better if the Army had been recruited on the old shortservice basis. . . .

Berlin, *October* 3, 1925—Last night the German mission left for Locarno. It consisted of the Chancellor, the Foreign Minister and the Secretary of State for Foreign Affairs. As regards the two latter, there can be no doubt that they start to meet the French and English Ministers with the determination to come to an agreement. The Chancellor is more doubtful, being apprehensive about his Reichstag majority unless he obtains, in addition to the Pact, subsidiary advantages for Germany. I had a long talk with him at the American Embassy the other night, and found that he either did not realize, or thought it good policy not to show, the enormous importance of the Pact for Germany. From being an ex-enemy, Germany becomes a Power with equal rights, whose frontiers will be guaranteed by a Treaty, the Treaty being guaranteed by England. Thus, both Germany and France have this security for the safety of their frontiers—that aggression brings in England against the aggressor.

As regards England, it may be said that we take a risk in guaranteeing both France and Germany against aggression from the other. But this guarantee is the best means of preventing aggression.

There can be no doubt that to wait for war to come about between France and Germany, and then to hold ourselves free to intervene, if we think our interests affected, is not only selfish but shortsighted, in that it makes war infinitely less improbable than under the Pact. Moreover, as guarantor we enjoy the prestige and the power of an arbiter.

The new constellation of Europe under the Pact is more advantageous to England than would be the maintenance of the post-War alliances under which France relied for her security partly on a large army, partly on military alliances with Yugoslavia, Poland, and Czechoslovakia. Under the Pact, these alliances will not immediately be given up, but they will cease to be the main protection, and in process of time will probably fade away.

Czechoslovakia is enthusiastically in favor of the Pact. It avoids for her the necessity of deciding between France, to whom they largely owe their independence and with whom they have a military alliance, and Germany, with whom they have long conterminous frontiers, and who buys 30 percent of their exports. . . .

Berlin, *November* 15, 1925—It seems to me difficult to exaggerate the importance of the Reparation Settlement in 1924 and the Treaty of Locarno in 1925, and it is satisfactory to recall that both these great advances towards the pacification of Europe have been carried through mainly on the initiative of England. Without English influence, exercised in the strongest manner, there would have been no Dawes plan, and still less would there have been a Locarno. We are sometimes reproached on the Continent with selfishness; let this be recorded to our credit.

Berlin, *November* 18, 1925—Germans say that the general failure here to appreciate the Pact is due, not to party politics, nor to militarism, nor even to war spirit, but simply and solely to want of political instinct.

The first and main gain is that Locarno puts an end to the war entente against Germany. It brings Germany into the European consortium of Western Powers, and finishes "the wicked disturber of the peace," "the aggressive militarist," and "the mad-dog" conception of the diplomatic position.

In addition to advantages on the broad issue, there are very distinct gains through the "reactions" in the occupied zone. These may be summarized as follows:

1. The immediate evacuation of the Cologne area, together with numerous concessions in regard to the degree of disarmament required by the Note of June 6.

2. A considerable reduction of the occupying forces and the liberation of a number of billets, schools, public buildings, etc., the requisition of which was probably the heaviest burden of the occupation.

3. By the reinstatement of the Reichskommissar Germany can make her views heard on all questions touching the interests of the Rhineland without the cumbrous intervention of diplomatic machinery in three capitals.

4. By the suppression of delegates, and the restriction of the powers of military courts, Germany recovers full civil sovereignty in the Rhineland. The population is spared the "humiliation" of being in constant contact with foreign officials, and any foreign interference in local politics is prevented.

Against these gains, impartial estimate might perhaps set certain losses. The principal of these is a weakening or abandonment of the Rapallo Treaty basis, but Rapallo has never been very satisfactory to Germany. It has given none of the commercial gains which were anticipated and not much of the diplomatic support; it has merely served to prevent Germany feeling out in the cold.

I still hold that prolonged cooperation between the German Right and the Russian Left is unthinkable, but I must admit that the other night at the Russian Embassy I was somewhat shaken to see how many gentlemen there were with stiff military backs and breasts bedecked with iron crosses, all partaking freely of Soviet champagne. . . .

Berlin, *January* 10, 1926—Another step forward. Germany has decided to send in her application for admission to the League of Nations. The debate in the Reichstag on this subject revealed considerable opposition, notably from Bavaria. It is said that even Hindenburg, who has proved an admirable President, is against joining the League now; he is believed to be in favor of waiting at least until September. The idea of those who advocate this course is that, by waiting a little longer, Germany can obtain larger counter-value for entering the League. I rejoin that once Germany is a member of the League she will be able to make her voice heard better than before, and that no counterconcessions can be expected for doing what is so much in Germany's own interest.

An event which greatly facilitated a solution regarding Geneva was the evacuation of Cologne. This came as a surprise here, and made an excellent impression. The opposition are always ready to taunt the Government with nonfulfillment by the Allies of the Locarno "Reactions." . . .

Berlin, *April* 5, 1926—My French colleague called this evening.

His first question was, "What do you think of the German-Russian Agreement?"

I said, "Does such an agreement exist? I have only heard of it as a probability and an intention—not as a matter concluded." He replied, "According to Hoesch's communication to Briand yesterday, the German Government have the intention of signing before the end of the present month." Hoesch declared that this would not be done as a result of the failure at Geneva, nor did it indicate any intention of abandoning the Locarno policy. It had been decided upon by the German Government as a result of Russian pressure, the Russians having declared that they would resume their complete liberty of action towards Germany if Germany decided to wait until after September before concluding an agreement with Russia.

The communication made by Hoesch to Briand concerning the proposed clauses of the agreement was identical with the terms already known to me, with one important addition, namely, a general engagement to discuss together all matters of common interest ("Engagement général de se concerter sur toutes les affaires communes"). Nothing about such a clause was said to me. It may be the most important of the whole draft convention, and certainly the one which will be most severely criticized in France and England.

The French Ambassador did not appear particularly alarmed by the idea of this projected Convention. It seemed to him more directed against England than against France, as the latter's relations with Russia were at the present moment quite friendly, outside the question of the debt.

He was anxious to know what the effect would be on English public opinion. I replied that it would be badly received at first, and would be considered as a device for Germany to pay out the Powers for the way she had been treated at Geneva. . . .

He appeared to share my view, that Stresemann was only entering into this agreement with Russia because he was afraid not to. . . .

Berlin, *October* 2, 1926—Now that Locarno has been in force for nearly a year, and that Germany is a member of the League of Nations, a definite period in history comes to a close. A fresh epoch for Europe commences, and the work here will assume a different and more normal character. The war spirit has been quelled, and the possibility of an era of peaceful development opens. . . .

During the years 1925–26 the German Ministers in charge of affairs have accomplished what even Bismarck and the post-Bismarckians attempted in vain. . . .

The outcome of events during the last two years has been this, that the object aimed at by former German statesmen has now been achieved by novel means in widely different—perhaps more difficult—circumstances. For it may be confidently said that the animosity between England and Germany has been in large measure appeased, the proof being that England is now brought in as an arbitrator, and as a guarantor of the territorial integrity, not only of France, but also of Germany. Moreover, it is mainly through English influence that Germany has obtained at Geneva a position acceptable to her national dignity.

As regards England, I hold that our new position as arbiter and guarantor is not only the more dignified and disinterested, but the more prudent. By our intervention in this new capacity, supported by Italy in a similar role, the risk of war between France and Germany is vastly diminished. With effective measures taken to protect the French frontier against Germany, and the German frontier against France, the worst danger-spot in Europe has been dealt with, and the menace of a new conflagration reduced, if not exorcised.

14. Out of the Wilderness

The remarkable economic recovery and apparent political stabilization of the Reich by 1929 attracted attention and commentary from many observers. Hugh Quigley, a British economist and civil servant, joined with Professor R. T. Clark of Manchester to make a detailed analysis of Weimar Germany at the end of its first decade. Their broadly favorable conclusions, particularly of the political situation, were characteristic of most non-Marxist writers of the time. All the greater, then, was the shock when the Weimar Republic began to crumble so soon thereafter.

SOURCE: Hugh Quigley & R. T. Clark, *Republican Germany: A Political and Economic Study* (London: Methuen Ltd., 1928), pp. 117–120, 122–126. Reprinted by permission of ABP International Ltd.

Although we are too near the event for final judgment, it is still possible to risk the statement that the formation of the Marx Cabinet and the intrigues attendant upon it mark the end of a period in German political history. Throughout 1927 that Cabinet functioned as a normal parliamentary Cabinet in possession of a parliamentary majority. The *regime* is not in question. Whatever monarchical principles the Nationalists had had, they sacrificed them for the solid fact of being able to carry on a conservative policy. For the first time, Germany became a united Republic, and President, ministers, and party leaders agreed to affirm their loyalty to the republican form of government. For the first time also, a Right Government could be trusted not to attempt to overthrow the Constitution, and, in spite of the animadversions of the Left, the reaction intends to be reactionary within the limits of the Constitution. Monarchism still survives, but it is gradually becoming the property of a sect more respectable, but not much more influential, than the section which has repudiated the old German god and gone back to Wotan. A less democratic system has many adherents, but the struggle will be fought out by parliamentary methods and change, if any, will require a national majority. . . .

At the moment of writing, Germany is indeed a definite force for peace in Europe. That is recognized abroad and the recognition has atoned for much. When as an equal Stresemann participated in those private negotiations that kept the peace in the Balkans and in Eastern Europe, when it was admitted abroad, and therefore could not be denied at home, that the policy pursued was a free one and that its spokesman had actually influenced, as agents of a German policy, the cause of international policy, much of the sense of humiliation passed away. The restoration of the Concert of Europe, however deplorable from the point of view of the League of Nations, restored self-respect to Germany, and the frank admissions of her former enemies have confirmed the restoration. The sense of outlawry has passed. It is true that the war-guilt clause still stands, but it is virtually a dead letter except in the eyes of legalists and reactionary politicians, for it is no use maintaining that a nation is a criminal and a pariah if her accusers cooperate with her on terms of perfect equality. Nothing is more significant in this connection than the reaction to Stresemann's experiment at the unveiling in autumn of the Tannenberg memorial. There Hindenburg read out a statement, carefully prepared by the Cabinet, formally repudiating war-guilt. It was in effect a national repudiation and could scarcely have been made more official. The consequences were curious. While certain sections abroad revived academic discussions of the issues involved and the French patriotic Press fulminated as usual, the declaration was received with sympathy where historical questions evoke interest, with indifference everywhere else. It had no international consequences. But it had all sorts of consequences in Germany. So much had the war-guilt question become a *chose jugée*—and not in the old Allied sense—that the declaration was made the occasion of violent attacks on the Government by the Opposition, not because they objected to its content, but because they considered that it might be used as a Left weapon against a Right Cabinet and for aid in the Socialist campaign against the President. Such consequences were unthinkable three years ago. When a nation can make its branding as a pariah an incident of party politics, the mark of the branding has disappeared. Stresemann had reason to be pleased with his experiment. . . .

Her policy, as guided so ably by Stresemann, does not always produce successes. Thus she has been able neither to secure general disarmament nor bring the Allied occupation to an end. That is undoubtedly a defeat for the Locarno policy, but it is not reckoned a defeat for German policy, although it can be used as a weapon against the Foreign Minister by party enemies. It does not arouse the indignation in Germany that one would expect, for it is realized that the refusal to evacuate is a confession of weakness on the part of France, and sooner or later evacuation will have to be ordered. A foreign policy based on peace and avoiding entangling alliances, with a clear sense of the realities of the situation and of the interests of Germany, and able to identify the morally righteous with the politically wise, is a strong foreign policy and the German nation recognizes it as such. The next Ministry may greatly vary Stresemann's language, but it will not greatly change its course. . . . Germany has been set free to take a creative interest in her domestic affairs. The issues that divide her people are no longer external or influenced predominantly by external events; they are those that divide nations everywhere—the struggles of interests, classes, and ideals within the frontiers. . . .

The tendency toward a four- and even a three-party system is growing and it is not really hindered by the appearance of small parties representing a definite social stratum or interest. A party representing the small or middle bourgeois may be relied on to support either the Liberals or the Conservatives, but once its support is pledged it disappears for the duration of the alliance into the larger party.

Before the war only the reckless prophesied on political futures; now only the foolish do so, but it is not too rash to expect a continuance of the swing to the Left and a Left victory following on the 1928 elections. The swing is normal and is the best evidence that the Constitution is functioning normally and satisfactorily. . . .

It may betray excessive optimism, but one may venture to declare that there is definite evidence that Germany has settled in solidity. That implies the opinion that the Republican system is secure unless extraordinary circumstances arise. The first noticeable thing is that to the average German the question of the *régime* is an academic question. It is true that the German has a genius for treating any question academically, but, prior to the end of 1925, the academic attitude was not apparent. Today, an average Anti-Republican will produce one hundred and one proofs of the undesirability of the Republican system and he will applaud vigorously the orator who presents him with a hundred and second, but he will take no action against it and when he goes to the poll it is no longer the supreme issue. Out of Anti-Republicanism of that sort it is impossible to create an Anti-Republican party, especially at a time when there is officially no Anti-Republican party and actually only one which, besides being Anti-Republican, is a lot of other things which academic Anti-Republicans dislike intensely. It is true that there exist all sorts of Anti-Republican organizations capable of noisy demonstration, but it is doubtful if—again given the continued absence of extraordinary circumstances—they can do more. It is equally true that an enormous amount of political and legal controversy goes on, but it is conducted mainly by the journalist. The agitation that forced the resignation of Seeckt because of the presence of Prince Wilhelm of Prussia at manœuvres has its counterpart in the artificial agitation against the naval authorities for allowing Prince Heinrich to be entertained on board the *Berlin* on its departure for foreign waters, but, while the former controversy agitated the nation, the latter agitated mainly party politicians and journalists. The notorious battle of the flags and the refusal of certain sections to hoist the black, red, and gold of the *Deutscher Bund*, officially proclaimed the national colors by the Weimar Constitution, was waged with a good deal of bitterness, but, when it came to ministers boycotting hotels and ex-Prussian captains barricading themselves in their rooms and defiantly shaking out black, white and red flags of enormous extent, the humorous side of the affair struck the nation, which, in its vast majority, sees no insult to Germany in preferring the flag of Lutzow's riders to that of the Hansa merchants *plus* that of the Hohenzollern dukes. The Republican *v.* Monarchist quarrel is real and deep-seated and it creates nasty incidents, but it will have dire political consequences till the Republican State fails in its duty as maintainer of order and upholder of law. So far it has done it, perhaps not quite impartially, for the Monarchist gets more easy treatment than the Communist, but that is true of all bourgeois States, and the pressure of public opinion is beginning to force a more even treatment.

The more statesmanlike conduct of the Allies has robbed the Monarchist of his best ally. It is no longer possible for him to complain that Germany is treated as a helpless inferior; the evidence to the contrary is too plain. He still indulges in polemics with his counterparts on the left bank of the Rhine, but he cannot rouse them more easily than he can his own countrymen, who have taken the measure of him and the French Chauvinist with considerable accuracy. That does not mean that the nation has simply accepted the Peace Treaty as the eternal basis of European relations. On the contrary, the opposition to the Treaty is as strong as ever, but the opposition to Treaty fulfillment has died away and

Monarchism is no longer identical with patriotism. It is only that the majority of the nation has become convinced that fulfillment is the quickest way to escape from the Treaty. It has already recovered Cologne and seen the Allied Commissions of Control depart; it knows that the rest of the Rhineland will be recovered in seven years; it knows that its reparation payments are an irksome but not an intolerable burden and are hurting the recipients quite as much as, if not more, than the payers; it does not and cannot forget the lost territory, but every day, that brings strength, brings the day of recovery nearer, and that strength requires unity to make it effective; it has the feeling that it is not for Germany to make the opportunity, but to be ready to seize the opportunity when others create it, as create it they must.

Germany is working in all her parts and a nation that works has little time for barren controversies, for, in the work itself, lie controversies that affect more deeply the life of the average German than the controversies on political philosophy and political history. Questions of tariffs, of socialization, of trustification, of the cost and distribution of food supplies, of wages, of municipal government, of housing, of general administration, education, and the Civil Service—these are the questions that fill the first place in his thoughts.

The lasting political struggle in Germany, the struggle between Left and Right, the struggle of democracy against reaction from the Right and reaction from the Left, perhaps against an unholy alliance of both, will be a severe one, but one sees as yet no reason to despair of the German Republic, to doubt of its future or to disbelieve in the possibility of a liberal Germany becoming one of the buttresses of peace in a Europe that has attained a settlement that corresponds to the deepest needs of Europe as a whole and is a beginning of the organization of Europe for the service of humanity. It may augur well for one's power of credulity to believe at the end of 1927 in the future of Germany, but to disbelieve in its future is to disbelieve in the future of Europe. Credulity is not necessarily a vice because it is the credulity of optimism.

IV

Depression and Politics, 1930–1932

THE GREAT DEPRESSION of 1929–1933 struck the various nations of Europe with differing severity, depending on the character of their governments and their economic strength at the time. Russia and Italy already had totalitarian regimes, which manipulated their respective economies and controlled the political reactions of their citizens. The peoples of Slavic central Europe, already mostly under semi-Fascist systems, slid into agrarian economic disaster. France, almost self-sufficient and with strong monetary reserves did not feel the full impact of the Depression until 1932–1936. England and Germany were the two major European nations that immediately felt the results of the worldwide breakdown in foreign trade and the ensuing collapse of the money markets. And of those two, only England had the strength of a tried and tested government.

The political system of Germany was weakly rooted and only grudgingly accepted by significant groups of its people. All Germans had barely begun to recover psychologically from the events of 1918–1924 before they were plunged again into insecurity and economic failure. All the vehemence of the resulting frustration, anger, and fear was directed with cumulative effect upon the unseasoned political structure of the Weimar Republic. For a time Chancellor Brüning guided the deteriorating society with the aid of constitutional emergency decrees. But his effectiveness weakened as the Reichstag became immobilized between those parties that still tried to make democracy work and those that even cooperated on occasion with each other to destroy it—the Nazis and the Communists. The nation was deluged with partisan speeches and propaganda in a psychologically exhausting series of election campaigns and other political confrontations. Brüning's fate—and that of the Weimar Republic as well—was sealed when conservative and opportunistic advisers importuned the semisenile President von Hindenburg to dispense with his chancellor's services.

15. From the Heart of Germany, 1931

William Harlan Hale is a writer and editor most recently working with the American Heritage Publishing firm. His article, which follows, was published in *The Nation*, a well-known liberal weekly. It followed developments in Germany with concerned foreboding, showing a naïve toleration for the good intentions of European communism while correctly anticipating the grim dimensions of later Nazi rule.

SOURCE: William Harlan Hale, "From the Heart of Germany," *The Nation*, no. 3463 (November 18, 1931), CXXXIII: 554–556.

Weimar, Thuringia, September 15

When you leave Berlin, with its political demonstrations, its daily tides of overheated newspapers, and its legions of glittering policemen murderously armed to the teeth, and come here to Weimar, you go into a sort of retirement. It is traditional that in this town of hallowed past the present world and its troubles should become unreal. You are expected to forget Hoover, unemployment, long-term credits, and Laval; the only world here traditionally considered real is the world of Goethe, Schiller, and their circle of poets, musicians, and brilliant amateurs. When great change strikes thoughtful Germany it comes last to Weimar, where the fascination of the past is still most vivid.

Now it has come to Weimar; the fever of confusion and despair has left no locality untouched. Start talking, even here, to the kindly people who sit next to you in a small restaurant, or on the terrace of the Belvedere palace, or in the park that Goethe so superbly laid out; you hear, over and over, "It can't go on." You might expect this in the centers of political agitation; it surprises you in the woodlands of Thuringia.

"It can't go on." The country is nearing the point where disaster is inevitable. An intelligent merchant here gave me the simile: Germany is like a formerly well-to-do citizen whose income enabled him to maintain a high standard of life. His income began to decline, but his whole arrangement of life forced him to keep the standard as high as before. His income dropped more rapidly; he had to borrow, he fell into an accumulation of debts, he had to borrow again. His intentions were of the best, but his vision was naturally limited and he could not see into the future. He trusted in a coming change for the better; he adhered to his old standard; and in order to get more credits he had to falsify the statements of his resources. He was not dishonest, he was merely blinded by himself and by circumstances. He could no longer pay the interest; his creditors realized that he could never pay back the capital. There was no way out of the collapse.

This is the national process: the growing unreality of wealth. Germany is surviving only on the basis of foreign capital; this can be withdrawn and the entire economic system wrecked in two weeks. There is no reliance to be placed on such an order. The structure of capitalism here is becoming, day by day, more wobbly. You stand by in a horrible fascination against the moment when the building will come crashing down with a great roar of bursting stone and timber. What is apparent even to the visitor in a German city is the fact that the middle class is dramatically on the point of vanishing. Every month thousands of people who traditionally belonged to that class—teachers, small professional men, shopkeepers, officials—are falling into the sea of the proletariat. When the factor is unemployment, that change is automatic and in its speed remorseless. When the factor is taxation, the change is more gradual but no less inevitable. There are thousands of trained officials in Germany who receive less than $500 a year. There are city doctors and sanitary officials who earn far below $1,000. Taxes, in no less than twenty varieties, remove about 50 percent of these sums. A new ordinance places a fine of 5 percent for every two weeks' delay in payment of taxes beyond the stated quarterly date. The fine adds up mechanically to 130 percent a year. The man who cannot pay his taxes on the appointed day is sooner or later lost. As the percentages on his payments roll up, his doom is sealed. Bankruptcy before the state naturally includes a surrender of real property; and with such Draconian mechanics proceeds the transition from landed middle class to shiftless proletariat.

Let no one imagine that the Prussian referendum of August 9 meant that the German people had discarded the intentions of radicalism. The referendum was followed in a few days by announcements of cuts of 15 or 20 percent in the already pathetically slender salaries of thousands of officials. Extensive reductions in the salaries of all public-school teachers are being considered. In the finest shopping streets in Berlin—the Friedrichstrasse and the Leipzigerstrasse—hundreds of thousands of square feet of select store and office space stand vacant. The *Wohnungsnot* of three years ago has so completely disappeared that the best modern cooperative settlements cannot begin to rent their flats—while in Berlin alone no fewer than 125,000 families are living in huts and tents in what are euphemistically called "orchard colonies." The dreaded *Hauszinssteuer* exacts ruinous tribute from all owners of occupied premises. The burden is so great that property values are virtually vanishing, since almost no buyer can afford to pay from $1,000 to $8,000 a year tax on his city house or country estate. The best homes are being deserted by their inhabitants just for the sake of spiting the government and preventing it from getting the taxes due. High mortgages on the finest metropolitan houses bring nothing but catastrophe when the sale value declines from $100,000 in 1916 to $15,000 in 1931. But with the doubling and tripling of taxes and the dizzy decline of wages and land values, there has been no adequate fall in the cost of living. Within the year the price of bread has risen 250 percent. These facts and situations do not discourage radicalism. They do not on the long term inspire enthusiasm for the existing order and the present government. The defeat of radical elements on August 9 was the expression of a popular desire for peace and order in a moment of utmost international crisis; the more thoughtful elements of the German nation dominated. But what was support for August 9 did not mean support for 1932 and thereafter.

To a foreign observer (who has no political passions one way or the other) there is manifest among even the higher middle groups of society an increasing skepticism of German social democracy. It is not merely a dislike for, or an indignation against, the party now in power; it is doubt as to the efficacy of the whole system. In point of fact, one hears few grave charges against the government; usually they are those of local extravagance or bureaucratic duplication, not those of corruption or hopeless blunder of policy. The admiration for Dr. Brüning as a man of heroic calm and courageous decision penetrates deep into the camp of his political opponents. No, it is skepticism about the present social democracy that one feels. Deeper than that, it is skepticism about the capitalist system. When Germany hears that America is menaced by 8,000,000 unemployed, is shutting down its most famous factories and letting its finest crops go to waste, it begins to feel that little help will come from us, that with all our notorious wealth we are no longer in a position to help. When Germany observes the failure of English exports to compete in the very colonies with the goods of China and Japan, when it sees the sacred pound sterling go wavering, when it realizes that England lost its war, it begins to doubt the potency of that much-advertised Anglo-German friendship. The people are being slowly and painfully convinced, after the short hysterical enthusiasm over the "Hooveryear," that the outside nations will do little for them. Self-help, they are told, must be the program. And when even the vast capitalist strengths of England and America cannot succeed in keeping their own houses in order, what chance is there for weak and tubercular Germany to accomplish that for herself?

There are, as is known, two ways out: Hitler's nationalism, and communism of the Russian brand. Both ideals are represented in Germany by powerful parties backed with considerable funds, able propaganda agents, and trained shock troops and marksmen. Young Germany is choosing between one and the other. Young Germany knows only this one thing: it will not follow the ways of its fathers, it will not pay reparations. The young men had nothing to do with the war, and they will not pay for it. They possess no accumulated wealth or inheritances which could prompt them to cling to the present order, with its moderate safety, rather than fly to revolution and financial crash. They have nothing to lose, and everything to gain, in an overthrow. What they have now is training, and no jobs; a very real Germanic strength, and nothing to apply it to. Overmature for their years, and overnervous and highstrung in their personalities, they are determined to carry through some reform which might make their lives worth living. Above all, I repeat: they will not pay reparations. . . .

Thus Germany confesses itself to be in a state of siege. The nation stands alone, and it feels its own foundations slowly weakening under it. It is the sick man of Europe—and its illness is the destiny of our civilization. With the most compelling line of forts in the world on one border, and the most compelling system of social reform in the world on the other, there is not much deep reality in the cutaway charms of Mr. MacDonald or the laconic visits of Mr. Stimson accompanied by Andy Mellon.

To reduce the German situation to such essentials as these is not to be a professional alarmist; it is merely to admit what everyone realizes today but often likes to gloss over in silence. It is merely to take as basic what the whole world is feeling—skepticsim of the power of international accords to cope with the forces of national-ism, French Caesarism, and the eternal hunger for war. It is to take as basic also a greater feeling—the doubt of the capitalist world, the insecurity, the weariness.

There are bright sides to the possibilities of a Communist Ger-many: the new order, with a program of central planning and administrative reform, would surely bring about an improvement in those domestic conditions which are now becoming insufferable. Communism regnant in Germany would assuredly not extinguish the country's disinterested world of scholarship and art and scien-tific research; would not submerge the entire population into an undifferentiated mass-existence; would probably not even begin in especially vicious bloodshed. Communism in Germany would have to adapt itself to a different plane of culture from that in Russia; for the German mind is modern, while the Russian may be said to be medieval.

Leaving aside all commercial considerations, there is a chief polit-ical reason to be fearful of a Communist Germany. The new order would carry with it the threat of a war to the end with France. What coordinate events and what consequences such a day would bring is in the power of no man to imagine.

And so, when I listened to a thoughtful German speak, as the sun went down beyond the gentle valley where Bach wrote his organ works, Goethe rounded out his "Faust," Schiller first pro-duced his dramas, and a hundred other preachers, poets, artists, and philosophers have performed their living work—when I listened to him speak of the cold inevitability of a conclusion, of an entire recommencement, and of a war, I found that not even here, above the silent town, was there any escape to be found from the rising tides that beat on the shores today.

16. Nazi-Communist Cooperation to Destroy the Weimar Republic

Between 1933 and 1939 there seemed to be at least one political-ideological certainty evident on the European scene: the vigorous and abiding antagonism between fascism and communism. It was forgotten that ever since 1920 the German Communists had considered the Social Democrats their greatest ideological enemies and that Nazis and Communists had sometimes cooperated tactically before 1933 to weaken and destroy the Weimar Republic, whose greatest support came from the Social Democrats. Proof of these cooperative ventures is scarce because evidence has been destroyed or is not accessible. The first of the following documents is from the state archives of Hanover; it ties in directly with the second item from the memoirs of Jan Valtin (Richard J. H. Krebs). Valtin's book was widely read when it appeared in early 1941, but it was soon overshadowed by the pragmatic realities of Western association with Russia invaded by the Nazis. Valtin was an active communist agitator and organizer in maritime unions during the 1920s. He worked for the Communist party in Germany, England, and Scandinavia from 1930 to 1934. He was caught by the Gestapo, imprisoned from 1934 to 1937, released as a counteragent and escaped to the United States in 1938. Careful cross-checking has borne out the essential validity of his account, which is one of the infrequent books on this dimension of political activity during the interwar decades.

a. Circular Letter of the Reichsbanner [Socialist Militia] of June 24, 1931; District Executive to all Local Groups in Hanover

SOURCE: Printed in Erich Matthias & Rudolf Morsey, *Das Ende der Parteien* (Düsseldorf: Droste Verlag, 1960), p. 220. Reprinted by permission of the publisher. Translation by the editor.

Dear Comrades!

In the face of current political tensions the Communists are again urging our comrades and Social Democratic Party members everywhere to join with them in a united front against fascism. Under all circumstances we must avoid letting our comrades participate in such action. For half a year now [our] "Iron Front" has effectively combined all the labor unions, the Social Democratic Party, the Reichsbanner, the workers' sports associations and other modern working-class organizations. The "Iron Front" is thus capable of staging far more effective marches and rallies than the Communists can with their so-called united front against fascism. We have no objection if Communists in the unions or other organizations want to join us in the "Iron Front"; in fact, as union members they have an obligation to do so. But if they do not join the "Iron Front," they prove that they are not basically interested in strengthening our organization and combined resistance against fascism. They are only trying to destroy the existing powerful antifascist movement in order to develop special agitation in their own interests.

In [the city of] Peine all the organizations participating in the "Iron Front" had agreed with the Communist Party to stage a combined march and rally.

We insisted basically, however, that during the march the Communists should not show identifiable antagonism against other organizations joined in the "Iron Front." The Communists would not agree and at the last minute it was specifically their leader who withdrew his group from the combined demonstration.

In addition, two days ago the [Communist] *Neue Arbeiter Zeitung* of Hanover had a longer editorial on the "united front." It stated that the Communists had absolutely no reason to make a so-called Burgfrieden [temporary pact in face of the enemy] with either the unions or the Social Democratic Party. They would continue as before unmasking the [Socialist] union and party leadership who [were not interested in the working class but] only anxiously sought to keep their little political jobs.

We can see from this evidence that the Communists are not really interested in fighting fascism but only seek to destroy other strong antifascist organizations.

Therefore, comrades, reject the "united front" and urge the Communists in the unions to join the "Iron Front."

With comradely greeting
"Freedom Heil"
The District Leadership
J. Lau   Aug. Sauder

b. From the Memoirs of Jan Valtin

SOURCE: Jan Valtin, *Out of the Night* (New York: Alliance Book Corp., 1941), pp. 250–255.

The Hitler movement was sweeping the country like a storm flood, washing away the parties in the middle. Because it was my business to fight it, at meetings, in the factories, in the streets and on ships, I studied its methods. The Nazis waged their campaigns with unlimited courage and ruthlessness, with devotion and cynicism. They promised higher wages to the workers, higher profits to industry, and well-paid jobs to the unemployed. They promised the liquidation of department stores to small traders. They promised land to the farmhands, tax-exemption and higher income to the farmers, and government subsidies and cheap labor to the large landowners. They promised to outlaw strikes and at the same time supported every strike to curry favor with the toilers. They ranted against capitalism and bargained with captains of industry behind the scenes. They held out the promise of careers and of power to students and intellectuals, who rallied to the Nazi banner by the thousands. Nazi propaganda was as quick as lightning, seizing upon every mistake made by other political groups. Hand in hand with this propaganda went a superbly organized terror. Merchants were terrorized into surrendering part of their profits to the Nazi Party. Liberals were terrorized until they dared not hold public meetings. Brown-shirted raiding detachments, schooled in the technique of terror, clubbed, stabbed, and shot opponents in daily affrays.

We raised the slogan, "Strike the Nazi wherever you meet him!" But it was a secondary motto for us. The paramount aim of the Communist Party was still the destruction of Social Democracy, the "principal foe" blocking the road toward a Soviet Germany. So it was that in organizing a maritime strike campaign, I concentrated my main efforts on the destruction of the socialist-controlled trade unions. With the aid of many hundreds of thousands of leaflets, we stirred up the discontent of the workers and lashed them to wild hatred against the employers, against the police, and against the Social Democratic leaders—who favored arbitration.

The tactics employed by the Comintern to wreck the socialist trade unions was that of the "united front." Every communist meeting, newspaper, leaflet raised the slogan of the "united front" on every occasion. In the beginning, because of my sincere belief in the desirability of cooperation with the socialists, I took it literally. I went to the headquarters of the socialist Transport Workers' Union in Bremen to propose to its chief a plan of united action in the strike then imminent. One of the numerous G.P.U. spies in our Party got wind of my visit, and sent a confidential report to Berlin, in which he accused me of secret counterrevolutionary negotiations with a notorious "Social-Fascist"—a term then in vogue among communists. The report was forwarded to Herrmann Remmele, communist Reichstag deputy, then touring Western Germany. He promptly collared me, and gave me a rough-and-tumble lecture on what the Comintern meant by the "united front."

Comrade Remmele made it clear that no "united front" was wanted unless it preserved communist leadership. The aim was to unite with the rank and file against the will of their socialist leaders. This was called the "united front from *below*," and was calculated to drive a wedge between the rival leaders and their masses, and to split the trade unions. All communist proposals were intentionally so worded as to be rejected by the socialist chiefs. These proposals invariably ended with the appeal, "Defend the Soviet Union, the fatherland of all workers!" The socialist leaders rejected this formula, and the communists then cried, "Traitors! Saboteurs of cooperation!" Thus the "united front" maneuver became one of the main causes of the impotence of organized German labor in the face of Hitler's march to power.

I bowed to Remmele's order. "That is the Party line," he said. "Any deviation from it is equal to treason!" Five years later this veteran of the Bolshevist movement, the author of a volume in praise of the Soviet Union, who had been condemned to prison in Germany and fled to Russia, came to the end of the "Party line." He was shot in the dungeons of the G.P.U. in Moscow as a "Gestapo spy."

The blind hatred for the Social Democrats took a decisive turn about the middle of January, 1931, when Georgi Dimitrov issued a secret memorandum of instructions to all leaders and subleaders of the communist columns. A special committee, headed by Thaelmann, Heinz Neumann, and Wollweber, was set up to carry the instructions into effect. Summed up in one sentence the instructions were: "*United action of the Communist Party and the Hitler movement to accelerate the disintegration of the crumbling democratic bloc which governs Germany."*

My chief aide, a leather-faced engineer named Salomon, and I stared at each other in consternation.

"Who is crazy?" Salomon muttered. "We—or the Central Committee?"

"Without the help of the Social Democratic Party, the German bourgeoisie cannot survive," Wollweber growled in a meeting of Party functionaries. "With the liquidation of the Social-Fascists, we are preparing the soil for civil war. We shall then give Hitler our answer on the barricades."

Those who objected were threatened with expulsion from the Party. Discipline forbade the rank and file to discuss the issue. From then on, in spite of the steadily increasing fierceness of their guerrilla warfare, the Communist Party and the Hitler movement joined forces to slash the throat of an already tottering democracy.

It was a weird alliance, never officially proclaimed or recognized by either the Red or the Brown bureaucracy, but a grim fact all the same. Many of the simple Party members resisted stubbornly; too disciplined to denounce openly the Central Committee, they embarked on a silent campaign of passive resistance, if not sabotage. However, the most active and loyal communist elements—I among them—went ahead energetically to translate this latest *Parteibefehl* into action. A temporary truce and a combining of forces were agreed on by the followers of Stalin and Hitler whenever they saw an opportunity to raid and break up meetings and demonstrations of the democratic front. During 1931 alone, I participated in dozens of such terroristic enterprises in concert with the rowdiest Nazi elements. I and my comrades simply followed Party orders. I shall describe a few of such enterprises to characterize this Dimitrov-Hitler alliance and to illustrate what was going on all over Germany at that time.

In the spring of 1931, the socialist Transport Workers' Union had called a conference of ship and dock delegates of all the main ports of Western Germany. The conference took place in the House of Labor in Bremen. It was public and the workers were invited to listen to the proceedings. The Communist Party sent a courier to the headquarters of the Nazi Party, with a request for cooperation in the blasting of the trade union conference. The Hitlerites agreed, as they always did in such cases. When the conference opened, the galleries were packed with two to three hundred Communists and Nazis. I was in charge of operations for the Communist Party and a storm troop leader named Walter Tidow —for the Nazis. In less than two minutes, we had agreed on a plan of action. As soon as the conference of the Social Democrats was well under way, I got up and launched a harangue from the gallery. In another part of the hall Tidow did the same. The trade union delegates were at first speechless. Then the chairman gave the order to eject the two troublemakers, me and Tidow, from the building. We sat quietly, derisively watching two squads of husky trade unionists advance toward us with the intention of throwing us out. We refused to budge. As soon as the first trade union delegate touched one of us, our followers rose and bedlam started. The furniture was smashed, the participants beaten, the hall turned into a shambles. We gained the street and scattered before ambulances and the *Rollkommandos* of the police arrived. The next day, both the Nazi and our own Party press brought out front page accounts of how "socialist" workers, incensed over the "treachery" of their own corrupt leaders had given them a thorough "proletarian rubdown."

On another occasion the German liberals were the victims. The Democratic Party had called a public mass meeting in defense of the German Constitution. It had summoned its military organization, the "Young German Knights," to protect this meeting against extremist raiders. A large police force also took up positions in the great hall. The day before the meeting, the Nazi Party had approached the Communist Party with a request for aid to smash the rally of the Democrats. A truce was established between the Red and Brown guerrillas. Both sides concentrated to wipe the Democrats off the political map. I was assigned to lead the Communist wrecking party; the Nazi faction was again under the command of Tidow, a soldier of fortune in the clique of Captain Roehm. Our hordes came early, filling the hall before the Democrats arrived in force. The main speaker of the evening was General von Lettow Vorbeck, the defender of German East Africa during the Great War. We granted Lettow Vorbeck a bare ten minutes of uninterrupted speaking. Then, at a signal, a group of Nazis and Communists in the front row of the auditorium began to shout the vilest terms of abuse at the General. Police and "Young German Knights" immediately intervened to silence the marauders. In a few seconds a grand battle was in progress. Bottles and chairs whistled through the air. Well over a thousand raiders tangled with hundreds of "Knights" and police and several thousand innocent listeners. Tidow's men and my own had brought with them itching powder, stink bombs, and a large number of white mice. The itching powder and the mice were used to drive the women present from the meeting. General von Lettow Vorbeck was locked in a lavatory beneath the stage. The police did not dare to use their weapons for fear of hitting noncombatants. Eventually, the police drove us into the street, where the affray continued far into the night. The mass rally of the Democrats was shattered beyond hope, like so many others of their meetings throughout the Reich.

Communist cooperation with the Hitler movement for reasons of political expediency did not stop at wrecking the meetings and demonstrations of opponents. In the spring of 1931, the German Nationalists moved for a plebiscite to oust the Social Democratic government of Prussia. Together with the followers of Hitler, they collected the number of signatures required by law to force the Berlin government to make the plebiscite mandatory. Tensely we Communists awaited the answer to the questions. "How are we to vote? If we vote with the Nazis, the Socialist government of Prussia might fall, and a combination of Hitlerites and Monarchists will come to power in Prussia, the dominant state within the Reich. Surely we are not to give our votes to make Hitler ruler of Prussia?"

The Communist high command, under Dimitrov, gave us the answer by telegram and letter, and through circulars, pamphlets, and headlines in the Party press. *Down with the Social Democrats, the chief enemy of the workers! Communists, your duty is to sweep the Socialist traitors out of the government offices!* So, while Communist and Nazi terror groups blazed away at each other in nightly skirmishes, Communists went loyally to the polls to give their votes in support of a drive launched by the Monarchist Hugenberg and the Fascist Hitler.

17. Hitler's Address to the Industrieklub, January 27, 1932

Already in the early 1920s, Adolf Hitler developed his talents as an indefatigable speaker, seeking to win converts with the messages he projected by his charismatic personality. In the good years of the later 1920s, his words fell on barren ground; but with the Nazi attack on the accelerated reparations schedules of the Young Plan (1929) and the onslaught of the Great Depression, he attracted ever-increasing attention. The smashing Nazi election victory of September 1930 marked his breakthrough to nationwide political prominence. Now he pressed ahead on every front, aided by the technological maturation of radio and newsreel, while also exploiting the theatrical potentialities of parades and rallies.

In January 1932 he maneuvered industrialist Fritz Thyssen to invite him to address the *Industrieklub* of Düsseldorf, a wealthy and influential organization of industrial magnates. For two and a half hours he belabored his initially skeptical audience, moving from political and philosophical platitudes to the struggles of his movement, to the alleged imminent threat of Bolshevism, and finally to urging reaffirmation of national solidarity backed by a powerful military establishment based on industrial might. He earned more than deafening applause; thenceforth the financial resources of some important industrialists were available to him, aiding him in his upcoming campaign against Hindenburg for the presidency. He lost the campaign, but he became more widely known than ever.

The following excerpts from his speech indicate his adroit exploitation of economic statistics and national sentiment to further the Nazi cause.

SOURCE: R. de Roussy de Sales, *Adolf Hitler: My New Order* (New York: Reynal & Hitchcock, 1941), pp. 108–111, 121–125.

Gentlemen, the development is clear for all to see: the crisis is very serious. It forces us to cut down expenses in every sphere. The most natural way of economizing is always to save in human labor-power. Industries will continuously be forced to ever greater rationalization, that means increase in achievement and reduction in the number of workmen employed. But if these workmen can no longer be given a place in newly started occupations, in newly developed industries, then that means that gradually three national banking accounts must be opened: the first account is called agriculture: from this national basic account men were formerly economized to constitute the second account. This second account was hand-work and later industrial production. Now an economy in man-power is being practiced on this second account and the men saved from this account are driven over into the third account—unemployment. With this word unemployment one is but shame-facedly seeking to put a better appearance upon hard facts: for the proper term is not "workless" but "existence-less" and therefore in truth "superfluous." It is the characteristic feature of our European nations that gradually a certain percentage of the population is proved statistically to be superfluous.

It is now quite clear that the necessity for supporting this third account thus falls upon the other two. That increases the pressure of taxation, and the consequence of that will be an enforced further rationalization of the method of production, further economy, and a still greater increase in the third account.

And to this must be added the fact that the fight which today all European nations wage for the world export-market results naturally in a rise of prices which in its reaction compels men to practice further economies. The final result which today can hardly be foreseen will in any event prove decisive for the future or for the downfall of the white race, and in especial of those peoples which in their narrow living space can establish economic autarchy only with very great difficulty. The further consequence will be that, for instance, England will carry through a reorganization with an eye to her internal market and for its protection will raise tariff barriers, high today and tomorrow still higher, and all other peoples, so far as they are in any way able to do so, will follow suit.

So far all those are in the right who regard the melancholy position of Germany as calling for special attention when considering our present distress, but they are wrong in seeking the cause of our distress in externals, for this position is certainly the result not merely of the external development but of our internal, I might almost say, aberration of spirit, our internal division, our internal collapse. . . .

Gentlemen, we know from our own experience that, through a mental aberration whose consequences you can in practice trace on every hand, Germany lost the War. Do you believe that when seven or eight million men have found themselves for ten or twenty years excluded from the national process of production that for these masses Bolshevism could appear as anything else than the logical theoretical complement of their actual, practical, economic situation? Do you really believe that the purely spiritual side of this catastrophe can be overlooked and that one day it will not transform itself into bitter reality—the evil curse following on the evil deed? . . .

The essential thing is to realize that at the present moment we find ourselves in a condition which has occurred several times before in the history of the world: already there have been times when the volume of certain products in the world exceeded the demand. Today we are experiencing the same thing on the largest possible scale: if all the motor-factories in the world today were employed a hundred percent and worked a hundred percent, then one could replace the world's entire stocks of motors in four and a half or five years. If all the locomotive-factories were employed a hundred percent they could easily renew the entire locomotive material in the world in eight years. If all the rail-factories and rolling-mills of the world were employed a hundred percent perhaps in ten to fifteen years one could put the whole system of railway-lines at present in existence once more round the world. And that holds good for nearly all industries. There has arisen such an increase in productive capacity that the present possible consumption market stands in no relation to this increased capacity. But if Bolshevism as a world-idea tears the Asiatic continent out of the human economic community, then the conditions for the employment of these industries which have developed on so gigantic a scale will be no longer even approximately realized. . . . When a politician or economist objects: that was, it is true, the case between Rome and Carthage, between England and Holland, or between England and France, but today the business world decides the matter, then I can only reply: that is not the spirit which formerly opened up the world for the white race, which for us Germans, too, opened the way into the economic life of the world. For it was not German business which conquered the world and then came the development of German power, but in our case, too, it was the power-State (*Machtstaat*) which created for the business world the general conditions for its subsequent prosperity. *In my view it is to put the cart before the horse when today people believe that by business methods they can, for instance, recover Germany's power-position instead of realizing that the power-position is also the condition for the improvement of the economic situation.* That does not mean that one should not forthwith try to oppose the malady which has seized upon our economic life, although one cannot immediately attack the source of the malady. But it does mean that every such external solution ignores the kernel of the problem, since it fails to recognize that there is only one fundamental solution. That solution rests upon the realization that economic systems in collapse have always as their forerunner the collapse of the State and not vice versa—that there can be no flourishing economic life which has not before it and behind it the flourishing powerful State as its protection—that there was no Carthaginian economic life without the fleet of Carthage, and no Carthaginian trade without the army of Carthage—that it goes without saying that also in modern times—when blow is met by blow and the interests of peoples clash—*there can be no economic life unless behind this economic life there stands the determined political will of the nation absolutely ready to strike—and to strike hard.* . . .

And now behind us there lie twelve years of fighting. That fight has not been waged in theory only and in the party alone turned into practice: we are also ready to wage that fight on the larger scale. I cast my mind back to the time when with six other unknown men I founded this association, when I spoke before eleven, twelve, thirteen, fouteen, twenty, thirty, and fifty persons; when I recall how after a year I had won sixty-four members for the Movement, how our small circle kept on growing, I must confess that that which has today been created, when a stream of millions of our German fellow-countrymen is flowing into our Movement, represents something which is unique in German history. The *bourgeois* parties have had seventy years to work in; where, I ask you, is the organization which could be compared with ours? Where is the organization which can boast, as ours can, that, at need, it can summon 400,000 men into the street, men who are schooled to blind obedience and are ready to execute any order—provided that it does not violate the law? Where is the organization that in seventy years has achieved what we have achieved in barely twelve years?—and achieved with means which were of so improvised a character that one can hardly avoid a feeling of shame when one confesses to an opponent how poverty-stricken the birth and the growth of this great Movement were in the early days.

Today we stand at the turning-point of Germany's destiny. If the present development continues, Germany will one day of necessity land in Bolshevist chaos, but if this development is broken, then our people must be taken into a school of iron discipline and gradually freed from the prejudices of both camps. A hard schooling, but one we cannot escape! . . .

People say to me so often: "You are only the drummer of national Germany." And supposing that I were only the drummer? It would today be a far more statesmanlike achievement to drum once more into this German people a new faith than gradually to squander the only faith they have. Take the case of a fortress, imagine that it is reduced to extreme privations: as long as the garrison sees a possible salvation, believes in it, hopes for it, so long they can bear the reduced ration. But take from the hearts of men their last belief in the possibility of salvation, in a better future—take that completely from them, and you will see how these men suddenly regard their reduced rations as the most important thing in life. The more you bring it home to their consciousness that they are only objects for men to bargain with, that they are only prisoners of world-politics, the more will they, like all prisoners, concentrate their thoughts on purely material interests. On the other hand, the more you bring back the people into the sphere of faith, of ideals, the more will it cease to regard material distress as the one and only thing which counts. And the weightiest evidence for the truth of that statement is our own German people. We would not ever forget that the German people waged wars of religion for 150 years with prodigious devotion, that hundreds of thousands of men once left their plot of land, their property, and their belongings simply for an ideal, simply for a conviction. We would never forget that during those 150 years there was no trace of even an ounce of material interests. Then you will understand how mighty is the force of an idea, of an ideal. Only so can you comprehend how it is that in our Movement today hundreds of thousands of young men are prepared at the risk of their lives to withstand our opponents. I know quite well, gentlemen, that when National Socialists march through the streets and suddenly in the evening there arise a tumult and commotion, then the *bourgeois* draws back the window-curtain, looks out, and says: Once more my night's rest disturbed: no more sleep for me. Why must the Nazis always be so provocative and run about the place at night? Gentlemen, if everyone thought like that, then no one's sleep at nights would be disturbed, it is true, but then the *bourgeois* today could not venture into the street. If everyone thought in that way, if these young folk had no ideal to move them and drive them forward, then certainly they would gladly be rid of these nocturnal fights. But remember that it means sacrifice when today many hundred thousands of SA and SS men of the National Socialist Movement every day have to mount on their lorries, protect meetings, undertake marches, sacrifice themselves night after night, and then come back in the gray dawn either to workshop and factory or as unemployed to take the pittance of the dole: it means sacrifice when from the little which they possess they have further to buy their uniforms, their shirts, their badges, yes, and even pay their own fares. Believe me, there is already in all this the force of an ideal—a great ideal! And if the whole German nation today had the same faith in its vocation as these hundred thousands, if the whole nation possessed this idealism, Germany would stand in the eyes of the world otherwise than she stands now! For our situation in the world in its fatal effects is but the result of our own underestimate of German strength. Only when we have once more changed this fatal valuation of ourselves can Germany take advantage of the political possibilities which, if we look far enough into the future, can place German life once more upon a natural and secure basis—and that means either new living-space (*Lebensraum*) and the development of a great internal market or protection of German economic life against the world without and utilization of all the concentrated strength of Germany. The labor resources of our people, the capacities, we have them already: no one can deny that we are industrious. . . .

And so in contrast to our own official Government I cannot see any hope for the resurrection of Germany if we regard the foreign politics of Germany as the primary factor: the primary necessity is the restoration of a sound national German body-politic armed to strike. In order to realize this end I founded thirteen years ago the National Socialist Movement: that Movement I have led during the last twelve years, *and I hope that one day it will accomplish this*

*task and that, as the fairest result of its struggle, it will leave behind
it a German body-politic completely renewed internally, intolerant
of anyone who sins against the nation and its interests, intolerant
against anyone who will not acknowledge its vital interests or who
opposes them, intolerant and pitiless against anyone who shall attempt once more to destroy or disintegrate this body-politic, and
yet ready for friendship and peace with anyone who has a wish for
peace and friendship.*

18. The Waning of the Weimar Era

Theodore Heuss had made a distinguished record as a writer and political figure long before he became the first president of the German
Federal Republic (1949–1959). As a young man he worked closely
with Friedrich Naumann, a prominent Wilhelmian Reichstag deputy
and writer who had tried to bring socialism and nationalism into creative democratic interrelationship. In the Reichstag of the late Weimar
Republic Heuss was one of a diminishing band of moderate liberals
who saw its political equilibrium give way to polarization and extremism. His memoirs and his Reichstag address of May 11, 1932 indicate
the rapid deterioration of the political climate in Germany. In contrast
to Hitler, Heuss made his appeal to reason and political decency, used
sophisticated irony instead of smears as he sparred with his Nazi opponents. His words proved then of little avail, but today they give
clear insight into the temper of those times.

SOURCE: Theodor Heuss, *Erinnerungen, 1905–1933* (Tübingen:
Rainer Wunderlich Verlag Hermann Leins, 1963), pp. 406–
408, 411–414. Reprinted by permission of the publisher. Germany, Reichstag, *Stenographische Berichte* . . . (V. Wahlperiode, 1930), 446: 2587–2593. Translations by the editor.

Our work in the Reichstag could not proceed as in previous
years. A somewhat qualified ministerial bureaucracy gained the
upper hand and generally governed on the basis of Article 48 of
the Constitution, to which Chancellor Brüning had accustomed
the president of the Reich. [A majority of] the Reichstag did not
object because they knew that in face of growing unemployment a
successor to Brüning could not stem the growth of the National
Socialists and Communists.

In the process of campaigning throughout the country I witnessed a complete collapse of traditional political behavior. Even in the cities, where one might have expected observance of political custom, groups of storm troopers attempted to disrupt meetings by singing songs; in Wiesbaden teenagers exploded firecrackers until the police stepped in and, as I heard later, thoroughly beat them up in the anteroom of the stately hall. My memories record some depressing experiences. Heinrich Himmler provided me with an anecdote for which I earned some applause, especially in [my native] Württemberg. When his party had become an important factor, he wrote (or had written) a little booklet on *The Reichstag of 1930*. He listed my name among its Jewish members. I faithfully took this pamphlet, replete with its nonsense and lies, to my rallies [and commented]: "I am descended on my father's side from a century-old family of Neckar boatmen and on my mother's, from many generations of foresters. These are two occupations in which there are statistically very few, if any, Jews, but these Nazis find out everything. . . . !" In Schwenningen I was greeted by the local Nazi paper as a "well-known Jew and Freemason," and the local Democrats urged me to sue for libel. I explained that this would be unwise because I had very close friends of Jewish descent, or friends who were members of the Freemasons, and they would be insulted by such a suit. But I did submit a "correction" [to the Nazi paper] in accordance with well established legal procedure: "It is untrue that, . . . but true that. . . ." Upon returning to Berlin, I found the editor's answer that they would accept only positive statements of truth. This was too much. Now I did complain to the courts, citing violation of the press law. The case came up in Tuttlingen; a former student of mine was an editor there and drew my attention to the "hearing." He wrote an amusing letter: every child in Württemberg knew full well that I was neither a Jew nor a Freemason. The judge levied a fine of thirty marks on the Nazi editor and stipulated that my correction be printed. This was done, but the editor also gave a glimpse of the years to come by adding that it was not at all certain that my grandparents had not been Jewish. Thus I received an early warning of this ancestor complex which later played such a tragic role in many families, but at the time, I considered it only as the impertinence of a shabby journalist. . . .

In the spring of 1932, complications in German domestic affairs intensified automatically because Hindenburg's seven-year term of office ended. In 1925 the National Socialists had unsuccessfully entered the contest for the presidency with Ludendorff as their candidate. Subsequently, under the influence of his second wife (who tried to found a new national pagan religion) General Ludendorff had forfeited his wartime fame and had disagreements with Hitler. When Ludendorff refused to join his old commander [Hindenburg] at the dedication of the Tannenberg Memorial, the complete break between the old comrades was apparent. This time the National Socialists would certainly send Hitler himself into the contest. He was already becoming a legendary figure, thanks to intensive propaganda and the success of his party in state elections. Brüning managed to convince Hindenburg to run again, even though he may have considered the eighty-four year old Field-marshall just an interim solution. Fearing Hitler's attraction, neither the Center nor the Social Democrats ran a candidate of their own [and supported Hindenburg]. The Communists again ran Thälmann, who got considerable support. Hugenberg, not wanting to lose influence with the Conservatives tried to run Colonel Düsterberg, a vice-chairman of the veteran's association "Stahlhelm," who had attracted some political attention. In the longer run the Colonel was never a real threat to the "Bohemian sergeant," as Hindenburg called Hitler, especially after Goebbels "revealed" in January of 1933 that Düsterberg's grandfather was Jewish. His public influence ended soon thereafter.

Hindenburg failed to get a plurality by only a small percentage of votes and won in the run-off of April 10, 1932. Düsterberg threw his support to Hindenburg and Hugenberg was neutral. Thälmann lost a million votes that obviously went to Hitler—it was an incredible task to push the superannuated Field-marshall in face of open discussions about his state of health and mind. In the end Brüning could take credit for the result as *his* achievement, to which he had devoted all of his remaining strength.

Yet, it was a pyrrhic victory. The Chancellor soon discovered that the governing technique of the last two years [by emergency decree] was coming to an end. Just as he thought that Germany's position in foreign affairs could be eased—negotiations with England and America continued in a favorable atmosphere and Herriot was the new premier in France—new difficulties constantly arose in the domestic sphere. Brüning's last parliamentary success was his request for a vote of confidence. I remember the situation very clearly, because I gave my farewell speech in the Reichstag on the same day, May 11, 1932. I engaged in a vigorous verbal exchange with the National Socialists, who appeared only occasionally at Reichstag sessions. Brüning was kind enough to speak after me so that the audience was rather large in expectation of his speech and I could nicely counter the interruptions of Goering, Goebbels, and Frank.

Let me quote from my speech to indicate the level of political argument and polemics in this confused period, with its techniques of interjection, verbal encouragement, and counterstatement.

Ladies and Gentlemen! The Reichstag suddenly finds itself in the strange position of receiving praise from the press which at other times would be questionable: it has become *"boring."* We should all note that the National Socialist German Workers' Party stated yesterday through representative Strasser that it would henceforth participate objectively in parliament where, up to now, it was only a source of disruption and opposition. Yes, the rumor is even heard in our land that henceforth these gentlemen will participate in our committees and their work. I believe that we are all very happy that these gentlemen are now cooperating. We should be grateful when Mr. Gregor Strasser faces the responsibility of re-ducing to legal language the great panoramic picture of Germany's future which he drew for us yesterday. (*Very good!*) In the proc-ess we shall all be able to examine the social, economic, and finan-cial prerequisites and effects of his proposals, a possibility which the gentlemen have never offered us before.

More of this later. First a few remarks about foreign policy. I refer to the speech to Mr. Goering, to his criticism of the Chan-cellor. Mr. Goering said in reference to the Disarmament Confer-ence that he could see nothing but failure after failure; nothing had come of it; only an entirely new type of German delegation could achieve anything in this area. Mr. Goering, I would not have expected you to repeat the propagandistic simplicities of your recent campaign speeches in the responsible chambers of the Reichstag. . . . You do not seem to have noticed, or you refuse to do so, that meanwhile something very substantial was achieved at the Disarmament Conference: the unfavorable text of the con-vention, with its tortuous excuses and dangerous possibilities, pre-viously rejected by Germany, has been superseded. We are now at the point where the disarmament clauses of the Versailles Treaty will serve as the model for discussions of the Disarmament Com-mission. We should be grateful to the Chancellor and Foreign Minister that instead of losing composure in February, or soliciting cheap domestic applause, they calmly fought for Germany's moral position with the steadfast responsibility of statesmen. Only naiveté or ill will can overlook the advantage of the fact that the same powers which forced disarmament upon us at Versailles, Italy, and America among them, are now prepared to impose the same obligations upon all the other powers. . . . This factor gives the whole problem of disarmament a totally new aspect. . . .

Colleague Goering spoke yesterday about the [favorable] results of the elections in Memel. I believe that everyone in this house regarded those developments with anticipation and a sure feeling for their outcome. Our colleague Goering claims that this was a positive result of the Hitler movement. Should we begin to discuss questions of the Germans abroad in terms of domestic party politics, and with such questionable evidence? No! Why not? Because this is almost the only area of German problems which we all, . . . have hitherto consciously and successfully excluded from political partisanship. (*Very good! from the benches of the government parties.*) I observe with great concern . . . that your [Nazi] group is trying to establish organizations with specific party leanings among the German minorities abroad. I will not elaborate now on the political tactlessness of National Socialist societies in "Bolzano" and "Merano." But a sense of responsibility on your part should recognize the dangers of involving Germans abroad and burdening them with the perils of internal German strife and possibly making martyrs of them, as you seem to have suggested in your speeches.

There is one other thing which I should mention, esteemed Mr. Goering. The principle which is the political premise of the National Socialists, namely that only he can be a "citizen" who is also a fellow German [*Volksgenosse*], will be especially dangerous for Germans abroad when other states and peoples realize its implications. This is already evident in Rumania, where some of the Rumanian nationalists refer to the 25 points of the National Socialist Party Program when they insult the German minority or question the citizenship of our Transylvanians. (*Hear Hear! at the left. Interjection from the National Socialists: they did this quite independently!*) The Rumanian nationalists are studying what you say about German minority problems. They are observing that the German National Socialists distinguish between the so-called "fellow Germans" and so-called "citizens" and treat them differently. Consequently, if other nations were to use the National Socialist principle of citizenship, which you want to use to discriminate against several hundred thousand Jews in Germany, then millions of fellow Germans abroad will find themselves imperiled. I fear that your argument will take root in other countries. (*Representative Dr. Frick: The Germans abroad are already suppressed because we, under your government, are too weak!*) Esteemed Dr. Frick, like you we know about the suppression of these fellow Germans, we also know that they receive from Germany every possible material and moral support in their struggle for political and cultural autonomy. Obviously you do not understand these matters because you never seriously analyzed them. (*Representative Goering: A powerful German Reich is the best support!*) Certainly, but you propagandize the Germans abroad in order to denigrate the mother country, this heart of everything German, and to rob this state of its moral strength and dignity! (*Active agreement from the Center and the Social Democrats. Rejection and continuous hooting from the National Socialists.*)

May I now continue and discuss foreign policy somewhat further? (*Representative Dr. Goebbels: What do you really want in this chamber? You no longer have any followers!*) Dr. Goebbels, I represent my own views here (*Representative Dr. Goebbels: We don't want to hear your views!*), and you will be so kind for a moment as to control your nervous agitation to your best ability. It will be my pleasure to converse with you later, but you should know that a code of behavior requires all members of the Reichstag to conduct themselves properly, politely, and honorably. This probably also pertains to you. (*Amusement and shouts from the Center and the Social Democrats.*) I therefore ask you to observe this injunction during my speech. (*Renewed merriment in the Center and by the Social Democrats*). . . .

It would be tempting for me to discuss History with Mr. Goering, but he no longer honors us with his presence. Yesterday he gave us Bismarck as an example, and told us that Bismarck had commanded the full support of the people for his foreign policy aims. In which history book did Mr. Goering study the Bismarckian era? (*Amused approval of the government coalition.*) Bismarck's ingenious successes in foreign policy, based on victorious wars, were great and lasting. But has Mr. Goering not noticed how Bismarck attempted to keep a broad stratum of Germans from exercising political powers (first those who were loyal to the Catholic Church, then the Socialists) and what a difficult heritage he left for the future? (*Quite right! from the Left.*) Did he not recognize—apparently not!—the tragic end of Bismarck? Because Bismarck reduced the power of the Prussian Landtag in the 1860s and excluded the German Reichstag from greater responsibility, he failed to construct a foundation from which he could extend his foreign policy. The grandson of the man whose power he so greatly enlarged [William II] was able to dismiss Bismarck because—and this is the tragedy of his domestic policy—he did not develop the power of popular participation in the affairs of state. (*Very good! from the government coalition.*) . . .

The German people face a strange peril. The economies of European countries, already challenged by the industrialization of overseas nations, are increasingly isolating each other with rising tariffs and monetary restrictions. Now we are urged to make a virtue of necessity, to accept this "autarkic" tendency [economic self-sufficiency] caused by distorted policies of financial and economic competition and to acclaim it as the new style for our economic future. . . . I would have liked to discuss autarky with Mr. Strasser. He advocates it with heroic national and political fervor, arguing that separation from things foreign is the prerequisite of freedom. One might approve the autarky which the National Socialists advocate if simultaneously one had the courage to say that the next task was then to organize famine in Germany for several millions more. (*Active agreement at the left.*) Autarky should be advocated only by those who can clearly recognize and explain this problem. . . .

Let me discuss the contents of Mr. Gregor Strasser's basic program. He indicates that it reflects the "new thought" (*Amusement on the left.*) which has already taken root in Germany, especially among many young people. To anyone with some theoretical training in economics, the new thought looks like a very old way of thinking (*Quite right! from the government coalition and the Social Democrats.*), a combination of German romanticism and early utopian socialism in the tradition of Weitling and Proudhon. But there are some strange discords as this enemy of liberalism speaks of re-establishing the "natural harmony" between economy and society. In fact, he reads just like a primer of classical liberalism. . . .

What does Mr. Strasser suggest? He proposes in a slightly embellished form that we return to the old idea of "creating new values" by financial credit and currency policy. . . . This whole doctrine is nothing but theoretical nonsense and a political danger for any government that might be seduced to manipulations of this kind. Inflation would be here tomorrow, for it is not just a mechanical question of quantitative money supply, but also a psychological problem. No matter how severe the effects of deflation may be, we expect the government to resist all experimentation with the currency, for the German people and their economy could not survive such ventures (*Quite right! from the Center*). . . .

Yesterday the Minister of Interior [Groener] described the S.A. [Storm Troopers] for us. We once read with interest Dr. Goebbel's announcement that the "new aristocracy," a new breed of leadership, was developing in the S.A. (*Laughter at the Left.*) We observe curiously that certain concepts of social philosophy, like those of Sorel and of Pareto, have taken root in German National Socialism. Note the concept of the "elite"—Mr. Strasser has written some splendid essays about it. But while the Nazis are still presenting themselves here as an "elite," their followers are already beginning to discover that they are just old party bosses. . . .

We have heard this new aristocracy praised for its discipline and ethical unity, yet anyone who has attended any S.A. meetings, as I often have, has not only heard a well-trained male choir, but has also experienced the fuss and fumes of firecrackers and stink bombs. This creates a rather unfavorable image of an elite representing the new aristocracy. We also know them well as tools of intimidation, of simple terror, and as a constant comfort for the frightened Philistines. Minister Groener, let me put just one question to you: if you observed so early, in my opinion with good reason, that a group had emerged that threatened the authority of the state, why did you not order the S.A. disbanded, why was it not already suppressed last October or November? I believe that many confrontations would have been resolved more easily if your decision had been made at that time. (*Very true! from the Center.*) . . .

Let me conclude. Because of Mr. Goering's speech and because of Mr. Strasser's announcement—(*Shout from the National Socialists: Did they make you uneasy?*)—No, for heaven's sake: I have had to endure so much stupid and even malicious nonsense from the National Socialists that my nerves are steeled. In fact, I have become quite immune. (*Laughter among the government coalition and the Social Democrats.*) As I contemplate what was served up again here, namely, the boast that something new is being generated by the German National Socialist Workers' Party, that a new Germanic type is being created, a new political style, then I am quite ready to recognize the fabulous achievements of propaganda, the technique of suggestion, the contrived alternation between victorious hero-saints and martyrs of persecuted innocence. In addition to these oscillating propagandistic ploys, we have learned something else, and I am grateful for those last eight days preceding the presidential election. At that time we simple folk bought the *Völkischer Beobachter* [the major Nazi newspaper] and day by day witnessed the praiseworthy physical, I emphasize *physical*, accomplishment of Mr. Adolf Hitler as he roared all over Germany in his plane. He took along a hack writer who composed a heroic epic of the flight; it was the worst trash produced in any German publication at the time. (*Continuous shouts from the National Socialists. Call to order.*) I believe that even Dr. Goebbels, who has some feeling for literary style, must have winced at this journalistic production. From all the poetic and sentimental agitation that we have heard during those eight days about the "Third Reich," the new Germanic type, the new style of the future Germany, it is obvious that this Third Reich, will be equipped from a clearance sale of newly varnished and refurbished white elephants of the Wilhelmian era; (*Active agreement from the Center and the Social Democrats.*) and of these, Gentlemen, I believe we have already had quite enough! (*Loud applause from the government coalition.*)

V

The "Conservative Revolution" and National Socialism, 1930–1933

HITLER'S STRONGEST political asset was his ability to formulate the aims of his movement so generally and yet in such diversity that there appeared to be something in his program, at some time, for nearly every German. He achieved one of his greatest successes of ideological obfuscation and political maneuver in his relationships with German conservatism.

At the height of the Wilhelmian Empire various conservatives— aristocrats, Junkers, the military officers, churchmen, and the new business-industrial leadership—were the elite that ruled Germany. But even at that time they already felt pressed by bourgeois liberalism, socialism, and secularism. As they sought to restrain the effective emergence of these forces, their sense of insecurity and apprehension grew. With the great defeat and revolution of 1918, they were removed from the levers of power, though their influence on German society remained strong enough to give them hope of returning to political authority. In competition with working-class and petit-bourgeois extremism, they also developed a thrust toward more radical activism. This was the "conservative revolution" of which there was talk and writing in the Weimar era, an amorphous collection of neoconservative ideological experiments, anxieties, and frustrations.

For several years before 1933, the Nazis adroitly played down the social radicalism of their original program and appeared to advocate a return to the more conservative order and values of the empire. The industrialist Hugenberg was one of the first prominent business magnates to collaborate with the Nazis. Subsequently Hitler attracted several sons of the Kaiser, Reichsbank president

Schacht, industrialist Thyssen, and finally the ambitious Prussian Catholic aristocrat, Franz von Papen, into juxtaposition and collaboration with National Socialism. These men hoped to ride to renewed power on a wave of Nazi votes.

As soon as he was in office, of course, Hitler rapidly dispensed with this traditional conservative baggage. Earlier a few perceptive men had warned that Nazism was not compatible with genuine German conservatism, but their warnings went unheeded. Within a year Vice-chancellor von Papen was demoted to ambassador— Hitler's advance man in Austria, then Turkey. The conservative military leaders increasingly incurred the Führer's disdain and rejection. The industrialists became materiel-producing servants for the Nazi juggernaut. The ultimate conservative confession of failure came in the abortive revolt of July 20, 1944, with its savage reprisals.

19. A Theory of the "Conservative Revolution"

Armin Mohler is a freelance writer and journalist of Swiss extraction. He spent the war years in Berlin and was the secretary of conservative philosopher Ernst Jünger from 1949 to 1953. Since 1964 he has worked with the Carl Friedrich von Siemens Foundation in Munich. The following selection is taken from the conclusion of his book, presently the most comprehensive historical analysis of the "conservative revolution" in the era of the Weimar republic.

SOURCE: Armin Mohler, *Die konservative Revolution in Deutschland, 1918–1932* (*Stuttgart: Evangelisches Verlagswerk, 1950*), pp. 206–209. Reprinted by permission of the publisher. Translation by the editor.

The ideas of Friedrich Nietzsche, particularly those developed in his conception of Eternal Recurrence, are central to a discussion of the disintegration of Western traditions and the emergence of neo-conservative thought. The cultural-intellectual developments of the last century should be viewed in the context of a duel between Hegel and Nietzsche. True, Nietzsche is himself a transitional figure who is still influenced by basic principles of his opponent. Yet, the world we live in today should be called the Age of Nietzsche, because all of the most important contemporary thought and imagery derives from him. Other original and creative thinkers have appeared since his time, but on closer observation they are all significant only in relationship to Nietzsche.

The term, "conservative revolution," designates the changes anticipated and expressed in Nietzsche's thought. It is a movement often directed against various secularized forms of Christianity and fundamentally against the entire Christian concept of the universe as well. The "conservative revolution" is an attempt to renew all aspects of life in most European countries. In this analysis our concern is limited to Germany, and we focus our attention on political ideas (where the term "German movement" might be synonymous with "conservative revolution") during the Weimar period. We can portray the "German movement" clearly between 1918 and 1932, because the characteristics were not distorted by the realization of its aims either in the previous Wilhelmian or later National Socialist contexts.

The "conservative revolution" seeks to encompass all aspects of life. Until now it has appeared only in a few initial manifestations; it is therefore essentially an intellectual movement and must be understood in an intellectual context not yet politically successful. Hugo von Hofmannsthal, who gave the term broader currency, sees the significance of the "conservative revolution" in two ways: first, in a yearning for unity and wholeness in place of separation (individualism) and division (dualism); secondly, in a search for ties, relationships, and loyalties in place of anarchic freedom. . . . The core of the "conservative revolution" is a belief in Eternal Recurrence, in which philosophically a cyclical world view is once again contrasted with a linear world view. All the other conceptions, such as "totality" or "bond," are encompassed by the theme of Eternal Recurrence.

In this frame of reference we consider the "conservative revolution" a negation not only of the idea of progress, but just as much, of Christianity. We do not overlook the fact that it still contains various Christian elements; but the small number of instances in which a Christian attitude is evident within the "conservative revolution" appear to be just residues of the original Christian position.

The model of Eternal Recurrence is only dimly recognizable in the political evolution of the "conservative revolution," but a careful observer will notice it everywhere. In a "linear" concept of life the recurrence of vanished worlds so essential to the "conservative revolution" is not possible; that requires a cyclical world view, where there are no differences of temporal distance or proximity. The efforts of one wing of the "conservative revolutionaries" to accelerate the rate of progress are really attempts to foreshorten the liberal era and force radical change. Even when these endeavors are manifested as "nihilism," i.e., as a determination to destroy the present, they at least are "limited" and derive from the hope that destructive radical change might create new social values.

The political "conservative revolution" in Weimar Germany can be divided into five groups which are related to five submodels. We call them submodels because initially they are visible to the observer as independent entities; only with time does the principal model of Eternal Recurrence (which encompasses all five submodels) become visible in relation to them. This grouping is a necessary simplification, for in reality the five groups are tightly interwoven. The first three groups are interrelated in theory, without immediate relevance to practical circumstances. First, is the national-folkish group, with its roots in the Germanic past and stress on inherent, intuitive qualities like "race" and "folk"; second are the "young conservatives" who seek a structured diversity reminiscent of the medieval Reich; and third are the "nationalist radicals" whose idealistic activism reveals a Prussian origin. The two other groups, in contrast to the first three, derive from a different ideological and psychological context, fluctuating between theory and action. . . . One of these is the "federated youth movement," the nationalist German successor to the idealistic youth movement of the turn of the century. The last group, "the rural-peasant movement" (which emphasizes cultural values that have been dormant for centuries) is just awakening; in its silent individuality it challenges the urban-industrial, progressive world.

The upshot of this analysis of the hapless Weimar Republic is that in perspective it appears like a mere transition from the Hohenzollern monarchy to National Socialism. It may be immediately useful to list an array of non-Marxist forces that opposed the Weimar Republic in such groups as "fascism," "cryptofascism," "parafascism," "nazism," or "nihilism"; but these categories are inadequate for a more profound interpretation that would do justice to reality. What happened in Germany in those days can only be understood by recognizing that there were two crosscurrents in conflict. On the one hand was the "conservative revolution," an intellectual movement which sought to supersede the Weimar interregnum with new conceptions of the cosmos; it achieved only partial formulation and had little success. Opposed to it was the victorious mass party of National Socialism, a crude conglomeration of diverse elements which superficially adopted conservative revolutionary ideas together with completely contradictory slogans. Though larger groups within the "conservative revolution" at first mistook National Socialism for a realization of their own goals, the fundamental antagonism soon became apparent. Though some individuals defected to National Socialism, the adherents of the "conservative revolution" are identified by the blood they later shed in their resistance to Hitler. It is still a moot question, of course, how much responsibility a cultural-intellectual movement like the "conservative revolution" must itself bear for the willingness of its adherents to see their ideas and ideals appropriated and misused for other political purposes.

20. Ideals and Aims of a "Conservative Revolutionary"

Hermann Rauschning came from a conservative Prussian landed family. As a young man he was a member of the prestigious Prussian *Kadettenkorps*. After World War I he moved to the free city of Danzig, where he became head of the government in 1932. In this role he was in frequent and crucial negotiations with Hitler and the National Socialists, who early considered Danzig a point of leverage for changing Germany's relations with Eastern Europe to Berlin's advantage. Rauschning broke with the Nazis when he had taken their full measure by 1934. Two years later he fled abroad and subsequently wrote several insightful and widely read popular books that indicated the mood and temper of national socialism in its early years of power.

SOURCE: Hermann Rauschning, *The Conservative Revolution* (New York: G. P. Putnam's Sons, 1941), pp. 189–201.

"What We Expect from National Socialism." This was the title of a little pamphlet that appeared in 1932. In it several authors collaborated, raising a number of questions. They included a Protestant and a Catholic clergyman, politicians and constitutional lawyers, university professors and schoolmasters. Each of them expressed from his own point of view the gravest doubts of Nazism, and their questions probed the weak spots in Nazi doctrine and practice. And all of them agreed that Nazism had it entirely in its power to meet these questions either in a generous and creative spirit or in such a way that it would bring the German people to ruin.

I will not deal in detail with this pamphlet, which would still repay reading and would give you a clear insight into our ideas at that time and into the fact that we did not plunge blindly into the "adventure" amid a mass of illusions. The writer of the introductory article, Professor Mannhardt, of the University of Marburg, was a friend of mine at the time. It happened that in the fateful summer of 1932 he took a team of students, mostly Germans living abroad, on a "study tour" eastward, coming to Danzig among other places. I was then president of our farmers' association, and I invited the young men to visit our principal agricultural estates. In conversation we came to the subject of that article. In that disturbed year, conversation with no political background was quite impossible.

The article and our conversation touched on five main points: Without a stratum among the people that carries its historical, intellectual, and political creative elements, without a stratum of true leaders, the greatest people sinks to the level of slumbering vegetation. Such a stratum is not to be confused with any social upper class, of whatever origin, based on blue blood or possessions. Germany has no such stratum at present, and it can come into existence only in a new process. The self-styled "geschichtsbefugte Oberschicht" of the Weimar regime is the antithesis of such a stratum. It is a clique for mutual boosting, an expression of the universal mediocrity. The German people is in a state of revolutionary upheaval. It is on the march. It has broken away from its past ideas and is in search of a new spiritual home. (General Smuts said the same thing a few years later, in a wonderfully vivid way, of all civilized humanity.) This movement is genuine and creative. It may enable our nation to take the lead in a great ascent of the peoples of the West. But this movement is elemental, an unbridled natural force. It needs to be given shape, to be disciplined, to be provided with political leadership. In order to be active and effective in the political world, it needs a political organ. That cannot develop automatically. It requires time and opportunity. It needs association with an existing political force. The force which is nearest to it, and which, consciously or not, has taken over much of it, is the National Socialist party. The great opportunity for the future is the fusing of the two. From this the great popular movement will gain political form and creative strength; the Nazi party will gain a genuine content. There is a great danger that Nazism may take advantage of the impulses of the popular movement, misusing it and making capital out of it. It might be that the party would remain what it is, the political movement of a stratum of asocial and declassed elements. The Nazi party shows signs of serious inadequacy. It may fall to pieces. It is even probable that it will fall to pieces. How are we to prevent its collapse from carrying with it into the abyss the great popular movement of renewal, and so leaving Germany in an even worse state than at present? How are we to prevent the great expenditure of energy from futility? The only way is to get rid of the Nazi leaders and replace them by a body of young men of experience, intelligence, and initiative, who will not seek their own advantage like the Nazi "elite" but the fulfillment of the tasks that face them.

One thing, we concluded, was necessary—to put to use the unquestioned stirring in our nation. Only with the aid of this could that venture into the unknown be attempted which opens every great epoch of history. The ordinary leaders, the "elderly statesmen," could be of no service at such times; but neither could the desperadoes help. The struggle must be entered on against the personal leadership of the Nazis, by producing from within the Nazi movement the only opposition that could be expected to be effective. The young had to be gained. The young could be won over only by the extremist parties and were to be had only for truly creative work.

We were attracted by an element that existed in Nazism and in no other German party. When one is compelled to venture into unfamiliar regions beyond the boundaries of ordinary routine, and to ignore the pretensions of the experts—and this happens at all times of great crises and changes—then the success of a great experiment depends above all on an immense faith and a vitality of far more than the normal temperature. Where did such a faith exist in Germany? Where had it been until recently in all the democratic countries? Was it not hesitation, skepticism, resignation, at best half-faith, that had been the true causes of the world's great disaster—the second thoughts that dim the bright colors of a resolve, the discretion that always makes action too late, the self-pity of those who groan at being required to restore to normality a world out of joint instead of devoting themselves to the enjoyment of life? This half-heartedness, this incomplete faith in the cause, this relief at finding reasons for doing nothing and dismissing the subject—all this existed over against a movement whose boundless faith seemed grotesque and infantile amid the skeptical environment of the time.

Does not men's unshakable faith in themselves and their mission always seem puerile and grotesque to the resigned skeptic? To those who had any feeling at all that the new and unfamiliar could be achieved only by strong faith, it was clear in the Germany of 1930–1933 that there was nothing to be hoped for from the "elderly statesmen." These men saw no necessity for any departure from the customary; they scarcely saw anything beyond the problems of the moment; they were completely immersed in detail.

In historic crises the saving act comes always from the outsiders, the men who are regarded as fools. In this Nazism there was faith, a truly ungovernable and unmannerly faith in itself. That was the attractive element in it. That was the secret of its sex appeal, not only to the masses, but to the intellectuals, although the latter saw plainly the alarming and menacing elements in the movement. It was not only by tricks and publicity dodges that the Nazi movement won over the masses but by this same unbreakable will and faith. Problems are mastered, not by superior intelligence and knowledge, but by the will that nothing can discourage.

There is no arguing with those people who to this day are convinced that all might have been different if only Nazism had been forcibly suppressed in time, that instead of a sanguinary war there would then have come world-wide economic and political harmony. No one is more convinced than I am that this catastrophe might have been prevented. I have no belief in any inexorable historic destiny. But great world crises cannot be overcome by petty means. Evolution in place of revolution would only have been conceivable if the men at the head ten to fifteen years ago had not merely kept watch for silver streaks on the horizon, for signs of the abatement of the crisis, and made this waiting their excuse for once more putting off the necessary but troublesome remedies, but had recognized the full dimensions of the change in our world and had been efficient helpers in the introduction of the new age.

But would this not have been asking too much? Were not these great men, personally great and clear-sighted as they may have been, petty and dependent as exponents of forces which they did not control but left to control them? Thus the whole development was inevitable. Any renewal was difficult to conceive without a decisive revolutionary move. Three things this man Hitler had, with his Nazism, that gave him the advantage over all other forces—the conviction that he stood at a critical turning point in history; a sovereign contempt for all accepted forms, all limits of the conventional, and all orthodox views; and the unshakable belief in his own mission.

Perhaps it is only possible for a man to attain Hitler's contempt for all that is conventional and usual and traditional if he has had such a life as Hitler's. But why was there not the same realization of the vast scope of the changes in our time in other quarters? Why was there not elsewhere that faith in a mission to help a new order into being?

The only thing that could have been effectively set against this Nazism was a great faith. Instead of that, the mark of the times was pusillanimity or baseless optimism.

To return to our talk in that early summer of 1932—what was it that we expected from Nazism? Nothing less than that it should make itself the instrument of the renewal of the German people by means of the values of Western civilization and German tradition. That it should serve this renewal, not make use of it for its own ends. Faith was what we expected from the masses led by it and readiness for sacrifice and discipline, without which the exceptional problems of the future were insoluble. It gave us the opportunity of forming a new political and intellectual elite, a body of leaders who would throw down the frontier posts of the past party formations. This could only be done if we ourselves, if conservative elements, entered the political movement in order to permeate it. "Into the Nazi movement" was not only the summons with which we parted from one another. It was also the advice of the former Minister Treviranus to the "Popular Conservatives," who had revolted like us from the reactionary activities of the unteachable Hugenberg. It was the only possible means of guiding the movement from within and gaining influence over it. Thus it had nothing of the Machiavellianism now charged against our endeavor after our failure. It was the obvious and the only thing to do. It may have been a mistake, but it was no guilty partnership in Hitler's machinations. Only the ideas of the need for inducing the masses to turn away from politics, and thus duping them, were mistaken and misleading.

How does a new elite come into existence? A body of leaders representing the historic continuity of the nation, when the old elite has been plowed under or has lost its energy? That is a question, my friend, which affects you, too, more than may willingly be admitted in public. It is the chief of all the questions that face every civilized nation today.

I do not want to burden you with Pareto and his theory of the rotation of elites. But this much I am bound to say: elites cannot be created, cannot be built up or, in spite of all our rational planners, "planned." If they no longer exist, if the natural process of their recruitment has broken down and an entirely new elite becomes necessary, it will install itself only in the course of a definite and positive historic process. It will take upon itself the responsibility for the fate of nation and state and society. It will identify itself with that fate, and in so doing it will make history.

Nazism, in its primitive but effective way, gave us, with its elite, a demonstration of how this is done. Our task was to prevent its party elite from becoming the only elite in Germany. No hierarchy of officials can take the place of a selected group of independent men. The nobility, the intellectuals, the big capitalists, the officials, the clubs, the industrial unions, corporations, religious fraternities—all had been tried. What method of selection of men remained? Nothing but the primitive process of personal rivalry.

Shall I give you a catalogue of all the things we wanted to achieve with the aid of Nazism? Tradition instead of radicalism, continuity instead of a rationally worked-out fresh start. Evolution instead of revolution. A form resulting from growth instead of a manufactured apparatus. Self-government instead of bureaucratism. Decentralization instead of centralization. Variety instead of uniformity. Personal initiative instead of tutelage. The individual instead of the collective. Property instead of independence on incomes drawn from the state. A Christian basis instead of that of the "enlightenment" of rationalism.

As I write these few words to you, I realize how little they convey and how easily all such generalizations may be misunderstood. It is so easy to reel them off. But was self-government, for instance, possible in these times? Was it not, in consequence of its expenditure of time and energy, a "hindrance to traffic"? Were they not all hindrances to business, these conservative ideas of ours of variety and individuality? Hindrances to business that stood in the way of a rational process and a common-sense order?

We were well aware of the existence of some of these deeper questions. There were other things we demanded that were of doubtful value, a fact of which we were understandably and pardonably unaware. There were many questions of detail which today have become by no means insignificant, and which some day will become important. Our aim was the setting up of units capable of supervision. Only so did there seem still to be any chance of saving democracy. In intellectual matters we tried, long before Nazism, to make use of the conceptions of home training and family culture, to return in education to the concrete and the things that may be comprehended through the senses. Not merely in the Pestalozzian sense, because it is picturesque, but for the sake of the preservation and further development of the variety, the wealth of distinctions, within Germany. What Professor Mannhardt called at that time the "popular German movement," a conception that has today been worn entirely threadbare and robbed of its value, described a movement for the bringing together of every German element, and it was no mere chance that these ideas arose outside Germany, among the Germans beyond the frontier and overseas, Germans who were suffering from the centralizing tendencies of the national democratic Succession States.

Thus our ideas were not concerned with what is called the state but with the renewal of the conception of the Reich, a "Third Reich," in any case, a special order which had nothing in common with the ideas of the French *État*. It never occurred to us that Nazism would usurp these ideas in order to misapply them to the single purpose of maintaining its power. In its activities we saw a tangled mass of conflicting tendencies which we might be able to unravel. In its program it placed the idea of the Reich in the foreground of its objectives. It promised to restore self-government. It had ideas of a new federative reconstruction of Germany. Even when the institution of the *Reichsstatthalter*, or governors of provinces, was introduced, it was still possible to regard this as a really brilliant idea of personal union of a federation of independent members. Was it not a fruitful idea to try to secure the union, not by bureaucratic means and in a written constitution, but through the personal influence of trusted men, of a sort of "high commissioners"?

There was also the phenomenon of the masses. How was it to be got rid of as a political force and a menace to any political order? We hoped for help from Nazism in this. We proceeded from the reflection that the masses can only be overcome through themselves. They must be made nonpolitical by a mass movement and then set limits to themselves, or, rather, give themselves a new form, in which they are no longer masses but an articulated, ordered community with a public function, though a restricted one.

I do not know to this day how far we were right in these ideas and how far our reflections were of doctrinaire origin. But this much I do know today; that for the sake of this argument we came to terms, and felt that we were bound to come to terms, with a side of Nazism of whose radically destructive nature we had at that time no conception, that of demagogy, propaganda, political intoxication, and hysteria. In accepting these things because we believed that there was no other way of gaining political power or of disciplining the masses, we were in error. I will not attempt to palliate or belittle the error by pointing out that other parties and political movements also made use of these expedients—less effectively, it is true, because with less cunning.

It had not occurred to us for a moment that in accepting demagogic methods we delivered ourselves up to a process that would "take charge" and compel us to resort to measures of exactly the opposite sort to those which we intended to take. The modern mass-democracy is faced with the question whether to make use of this new technique of mass psychology in political controversy or to abstain from it. There will be practical politicians everywhere who, undisturbed by the question of the immorality of these means, will attend only to that of their efficacy and utility. To all those who are trying to copy the Nazi or Fascist tricks I can only say that mass propaganda is not only immoral but inexpedient, because, while it may help to overcome momentary difficulties, it brings to life no real and lasting forces.

In all this I have said nothing on one point which you will want answered as the most essential of all: the question how it was possible for us to associate ourselves with the Nazi playing at soldiers, the militant organizations and the intention of thorough-going rearmament. I will add only the following to what I wrote to you not long ago—that that which I described as a rebirth out of the element of the army is perhaps being made clearer by the latest developments. I mean simply that it is not enough to have a constitution in order to be certain of a state in the leadership of the nation. I mean that a state is always in the first place an organization for practical activity. At times of failing energies the state must fall back on the element in which such an organization pre-eminently exists. This, usually, is the army; or, if there is none, the nucleus of an army in the unions of men trained in defense. The state becomes what it is in the creative times of its birth—the active association of all conscious elements of will and vitality. It is exactly that that we wanted during the crisis of the Weimar Republic in the renewal of our people's army. So, at least, we saw it.

21. Warnings from an Anti-Nazi Conservative

Ewald von Kleist-Schmenzin was a Prussian Junker and jurist; prior to 1933 he held several intermediate official positions in his native Pomerania. As a member of the German National party and the veterans organization, *Stahlhelm*, he had ample opportunity to take the measure of his fellow-conservatives and the Nazis. In 1933 he was twice arrested for showing his conservative (but not Nazi) colors. He had connections with several groups ultimately involved in the anti-Hitler revolt of July 20, 1944. The Nazis never forgave him for the kind of outspoken opposition which he expressed in his pamphlet of 1932, reprinted below, and beheaded him for complicity in the plot.

SOURCE: Ewald von Kleist-Schmenzin, *Der National Sozialismus. Eine Gefahr* (Berlin: Verlag Neue Gesellschaft, 1932). Reprinted in H-A. Jacobsen and W. Jochmann, eds., *Zur Geschichte des Nationalsozialismus. Ausgewählte Dokumente* (Bielefeld, 1961). Translation by the editor.

NATIONAL SOCIALISM: A MENACE

The impact of National Socialism is assuming dimensions which threaten our future. National Socialism has caused a complete change of attitude among a large number of people, particularly workers, who were originally just nationalistically minded. These people, who were unmoved by the socialistic demands and slogans of the Social Democrats, have adopted these same demands and slogans when they were offered in nationalistic wrappings. Now they are firmly convinced of their truth, and most of them turn with hatred against any kind of personal property. The ideal of nationalism pales into a slogan. The party is made an equivalent of the nation, and loyalty to the fatherland is transferred to the party. The intuitive contradiction between religion and fanatic hatred of private property is gradually leading to disdain and even fervent rejection of religion. The same is true of their attitudes toward monarchy, reverence, tradition, obedience outside of the party discipline, and so on. Mere mention of the word, "religion," has caused eruptions of animalistic rage among the National Socialists. Basically dependable workers neglect their duties under the influence of National Socialism. It appears that this anti-Establishment attitude is being passed on to children as well, in a way previously known only in the Communist districts of large cities. The discipline of the Storm Troopers should not divert us from this fact. The indoctrinated belief in the unique salvation and redeeming qualities of National Socialism, and in Hitler personally, fosters an incredible intolerance. In villages where conservative Nationalists and Social Democrats once lived together tolerably, those Nationalists and National Socialists now often oppose each other like enemy nations. Similar destructive effects are evident among National Socialist farmers, notably the younger ones. Laborers, artisans, lesser job holders and others might go Social Democratic in the foreseeable future, but are more likely to join the Communists. Declining Marxism is reviving because of Hitler; that is the harvest of his dragon's seed.

The devastating effects of National Socialism are making themselves felt in every aspect of life. The fanatic Nazi followers are loyal only to their party. They undercut proper decision-making, even in nonpolitical organizations, and employees neglect their work. In short, everywhere the conditions for living together in human and governmental association are being destroyed.

The youth and educated classes who have succumbed to National Socialism are uprooted and constitute a threat to the future. In general, it is no longer true, except in isolated cases, that National Socialism makes nationalism attractive to Marxists. Those Marxists whom the Nazis converted had already recognized the inadequacy of Marxism in the face of economic distress and would have abandoned it sooner or later. Some of these converts hope to foster the class struggle more successfully with nationalist slogans than international ones. Others were ready for a genuine inner conversion and, attracted by nationalist slogans, are now hooked by the National Socialist ideology that forces them back to socialistic thinking.

These circumstances cannot necessarily be ascribed to all National Socialists, but generally things are developing thus and, in fact, have accelerated in the last few weeks. The National Socialist assault on the very foundation of human and political life is even more dangerous than that of the Social Democrats. Because of its misleading name and the deliberate duplicity of its leadership, people who would normally resist an open attack on their way of life succumb to National Socialism. Public National Socialist agitation is unprincipled and thorough, especially in small gatherings; but the propaganda on a personal level is even more ruthless. Even in this region, where the National Socialists still pretend to support conservative national views and behave somewhat peaceably, their person-to-person agitation consists of an alarming amount of purely Communistic hatemongering. This incitement to destruction persists and engulfs all the other professed national aspirations. One is constantly amazed how few people see, or want to see, this danger.

National Socialism would never have taken this dangerous upsurge if nationally minded groups had openly divorced themselves from it. The view tolerated in those groups, that National Socialism should be seen as a nationalist movement with just a few shortcomings, has produced danger for our future that can only be countered by the greatest of effort. During the second presidential election, the slogans of the *Reichslandbund*, the Crown Prince, the United Patriotic Associations, and others . . . were so bereft of political instinct that they drove hundreds of thousands of nationalists over to Hitler and exposed them to spiritual corruption and brain washing. There were also failings on the part of the German National Peoples Party. At very least after the Harzburg Meeting [a demonstrative gathering of some conservatives and Nazis], or by the time that candidates were nominated for the first presidential ballot, it was clear that a workable coalition would never be possible with National Socialism and Hitler. After that, all the divisive and incriminating remarks of Hitler should have been used against the Nazis, with dignity but with ruthlessness, to expose the true nature of this party. But that occurred only partially and insufficiently. This weakness caused the loss of many nationalist adherents because they were left in confusion as to the nature and goals of National Socialism and Hitler.

The flow of followers to Hitler is largely a movement of fear and desperation. In fear of what may yet come, people flock to the National Socialist Party in senseless despair because they hope that the mass of voters, by casting like ballots, can avert the troubles threatening us and can above all spare the individual from personal involvement. Many of them put all their hopes in Hitler and do not want to see the shortcomings of National Socialism. Those who stick with the German National Party only do so because they believe that a counterbalance is still somehow necessary. No wonder there is such confusion of thought. If political action is to be successful for Germany's future, . . . our struggle against the aberrations of National Socialism must be waged promptly, with dignity and earnestness, but with rigorous determination.

Religious attitudes are crucial in separating conservative thinking from National Socialism. The foundation of conservative policy is that obedience to God, and faith in Him, must determine the whole of public life. National Socialism is based on a fundamentally different point of view in which questions of faith must, of course, be dropped as irrelevant. Hitler actually recognizes race and its demands as the highest law of governmental action; if at times he says otherwise, that does not make any difference. His materialism cannot be reconciled with Christianity. According to Hitler, the state does not have the responsibility to foster creativity, but only to guard the racial heritage! . . . Hitler is primarily interested in breeding healthy bodies; he stresses emphatically that building character is only of secondary importance. This conviction is unacceptable. . . . Inseparably connected with National Socialism are a superficial search for happiness and a streak of liberal rationalism that is expressed in its motto, group welfare has priority over individual desire. National Socialism leans increasingly toward the liberal conception of the greatest good of the greatest number. For us, the nation *per se* is not the ultimate measure, but rather the will

of God which obligates us to live for the nation. That is a fundamental difference.

It is difficult to tell how National Socialism officially views mar-
riage and the family, but it is evident from numerous comments of
well-known Nazis that they accept many views which we must
resolutely reject.

It is certain that National Socialism does not favor monarchism
and is definitely republican in conviction. The core of its domestic
political program is synonymous with Social Democracy on economic, social, and tax policy, and largely also in agrarian proposals.
Hitler is demanding continuation of the socialist policy which
contributed to our economic collapse and harmed the workers as
well. His excessive agitation against property and capital and his
unscrupulous provocation of people to militancy, threaten to destroy every possibility of reconstruction by arousing instincts of
envy that will not easily be controlled.

Hitler has declared that efforts to forge a united front are superfluous. How could an honest coalition be established with such a
man?

The National Socialists said they were prepared to join a cabinet
formed by Democrat Gessler as Chancellor and with Brüning as
Foreign Minister. Where does that leave their loud campaign
against the Establishment with which they meant to catch the
voters? Hitler has declared to a foreign correspondent that the
Versailles Treaty cannot simply be torn up but must be replaced at
a conference by a new one. Where does that leave the campaign he
has hitherto fought against our foreign policy? Where does that
put the slogan of a struggle for freedom? Hitler stated publicly in
Lauenburg that he was not prepared to defend our borders against
a Polish invasion as long as the present government was in power.
This statement has been repeated and confirmed in writing by
other National Socialists who were present. This declaration
openly means abandonment of the German nation and actually
encourages the Poles to invade. *Hitler and the party have publicly
set themselves above the fatherland*. Given such an attitude, can
one expect them to join a coalition government and conduct
foreign policy in the national interest?

A glance at National Socialist newspapers, pamphlets, and other
propaganda should convince anyone (who is still willing to look)
of the unscrupulous dishonesty of the movement and its leaders.

Their arguments can be cited both for and against almost any position. Since people are not aware of this duplicity, it is no wonder that they succumb to National Socialism in their ignorance. We can no longer tolerate the pretence that National Socialism is the one movement that can save the nation. This delusion must be destroyed together with the totally false image that the people have of Hitler. In light of the foregoing, I ask: have we conservatives anything left in common with National Socialism? Surely we must recognize that its essential assumptions are a menace to the nation and to unselfish patriotic convictions. The many respectable groups presently cooperating with National Socialism will progressively have less power to influence the nature of the movement. In the French Revolution, with its appeal to national striving for freedom and socialism, a vanguard of selfless and confused visionaries prepared the way for destruction; similarly under National Socialism the nationalist elements will involuntarily set the stage for a national disaster. A National Socialist government will inevitably end in chaos. Their rulers would soon be swept away by the unmanageable tide of upheaval they created. We conservative nationalists should no longer abet the destruction caused by Nazi slogans of national interest and by Hitler's romantic image.

Hopes for a coalition government are at the moment nonexistent, but even if one could assume the prospects were favorable, how promising would they be? We conservatives are united in our common determination to supplant the present democratic leaders. We only seek this change so that a different policy can be pursued, one which will save the nation. The National Socialists, however, want to overthrow the present governmental system in order to assume power themselves. Once arrived, they will do all they can to dissolve the coalition and would ally with any other faction if necessary. Considering their numerical strength, the National Socialists would certainly not leave the important offices to administration experts. We would achieve nothing but support of a policy that would be more disastrous than the previous one. It would be a fateful error to assume that National Socialism could ever abandon its ambitions for total control. These intentions are as determined as the claim of the Roman Catholic Church to absolute rule. Only in defeat can National Socialism be coerced to offer limited cooperation.

To summarize: it is the task of all conservative forces, like the

German National Peoples Party and other patriotic organizations, resolutely to renounce cooperation with the politically fashionable Nazi disease; for the sake of Germany's future, we cannot tolerate the destruction of the remaining genuine conservative principles that are a necessary part of the foundations of the new state. We must give up the mistaken belief that favorable political change can only be brought about by the enervating elections that characterize this parliamentary system. We must redouble our political action and bring it elsewhere to bear on the political process. The thought and action of the people must be focused on crucial matters. It is always just a few individuals who institute crucial and favorable political change. But behind them must stand dedicated men whose every thought and action is determined by unselfish patriotism, who are united by a deep inner communion and whose whole posture is determined by unshakeable faith.

VI

National Socialism Seizes Power, 1933

THE NAZIS suffered such a serious setback in the Reichstag elections of November 1932 that the *New York Times* predicted in its New Year's preview of January 1, 1933, that Hitler's movement was no longer a threat. But the *Times*, and many others, were wrong. The government of General von Schleicher quickly fell into disarray. Von Papen negotiated again with Hitler and brought renewed pressure on Hindenburg. On January 30, 1933, the aged president reluctantly made Hitler chancellor of a coalition cabinet in which three Nazis seemed to be overwhelmingly counterbalanced by the presence of nine reliable conservatives, with von Papen as vice-chancellor. Another round of elections was called for March 5, 1933, to confirm or reject the new government.

If the conservatives were confident that they had Hitler safely fenced in, the Nazis were jubilant that they could now fully command public attention and use any means to stimulate, confuse, cajole, or force Germans into voting for them. Their propaganda onslaught began with Hitler's proclamation of February 1 and culminated, after the Reichstag fire of February 27, in a five-day frenzy of theatrical politics, suppression, and terror unequalled in the history of any other modern nation. "Give me four years time," Hitler cried, "and you will not recognize Germany!" The results of the last election of the Weimar republic showed that still Hitler could not get a clear majority in his own right. He had to continue with the conservatives, combining his 44 percent of the vote with von Papen's 8 percent to give their government a 52 percent support, just barely a legal majority.

Thereafter it was a complicated game for Hitler. Publicly he paraded solemnly with the conservatives, flew his swastika banners alongside the officially re-established imperial German colors, and tolerated a momentary revival of Prussian traditions and symbols. Beneath the surface, however, his system was already at work: suppressing Communists and Socialists; establishing extralegal judicial procedures that led into concentration camps; forcing early retirement upon unenthusiastic public officials; reducing the opposition press with a variety of technical devices; and pressing a Nazi image upon all organizations of education and culture. Only two opponents were openly and ruthlessly attacked, the "Marxists" (with little distinction between Communists and Social Democrats) and the Jews. That much violence was publicly tolerated at the time. Many of the Germans who cheered an imminent return of good times and accepted the Nazi procedures of "reeducation," "rehabilitation," or "adjustment of social ratios" would only learn what it was really all about when they were themselves later entrapped in the Nazi network.

22. Hitler's Proclamation to the German Nation, February 1, 1933

SOURCE: R. de Roussy de Sales, *Adolf Hitler: My New Order* (New York: Reynal & Hitchcock, 1941), pp. 142–147.

More than fourteen years have passed since the unhappy day when the German people, blinded by promises from foes at home and abroad, lost touch with honor and freedom, thereby losing all. Since that day of treachery, the Almighty has withheld his blessing from our people. Dissension and hatred descended upon us. With profound distress millions of the best German men and women from all walks of life have seen the unity of the nation vanishing away, dissolving in a confusion of political and personal opinions, economic interests, and ideological differences. Since that day, as so often in the past, Germany has presented a picture of heartbreaking disunity. We never received the equality and fraternity we had been promised, and we lost our liberty to boot. For when our nation lost its political place in the world, it soon lost its unity of spirit and will. . . .

We are firmly convinced that the German nation entered the fight in 1914 without the slightest feeling of guilt on its part and filled only with the desire to defend the Fatherland which had been attacked and to preserve the freedom, nay, the very existence, of the German people. This being so, we can only see in the disastrous fate which has overtaken us since those November days of 1918 the result of our collapse at home. But the rest of the world, too, has suffered no less since then from overwhelming crises. The balance of power which had evolved in the course of history, and which formerly played no small part in bringing about the understanding of the necessity for an internal solidarity of the nations, with all its advantages for trade and commerce, has been set on one side. The insane conception of victors and vanquished destroyed the confidence existing between nations, and, at the same time, the industry of the entire world.

The misery of our people is horrible to behold! Millions of the industrial proletariat are unemployed and starving; the whole of the middle class and the small artisans have been impoverished. When this collapse finally reaches the German peasants, we will be faced with an immeasurable disaster. For then not only shall a nation collapse, but a two-thousand-year-old inheritance, some of the loftiest products of human culture and civilization.

All about us the warning signs of this collapse are apparent. Communism with its method of madness is making a powerful and insidious attack upon our dismayed and shattered nation. It seeks to poison and disrupt in order to hurl us into an epoch of chaos. . . . This negative, destroying spirit spared nothing of all that is highest and most valuable. Beginning with the family, it has undermined the very foundations of morality and faith and scoffs at culture and business, nation and Fatherland, justice and honor. Fourteen years of Marxism have ruined Germany; one year of Bolshevism would destroy her. The richest and fairest territories of the world would be turned into a smoking heap of ruins. Even the sufferings of the last decade and a half could not be compared to the misery of a Europe in the heart of which the red flag of destruction had been hoisted. The thousands of wounded, the hundreds of dead which this inner strife has already cost Germany should be a warning of the storm which would come. . . .

In those hours when our hearts were troubled about the life and the future of the German nation, the aged leader of the World War appealed to us. He called to those of us in nationalist parties and leagues to struggle under him once more, in unity and loyalty, for the salvation of the German nation. This time the front lines are at home. The venerable Reichspräsident has allied himself with us in this noble endeavor. And as leaders of the nation and the national Government we vow to God, to our conscience, and to our people that we will faithfully and resolutely fulfill the task conferred upon us.

The inheritance which has fallen to us is a terrible one. The task with which we are faced is the hardest which has fallen to German statesmen within the memory of man. But we are all filled with unbounded confidence for we believe in our people and their imperishable virtues. Every class and every individual must help us to found the new Reich.

The National Government will regard it as its first and foremost duty to revive in the nation the spirit of unity and cooperation. It will preserve and defend those basic principles on which our nation has been built. It regards Christianity as the foundation of our national morality, and the family as the basis of national life. . . .

Turbulent instincts must be replaced by a national discipline as the guiding principle of our national life. All those institutions which are the strongholds of the energy and vitality of our nation will be taken under the special care of the Government.

The National Government intends to solve the problem of the reorganization of trade and commerce with two four-year plans:

The German farmer must be rescued in order that the nation may be supplied with the necessities of life. . . .

A concerted and all-embracing attack must be made on unemployment in order that the German working class may be saved from ruin. . . .

The November parties have ruined the German peasantry in fourteen years.

In fourteen years they have created an army of millions of unemployed. The National Government will, with iron determination and unshakable steadfastness of purpose, put through the following plan:

Within four years the German peasant must be rescued from the quagmire into which he has fallen.

Within four years unemployment must be finally overcome. At the same time the conditions necessary for a revival in trade and commerce are provided.

The National Government will couple with this tremendous

task of reorganizing business life a reorganization of the administrative and fiscal systems of the Reich, of the Federal States, and the Communes.

Only when this has been done can the idea of a continued federal existence of the entire Reich be fully realized. . . .

Compulsory labor-service and the back-to-the-land policy are two of the basic principles of this program.

The securing of the necessities of life will include the performance of social duties to the sick and aged.

In economical administration, the promotion of employment, the preservation of the farmer, as well as in the exploitation of individual initiative, the Government sees the best guarantee for the avoidance of any experiments which would endanger the currency. . . .

As regards its foreign policy the National Government considers its highest mission to be the securing of the right to live and the restoration of freedom to our nation. Its determination to bring to an end the chaotic state of affairs in Germany will assist in restoring to the community of nations a State of equal value and, above all, a State which must have equal rights. It is impressed with the importance of its duty to use this nation of equal rights as an instrument for the securing and maintenance of that peace which the world requires today more than ever before.

May the good will of all others assist in the fulfillment of this our earnest wish for the welfare of Europe and of the whole world.

Great as is our love for our Army as the bearer of our arms and the symbol of our great past, we should be happy if the world, by reducing its armaments, would see to it that we need never increase our own.

If, however, Germany is to experience this political and economic revival and conscientiously fulfill her duties toward the other nations, one decisive step is absolutely necessary first: the overcoming of the destroying menace of communism in Germany. We of this Government feel responsible for the restoration of orderly life in the nation and for the final elimination of class madness and class struggle. We recognize no classes, we see only the German people, millions of peasants, bourgeois, and workers who will either overcome together the difficulties of these times or be overcome by them. We are firmly resolved and we have taken our oath. *Since the present Reichstag is incapable of lending support to this work, we ask the German people whom we represent to perform the task themselves.*

Reichspräsident von Hindenburg has called upon us to bring about the revival of the German nation. Unity is our tool. Therefore we now appeal to the German people to support this reconciliation. The National Government wishes to work and it will work. It did not ruin the German nation for fourteen years, but now it will lead the nation back to health. It is determined to make well in four years the ills of fourteen years. But the National Government cannot make the work of reconstruction dependent upon the approval of those who wrought destruction. The Marxist parties and their lackeys have had fourteen years to show what they can do. The result is a heap of ruins.

Now, people of Germany, give us four years and then pass judgment upon us. In accordance with Field Marshal von Hindenburg's command we shall begin now. May God Almighty give our work His blessing, strengthen our purpose, and endow us with wisdom and the trust of our people, for we are fighting not for ourselves but for Germany.

23. Pages from Goebbels' Diary, January–May, 1933

Joseph Goebbels, a man of great talent in public relations and enormous energy, was Hitler's most important associate in the Nazi party. As district leader of Berlin, he successfully fought his opponents in the streets and in the press—he was editor of the Berlin Nazi daily, *Der Angriff* [*The Attack*]. He clearly outdid the Führer as a speaker, but his personality aroused misgiving instead of devotion. He prostituted his considerable intellectual abilities to insane ends and was the only important Nazi to die with Hitler in the ruins of the Reich chancellory.

The following excerpts from his diary indicate his ruthless effectiveness as a propagandist. They illuminate four major events in the Nazi consolidation of power: (1) media manipulation after the Reichstag fire, February 27; (2) the shotgun wedding of National Socialism with Prussian-German tradition at the Potsdam Garrison Church ceremonies of March 21; (3) instigation of the anti-Jewish boycott of April 1; and (4) the transformation of May Day, the great working-class holiday, into a celebration of Nazi solidarity. The diary was published in Germany in early 1934. With its omission of major facts or deliberate distortion of them, it became a further weapon in the Nazi propaganda arsenal.

SOURCE: Joseph Goebbels, *My Part in Germany's Fight* (London: Hutchinson Publishing Group Ltd., 1935), pp. 207–208, 211, 219–227, 234–238, 251–253. Reprinted by permission of the publisher.

January 30th, 1933.

It seems like a dream. The Chancellory is ours. The Leader is already working [there]. We stand in the window upstairs, watching hundreds and thousands of people march past the aged President of the Reich and the young Chancellor in the flaming torchlight, shouting their joy and gratitude.

At noon we are all at the Kaiserhof, waiting. The Leader is with the President of the Reich. The inward excitement almost takes our breath away. In the street the crowd stands silently waiting between the Kaiserhof and the Chancellory. What is happening there? We are torn between doubt, hope, joy, and despair. We have been deceived too often to be able whole-heartedly to believe in the great miracle.

Chief-of-Staff Röhm stands at the window the whole time, watching the door of the Chancellory from which the Leader must emerge. We shall be able to judge by his face if the interview was happy.

Torturing hours of waiting! At last a car draws up in front of the entrance. The crowd cheers. They seem to feel that a great change is taking place or has already begun.

The Leader is coming.

A few moments later he is with us. He says nothing, and we all remain silent also. His eyes are full of tears. It has come! The Leader is appointed Chancellor. He has already been sworn in by the President of the Reich. The final decision has been made. Germany is at a turning-point in her history. . . .

The day passes like a dream. Everything is like a fairy tale. Slowly the evening closes in over the Capital of the Reich. At seven o'clock Berlin resembles a swarming beehive. And then the torchlight procession begins. Endlessly, endlessly, from seven o'clock in the evening until one o'clock in the morning crowds march by the Chancellory. Storm Troopers, Hitler-youths, civilians, men, women, fathers with their children held up high to see the Leader's window. Indescribable enthusiasm fills the streets. A few yards from the Chancellory, the President of the Reich stands at his window, a towering, dignified, heroic figure, invested with a touch of old-time marvel. Now and then with his cane he beats time to the military marches. Hundreds and thousands and hundreds of thousands march past our windows in never-ending, uniform rhythm.

The rising of a nation!

Germany has awakened!

In a spontaneous explosion of joy the people espouse the German Revolution. . . .

February 3rd, 1933.

I talk over the beginning election campaign in detail with the Leader. The struggle is a light one now, since we are able to employ all means of the State. Radio and Press are at our disposal. We shall achieve a masterpiece of propaganda. Even money is not lacking this time.

The only difficulty lies in the organization of the contest. We decide that the Leader is to speak in all towns having their own broadcasting station. We transmit the broadcast to the entire people, and give listeners-in a clear idea of all that occurs at our meetings.

I am going to introduce the Leader's address, in which I shall try to convey to the hearers the magical atmosphere of our huge demonstrations.

Late at night the Leader flies to Munich to attend some urgent conferences.

The Radio causes me some trouble. All the important positions are still held by the same old-System profiteers. They have to be got rid of as soon as possible, that is before the fifth of March, lest they endanger the election.

The Propaganda Department of the Reich is moving to Berlin, in order to be able to direct the contest with all its forces concentrated.

The agitation in rough outline is ready. So we can set to work immediately. We have not much time to lose.

Deliver an address to the Hitler-youths at Ulap in the evening. It is wonderful to be among these boys, and able to speak to them in their own fashion. . . .

February 21*st*, 1933.

We decide to call up the German people on March 4th for a "Day of the Awakening Nation." The Leader is going to deliver an address to the whole Reich in the evening from Königsberg. In an unprecedented concentration of all the possibilities of propaganda, the campaign is to be brought to its culminating point. That will bring the last wobblers over to our side. Our propaganda is acknowledged not only by the German, but also the international Press, to be a model, and unique. We have gained such extensive experience in this matter during the past election campaign that we are able to win a victory over our adversaries without difficulty by our better methods. As it is, the other side is so intimidated that it hardly utters a sound. We will now show them what one can do with the Apparatus of the State, if one understands how to use it.

The rotary presses are thundering and vomiting forth our election material by the million. A wonderful song of political force and activity.

In the evening we go to the Opera with the Leader, for recreation, and for the first time hear Wagner's *Liebesverbot*. This work already contains much of what came later in Wagner's work. Although the compositon is as yet primitive, the music on the whole is bold, and handled in a masterly manner.

At home the Leader tells us about the Kapp-Putsch, and all the other unsuccessful enterprises in which he somehow always took part. He was always for direct action; and if he was unable to undertake action of his own, on principle he took part in the actions of others.

One could listen to the Leader for hours. . . .

February 27*th*, 1933.

The vast propaganda action for the "Day of the Awakening Nation" has been settled in every detail. It will be a wonderful spectacle throughout Germany.

The Leader is back from Munich. His speeches there and at

Nuremberg have been a huge success. He is delighted with the result of our campaign.

Give instructions to the Press for the preparation of the "Day of the Awakening Nation!" We now are concentrating the entire public interest on this sole point. We shall succeed in making this day an unheard-of success.

Work at home in the evening. The Leader comes to dine at nine o'clock. We have some music and talk. Suddenly a 'phone call from Dr. Hanfstaengl: "The Reichstag is on fire!" I take this for a bit of wild fantasy and refuse to report it to the Leader. I ask for news wherever possible and at last obtain the dreadful confirmation: it is true! The great dome is all ablaze. Incendiarism! I immediately inform the Leader, and we hasten at top speed down the Charlottenburg road to the Reichstag. The whole builing is aflame. Clambering over thick fire-hoses we reach the great lobby by gateway number two. Goering meets us on the way, and soon von Papen also arrives. That this is the work of incendiaries has been ascertained to be the fact at various spots. There is no doubt but that Communism has made a last attempt to cause disorder by means of fire and terror, in order to grasp the power during the general panic.

The decisive moment arrives. Goering is amazingly active. Not for a moment does the Leader lose his composure; wonderful to watch him giving his orders here, the same man who sat at table with us, chatting cheerfully, half an hour ago.

The Hall of Full-session presents a desolate spectacle of devastation. The flames have reached the ceiling, which threatens to crash every moment.

Now we have to act.

Goering at once suppresses the entire Communist and Social Democrat Press. Officials of the Communist Party are arrested during the night. The S.A. is warned to stand by for every contingency.

Dash to the district, to inform everybody, and to prepare for all eventualities. The Leader confers with a hurriedly summoned Cabinet council. We meet again shortly after at the Kaiserhof and discuss the situation. One culprit has already been caught, a young Dutch Communist called van der Lubbe.

Drive with the Leader to the editorial office of the *Völkische*

Beobachter. We both set to work there at once, writing leading articles and proclamations. I retire to the district hall, to be able to dictate without being interrupted. In the middle of the night Councillor of State Diels, of the Prussian Ministry of Interior, comes to give me a detailed report as to all the steps that have hitherto been taken. The arrests have been effected without difficulty. The entire Communist and Democratic Press is already suppressed. If resistance is offered, it will be "line clear" for the S.A.

It is already morning when I meet the Leader again at the Kaiserhof. The Press is in order. The direction of our action has been set by events themselves. Now we can set to work with a vengeance. The Communists will have been very much mistaken. They have proposed our downfall, but have dealt themselves the mortal blow.

Two S.A. men shot in Berlin during the night. They will not go unrevenged.

Spent, and fagged out, I get home at eight in the morning. One hour's sleep and then it is "shoulder to the wheel" again at once.

February 28th, 1933.

Compose an effective placard against the Socialists and Communists. No Marxist papers are published in the whole Reich any more. Goering has initiated energetic measures in Prussia against the "Red" parties; it will end with their complete destruction.

The Cabinet has issued a sharp decree against the Communist Party. This decree provides for capital punishment. This is necessary. The people demand it.

Arrests upon arrests. Now the "Red" pest is being thoroughly rooted out. No sign of resistance anywhere. The opponents seem to be so overwhelmed by our energetic action that they dare no longer offer resistance.

Inspect the effects of the fire in the Reichstag. The Hall of Full-session is a sad picture of devastation. Wreckage upon wreckage. The Communist Party will have to pay for it dearly. Indescribable indignation at this cowardly *attentat* is universally expressed.

Now work proceeds smoothly. The worst is over. We hope that the last breakdown is happily overcome. Only a few days more and we shall be able to celebrate our great triumph.

To live is again a joy. . . .

March 4th, 1933.

The S.A. marches through Berlin in endless columns. Last preparations for the election. The struggle has reached its climax. The whole line to Hamburg is shrouded in fog; so we cannot start by plane, but have to go by train. Work, and confer, on the way. Things at Hamburg hang by a hair. Directly after the election we shall take energetic measures there. The meeting is excellently prepared, and the Leader delivers by far the best address of this campaign. He rises to marvelous heights of oratory. The audience is greatly enthused.

Fly back to Berlin early next morning; effect an intermediate landing, and start again at once, after having got through the most urgent work, on a lovely trip to Königsberg. The great "Day of the Awakening Nation" has come. Land at two o'clock in the coronation town of Königsberg.

The last preparations made for the meeting in the evening. All will go off splendidly.

I outline the day's events, and describe the anticipated effect the celebration will have. The Leader speaks with utmost fervor and devotion. When at the end he mentions that the President of the Reich and he had clasped hands—the one having released Prussia from the enemy as a Field-Marshal, the other having done his duty in the West as simple soldier—solemn silence reigns and deep emotion holds the whole assembly. The Netherland Hymn of Thanksgiving, the last verse of which is drowned in the clamor of the bells from the Königsberg Cathedral, forms a mighty chorus to crown his speech. This hymn goes throbbing on the ethereal waves of the Radio over the whole of Germany. Forty million people are now standing in the squares and in the streets, or are sitting in the Bierhallen and their homes by the Radio, and become conscious that the new era has dawned. At this moment hundreds of thousands will decide to follow Hitler, and fight in his spirit for the revival of the nation.

We hear at the aerodrome it is impossible to fly tonight. The route is shrouded in dense fog, and therefore a landing at Berlin is out of the question. We have to return to the hotel, where we find a pile of telegrams from all parts of the Reich. Indescribable enthusiasm reigns in Berlin. The whole city has risen. Throngs of people are marching through the streets singing. The S.A. has marched to the strains of the band through the Brandenburger Tor. Hundreds of thousands upon hundreds of thousands are on foot in the city, as well as the suburbs. All over the country the fires of freedom are blazing on the hill-tops. The whole of Germany resembles a great, luminous beacon. All has come true as we hoped for, the "Day of the Awakening Nation." A rising of the people!

March 5th, 1933.

Before leaving Königsberg we go to a small polling booth and record our votes. The Returning Officer is highly astonished to see the Leader suddenly step into his office and cast his voting paper into the ballot-box like everybody else.

Beneath us lie the fog-banks and rain-clouds, the motors thunder their jubilant song. The sun burns down on us. At one o'clock we break through the fog and shoot down on to the Berlin aerodrome. The whole city is one mass of flags.

It will be a splendid victory.

In the afternoon we are assembled at the Chancellory, anxiously waiting for the first results to come through. The Leader is as quiet and composed as ever; this time things can hardly go wrong.

Hear the *Walküre* in the evening at the State Opera. Wagner's sublime music is mingled with the sound of marching of the Stahl-helm who have celebrated their great day in Berlin, and are now passing the Opera House.

Then the first results come through. Success upon success, fantastic and incredible.

When we get back to the Chancellory after the performance the victory is ours. It is far greater than any of us had dared to hope. But what do figures signify any longer? We are masters of the Reich and of Prussia; all other parties have been definitely beaten.

Long work crowned by success at last!

Germany has awakened!

South Germany has specially taken the lead in the entire electoral success. That is all the more gratifying since it enables us to take radical measures against a policy of Separatist Federalism.

Berlin alone records over a million votes. Incredible figures! We are all intoxicated with success. New and quite unforeseen surprises turn up every hour. The Leader is overjoyed.

Down in the Wilhelmplatz huge motley crowds of people congratulate the Leader. So there we are! Now the constructive part of the German Revolution can begin.

Drop into bed at four in the morning dead-tired but thoroughly happy. Now we have achieved our aim! . . .

March 22nd, 1933.

The great day of Potsdam will be unforgettable in its historical significance.

In the morning I drive with the Leader to the Luisenstädtische Friedhof (cemetery). We do not go to church, but visit the graves of our dead comrades.

On our way from Berlin to Potsdam we pass through huge crowds of cheering people. Potsdam is smothered in flags and green garlands. Only with difficulty can the road be cleared for the Cabinet and the Members of Parliament to pass. We are nearly suffocated by the multitude. Hindenburg enters the Garrison Church (Garnisonkirche) together with the Leader. A deep silence reigns. Briefly and solemnly the President of the Reich reads his message to the Members of the Reichstag and the German people. His voice is clear and firm. In our midst stands a man who unites whole generations.

Then the Leader speaks. His tone is dominating and when he ends we are all much moved. I sit near Hindenburg and observe tears in his eyes. All rise from their seats and enthusiastically acclaim the ancient Field-Marshal, who shakes hands with the young Chancellor.

An historical moment! Germany's shield of honor has been washed clean. The banners with our eagles are rising once more.

Hindenburg deposits laurel wreaths at the tombs of the great Prussian kings, amidst the salvos of the guns.

Now the trumpets blare forth, the President of the Reich stands on an elevated platform, the Field-Marshal's baton in his hand, and salutes the Reichswehr, S.A., S.S., and Stahlhelm, who march past him.

He stands there at the salute; the whole scene is bathed in sunshine; the hand of God is held in invisible benediction over the gray town of Prussian grandeur and duty.

The Cabinet sits in council at noon in the Ministry of the Interior. A bill about the unauthorized wearing of uniforms, which provides heavy penalties, is passed. The Full-session sits in council. The burned-out Reichstag offers no accommodation for it. We have moved into the Kroll Opera House.

It is a solemn moment when the Leader enters the Kroll Opera House. Formalities are settled in half an hour which formerly took nearly a week. Goering is re-elected President, and introduces himself with a firm and manly speech.

In the evening it is hardly possible to get through the huge crowds of people marching down the Linden in endless torchlight procession. Trams and buses are full of singing and cheering men, women, and children. An amazing, unique spectacle. If one were recognized, one would probably be suffocated.

A lovely performance of the *Meistersinger* at the Linden Opera ends the evening. Everything is steeped in music! Now the radiant "Awake" Chorus has regained its true significance.

Late in the evening General von Epp gives me a description of the events in Bavaria. Everything has passed off quickly and with precision. The resistance offered by the Königsmacher was merely ludicrous. It was broken at once.

Wednesday: I finally move into the Ministry. My new rooms are quite to my taste, sunny and airy. Here it is possible to work.

My builders and bricklayers and I spend the evening together. They are old S.A. comrades. I give them their treat. They are fine chaps who, of course, were only too glad to help me play the bureaucrats that trick.

March 24th, 1933.

The Leader delivers an address to the German Reichstag. He is in good form. His speech is that of an expert statesman. Many in the House see him for the first time, and are much impressed by his demeanour. A two-hours' interval offers the parties the opportunity to decide about their attitude.

The leader of the Socialists, Wels, actually returns a reply which is one long woeful tale of one who arrives too late. All we have accomplished the Social Democrats had wanted to do. Now they complain of terrorism and injustice. When Wels ends, the Leader mounts the platform and demolishes him. Never before has anyone been so thoroughly defeated. The Leader speaks freely, and well. The House is in an uproar of applause, laughter, and enthusiasm. An incredible success!

The Zentrum, and even the Party of the State (Staatspartei), affirm the law of authorization. It is valid for four years and guarantees freedom of action to the Government. It is accepted by a majority of four to five; only the Socialists vote against it. Now we are also constitutionally masters of the Reich.

A member of the Cabinet, Labor-Commissioner Gereke, is accused of heavy offences. The Cabinet unanimously carries a motion to have him arrested at once. Only thus is it possible to eradicate corruption. One must show no mercy, neither to the humble nor to the mighty.

Friday: In the Cabinet, Hugenberg thanks the Leader for the adroitness and straightforwardness of his policy, and especially for the spendid snubbing he gave the Marxist leader, Wels.

I bring forward the Bill to make the first of May a national holiday for the whole German people, as the first introduced into Parliament, and am entrusted by the Cabinet with carrying it through. We will plan it on a vast scale, and for the first time unite the whole German people in one sole demonstration.

Now the discussions with the Trade Unions begin. We shall not have any peace before we have entirely captured these.

The horrors propaganda abroad gives us much trouble. The many Jews who have left Germany have set all foreign countries against us. Now we have to suffer from the omission of the former Government to make propaganda abroad. We are defencelessly exposed to the attacks of our adversaries.

We are already beginning to prepare for the 1st of May. This festival is to be a brilliant piece of organization and demonstration.

Write a convincing and well-founded article for a large English paper against the horrors propaganda. We do what we can. But this is quite inadequate. . . .

March 27th, 1933.

Dictate a sharp article against the Jewish horrors propaganda. The proclamation of the boycott already makes the whole clan tremble in their shoes. One has to employ these methods. Generosity does not impress the Jews. One has to show them one is equal to anything.

Transmit my article at once to Munich by wire, so as to have it delivered to the Leader. He will decide when the boycott is to take place.

The Jewish Press is whimpering with alarm and fear. All Jewish organizations proclaim their loyalty to the Government.

We work through interviews as much as possible; but only a really extensive movement can now help us out of our calamity.

A beautiful spring smiles over Germany. . . .

May 1st, 1933.

The great Day of the German Nation has arrived. Yesterday it looked like rain, but today the sun is shining gloriously. Real Hitler weather! All will now go off splendidly. Things depend no longer on the way the day passes off, but on the intrinsic value of this national gesture and the meaning that attaches to it.

In the morning the Berlin school-children parade in the Lustgarten. Already the road there presents an overwhelming spectacle. Wherever one looks, Unter den Linden, all over the Lustgarten, children, children, and still more children. I speak to them from the depth of my heart.

It is easy to speak to children if one understands their little souls. Then wild shouts of joy! The President of the Reich and the Leader appear, sitting side by side in the car. Age and youth united! A beautiful symbol of the new Germany which we have erected.

Proud and happy, Harald presents a large bunch of roses to President Hindenburg.

The President speaks to the children as if he were a contemporary of our own. He tells them to be loyal, persevering, industrious, and full of respect toward the past. The Leader gives three cheers for him, in which the children join with enthusiasm and fervor.

Our passage through the crowd of boys and girls resembles a triumphal procession. The Tempelhofer Feld teems with the multitude. Berlin is already on its way there, lock, stock, and barrel, workmen and *bourgeois*, high and humble, employers and employees; now these differences are obliterated and the German People only is on the march.

A few years ago the machine-guns were rattling in Berlin.

In the aerodrome we receive the workmen's delegations from the entire Reich, who have come to Berlin by air. The faces of these serious, stalwart men express pure joy. At midday they are invited by the Leader to lunch and afterwards they are received by the President of the Reich. This reception is deeply affecting in its monumental simplicity. The great soldier of three wars, the guardian angel of the German nation, stands in the midst of the poorest of the land and holds out his hand to enter into an alliance with them.

Now the multitude is slowly winding its way through Berlin. An endless continuous stream of men, women, and children flows to the Tempelhofer Feld. Toward seven in the evening the report comes through that a million and a half people have assembled there. Similar news come from towns and villages all over the country.

I sit in the rear of the Leader's car as he drives in triumph through the masses of working people lining the streets from the Chancellory to the Tempelhofer Feld. An indescribable drive! In the Tempelhofer Feld it is impossible to survey this enormous ocean of people. Dazzling rays of the flashlights sweep over it, and one recognizes nothing but a gray mass, shoulder to shoulder.

I say a few introductory words, and then proclaim a minute's interval of silence in honor of the Essen miners who have come to grief the same day. The whole nation stands motionless. This silence is universally observed, intimated by wireless, throughout towns and countries. A touching moment of unity and alliance of all classes and professions.

Then the Leader speaks. He once more summarizes what we are and what we wish to achieve. He invests Work with a new ethic. The working classes now comprise all true Germans. The nation has regained its real meaning.

Now we will work and not despair.

Germany is at stake, its future, and the future of our children.

A wild frenzy of enthusiasm has seized the crowd. Grandly and trustfully the Horst-Wessel Hymn rises to the eternal evening sky. The voices of the million and a half gathered in the Tempelhofer Feld are borne on the ether over the whole country, over towns and villages, and choruses will be joining everywhere, by the workmen of the Ruhr district, the sailors in the Hamburg harbor, the woodcutters from Bavaria, and the lonely peasant up in the north by the Masurian lake-sides. Nobody can hold himself aloof;

here we all belong together, and it is no longer a hollow phrase: to say we have grown to be one sole people of brothers.

And he who showed us the way is now standing upright in his car, on his way back to his workroom in the Wilhelmstrasse, through a "Via triumphalis" formed around him by the living bodies of men.

Tomorrow we shall seize the houses of the Trade Unions. There will hardly be any resistance anywhere. The struggle is going on!

Up in the Chancellory we stand with the Leader in the window of his home. The songs and cheers of the crowds marching off from the Tempelhofer Feld reach us from afar.

Berlin does not dream of going to rest, and in unison with this huge city the entire Reich is yet thrilling with joy and emotion, and is conscious of the great hour that compasses the junction of two eras, the past and the future.

This moment a column of marchers turns into the Wilhelmstrasse. Swastika banners float above it and the red flags are dipped before the Leader to greet him and his work in silence and veneration.

And out of the youthful throats Horst-Wessel's eternal hymn bursts forth: "Now Hitler's flags are flying far and wide. . . ."

We remain together till daybreak.

The long night is over.

The sun has risen again on Germany!

24. Final Reichstag Address of Otto Wels, March 23, 1933

Between 1912 and 1933 Social Democrat Otto Wels was a deputy in the imperial Reichstag, the Weimar Constituent Assembly, and the Reichstag of the republic. A member of the Social Democratic Central Committee from 1913 onwards, he became head of the party in 1931 and led its parliamentary delegation at the last meeting of the Weimar Reichstag. Hitler made every effort to come to power legally and needed a constitutional two-thirds majority to approve the "Enabling Act," a grant of extraconstitutional powers allegedly required to initiate immediate economic measures to combat the Great Depression. Many deputies voted to grant these powers to a government apparently dominated by the traditional conservatives; but, in fact, it turned out that they destroyed the Weimar Republic. As the speech indicates, Wels and the Social Democrats remained in resolute opposition. Later that year Wels fled to Prague to direct the continuing anti-Nazi activities of the Socialists from there.

SOURCE: Germany, Reichstag, *Stenographische Berichte . . .*, VIII (V. Wahlperiode 1933), 457: 32–34. Translation by the editor.

Ladies and gentlemen of the Reichstag. We Social Democrats agree emphatically with the demand for equality in foreign affairs, which the Chancellor has expressed, all the more so because we have always fought for that demand in principle. In this connection let me comment personally that I was the first German who opposed the falsehood of Germany's sole guilt for the outbreak of the World War before an international audience at the Berne [Socialist] Conference in 1919. No principle of our party has ever prevented, or been able to prevent, us from supporting the equitable claims of the German nation in face of the other peoples of the world.

The Chancellor made a statement day before yesterday at Potsdam which we support. He said: "It was the fallacious formula of permanent victory and permanent defeat which created the absurdity of reparations and the resultant world economic catastrophe." This formula applies no less to domestic policy; here, too, a theory of permanent victors and vanquished is, as the Chancellor said, absurd.

The Chancellor's speech also reminds us of another address given in the National Assembly on July 23, 1919, in which was stated: "We are disarmed; but to be disarmed is not to be dishonored. Certainly our opponents wish to dishonor us, there is no question of that. But we believe that the effort to dishonor us will at sometime backfire upon its perpetrators. For it is not our honor which perishes in this world tragedy." (*Interjection from the National Socialists: Who said that?*)

It was stated in the declaration which a government led by Social Democrats issued in the name of the German people to the whole world four hours before an anticipated expiration of the Armistice and in order to inhibit the further advance of the enemy. That statement is today a valuable supplement to the Chancellor's declaration.

There is no boon in peace by force, especially in domestic affairs. A genuine national community cannot be founded upon such a peace. Its first precondition is equal application of law. Government may protect itself against extravagances of polemics; it may prevent with severity any provocation of violence and violence itself. That is proper as long as the law is enforced equally and impartially on all sides and if people cease treating defeated opponents as outlaws. Liberty and life may be taken from us, but not our honor.

After the persecution which the Social Democratic party has recently suffered, no one can fairly demand or expect it to vote for the proposed Enabling Act. The elections of March 5 gave a majority to the government parties, and therewith they have the opportunity to govern within strict and literal construction of the constitution. The opportunity, indeed, becomes a duty. Criticism is healthy and necessary. As long as there has been a Reichstag, never has the control of public affairs by the elected representatives of the people been so cut off as right now, and as is even further planned under the new Enabling Act. The consequences of such omnipotent government must be all the more oppressive, since the press is to be deprived of its basic freedom.

Ladies and gentlemen. The situation which prevails in Germany today is often portrayed in glaring colors. As usual, there is much exaggeration. As far as my party goes, I can say we have not asked Paris for intervention, nor secretly sent millions of marks to Prague, nor transmitted exaggerated reports abroad. It would be easier to confront these distortions at home if our news media made an effort to distinguish truth from falsehood. It would be better still if we could testify with a clear conscience that full rights and protection under the law had been re-established for all. That, gentlemen, is up to you.

The gentlemen of the National Socialist party call the movement which they have unleashed a national revolution, not a national socialist one. The connection between their revolution and socialism has so far been limited to attempts to destroy more than two generations of Social Democratic ideas and ideals. If the gentlemen of the National Socialist Party wanted to enact genuine socialist legislation, they would not need an Enabling Act. They could be certain of an overwhelming majority in this house. Any proposal of yours in the interest of workers, farmers, office workers, or bourgeois officials would be approved, if not unanimously, at least by a strong majority.

But the fact is that you want first to eliminate the Reichstag in order to foster your kind of revolution. But destruction of the status quo is not yet a revolution. The people expect positive accomplishments. They expect effective measures against the terrible economic misery that prevails in Germany and in the whole world. In the most difficult of times, we Social Democrats have upheld our responsibility and have been ridiculed for it. Our contributions to the rehabilitation of the state and the economy, and to the liberation of the occupied [Rhineland] areas, will be recognized by history. We have created equal rights for all and a socially responsible labor law. We have helped create a Germany where not only princes and barons, but also working men have access to leadership in government. We cannot undo these advances without abandoning our own leadership. It will be fruitless to reverse the wheel of history. We Social Democrats know that one cannot eliminate the facts of political power by sheer denial of rights. We recognize that the politics of power prevail for the moment. But the people's sense of justice is also a political force, and we will never cease appealing to it.

The Weimar constitution is not a socialist constitution. But we support the principles of a constitutional state, of equal rights, and of social rights which are set forth in it. In this historic hour, we German Social Democrats solemnly reaffirm the principles of humanity and justice, of freedom and socialism. No Enabling Act gives you the power to destroy ideas which are eternally indestructible. You yourselves have professed socialism. Earlier anti-Socialist laws did not destroy Social Democracy. German social democracy will draw new strength from renewed persecution.

We salute the persecuted and oppressed. We salute our friends in the Reich. Their steadfastness and faithfulness merit our admiration. The courage of their dedication and their unbroken confidence vouch for a brighter future.

25. Against the Un-German Spirit

The thoughts and practises of Nazism included rewriting history and reviving Germanic customs from the past. The medieval business of book-burning gave a dramatic impact to political revision of popular notions about German history and culture. On May 10, 1933, a large group of Nazi students at the University of Berlin welcomed Dr. Goebbels to the festive occasion of intellectual revision and intimidation described below.

SOURCE: *Fränkischer Kurier*, May 12, 1933. Translation by the editor.

Berlin, May 11, 1933. On Wednesday night the Student Activist Committee, "Against the un-German Spirit," staged a rally with the slogan "The German spirit awakes!" It culminated at midnight with the symbolic act of burning some 20,000 politically and morally un-German books. . . .

The burning of seditious writings was the focal point of these midnight ceremonies in all German university communities. The books were committed to the flames with the following incantations:

1st Crier: Down with class struggle and materialism! In the name of national cohesiveness and idealistic life, I commit the writings of [Karl] Marx and [Karl] Kautsky to the flames.

2d Crier: Down with decadence and moral decay! In the name of discipline and morality in family and state, I commit the writings of Heinrich Mann, Ernst Gläser, and Erich Kästner to the flames. [All were writers critical of superpatriotism.]

3d Crier: Down with turncoats and political traitors! In the name of dedication to the people and the state, I commit the writings of Friedrich Wilhelm Förster to the flames. [An anti-Prussian pacifist.]

4th Crier: Down with corruptive overemphasis of baser impulses! In the name of the nobility of the human soul, I commit the writings of Sigmund Freud to the flames.

5th Crier: Down with the falsification of our history and the degradation of its great personalities! In the name of reverence for our great past, I commit the works of Emil Ludwig and Werner Hegemann to the flames. [Both were writers of popularized pseudopsychological history.]

6th Crier: Down with antipopular journalism in the democratic-Jewish style! In the name of responsible cooperation of the press in the work of national reconstruction, I commit the writings of Theodor Wolff and Georg Bernhard to the flames. [Editors of the liberal *Berliner Tageblatt* and *Vossische Zeitung*.]

7th Crier: Down with literary betrayal of the soldiers of the World War! In the name of educating our people in the spirit of valor, I commit the writings of Erich Maria Remarque to the flames. [Author of *All Quiet on the Western Front.*]

8th Crier: Down with degradation of the German language! In the name of fostering this precious possession of our people, I commit the writings of Alfred Kerr to the flames. [An expressionist literary critic.]

9th Crier: Down with impudence and pretension! In the name of honor and reverence for the immortal spirit of the German people may the flames also devour the writings of [Kurt] Tucholsky and [Carl von] Ossietzky! [Both were editors of the pacifist *Weltbühne.* Ossietzky received the Nobel Peace Prize in 1935 while a prisoner at Dachau concentration camp; later he was murdered there.]

26. Anti-Semitic Hate Propaganda

Julius Streicher looked his part: a stocky, brutal, loud-mouthed bully with a thick neck. An early convert to the Nazi party, he helped organize the Storm Troopers and in 1922 began editing *Der Stürmer* [*The Storm Trooper*], a vicious anti-Semitic hate sheet. Advertised as a "German weekly in combat for truth," it featured coarse cartoons, character assassination, and sensational feature articles (often with pornographic innuendo) about "international Jewry." Since most Germans refused to buy the paper, it was often distributed free of charge and always prominently displayed on thousands of bulletin boards, with heavy wire mesh protection, throughout Germany. Its very obscenity made it attractive, particularly to adolescents, and inevitably it made some impact on public attitudes. The following excerpts are characteristic of its tone and message.

SOURCE: *Der Stürmer*, no. 27, vol XI (1933). Translation by the editor.

THE PAN-JEWISH WORLDWIDE ATTACK
SECRET PLANS AGAINST GERMANY REVEALED
THE JEWISH WORLD CONFERENCE

On June 19, 1933, the "Rotterdamsche Courant," a Dutch news service, issued a typical release to the world press. In London the so-called World Economic Conference is still in session, where there is much idle chatter but little action. The Jews have now decided to exploit the conference for their own purposes. They have called a *Jewish World Conference* for July 15. The purpose of this meeting is to make decisions and issue instructions directed against National Socialist Germany. These decisions and instructions will then be presented to the World Economic Conference. At the same time international Jewish policy is to be consolidated and more uniformly administered. The conference is being called by the Jewish money kings of England, the Anglo-Jewish Industrial and Commercial Union. The conference will be organized by Jewish lawyer Samuel Volkmeyer from America and by the prominent English Jewish industrialist, Lord Melchett.

The world Jewish elite will confer: the chief rabbis (they are the political leaders of world Jewry) and the Jewish millionaries and billionaires, the bank and exchange moguls, the trust organizers, and big Jewish industrialists. These are the Jews whom Walter Rathenau already designated before the war in the *Neue Freie Presse* of Vienna: "Three hundred men, all of whom know each other well, govern the destiny of the world; nothing occurs without their will; they are the true rulers, the actual uncrowned kings."

These three hundred men will devise and implement the intensified Pan-Jewish economic boycott against Germany. They will try to injure Germany until they feel it has given up its anti-Jewish attitudes or is forced to its knees. They will leave nothing untried. They will lie and slander; time and again they will try to inflame the whole world against Germany. They will use all the methods that a Jewish mind can devise. The Jews know: Germany's victory in its domestic and foreign struggle for independence will mean the end of Pan-Jewish power. . . .

Exterminate Them!

In 1897, the Jew thought he was so safe that he wrote in the Protocols of Zion:

"Even if a spiritual hero should arise in the opposing camp and risk doing battle with us, he will have to succumb. For the novice cannot measure up to the proven warrior. The struggle between us and him would be more merciless than the world has ever seen, but the spiritual hero would come too late."

The Jew has miscalculated. The hero has not come too late. He took up the struggle against Jewry and achieved victory. The whole world knows who this hero is. He is Adolf Hitler, the leader of the German liberation movement. Facing the Führer and his blows, the Jew fell to the dust. He now sees the enormous danger threatening him. He is exposed; his criminal plans are revealed. And now a struggle begins the like of which the world has never seen. World Jewry is up against Adolf Hitler. World Jewry is up against Germany. The Jews are going to wage this conflict without mercy. We must also wage it against Pan-Jewry without mercy. The Jews are a people of the devil. They are a people of criminals and murderers. Therefore, the Jewish people must be exterminated from the face of the earth. . . .

THE JEWISH RAILROAD STATION

On the railroad line between Erfurt and Meiningen is a station named "Simson Works" in bright letters. The Simson Works rank among the largest arms factories in Germany. When Catholic-Socialist traitors ruled Germany, the Simson Works were suppliers of the German army. The factory belongs to the Jewish Simson brothers, so the railroad station has a Jewish name. For a long time, the people have called it simply "Jews' Station." The national railroad provides the Jews Simson with cheap publicity, since the station is listed under the Jewish name in all rail schedules and route plans.

In the last few months, all public streets and squares in Germany once named after Jews were renamed. Today, you will find neither a Rathenau Street nor a Karl Marx Street. The disgrace of past years has been erased. But the national railroad still appears to be happy with the Simson station. Otherwise, it would have given it a German name long ago. The *Stürmer* expects that responsible officials will quickly accomplish a task that should have been completed long ago. It is a disgrace that today a German railroad station should still be named after a Jew. . . .

HOW THEY LOITER ABOUT
IMPUDENT AND PROVOCATIVE JEWISH BEHAVIOR
AFTER THE JEHOVAH SERVICES

If a German goes to church he enters and leaves solemnly. Especially when he leaves the Lord's House, he is in no mood to gather in the street for chatter about business and deals. The Jew knows nothing of such devout solemnity. Whoever goes to the synagogues at Spital Square or on Essenwein Street will witness quite a sight at the beginning or the end of the Sabbath, or on any other Jewish holiday, when the services are over. To see these Jewish faces and figures all together is a sight that affronts any aesthetic sense. But it is even more disgusting to have to watch them gather in groups and bunches. The way they begin haggling, gesturing, and jabbering just like Jews do—it makes one sick. The way they stand around in greasy caftans, with drooping curls about their temples, drivelling mouths and shining wild eyes.

They impudently scrutinize every passerby from head to toe. This foreign race of vultures stands in everyone's way, blocks traffic, and never thinks of stepping aside when someone approaches. The behavior of this herd is a provocation, an impudent challenge to all Germans. If they do not stop their idle and indecent loitering, appropriate measures will have to bring them to reason. . . .

Exposed in Neustadt

Frau Kunigunde Lunz, mother of a petty officer of the conservative "Stahlhelm" Veterans Organization in Neustadt (Aisch) buys from the Jew Schwab and proudly declares everywhere that now, especially, she buys in Jewish shops.

We just wonder what this Frau Kunigunde Lunz has to be so proud about. It must be her stupidity and the fact that she still is one of the few who refuse to learn and would rather be cheated by a Jew than buy from her fellow Germans. Or is she proud that her son is a junior officer in the "Stahlhelm"? But she really should not be proud of that. Her son is not in the best company. . . .

Is the "Stahlhelm" Nationally Dedicated or Is It a Jewish Protection Brigade?

Lately in Neustadt (Aisch), the "Stahlhelm" has been strutting around quite a bit. As long as there was need to fight against the recently crushed Establishment and for a national regime, nothing was heard from these gentlemen. Now these busybodies are suddenly evident.

One of their chief operators is a certain Karl Meister, a Jew's servant of the vilest sort. What this gentleman does, and how he earns his money, is cloaked in deepest obscurity. It is only known that he is on good terms with the wife of Jew Stein in Neustadt (Aisch) and that he often travels with Jewish hops-dealer Fuld of Nürnberg.

Tell me with whom you associate and I will tell you who you are. . . .

WHAT MUST BE DONE!

1. Renewal of all business directories in the Reich with the Jewish and non-Jewish firms distinctly separated.

2. Addition of a further business directory in which exclusively non-Jewish firms are listed, that is, those which are not yet too heavily dominated by Jewish capital. . . .

PUBLIC ANNOUNCEMENT
City of Fürth

In reference to the ordinance of April 22, 1933, regarding admission of physicians to practice under national health insurance, the following are excluded, since as Aryans or non-Aryans they were close to the Communist Party, or as non-Aryans they participated neither in the World War nor in suppressing Spartacist disturbances:

Dr. Alfred Beselau, general practitioner
Dr. Dora Heilbronn, pediatrician
Dr. Berthold Heilbrunn, general practitioner
Dr. Adolf Hollerbusch, general practitioner
Dr. Irma Kraus, general practitioner
Dr. Franz Loose, oculist
Dr. Joseph Oppenheimer, general practitioner

VII

The National Socialist Consolidation of Victory, 1933–1937

THE STUDENT of today who looks back upon the Nazi era most probably finds his attention drawn to its dreadful culmination in war, destruction, and mass-murder across the continent of Europe. Inevitably he will wonder what happened to that 48 percent of the German electorate which voted neither Nazi nor conservative nationalist in the last free election. Those millions of non-Nazi voters were not apathetic on the issues of National Socialism; the vehemence of the election campaigns had forced them to make a distinct choice, and it was not for the Nazis. Once firmly established in power, the Nazis sought to win over or digest these citizens into their system. Terror and imprisonment engulfed the opposition chiefs of the Left. The confusion of symbols and appeals to patriotism, or rank opportunism, divided and deflected the elite of the Center and Right. Deprived of their leadership, the masses of non-Nazi Germans were targets for conversion by organizational pressure in every aspect of their daily lives. Four of the most important pressure areas are described in the selection which follows: (1) Nazified education; (2) the Labor Service, which combined military training with social idealism; (3) the tremendously successful leisure time and travel operation called "Strength through Joy"; and (4) the systematic exploitation of cultural pursuits for political impact.

27. *An Australian Views the Third Reich*

Between 1935 and 1937 Professor Stephen H. Roberts of the University of Sydney made an intensive study of the new Nazi regime. For more than a year this recognized Australian expert in European history traveled the length and breadth of the Reich, taking full advantage of unique privileges granted him by the German foreign office and Nazi party agencies but firmly preserving his independence of observation and judgment. The result was an impartial contemporary study of Nazi Germany written with unusual vividness. It remains the single best evaluation of the Third Reich during its peacetime phase.

SOURCE: Stephen H. Roberts, *The House that Hitler Built* (London: Methuen & Co., 1938), pp. 211–217, 224–228, 241–254, 254–257. Reprinted by permission of ABP International Ltd.

EDUCATION

The Nazis have laid a heavy hand on education. They know that the textbooks of today are shaping the political realities of the decades to come, and accordingly have made every part of education—curiously enough, even mathematics—a training ground in Nazi ideology. As soon as the child enters an elementary school (*Grundschule*) at the age of six, his days are given over to the idealizing of the Nazis. He counts up Storm Troopers, he sews crude figures of Black Guards, he is told fairy stories of the Nazi knights who saved the civilized maiden from the bad Russian gnomes, he makes flags and swastikas. After four years of this, he emerges to the *Volkschule* or *Mittelschule*, thinking of Hitler and his cabinet in the way that we regard Christ and His disciples. Their schoolwork is secondary to their activities in the youth organizations, especially when they reach the secondary school stage.

The whole of their education is tendentious. One of the earliest reforms of National Socialism was Dr. Frick's ban on the older form of education that failed to preach morals. Frick upbraided the teachers for having fallen behind in the national regeneration and warned them that they had to atone for their past faults by intense propaganda for the Nazis in the future. His warning particularly applied to the teaching of history. History was not a matter of objective fact, he told them, but a machine for inculcating German patriotism. All great men of the past were connected with Germany in some way or other, said Frick; all life-giving streams of civilization were due to the penetration of German blood or influence, all German history has been a struggle against encircling enemies, and never more than since brutal Imperialists forced her into a war of self-defence in 1914 and diabolically ground her to the dust. All world-history since the war has meaning only as bearing on the rise of Adolf Hitler; no other fact in the world counts as much as the new-found regeneration of the nation and the rise of the *Führer*.

This was the pattern to which the facts had to conform. When they could not be made to do so, they omitted whole slabs of them. "How can you do this?" I asked a noted German historian, and he replied, "My children must eat"; and, in several other cases, the reply was that the means justified the end. The German nation was being benefited by the false teaching, and, after all, said one historian, what difference was there between propaganda in peacetime and propaganda in wartime, especially nowadays when actual military operations were probably the least important part of war? There is probably nothing more revolting in Germany, not even in the stories of physical atrocities, than the degradation of professional historians.

Rust and Hinkel are the administrative leaders of German education today. Bernard Rust was, for over twenty years, a schoolteacher in Hanover, but his experiences as a battalion commander in the war made him chafe at the restrictions to which he was submitted. He sought relief by interfering in provincial politics. At last his extremely pugilistic nationalism lost him his job. A schoolmaster cannot very well conduct a vendetta against the parliament of his province. At this time Rust was approaching his fiftieth year, and he was saved from starvation only because the Nazis elected him to the Reichstag and made him leader of the Hanoverian group of the Party. His promotion was rapid. He became first Commissioner and then Minister of Education in Prussia, and later, in the whole Reich, distinguishing himself at each stage by his efforts to subordinate education to Hitlerite doctrines. He claimed that even scientific subjects could be used as media for instruction in National Socialism. His doctrines naturally reflected his personal experiences, and he approached his task with a bitter feeling against the professional leaders of education in Germany, against those who merely did their jobs without interfering in politics. Rust is a sallow little man with habitually clenched teeth. Forever spoiling for a fight, he is never happy unless knocking down obstacles.

Subtlety means nothing to him; he prefers to use his head as a battering ram.

At present, then, education is a weapon in the fight for a Nazi *Weltanschauung*. Preference is given at all stages to Nazis. Most of the scholarships are reserved for children who have been members of some Party organization. With a few exceptions, non-Aryans are excluded, and plans are being made for the segregation of such children in special schools of their own. For nine out of ten such unfortunates, education necessarily ends at the high school stage. The professions are closed to them.

Yet there is another side to the educational question in Germany. The Nazis have introduced order and efficiency in administration. Previously the educational system was cluttered up by too many administrative organizations. Much dead wood existed, and the ruthless pruning of Dr. Rust did much good. Moreover, it would be erroneous to assume that the earlier system was free from political elements. Many German teachers had adopted a defeatist attitude and this penetrated their whole teaching. In some of the larger cities, the children of the poorer districts were being taught Bolshevik ideas; and, throughout Germany, much evidence existed to support Rosenberg's attacks on *Kultur-Bolschevismus*. This applied particularly to art, music, literary criticism, and history, and was quite as destructive as the superpatriotism of the Nazis—in some ways more so. Despite the good points of the German system under the Republic, it had lost much of its objectivity. Even where it was not openly subversive it suffered from faults of emphasis, such as the discarding of many nonpractical subjects as mere frills. It would thus be a great mistake to assume that the Nazis took over an educational system as detached from politics, say, as the British system. Of course, this does not excuse the new Nazi tendentiousness; but it explains why, quite apart from their concept of politicalized education, they were so concerned about the "purification" of teaching. I have seen curricula from working-class schools of Berlin and Hamburg that are grotesque travesties on education; yet these had received the blessing of the Republican authorities. As recent German writers have pointed out, it was not the Nazis who started the idea of making education a field for *Kulturwaffen*—a clash between rival systems of *Kultur:* the Communists set the ball rolling, the Hitlerites merely kicked the goal. . . .

The Labor Service

The Labor Service seems to me one of the most desirable of the Nazi experiments, at least under German conditions. Long before Hitler came to power, when he was evolving the shadow organizations of his ultimate State, he appointed Konstantin Hierl to work out a system whereby the youth of the nation, irrespective of social class, could be put through the mill of compulsory labor service. Hierl was a professional soldier with over thirty years service, and had obtained a reputation first as Director of the War Academy in Munich and later at the War Ministry. During the Spartacist troubles, he had raised the "Hierl Detachment" and driven the Socialists out of Augsburg, so that his Nationalist sympathies were beyond doubt. In short, he was just the man to build up a nationwide labor service along military lines, and this was the task Hitler allotted him when he became an organizing leader (*Organisationsleiter*) at Party Headquarters in Munich eight years ago.

About that time there was much discussion of voluntary labor service as a method of alleviating unemployment, and the Brüning Government passed a law in July 1931, allowing such camps. Political rivalries entered, however, and the Nazis proceeded to organize their own camps. Hierl called a meeting of leaders in the Kurmark region and, in the first weeks of 1932, mustered the first camp at Hammerstein in the Grenzmark. A few months later, the state of Anhalt—in this as in so many other ways a nursery of Nazi idea—made such service Statewide.

Next year, fifty-eight-year-old Colonel Hierl became Secretary of State for Labor Service. He had a plan and a theory. "The Hierl Plan," as worked out in his book, *Sinn und Gestaltung der Arbeitsdienstplicht*, went far beyond unemployment. It was to be a cardinal feature in building up the New Germany. It was far less economic than social. The idea behind it all was that manual labor provided the best means of breaking down social barriers and molding the character of the young. Every young man would find himself in the regenerating process of hard physical work; he would realize the comradeship of his fellows; he would learn discipline; he would come into contact with the German soil for which he was to be trained to die. Boys from all parts of Germany and from all social classes were to be flung into camps, where their bodies were to be made fit by hard labor and their minds were to be molded along the desired national lines. Incidentally they would relieve the congestion on the labor markets and accomplish works that could not otherwise be brought about. "Labor service shall be the proud privilege of German youth and shall be service to the whole *Volk*," cried Hierl. In brief, his theory was far more concerned with the physical and mental wellbeing of the youth of the country than with economic gain or loss. That is where it differed from earlier experiments, and that is where the *Arbeitsdienst* of Germany remains unique.

The voluntary camps worked well, but Hierl was eagerly awaiting the day when labor service would be universal and compulsory. That day came on June 26th, 1935, when the Reich Labor Service Law was promulgated. It provided that every German man should serve for six months in a labor service camp at some time between his eighteenth and twenty-sixth birthdays. The authorities would have preferred a clear-cut scheme whereby every boy should serve for six months in a camp and then, immediately on achieving his twentieth year, go to a military camp and serve his period as a conscript. But this was impossible because facilities did not exist and any such limitation would have kept out ardent Nazis who were a few years older—just the kind of men who were to provide the camps with leaders.

At present, 200,000 men serve in such camps for six months. Usually men who are called up for the summer term of duty go on to the Army at the end of their service, and those who serve in winter, persons like farmers and waiters, can pursue their ordinary avocations in summer. A camp-leader once told me that, in the villages, boys who were thought to be opposed to Hitlerite ideas usually found themselves put down for the winter term in labor service camps, because the work is naturally less pleasant in winter than in summer.

The camps are organized on thoroughly military lines. Discipline is rigid; the boys wear uniforms like soldiers; the only difference is that they carry spades instead of rifles and work in the fields. Three aims are sought—physical exercise, intensive drill, and training of the mind; and each day is divided between the three, although, as the Nazi literature on the subject points out, the training in National Socialism principles comes first and "permeates the service from early morning until bed time." That is why the Army is said to have opposed the scheme from the first—because the boys are too well-trained in the Nazi way before the Army gets hold of them.

Everything goes according to routine. At each of the thirteen hundred camps in Germany, every boy will be doing the same thing at a given time. Individualism has no place in the scheme. Take a typical summer's day in a camp I saw near Potsdam. Reveille comes at five o'clock. After ten minutes of exercises, an hour is allowed for dressing and putting the bunks in order. Then comes a mass parade and the ceremonial raising of the swastika flag, with its emblems of a spade and two ears of corn. This is followed by an allocation of the tasks for the day, and the men swing off in platoons to march to the fields where they are working, or, if the distance is too great, go by bicycles. They work from half-past six till a quarter-past two, with half an hour's break for an early morning meal at ten o'clock. In all, counting the meal-time and the march from and to the camp, they work for eight hours in summer and seven in winter.

But at three o'clock, after they have eaten their dinner, the novel features of camp life appear. If it is summertime, each man must take an hour's rest on his bed after dinner, but in winter, the ordinary duties go on. After a short political talk, they go out for athletics or drill and return, a little after five o'clock, for lectures on the New Germany or on international affairs. When I visited the camps, these talks were usually highly tendentious accounts of events in Abyssinia or the decline of democracy. The boys then go out to a roll call ceremony and the lowering of the flag. This brings them to a little after seven, when they have half an hour for supper. After this, they have an organized evening of singing or discussions on Nazi literature, or a *Feierabendgestaltung*. The evenings are usually rather jolly, because, as one supervisor told me quite seriously, "they drink nothing intoxicating, and are only allowed beer." Thus it will be seen that it is a strictly regimental life from five o'clock in the morning until the "lights out" signal at ten in the evening. It is impossible, for instance, for a boy to perform his physical tasks and keep his mental processes to himself. The whole time, there is deliberate leading of his mind in certain directions. He is given a hearty and healthy life, with a premium on good-fellowship and physical well-being, but mental freedom is taken from him. He must think as the masses do, his mind must move along the orderly channels worked out at Hierl's headquarters in the Potsdam Park. For the mass of average boys, the life seems a happy one, but for the wayward minority, Hierl prescribes regimentation. The stress is on the group and on turning out identical specimens, and that is why I think the future of Germany depends far more on one rebel boy in a camp than on the 130 normal "hearties." The Nazi creed, however, is "*Volk* before Self," and they believe that the *Volk* finds its best expression when the Self is completely subordinated.

The service is organized down to the last button of the last man. There are thirty "Service-districts," corresponding to the political districts of the Reich. Each of these is divided in anything up to ten groups, each group has six to ten *Abteilungen,* each of which occupies a camp. In the whole of Germany there are 1,260 camps. Each camp is a duplicate of the other. The barracks are standard and built round a square. One side is given over to administration and meeting-rooms, each of the other three has a self-sufficient community. Every camp has exactly 152 men, of whom seventeen are executive officials. Each of the three *Züge* or wings houses forty-five men, who in turn are subdivided into three troops of fifteen. Everybody is plastered with badges of rank, for the Service has a military hierarchy with no less than fifteen distinct grades. In a word, in time of emergency, the *Arbeitsdienst* could immediately put 200,000 drilled and well-organized infantrymen into the field.

The system of training is equally intricate. Hitler realized from the outset that one of Germany's problems was to provide leaders for the various branches of his movement, and the labor service, in addition to being what he calls a school for the entire nation, is an admirable training-ground for leaders of all kinds. The boys who have graduated through the various Nazi youth organizations now take on the wider responsibilities of adult leadership, and in many ways the training institutions of the labor service—the troop-leaders' school, the *Feldmeistersschule,* the *Bezirksschule,* and the *Reichsschule*—are determining the nature of the Nazi State of the future.

After his labor service and military training, the future leader signs on for ten years and receives a specialized training in the psychology of leadership and in the technical engineering aspects of the work. At any given moment, there are at least 25,000 leaders working in the camps, and, in addition to these who have chosen the labor service for their lifework, far greater numbers, after the discipline received during their service, have been absorbed in other departments of the Nazi State where a premium is placed on intelligent and obedient leadership.

Although it is forever being asserted that the main aim of the labor service is to train the mind and bodies of Young Germany, the economic aspects are not lost sight of. Here we have a body of 200,000 lusty young men, who receive twenty-five pfennigs a day as pocket-money, and whose keep never costs more than eighty-two pfennigs a day. That is to say, it is a disciplined labor supply for a little over a mark a day, a supply that can be sent anywhere and put to any kind of work.

So far the service has been used mainly to reclaim lands that can be used in the fight to make Germany self-sufficient in her food-stuffs. It is in keeping with the Nazi cult of *Blut und Erde* to bring the adolescents into close contact with mother earth, and wrest waste-lands away from destruction. There is something satisfying to them in triumphing over Nature. There were marshes to drain, swamps and moorlands to clear, erosions to be stopped, canals and irrigation channels to be built, land to be reclaimed from the sea, and public amenities to be created. Eight million hectares can be won back to cultivation, cry the leaders, four provinces the size of Saxony can be gained to the Reich without any war save with Nature.

It is impossible to estimate just what has been achieved. Hitler inaugurated "the Fight against Water" with great éclat in 1934, and announced at the Party Congress of 1935 that the first fifty peasants had already been settled on reclaimed marshes. The greatest concentration of camps was in Oldenburg and Westphalia, but the most far-reaching plans were in the southwest, in the area between the Rhine and the Danube. It is still too early to assess the economic results as a whole; all that one can do is to say that the workers are building up potential wealth for the nation.

It has been asserted that the Labor Service Army constitutes slave-labor which competes with private enterprise. The authorities deny this and point out that none of their activities affect the labor market. Land is being reclaimed that would not otherwise have been touched; forests are being cleaned up and tasks that would otherwise be too expensive (such as the tapping of pine trees to secure the resin that will ultimately make Germany independent of foreign supplies of turpentine) are being carried out; and the sea is being pushed back. It is hotly denied that the labor service youths are being employed in road-making, which absorbs so many of the ordinary unemployed, except for scenic roads in the forests. One must add that, from one's own experience in Bavaria and in the Black Forest, a very liberal interpretation is given to the word "scenic" in this connection.

It is also claimed that the system often means the use of labor at State cost to improve the lands of individual farmers; but, in answer to this, Hierl maintains that the system is proof against abuse. No schemes of reclamation are undertaken if they improve the land of one farmer alone. Usually, in a district in which there is waste land or where erosion is eating into the fields, the community appoints a committee which gets in touch with the nearest *Arbeitsdienst* office. All claims are most carefully considered on their merits before a decision is reached, and it does seem as if illicit individual gain has been effectively ruled out.

The whole experiment is a fascinating one for foreigners. One of the most typical sights in Germany is to come upon platoons of labor service men swinging along country tracks with shovels carried like rifles at the slope, or to see masses of browned boys working lustily in the fields and stripped to the waist in all weather. In the remotest woods one sees a red flag with a black spade worked in its midst and, as one approaches, a brown-clad sentry smartly springs to attention and brings his aluminiumed spade to the present, and somehow it does not seem absurd to be saluted with a spade. . . .

ORGANIZED TRAVEL MOVEMENTS

From the human point of view, one of the most interesting experiments in Germany has been the attempt to supplement wages by providing facilities for travel or enjoyment. A most popular section of the Labor Front is the department known as "Strength through Joy" (*Kraft durch Freude*). This was set up at the end of 1933, and only the lower paid workmen can take advantage of its facilities. The limit is a variable one. A typist cannot enter the organization if she earns more than 150 marks a month, whereas a worker with four children is still eligible even if he earns as much as 500 marks.

The idea is to get the workman away from his everyday surroundings. Any workman who wishes to travel gets into touch with the works member of the "confidential council" (set up by the Labor Front) and thus with the district office of the movement. He receives a card which is stamped with his weekly contribution and, when he has saved enough money, he goes on one of the trips. In the first year of operations, 3,000,000 workers took such trips, and this year the number is expected to exceed 6,000,000. When the hotels were filled, the trippers went on hired boats. Today six vessels go to Madeira or Norway, and the Labor Front is building boats of its own. Last summer 150,000 workers took sea trips, a week's cruise to Norway costing less than thirty marks.

In addition, eighty recreation homes have been built, and at present the Government is constructing a huge spa on the island of Rügen to accommodate 20,000 people. Seaports are being organized along the entire northern coast, and there is barely a region of Germany that is not being opened up by some form of this tourist activity. The motorist in Germany encounters the huge buses with the *K.d.F.* symbol in the most inaccessible spots and frequently finds towns overrun by them, until his zest for the organization almost changes into a feeling of exasperation.

The amazing feature is that, apart from administrative personnel, the scheme is claimed to be self-supporting, because hotel proprietors and railway owners are satisfied with smaller profits in order to get the extra business. The central authorities in Berlin told me that this applied to building ships of their own, but I fail to see how huge liners can be made to pay at a daily rate of six and a half marks per person.

Nevertheless, *Kraft durch Freude* appears to be an excellent device for providing holidays for people who would not otherwise get them. Its varying success in different districts provides a kind of social barometer. At headquarters in Berlin, regional graphs (which cover whole walls) enable the authorities to see at a glance how many people from each town are taking holidays, where they are going, how many more or less are going than at this time last year. They are multicolored marvels of statistical ingenuity and, if accurate, afford excellent data about the prosperity and loyalty of each region in Germany. I investigated the applications from Silesia and the distressed Rhineland area and was amazed to find no essential difference from elsewhere.

Another department of the organization arranges theatre facilities for the same class of people. A census of the great Siemens factories taken when the Nazis came to power showed that three-quarters of the people never went to theatres. The Government therefore arranged with theatrical managers that blocks of seats should be made available to workers at special rates. Workmen who received good reports thereupon take part in a ballot for these seats, so that for seventy-five pfennigs, a man may find himself in the front row of the stalls or up in the gallery.

The position here is rather complicated, because the Propaganda Ministry frequently intervenes, giving grants in special cases and sometimes taking over whole theatres. Some propagandist plays may be opened to the public for nothing, while, at other times, the Ministry takes over an ordinary commercial theatre when some play or picture with an historical moral is being presented. There may be a direct grant for a given play, or merely indirect aid through a reduction of taxes; and, to complicate matters, such grants may come either from the Labor Front or from the Propaganda Ministry. The upshot of it all is that a worker may go to selected plays for seventy-five pfennigs, to operas for ninety pfennigs, and to ordinary plays in outside theatres for half the ordinary rates. Officially no compulsion is exerted on owners of theatres, only "persuasion." The Labor Front argue that the owners welcome their intrusion because empty seats are filled and plays booked in advance; but it is obvious how such a system must work in the direction of making the theatre a subsidiary propagandist body for the Party.

Films, other than moralizing historical presentations, are outside this scheme in the towns. But, in the country districts, film shows and concert parties circulate in parts where otherwise they would not pay. There is a definite move to educate the musical taste of the people, in the direction of chamber music, for instance. Orchestras are sent round to factories, and, for a few pence, workers can hear conductors like Feuchtwangler.

Already 25,000,000 people a year benefit from these facilities, and, once again, it is claimed that the State pays nothing, although obviously the subventions from the Propaganda Ministry and the losses in taxes must be counted on the debit side. If one puts aside the propagandist element, one must admit that this movement is definitely providing facilities that would not otherwise exist, although it is at first a little strange to pay many marks for a seat in a theatre and find a neighbor who has paid only a few pfennigs. The system reaches its height in the *People's Theatre* in Berlin, the former circus in which Max Reinhardt staged his most flamboyant spectacles. The great circular building has now become a People's Theatre, at which two-thirds of the seats are reserved for workers. Last year the productions varied from *Peer Gynt* and *The Merry Wives of Windsor* to operettas of Strauss and Lincke. It must be added, however, that a popular revue, *Let's Have a Good Time*, had by far the longest run.

A further department of the "Strength through Joy" movement is that which provides facilities for cheap sport. This arouses more attention in Germany than it would in a British country, and my mentors could not understand my lack of interest in this phase of their activities, a phase of which they were particularly proud. The idea that sport was not a matter for the Government found no support with them; and I had to listen to accounts of the intricate organization for popularizing sport amongst the German masses. The Labor Front provided funds for endowing this department, and a huge pyramid of committees was set up from factory to the whole Reich. It was all taken very seriously. Lectures are a regular part of the program, and the aim is to improve the bodies of the Germans, and in no sense to create new records. It was in the academically serious atmosphere of this department that I felt myself most a foreigner in Germany.

No arrangements are made for football and handball, on the ground that these are already too popular, but a workman can obtain an evening's sport by paying twenty pfennigs, or, if he wants instruction in swimming, ten pfennigs more. The accompanying lectures even in central Germany, go as far afield as sailing and skiing. From a little over half a million in the first year, the number of people using these facilities has swollen to 6,000,000 a year. This was stressed as one of the greatest achievements of the new régime, and my arguments that British sport needed no such State aid were received with kindly sympathy as still another instance of how we were losing the race. Even my aide from the Foreign Office, a man who had taken a degree in an English University, thought my attitude to Government-organized sport—so palpably one of the most cherished achievements of the Third Reich—a little flippant. For the women, there is a special department called "Jolly Gymnastics and Games." It should be added that only "citizens" may share in this comradeship of sportsmen; in other words, Jews and part-Aryans are excluded.

And so, runs a piece of propaganda, "the contentment of the day's work vibrates into the leisure hours in which fresh strength is gained for the next working day," and, at the same time, one's pride of nationality and heritage is increased. At first I was inclined to interpret "Strength through Joy" as a spectacular embellishment of government, but, after further investigation, I realized that it was one of the most striking forms of social service I had yet seen and, at the same time, a most efficient method of propaganda. The Germans rank it with the Labor Service camps as a great instrument of national regeneration and one of their most original contributions to social history. It is an officially organized campaign for *Health, Joy, and Homeland*, and, as such, is a cult peculiarly Teutonic. Nevertheless, propaganda apart, it is a most attractive organization. Beethoven for sixpence, Bavaria for eighteenpence, and Norway for six shillings a day, the sea for the mountaineer and the mountains for the sailor—its prospects are most alluring, and I regretted my inability to accept Dr. Ley's invitation to go on a cruise to the Norwegian fjords—eight days for twenty-two marks —if I insisted on paying for myself. . . .

CULTURE

It was part of the Nazi creed that no aspect of life could stand outside the totalitarian State. Instead of the democratic licence that had hitherto prevailed in literature, art, and the drama, there had to be organized development. As soon as the régime was established, therefore, the Government proceeded to institute a series of trusts that would cover the whole cultural field.

In October 1933, a Reich Chamber of Culture was set up, under the ubiquitous Dr. Goebbels. This consisted of seven Chambers, each dealing with some aspect of cultural life (Literature, Press, Broadcasting, Theatre, Music, Art, Films). Each of these has a president and an executive board, and includes professional organizations from the whole of Germany. The presidents come together from time to time and meet as the Reich Advisory Board of Culture. Although the organization is now completed, Dr. Goebbels recently admitted that the task had been very difficult, and that his first two years' labor were slower than they otherwise would have been, because of "the self-willed nature peculiar to people of intellect and artistic temperament." Oddly enough, according to Goebbels, the men of culture proved amazingly conservative. An official account said: "The will to something new almost invariably met with inherent opposition which the Minister ascribes as much to latent obstinacy as to the initial recoil from the inrush of revolutionary ideas to which people of intellect are naturally more susceptible" [*sic!*]. It was therefore counted as a concession when, in November 1935, Goebbels set up a Reich Senate of Culture composed of competent intellectuals.

The functions of these cultural bodies are said to be, firstly, the provision of uniform and spirited leadership; secondly, the sifting of the worthwhile from the mediocre; and thirdly, setting forth juridical standards. I am not certain what the last means, but it is obvious that the scheme places all control of cultural life in the hands of Dr. Goebbels, "as *spiritus rector*" runs one account. The real aim is to develop culture along National Socialist lines. The Statute instituting the Chamber of Culture specifically stated that "it is the business of the State to combat injurious influences and encourage those that are valuable, actuated by a sense of responsibility for the wellbeing of the National Community." In another place, it states that "all creative forces in all spheres must be assembled under Reich leadership with a view to the uniform moulding of the will." Beyond this, it goes on, creative effort is to be individual and unrestricted.

It is only necessary to supplement this astounding view of culture by stating that membership of one of the Chambers is compulsory for every intellectual or artist, and that expulsion due to "cultural misbehavior" means starvation.

The executive president of the Chamber of Culture is Hans Hinkel, one of the oldest members of the Party. After a few months of fighting in the war, he enlisted in the Oberland Free Corps after the Armistice and was so active in sabotage in the Rhineland that the French sentenced him to eight years' imprisonment. He then became a reporter on the first National Socialist newspaper to be established in North Germany and later on Hitler's *Völkischer Beobachter*. After the Revolution, this thirty-two-year-old reporter became director of cultural organizations in Prussia and later head of the Theatre Union. Today he enforces the cultural ideas of Goebbels throughout Germany, and no more need be said than that his actions are a reflection of his training.

The Chamber of Culture is now four years old and, in so far as its goal was the subordination of cultural life to Nazi ideals, it has been completely successful. In each of its seven sections there has been a purge of undesirables and a unification of outlook. The creation of art was not part of the Chamber's functions. As Goebbels has repeatedly said: "The uniform moulding of the will" was more important.

Turning to each of the divisions of culture we may see how Hinkel's "molding" worked out. Literature was placed under Hans Blunck, a retired civil servant. His theory is that contemporary literature goes back to the period of Romanticism, but a Romanticism purged of the egotism and the undue subjectivity of liberalism. He holds that the writers of Nazi Germany now represent a synthesis between two groups. On the one hand were "the writers of the people" who reacted from individualism to an emphasis on the responsibility of the individual to his community. They were led by the moralizing historical novelist, Edwin Kolbenheyer, and it was only the connecting link of a common nationalism that drew them into the fold of the second group, the adolescents of the Nazi Youth Movement who clamored for revolt and romantic nationalism. They were the writers of the *Fronde*, and their viewpoint was that of the eternal opposition, save that they were destined at an early age to become the official spokesmen of the New Germany. According to Blunck, their strength lay in the application of their talent to such political topics as treaty-revision; they transmuted politics by applying "the eternal German romanticism." Skepticism and negation were swept aside, and in their place was a new creative will. As Blunck naïvely concludes when writing of the men in charge of German literature at the moment, "every one of them has produced a life's work, which at this late stage is appearing before the public for recognition and appreciation for the first time."

The literary output of these "secret poets," as Blunck calls them, these rulers of Germany whose transformation from fighting opposition to official beatitude occurred with surprising uniformity on January 30th, 1933, is not of high quality. Hitler, Rosenberg, and von Schirach are Germany's best sellers. *Mein Kampf* certainly does not sell for its literary merits, while the turgid outpourings of Rosenberg have only to be compared with a Swift or a Bolingbroke to be revealed in all their weakness. Von Schirach is described by Germans as a great lyrist, but to the outsider his verses are but the jingles of an undeveloped adolescent. These men are supposed to be links with the *Burschenschaft* of 1848 or the great national revival against Napoleon; but their writings lack fire and expression.

There is a marked paucity of literary output in Nazi Germany. Political tracts and heavy histories and works on military science sell well. While pornographic literature has disappeared (one of the salutary results of the new régime), the censorship on all remaining books is as harsh as in the first days of Hitlerism. A striking feature is the vogue for translations of foreign novels, although this is probably only an expression of the German lack of creation.

On the other hand, Goebbels is probably right when he says that he anticipates a greater productivity once the transition period is over. The exalted mysticism and the fervid patriotism of the new régime lend themselves to a peculiar mixture of expressionism and realism, a combination of idealism and actuality—everything that the German means when he speaks of *der neue Zeitgeist*. The individualist must shackle his belief to this standard or be for ever silent, and it must be remembered that the German system of education produces a type of mind that will find its form of revolt, not in opposition to the governing régime, but in romantic expressions of self-sacrificing patriotism that outrival those of his teachers. The adolescent will be more divinely mad than his mentors, and will allow himself the indulgence of a mystical exaltation that takes the form of a delight in sacrifice and immolation. By abnegating his individualism, he is finding the strongest expression for that individualism, and is thus unconsciously revenging himself on his instructors who teach the all-embracing virtues of uniformity. But whether this will produce the variety essential to literature is another question. Hans Blunck cannot have it both ways. He contends that the strength of the present official writers (who now "are revealing an almost immeasurable wealth of talent in all domains of creative art") was due to their campaigns against authority in their youth, their *Sturm und Drang* period; but, if this be so, what can provide the *Fronde* of the coming generation? Germany is relying on romanticism, on "the deep passion to be allowed once more to accept the Mother as holy and the Child as a miracle"; but it remains to be shown whether romanticism can flourish as an inspiration to young writers when it is officially directed and its various stages controlled by a Reich Literary Chamber which must report in turn to a Reich Chamber of Culture and to a Minister of Propaganda.

Hitlerism was associated with intellectual intolerance from the outset, although they called it the elimination of decadent thought. One of Dr. Goebbels's most spectacular efforts was in organizing the street riots in the winter of 1930 that resulted in the withdrawal of the film *All Quiet on the Western Front* from all Berlin theatres. The French pacifist film *The Wooden Cross* met a similar fate when the Nazis came to power. The youth of Germany were to be taught that war was fine, ennobling, romantic, chivalrous; and truth was to be cast aside. Germany is one of the two countries in Europe today in which youth does not revolt against the idea of war.

One of the most disgusting episodes of the régime was Goebbels's famous bonfire of "undesirable" literature. This product of seven universities even enlisted the aid of immature university students to pick books from their libraries and add fuel to his bonfire in the Opera-platz in Berlin. He even had the audacity to quote from a Renaissance scholar who welcomed the breaking of the bonds of medieval darkness in these words: "O Century! O Science! What a joy to be alive!" To this accompaniment, the works of Remarque, Freud, Schnitzler, Marx, Gide, Zola, Proust, Helen Keller, Einstein, Ludwig, the two Manns, Wells, and even Jack London and Upton Sinclair were burnt, together with tens of thousands of other books.

Copies of all these offerings to the flames were kept in Berlin and Munich. At Party Headquarters I was taken through room after room of confiscated literature. Since most of it is easily accessible in any good British library, I evinced no desire to work on it; but I was nevertheless informed that the records were all available to me except the confiscated literature. The custodian was a very intelligent man, a trained research worker. I asked: "How could I write of National Socialism without considering the case of both sides?"

In answer, he conducted me to another library which contained every sympathetic account ever written of Hitler, down to cuttings from local newspapers in small Australian towns, of which I, an Australian, had never heard. "Here is the truth," said the librarian, "and, in depicting the truth, one has no need of filth and lies." In that building, although I raised the issue with many officials, not one would admit that it was necessary to cover all sources, friendly or inimical, in writing modern history. They are so convinced of the success of their propaganda that the propaganda has become truth to them, as unassailable as Holy Writ. To my riposte that most of the forbidden books were in the British Museum, they answered that such negligence accounts for the decadence of Britain and that a clean broom like Hitler is needed. They were genuinely sorry for a government which permitted free discussion of social and political problems; and many of them refused to believe that a Conservative Ministry allowed the open sale of Communist literature. Asked whether the restrictions on literature were mere phases of the transitional period, they all replied to the effect that the restrictions would become needless once the whole nation was educated up to Hitlerism. To lift them was unthinkable: one man said that, if they did that, they would be like a doctor who offers noxious drugs to unbalanced patients. My argument that a drug-taker, cured of his vice and fully convinced of the benefits of health, could face a whole drug-cabinet without giving way, was passed over in silence. Rigid control of the mind is so much an engrained principle of National Socialism that it was almost heresy to question it. Intellectual detachment is treason to them (had not Göring once said in public: "I am not concerned with both sides. I see only those who are for National Socialism and those who are against it, and I know how to deal with the latter!").

VIII

The Road to War, 1936–1939

BETWEEN 1930 and 1936 the National Socialists blew hot and cool on the issues affecting war and peace. Hitler vowed to overthrow the Versailles settlement and restore equality for the Reich among its neighbors. He also conjured up the vision of a peaceful Germany in harmony with a Europe restored to balance and security for all. In the spring of 1933 he conferrred diligently in a four-power conference; in the autumn he explosively walked out of the League of Nations. In March of 1935 Hitler startled Europe with full-scale rearmament; two months later he soothed the powers with fervent pleas for peace and subsequently negotiated a naval agreement with Britain. A year later he suddenly smashed the Locarno treaties by marching into the demilitarized Rhineland and won resounding approval from Germans by also portraying his action as strengthening the prospects for peace. All of these events won the favor of a sizeable majority of Germans, for they satisfied national grievances felt since 1919. Indeed, Hitler probably won considerable additional support because he was a man of action—and a successful one.

Among the peoples of the other European powers, however, Hitler's meager credibility as a man of peace wore very thin. He tried to use the Olympic Games of 1936 at Berlin as another device publicly to parade his affirmations for international amity. But privately, in the innermost councils of the Third Reich, he argued that the time for decision was close at hand. With one exception all the following documents were used at the Nuremberg Trials as evidence of Nazi conspiracy and aggression.

28. Führer Memorandum on the Tasks of a Four-Year Plan, 1936

Professor Albert Speer, the Führer's architect, certified in 1945 that this unsigned memorandum was handed personally to him by Hitler. The Führer commented at the time that the "lack of understanding on the part of the Reich ministry of economics and the opposition of the German business world" had prompted him to establish a four-year economic mobilization plan under the direction of Reichminister Hermann Goering.

SOURCE: Germany, Auswärtiges Amt. *Documents on German Foreign Policy*, Series C (Washington, D.C., 1949), V: 853–857, 859–862.

[Obersalzberg, August, 1936]

THE POLITICAL SITUATION

Politics are the conduct and the course of the historical struggle for life of the peoples. The aim of these struggles is the assertion of existence. . . .

No State will be able to withdraw or even remain at a distance from this historical conflict. *Since Marxism, through its victory in Russia, has established one of the greatest empires in the world as a forward base for its future operations, this question has become a menacing one. Against a democratic world ideologically rent within itself stands a unified aggressive will founded upon an authoritarian ideology.* The means of military power available to this aggressive will are meantime increasing rapidly from year to year. . . .

Germany will, as always, have to be regarded as the focal point of the Western world in face of the Bolshevist attacks. I do not regard this as an agreeable mission but rather as a handicap and encumbrance upon our national life regrettably resulting from our position in Europe. We cannot, however, escape this destiny. . . . *A victory of Bolshevism over Germany would not lead to a Versailles Treaty but to the final destruction, indeed to the annihilation of the German people.*

The extent of such a catastrophe cannot be foreseen. How, indeed, would the whole of densely populated Western Europe (including Germany), after a collapse into Bolshevism, live through probably the most gruesome catastrophe for the peoples which has been visited upon mankind since the downfall of the States of antiquity? *In face of the necessity of defence against this danger, all other considerations must recede into the background as being completely irrelevant.*

GERMANY'S DEFENSIVE CAPACITY

Germany's defensive capacity is based upon several factors. I would give pride of place to the intrinsic value of the German people *per se.* A German people with an impeccable political leadership, a firm ideology and a thorough military organization certainly constitutes the most valuable factor of resistance which the world of today can possess. Political leadership is ensured by the National Socialist Party; ideological solidarity has, since the victory of National Socialism, been introduced to a degree that had never previously been attained. It must be constantly deepened and hardened on the basis of this concept. This is the aim of the National Socialist education of our people.

Military development is to be effected through the new Army. *The extent and pace of the military development of our resources cannot be made too large or too rapid!* It is a capital error to think that there can be any argument on these points or any comparison with other vital necessities. However much the general pattern of life of a people ought to be a balanced one, it is nonetheless imperative that at particular times certain disturbances of the balance, to the detriment of other, less vital, tasks, must be adopted. *If we do not succeed in developing the German Wehrmacht within the shortest possible time into the first Army in the world, in training, in the raising of units, in armaments, and, above all, in spiritual education as well, Germany will be lost!* The principle applies here that the omissions of peacetime months cannot be made good in centuries. . . .

GERMANY'S ECONOMIC POSITION . . .

We are overpopulated and cannot feed ourselves from our own resources. . . .

The final solution lies in extending the living space of our people and/or the sources of its raw materials and foodstuffs. It is the task of the political leadership one day to solve this problem.

The temporary easing can only be brought about within the framework of our present economy. In this connection, the following is to be noted: . . .

It is not sufficient merely to draw up, from time to time, raw material or foreign exchange balances, or to talk about the preparation of a war economy in time of peace; on the contrary, it is essential to ensure peacetime food supplies and above all those means for the conduct of a war which it is possible to make sure of by human energy and activity. And I therefore draw up the following programme for a final solution of our vital needs:

1. Like the military and political rearmament and mobilization of our people, there must also be an economic one, and this must be effected in the same tempo, with the same determination, and, if need be, with the same ruthlessness as well. . . .

2. For this purpose, in every sphere where it is possible to satisfy our needs through German production, foreign exchange must be saved in order that it can be applied to those requirements which can under no circumstances be supplied *except* by imports.

3. Accordingly, German fuel production must now be stepped up with the utmost speed and be brought to final completion within eighteen months. This task must be attacked and carried out with the same determination as the waging of war; for on its solution depends the conduct of the future war and not on the laying in of stocks of petroleum.

4. It is equally urgent that the mass production of synthetic rubber should be organized and secured. . . .

5. The question of the cost of these raw materials is quite irrelevant, since it is in any case better for us to produce in Germany dearer tyres which we can use, than for us to sell theoretically cheap tyres for which, however, the Ministry of Economics can allocate no foreign exchange and which, consequently, cannot be produced for lack of raw materials and consequently cannot be used at all. . . .

It is further necessary to increase the German production of iron to the utmost. The objection that we are not in a position to produce from the German iron ore, with a 26 percent content, as cheap a pig iron as from the 45 percent Swedish ores, etc., is irrelevant because we are not in fact faced with the question of what we would *rather* do but only of what we *can* do. . . .

It is further necessary to prohibit forthwith the distillation of alcohol from potatoes. Fuel must be obtained from the ground and not from potatoes. Instead, it is our duty to use any arable land that may become available, either for human or animal foodstuffs or for the cultivation of fibrous products.

It is further necessary for us to make our supplies of *industrial* fats independent of imports as rapidly as possible and to produce them from our coal. This task has been solved chemically and is actually crying out to be done. The German economy will either grasp the new economic tasks or else it will prove itself quite incompetent to survive in this modern age when a Soviet State is setting up a gigantic plan. *But in that case it will not be Germany who will go under, but, at most, a few industrialists.*

It is further necessary to increase Germany's output of other ores, *regardless of cost,* and in particular to increase the production of light metals to the utmost in order thereby to produce a substitute for certain other metals.

It is, finally, necessary for rearmament too to make use even now whenever possible of those materials which must and will replace high-grade metals in time of war. *It is better to consider and solve these problems in time of peace than to wait for the next war, and only then, in the midst of a multitude of tasks, to try to undertake these economic researches and methodical testings too.*

In short: I consider it necessary that now, with iron determination, 100 percent self-sufficiency should be attained in all those spheres where it is feasible, and not only should the national requirements in these most important raw materials be made independent of other countries but that we should also thus save the foreign exchange which in peacetime we require for our imports of foodstuffs. *Here I would emphasize that in these tasks I see the only true economic mobilization and not in the throttling of armament industries in peacetime in order to save and stockpile raw materials for war.*

But I further consider it necessary to make an immediate investigation into the outstanding debts in foreign exchange owed to

German business abroad. There is no doubt that the outstanding claims of German business are today quite enormous. Nor is there any doubt that behind this in some cases there lies concealed the contemptible desire to possess, whatever happens, certain reserves abroad which are thus withheld from the grasp of the domestic economy. I regard this as deliberate sabotage of our national self-assertion and of the defence of the Reich, and for this reason I consider it necessary for the Reichstag to pass the following two laws: (1) a law providing the death penalty for economic sabotage, and (2) a law making the whole of Jewry liable for all damage inflicted by individual specimens of this community of criminals upon the German economy, and thus upon the German people. . . .

Nearly four precious years have now gone by. There is no doubt that by now we could have been completely independent of foreign countries in the sphere of fuel supplies, rubber supplies, and partly also iron ore supplies. Just as we are now producing 700,000 or 800,000 tons of petroleum, we could be producing 3 million tons. Just as we are today manufacturing a few thousand tons of rubber, we could already be producing 70,000 or 80,000 tons per annum. Just as we have stepped up the production of iron ore from 2½ million tons to 7 million tons, so we could be processing 20 or 25 million tons of German iron ore, and if necessary even 30 million. There has been time enough in four years to discover what we cannot do. It is now necessary to state what we can do.

I thus set the following tasks: (1) The German army must be operational within four years; and (2) the German economy must be fit for war within four years.

29. Minutes of the Conference in the Reich Chancellery, Berlin, November 5, 1937

This is an excerpted version of the crucial Hossbach Memorandum. Having initiated German economic mobilization the year before, Hitler now revealed to a tiny circle of top officials how he viewed the international situation, the potential advantages for Germany which he saw therein, and the time span within which he felt Germany would have to move to attain his objectives. Much of the text here, and in other

documents of this chapter, is excluded because the Führer was so ver-
bose and repetitive.

SOURCE: Germany. Auswärtiges Amt. *Documents on German
Foreign Policy*. Series D (Washington, D.C., 1949), I: 29–31,
34–36, 38–39.

November 10, 1937

Present: The Führer and Chancellor,
Field Marshal von Blomberg, War Minister,
Colonel General Baron von Fritsch, Commander in
Chief, Army,
Admiral Dr. h. c. Raeder, Commander in Chief, Navy,
Colonel General Göring, Commander in Chief, *Luft-
waffe*,
Baron von Neurath, Foreign Minister,
Colonel Hossbach.

The Führer began by stating that the subject of the present
conference was of such importance that its discussion would, in
other countries, certainly be a matter for a full Cabinet meeting,
but he—the Führer—had rejected the idea of making it a subject
of discussion before the wider circle of the Reich Cabinet just
because of the importance of the matter. His exposition to follow
was the fruit of thorough deliberation and the experiences of his
four and one-half years of power. He wished to explain to the
gentlemen present his basic ideas concerning the opportunities for
the development of our position in the field of foreign affairs and
its requirements, and he asked, in the interests of a long-term German policy, that his exposition be regarded, in the event of his
death, as his last will and testament.

The Führer then continued:

The aim of German policy was to make secure and to preserve
the racial community and to enlarge it. It was therefore a question
of space.

The German racial community comprised over 85 million people
and, because of their number and the narrow limits of habitable
space in Europe, constituted a tightly packed racial core such as
was not to be met in any other country and such as implied the
right to a greater living space than in the case of other peoples.

. . . Germany's future was therefore wholly conditional upon the solving of the need for space, and such a solution could be sought, of course, only for a foreseeable period of about one to three generations.

Before turning to the question of solving the need for space, it had to be considered whether a solution holding promise for the future was to be reached by means of autarchy or by means of an increased participation in world economy.

Autarchy: . . .

It was not possible over the long run, in a continent enjoying a practically common standard of living, to meet the food supply difficulties by lowering that standard and by rationalization. Since, with the solving of the unemployment problem, the maximum consumption level had been reached, some minor modifications in our home agricultural production might still, no doubt, be possible, but no fundamental alteration was possible in our basic food position. Thus autarchy was untenable in regard both to food and to the economy as a whole.

Participation in world economy:

To this there were limitations which we were unable to remove. The establishment of Germany's position on a secure and sound foundation was obstructed by market fluctuations, and commercial treaties afforded no guarantee for actual execution. In particular it had to be remembered that since the World War, those very countries which had formerly been food exporters had become industrialized. We were living in an age of economic empires in which the primitive urge to colonization was again manifesting itself; in the cases of Japan and Italy economic motives underlay the urge for expansion, and with Germany, too, economic need would supply the stimulus. For countries outside the great economic empires, opportunities for economic expansion were severely impeded. . . .

The development of great world political constellations progressed but slowly after all, and the German people with its strong racial core would find the most favorable prerequisites for such achievement in the heart of the continent of Europe. The history of all ages—the Roman Empire and the British Empire—had proved that expansion could only be carried out by breaking down resistance and taking risks; setbacks were inevitable. There had never in former times been spaces without a master, and there were none today; the attacker always comes up against a possessor.

The question for Germany ran: where could she achieve the greatest gain at the lowest cost. . . .

Germany's problem could only be solved by means of force and this was never without attendant risk. The campaigns of Frederick the Great for Silesia and Bismarck's wars against Austria and France had involved unheard-of risk, and the swiftness of the Prussian action in 1870 had kept Austria from entering the war. If one accepts as the basis of the following exposition the resort to force with its attendant risks, then there remain still to be answered the questions "when" and "how." In this matter there were three cases to be dealt with:

Case 1: Period 1943–1945. After this date only a change for the worse, from our point of view, could be expected.

The equipment of the army, navy, and *Luftwaffe*, as well as the formation of the officer corps, was nearly completed. Equipment and armament were modern; in further delay there lay the danger of their obsolescence. In particular, the secrecy of "special weapons" could not be preserved forever. The recruiting of reserves was limited to current age groups; further drafts from older untrained age groups were no longer available.

Our relative strength would decrease in relation to the rearmament which would by then have been carried out by the rest of the world. If we did not act by 1943–45, any year could, in consequence of a lack of reserves, produce the food crisis, to cope with which the necessary foreign exchange was not available, and this must be regarded as a "waning point of the regime." Besides, the world was expecting our attack and was increasing its countermeasures from year to year. It was while the rest of the world was still preparing its defenses that we were obliged to take the offensive.

Nobody knew today what the situation would be in the years 1943–45. One thing only was certain, that we could not wait longer.

. . . The necessity for action before 1943–45 would arise in cases 2 and 3.

Case 2: If internal strife in France should develop into such a domestic crisis as to absorb the French Army completely and render it incapable of use for war against Germany, then the time for action against the Czechs had come.

Case 3: If France is so embroiled by a war with another state that she cannot "proceed" against Germany. . . .

If the Czechs were overthrown and a common German-Hungarian frontier achieved, a neutral attitude on the part of Poland could be the more certainly counted on in the event of a Franco-German conflict. Our agreements with Poland only retained their force as long as Germany's strength remained unshaken. In the event of German setbacks a Polish action against East Prussia, and possibly against Pomerania and Silesia as well, had to be reckoned with.

On the assumption of a development of the situation leading to action on our part as planned, in the years 1943–45, the attitude of France, Britain, Italy, Poland, and Russia could probably be estimated as follows:

Actually, the Führer believed that almost certainly Britain, and probably France as well, had already tacitly written off the Czechs and were reconciled to the fact that this question would be cleared up in due course by Germany. Difficulties connected with the Empire, and the prospect of being once more entangled in a protracted European war, were decisive considerations for Britain against participation in a war against Germany. Britain's attitude would certainly not be without influence on that of France. An attack by France without British support, and with the prospect of the offensive being brought to a standstill on our western fortifications, was hardly probable. Nor was a French march through Belgium and Holland without British support to be expected; this also was a course not to be contemplated by us in the event of a conflict with France, because it would certainly entail the hostility of Britain. It would of course be necessary to maintain a strong defense on our western frontier during the prosecution of our attack on the Czechs and Austria. And in this connection it had to be remembered that the defense measures of the Czechs were growing in strength from year to year, and that the actual worth of the Austrian Army also was increasing in the course of time. Even though the populations concerned, especially of Czechoslovakia, were not sparse, the annexation of Czechoslovakia and Austria would mean an acquisition of foodstuffs for 5 to 6 million people, on the assumption that the compulsory emigration of 2 million people from Czechoslovakia and 1 million people from Austria was practicable. The incorporation of these two States with Germany meant, from the politico-military point of view, a substantial advantage because it would mean shorter and better frontiers, the freeing of forces for other purposes, and the possibility of creating new units up to a level of about twelve divisions, that is, one new division per million inhabitants.

Italy was not expected to object to the elimination of the Czechs, but it was impossible at the moment to estimate what her attitude on the Austrian question would be; that depended essentially upon whether the Duce were still alive.

The degree of surprise and the swiftness of our action were decisive factors for Poland's attitude. Poland—with Russia at her rear—will have little inclination to engage in war against a victorious Germany.

Military intervention by Russia must be countered by the swiftness of our operations; however, whether such an intervention was a practical contingency at all was, in view of Japan's attitude, more than doubtful. . . .

In appraising the situation Field Marshal von Blomberg and Colonel General von Fritsch repeatedly emphasized the necessity that Britain and France must not appear in the role of our enemies, and stated that the French Army would not be so committed by the war with Italy that France could not at the same time enter the field with forces superior to ours on our western frontier. General von Fritsch estimated the probable French forces available for use on the Alpine frontier at approximately twenty divisions, so that a strong French superiority would still remain on the western frontier, with the role, according to the German view, of invading the Rhineland. In this matter, moreover, the advanced state of French defense preparations must be taken into particular account, and it must be remembered apart from the insignificant value of our present fortifications—on which Field Marshal von Blomberg laid special emphasis—that the four motorized divisions intended for the West were still more or less incapable of movement. In regard to our offensive toward the southeast, Field Marshal von Blomberg drew particular attention to the strength of the Czech fortifications, which had acquired by now a structure like a Maginot Line and which would gravely hamper our attack.

General von Fritsch mentioned that this was the very purpose of a study which he had ordered made this winter, namely, to examine the possibility of conducting operations against the Czechs with special reference to overcoming the Czech fortification system; the General further expressed his opinion that under existing circumstances he must give up his plan to go abroad on his leave, which was due to begin on November 10. The Führer dismissed this idea on the ground that the possibility of a conflict need not yet be regarded as so imminent. To the Foreign Minister's objection that an Anglo-French-Italian conflict was not yet within such a measurable distance as the Führer seemed to assume, the Führer put the summer of 1938 as the date which seemed to him possible for this. In reply to considerations offered by Field Marshal von Blomberg and General von Fritsch regarding the attitude of Britain and France, the Führer repeated his previous statements that he was convinced of Britain's nonparticipation, and therefore he did not believe in the probability of belligerent action by France against Germany. Should the Mediterranean conflict under discussion lead to a general mobilization in Europe, then we must immediately begin action against the Czechs. On the other hand, should the powers not engaged in the war declare themselves disinterested, then Germany would have to adopt a similar attitude to this for the time being.

Colonel General Göring thought that, in view of the Führer's statement, we should consider liquidating our military undertakings in Spain. The Führer agrees to this with the limitation that he thinks he should reserve a decision for a proper moment.

The second part of the conference was concerned with concrete questions of armament.

HOSSBACH

Certified Correct:
  Colonel (General Staff)

30. Hitler Speaks to the German Press after the Humiliation of Czechoslovakia, November 10, 1938

Six weeks after the Munich Conference, Hitler met on November 10, 1938, in the city of his victory with some four hundred selected top members of the German press. The text of his confidential, rambling, self-congratulatory address was recorded at the time, but not published. It was included in a great mass of recordings confiscated by the British in 1945; neither the text, nor its significance, came to light until 1958. Few documents in modern history can equal this account of deliberate misuse of the press and public confidence in its validity.

SOURCE: Wilhelm Treue, "Rede Hitlers vor der deutschen Presse (10 November 1938)," *Vierteljahrshefte für Zeitgeschichte* (1958), VI: 181–191. Reprinted by permission of the publisher. Translation by the editor.

The achievements of this year, 1938, were primarily due to the immense education impact of National Socialism upon the German people. The fruits of this endeavor are now beginning to ripen. The German people passed their test in recent months with flying colors, better than any other European nation. These achievements obviously are further attributable to the decisiveness of our leadership. You may believe me, gentlemen, that it was not always easy to make these decisions in the first place, and secondly, to stick to them. The whole nation of course, particularly its intellectual circles, did not support these decisions; there were naturally many intelligent people—at least they think they are intelligent— who raised more doubts than gave approval. It was thus all the more important, ever since last May, to maintain and carry out these decisions with iron determination against all opposition. A further reason for our success and triumph was the preparation which we made in many areas, primarily in military armament. A large number of measures undertaken this spring had to take effect at the precise time and did so. Foremost was the massive construction of fortifications in the west. In the end, an adroit utilization of circumstances was perhaps the most important reason for our triumph. The general world situation seemed to me more favorable than ever for pressing our demands. Beside all this, we must not forget that there was another decisive factor, namely, *propaganda*, not only propaganda within the country but also the propaganda abroad. If *this* time—as I have already stressed—the German people took an attitude differing from that of many other peoples then this result must be ascribed to our continued work of enlightenment, to the propaganda with which we laid hold of the German people. And here the press has played a major role.

This past year we set several tasks for accomplishment by propaganda—and I note the press, here assembled, as the most important of our instruments. Our *first task* was the gradual preparation of the German people. For *decades* circumstances have forced me to talk of almost nothing but peace. Only by continuously stressing a German will and intention for peace was I able to win freedom, step by step, for the German people and to give them the strength that is always a necessary prerequisite for the next move. It goes without saying that decades of such peace propaganda have their dubious results as well; they can all too easily convince many people that the present regime will preserve peace under any circumstances. . . . It has now become necessary to change the psychological climate of the German people and to make them understand that there are objectives which must be attained by force when they cannot be gained by peace. It was thus essential not to advocate force as such, but rather to illuminate certain foreign developments for the German people in such a way that the *inner voice* of the people itself slowly began to demand force. . . . This endeavor took months; it was begun according to plan, carried on, and strengthened according to plan. Many did not understand it, gentlemen; many were of the opinion this was all a bit exaggerated. These are the overbred intellectuals who have not the faintest idea how a people can ultimately be stimulated to stand their ground even when thunder and lightning begin.

Our *second* task was to expose the world to this propaganda from a whole series of viewpoints. (1) It was necessary to show the rest of the world those problems which struck us as naturally urgent and grave. (2) It was necessary to make it clear to the rest of the world that the German nation was gradually coming to the point where it had to be taken seriously. (3) A convincing impression had to be conveyed of the solidarity of the German people. In these efforts our press was used substantially. It was also necessary to use the press and other propaganda to intimidate the enemy close by, namely in Czechoslovakia. There were no doubt some who did not understand many of the measures which were taken in these years. Gentlemen! After May 21, 1938, it was crystal clear that this problem had to be solved, one way or another! Any further postponement could only aggravate the question and make the solution more bloody. Today we know that it was absolutely the last moment to settle this matter as it has now been done. One thing is certain, gentlemen: even a delay of only one or two years would have put us militarily in an extremely difficult position. Our enemies in the rest of the world would have remained. The aircraft carrier poised at the heart of Germany [Czechoslovakia] would have armed and strengthened itself, and all the additional weapons of our own armament would have been gradually pre-empted by the need of dealing militarily first with this area.

The problem had to be solved this year, no matter what the circumstances. Postponement was now no longer possible. Here for the first time our preparations had to be planned and carried out with war ultimately in mind; they were so massive that it no longer seemed reasonable to camouflage them. We simply could no longer assume that in these circumstances the rest of the world would have been misled by any of our [customary] deceptions. I think this gramophone record, the pacifist one, is finished for us. I was convinced that only the other way was still open, namely to speak the truth brutally and relentlessly, no more and no less. I was convinced that in the long run this action would have the most crippling effect upon our immediate adversary. I was asked: "Do you think that is right? For months there has been continuous firing day and night in every gunnery range around Czechoslovakia; Czech pillboxes have been fired upon constantly; live ammunition is being fired constantly; you are drawing everybody's attention." I was convinced that by continued activity I would slowly but surely destroy the nerves of these gentlemen in Prague. And the press also had to help in this effort. It had to help by slowly unnerving these people; and, in fact, they did not stand fast. At the moment of final and decisive pressure, the others finally lost their nerve without the necessity of our actually taking up arms. That was one of the most essential tasks of our press campaign, obviously not understood by many. . . . But believe me, our methods were necessary. And ultimately it is success that counts.

Let me now confirm the fact that our propaganda worked superbly this year, quite superbly, and that the press adapted itself well to this work. It was a delight for me to read these many German newspapers every day. I really had to admit that this propaganda was bound to affect the German people in the long run, that it could not avoid influencing other countries, and that the nerves of the responsible gentlemen abroad (especially those in Prague) could not hold out against it. Praise and thank God, they all know German and all read our newspapers. . . . Success, as I have already said, is decisive; and this, gentlemen, is an enormous one. It is fantastic, so great that we today can hardly begin to measure it. I was most aware of its magnitude the moment I first stood along the line of Czech pillboxes. There I learned what it means to acquire a front of nearly 1,300 miles of fortifications without firing a shot. Gentlemen, this time we have acquired ten million people and more than a hundred thousand square kilometers of territory by propaganda in service of a cause. That is a tremendous achievement.

These events give us an understanding of Napoleon's victories. He achieved them not only as a strategist or ingenious commander; he was preceded by the "Marseillaise," and the ideas of the French Revolution and actually reaped what this revolution had earlier sown. From all of this we must draw one basic conclusion: the press, gentlemen, can achieve fantastic results and can have fantastic effects when it becomes a means to an end. . . .

We in Germany have consistently striven to shape the press into just such a weapon. . . . Now, once again, we have great tasks ahead of us. There is one *above all*, gentlemen: we must now proceed, *step by step*, to strengthen the self-confidence of the German people! I know that is a task which cannot be completed in one or in two years. We need public opinion that is strong, *firmly rooted in self confidence*, if possible, even reaching the intellectual circles. (Laughter in the audience). . . .

We must succeed in giving our people confidence based on our own most recent history and our own ideology, in order to complete the great political tasks of the future. The Führer of this nation can achieve no more than the nation itself gives him. That is a law of irrefutable validity and significance. . . . I must have behind me a faithful, united, confident and trusting German people. It is our mutual and formidable task to achieve that objective, and it is a fabulous task. It is really something, mark you, to *make* history. Today we are in a marvelous time of which we can say that history really was made, that we did not waste time, that we did not exhaust ourselves writing about things just for the sake of writing, or that we talked just for the sake of talking. Indeed, it has all led to results and especially to an historical outcome that we can proudly serve up compared to earlier generations. And that is our common accomplishment, not just mine alone, but the accomplishment of all the hundreds of thousands standing behind me, and marching with me. . . .

It is necessary that you men of the press adhere blindly to the principle: "The leadership acts correctly." Gentlemen, we must all claim some license for ourselves to make mistakes. Even newspapermen are not free of this danger. We can all only prevail if we do not mutually illuminate our mistakes before the world, but rather seek to emphasize the positive. In other words, the basic correctness of the leadership must always be stressed. That is the decisive point. Above all, mark you, that is necessary for the people's own sake. I hear so often, even today, questions—liberalistic lapses—like: "Well, shouldn't we perhaps leave it up to the people this time?" Mark you, gentlemen, I believe I have accomplished quite a bit, in any case more than a shoemaker or milkmaid. Nevertheless, it is possible that I do not entirely agree in the judgment of a problem with other gentlemen who have accomplished just as much. But it is certain that a decision must now be reached. It is quite impossible that I leave the making of this decision, on which we do not all quite agree, in the hands of the milkmaids, dairy farmers, and shoemakers. That is out of the question. Therefore, it is entirely irrelevant whether such a decision is ultimately entirely right—that is *totally unimportant*. What is decisive is that the entire nation stand in closed ranks behind such a decision. It must be a united front, and then whatever is not entirely right about the decision will be made good by the resolve with which the entire nation stands behind it.

This is important for the years to come, gentlemen! Only this way will we free our people from the kind of doubt which only makes them unhappy. The vast majority has but *one single desire:* that they be well led, that they be able to trust their leadership, that the leaders not argue among themselves, but stand solidly in front of them. Believe me, I know. . . . When they see this picture, the Führer with all his men at his side, that calms the people enormously and that makes them *happy!* They *want* that! Thus it was earlier in German history. The people are always happy when some stand together above them as leaders; it strengthens the mutual cohesiveness of the people below as well. This we must understand; thus we must all act so as to keep and continue that impression among the people. They must be convinced that their leadership is *acting correctly* and that everyone is in agreement.

And then it will be very easy for the leadership to assert itself psychologically in critical situations against the surrounding world.

There is just one thing I would like to say in conclusion, gentlemen: in liberal countries the function of the press is seen as: *the press plus the people against the leadership*. Here it must read: *leadership plus propaganda and press, etc. guiding the people!* . . . And in presence of the people itself, this leadership must appear as a single dedicated body. Opinions can be exchanged privately among ourselves. In presence of the *people*, there is just one opinion. Gentlemen, that is a perfectly clear principle! If we can enforce it completely, then the German people will become great and powerful *by virtue of this leadership*. Then we will not be standing in 1938, at the end of a historical epoch, but *we* will surely be standing at the very *beginning* of a greater one.

I believe in this future for the German people. Perhaps there used to be many who asked: "The Führer is certainly a dreamer—why does he believe in such possibilities?" Very simple, gentlemen. History is made by men. It has been made by men before and is being made by men today. What matters is the worthiness of these men, and after that their number. The worthiness of the German people is incomparable. I will *never* let myself be convinced that any other people could be *more* so! I am convinced that our people, especially today with their gradual racial improvement, represents the greatest worthiness that can be found on earth. . . .

Whoever doubts the future of this greatest bloc of mankind, or does not believe in its future, is only a weakling himself. We once *were* the greatest Reich. Then we grew tired and weary; we exhausted our strengths in a process of internal disintegration and thus lost stature in the eyes of the world. Now after a crisis of three or four hundred years, the recovery of our people has begun. And I know for certain, we are now standing at the beginning of our German life and thus of our German future. It is the greatest good fortune for all of us that we are permitted to prepare for, indeed to help mold this future, and to assist in achieving it. The opportunity must fill us with the deepest satisfaction; everything else disappears into an empty void in face of it. This conviction once led me out from a military hospital to this very moment when I am standing before you. And this conviction must motivate us all on the road ahead for our German people. I am convinced that it will be a road to greatness, a road to a great future for our German nation. Let me thank you once again for your cooperation.

31. The Führer Conference of May 23, 1939

As seen from the preceding documents, Hitler did not plan for war according to a strict time table. He took account of internal preconditions, prepared Germany economically and psychologically (as well as militarily), and concurrently tried to manipulate the changing international scene to Germany's advantage. These efforts reached a climax by the spring of 1939. In mid-March German troops occupied Prague; a week later the Nazis pressed stiff demands upon Poland over Danzig and the "Polish Corridor." Britain and France responded with pledges to preserve Polish sovereignty (March 31), subsequently extending these guarantees to Rumania and Greece (April 13) after Italy had seized Albania. On April 28 Hitler dramatically denounced Germany's peace pact of 1934 with Poland and the Anglo-German Naval Treaty of 1935. Just before the conference described below, Mussolini and Hitler proclaimed that the Rome-Berlin Axis was transformed into a firm military alliance. Now Hitler gathered his military chiefs to consider the potentialities of the immediate future.

SOURCE: Germany. Auswärtiges Amt. *Documents on German Foreign Policy*. Series D (Washington, D.C., 1956), VI: 574–580.

[no place, no date]

TOP SECRET

To be handled by officer only. . . .

    Subject: *Briefing on the Situation and Political Objectives*
        The Führer gave as *the purpose of the conference:*
1. Review of the situation.
2. To set the Armed Forces the tasks arising from the situation.
3. Definition of the conclusions to be drawn from these tasks.
4. Ensuring that secrecy is maintained on all decisions and measures resulting from these conclusions. Secrecy is the prerequisite for success.

The gist of the Führer's statements is as follows.

Our present position must be viewed under two aspects.
    a. Actual development from 1933–1939.
    b. Germany's never-changing situation.

From 1933–1939 progress in all spheres. Our military situation improved enormously.

Our situation *vis-à-vis* the surrounding world has remained the same.

Germany was outside the circle of the Great Powers. A balance of power had been established without Germany's participation.

This balance is being disturbed by Germany claiming her vital rights and her reappearance in the circle of the Great Powers. All claims are regarded as "breaking in." . . .

After six years the present position is as follows:

The national political unification of the Germans has been achieved bar minor exceptions. Further successes can no longer be won without bloodshed.

The delineation of frontiers is of military importance.

The Pole is not a fresh enemy. Poland will always be on the side of our adversaries. In spite of treaties of friendship Poland has always been bent on exploiting every opportunity against us.

It is not Danzig that is at stake. For us it is a matter of expanding our living space in the East and making food supplies secure and also solving the problem of the Baltic States. Food supplies can only be obtained from thinly populated areas. Over and above fertility, the thorough German cultivation will tremendously increase the produce. . . .

There is therefore no question of sparing Poland and we are left with the *decision:*

To attack Poland at the first suitable opportunity. . . .

What will this conflict be like?

England cannot finish off Germany with a few powerful blows and force us down. It is of decisive importance for England to carry the war as near as possible to the Ruhr. French blood will not be spared (West Wall!!). The duration of our existence is dependent on possession of the Ruhr. . . .

Therefore, if England wants to intervene in the Polish war, we must make a lighting attack on Holland. We must aim at establishing a new line of defence on Dutch territory as far as the Zuyder Zee. The war with England and France will be a war of life and death.

The idea of getting out cheaply is dangerous; there is no such possibility. We must then burn our boats and it will no longer be a question of right or wrong but of to be or not to be for 80,000,000 people.

Question: Short or long war? . . .

England is the motive force driving against Germany. Her strength lies in the following:

1. The Briton himself is proud, brave, tough, dogged, and a gifted organizer. He knows how to exploit every new development. He has the love of adventure and the courage of the Nordic race. The increase in quantity involves a lowering of quality. The German average standard is higher.

2. England is a World Power in herself. Constant for three hundred years. Increased by alliances. This power is to be regarded as embracing the whole world not only physically but also psychologically.

Add to this immeasurable wealth and the solvency that goes with it.

3. Geopolitical security and protection by a strong sea power and valiant air force. . . .

Planning must be based on the most *unfavorable* conditions.

1. *The aim* must be to deal the enemy at the start a smashing blow or *the* smashing blow. Here right or wrong, or treaties, play no part.

This is only possible if we do not "slide" into a war with England on account of Poland.

2. *Preparations* must be made for a *long war as well as* for a surprise *attack* and every possible intervention by England on the Continent must be smashed.

The Army must occupy the positions important for the Fleet and the Luftwaffe. If we succeed in occupying and securing Holland and Belgium, as well as beating France, the basis for a successful war against England has been created.

The Luftwaffe can then closely blockade England from western France and the Fleet undertake the wider blockade with submarines.

Results:

England cannot fight on the Continent.

The daily attacks by the Luftwaffe and the Fleet sever all vital arteries.

Time will decide against England.

Germany does not bleed to death on land.

The necessity of *such conduct of the war* is proved by the World War and military operations since. The World War *compels* us to draw the following *conclusions* for the conduct of war.

1. Had the Fleet been stronger at the beginning of the World War or had the Army been switched to the Channel Ports the war would have had quite a different outcome.

2. A country cannot be forced down by the Air Arm. All objectives cannot be attacked simultaneously and a few minutes' interval brings into action anti-aircraft devices.

3. It is important to use all means ruthlessly.

4. Once the Army in cooperation with the Luftwaffe and the Fleet has taken the most important positions, industrial production will cease to flow into the bottomless Danaid cask of the Army's battles but will be available for the benefit of the Luftwaffe and the Fleet.

Therefore the Army must be able to capture these positions. *The attack must be prepared according to plan.*

Study of this is the most important task.

The *aim* will always be to force England to her knees.

The effect of any weapon will decide a battle only as long as the enemy does not possess it.

This goes for gas, submarines and the Luftwaffe.

This applied to the Luftwaffe as long as, for instance, the English Fleet had no defence against it but that would no longer be so in 1940 and 1941. Against Poland, for instance, tanks will be effective as the Polish Army lacks defence against them.

Where the effect can no longer be regarded as decisive it must be replaced by surprise and masterly handling.

This is the *programme of attack.*

The programme demands

1. The correct assessment of weapons and their effects, e.g.,
   a. battleships or aircraft carriers: which is the more effective both in single cases and considered as a whole? The aircraft carrier is the better protection to a convoy.
   b. Is air attack on a factory more important than that on a battleship? Where are the bottlenecks in manufacturing?

2. Rapid mobility of the Army. It must move straight from its barracks to overrun neighboring countries.
3. Study of the enemy's vulnerable points. These studies must not be left to the General Staff. Secrecy would then no longer be assured.

The Führer has therefore decided to order the setting-up of a small *planning staff in the OKW*, composed of representatives of the three branches of the Armed Forces and calling in, whenever necessary, the three Commanders-in-Chief or their Chiefs of Staff. The staff will have to keep the Führer currently informed and report to him.

This planning staff will undertake the planning preparations for the operations to the utmost degree and the resultant technical and organizational preparations.

The object of any of the schemes drawn up is the concern of no one outside the staff.

However much our enemies may increase their armaments they must, at some time or other, come to the end of their resources and our armaments will be the greater.

French age groups yield only 120,000 recruits!

We shall not be forced into a war but we will not be able to avoid one.

Secrecy is the decisive prerequisite for success. Our objects must be kept secret from both Italy and Japan. As for Italy, we shall continue to abide by the Maginot Line breakthrough, which is to be studied. The Führer thinks this breakthrough possible.

On studying the problem as a whole, coordination (grouping together) of the branches of the Armed Forces is important.

The object—
1. Study of the problem as a whole,
2. Study of how to set about it,
3. Study of the resources needed,
4. Study of the necessary training.

Members of the staff must be men of great imagination and the highest specialist competence as well as officers of sober and critical judgment.

Principles to be applied to this work.
1. No one to be initiated who does not have to be.

2. No one to know more about it than he has to.

3. When is the latest for him to know? No one to know anything sooner than he has to.

In reply to Field Marshal Göring the Führer lays down that:

a. the branches of the Armed Forces determine what is to be constructed;

b. nothing will be changed in the shipbuilding programme;

c. the armaments programme will be completed by 1943 or 1944. Certified correct.

SCHMUNDT, Lt. Col.

32. Speech by the Führer to the Commanders-in-Chief, August 22, 1939

During the summer of 1939 Germany intensified her quarrel with Poland. Berlin disregarded repeated warnings from London and Paris as it pressed its demands upon Warsaw. In late June German "volunteers" began to appear in Danzig to support the "defense" of the isolated free city. The announcement of the Nazi-Soviet nonaggression pact (which also had a secret protocol providing for economic aid, a Fourth Partition of Poland and discussion of other disputes in Eastern Europe) precipitated the crisis which led to war. The terse wording of the following unsigned memorandum indicates that it is not the full text of Hitler's address, but rather a compressed set of notes.

SOURCE: Germany. Auswärtiges Amt. *Documents on German Foreign Policy*, Series D (Washington, D.C., 1956), VII: 200–204.

I have called you together to give you a picture of the political situation, in order that you may have some insight into the individual factors on which I have based my decision to act and in order to strengthen your confidence. . . .

1. First of all two personal factors:

My own personality and that of Mussolini.

Essentially all depends on me, on my existence, because of my political talents. Furthermore, the fact that probably no one will ever again have the confidence of the whole German people as I have. There will probably never again in the future be a man with more authority than I have. My existence is therefore a factor of great value. But I can be eliminated at any time by a criminal or a lunatic.

The second personal factor is the Duce. His existence is also decisive. If anything happens to him, Italy's loyalty to the alliance will no longer be certain. The Italian Court is fundamentally opposed to the Duce. Above all, the Court regards the expansion of the empire as an encumbrance. The Duce is the man with the strongest nerves in Italy.

The third personal factor in our favor is Franco. We can ask only for benevolent neutrality from Spain. But this depends on Franco's personality. He guarantees a certain uniformity and stability in the present system in Spain. We must accept the fact that Spain does not as yet have a Fascist party with our internal unity. . . .

It is easy for us to make decisions. We have nothing to lose; we have everything to gain. Because of our restrictions our economic situation is such that we can only hold out for a few more years. Göring can confirm this. We have no other choice, we must act. Our opponents will be risking a great deal and can gain only a little. Britain's stake in a war is inconceivably great. Our enemies have leaders who are below the average. No personalities. No masters, no men of action. . . .

The creation of Greater Germany was a great achievement politically, but militarily it was doubtful, since it was achieved by bluff on the part of the political leaders. It is necessary to test the military [machine]. If at all possible, not in a general reckoning, but by the accomplishment of individual tasks.

The relationship with Poland has become unbearable. My Polish policy hitherto was contrary to the views of the people. My proposals to Poland (Danzig and the Corridor) were frustrated by England's intervention. Poland changed her tone toward us. A permanent state of tension is intolerable. The power of initiative cannot be allowed to pass to others. The present moment is more favorable than in two or three years' time. An attempt on my life or Mussolini's could change the situation to our disadvantage. One cannot for ever face one another with rifles cocked. One compromise solution suggested to us was that we should change our convictions and make kind gestures. They talked to us again in the language of Versailles. There was a danger of losing prestige. Now the probability is still great that the West will not intervene. We must take the risk with ruthless determination. The politician must take a risk just as much as the general. We are faced with the harsh alternatives of striking or of certain annihilation sooner or later.

Reference to previous hazardous undertakings.

I should have been stoned if I had not been proved right. The most dangerous step was the entry into the neutral zone [demilitarized Rhineland, 1936]. Only a week before, I got a warning through France. I have always taken a great risk in the conviction that it would succeed.

Now it is also a great risk. Iron nerves, iron resolution.

The following special reasons fortify me in my view. England and France have undertaken obligations which neither is in a position to fulfil. There is no real rearmament in England, but only propaganda. A great deal of harm was done by many Germans, who were not in agreement with me, saying and writing to English people after the solution of the Czech question: The Führer succeeded because you lost your nerve, because you capitulated too soon. This explains the present propaganda war. The English speak of a war of nerves. One factor in this war of nerves is to boost the increase of armaments. But what are the real facts about British rearmament? The naval construction programme for 1938 has not yet been completed. Only the reserve fleet has been mobilized. Purchase of trawlers. No substantial strengthening of the Navy before 1941 or 1942. . . .

France is short of men (decline in the birth rate). Little has been done for rearmament. The artillery is obsolete. France did not want to embark on this adventure. The West has only two possibilities for fighting against us:

1. Blockade: It will not be effective because of our autarky and because we have sources of supply in Eastern Europe.

2. Attack in the West from the Maginot line: I consider this impossible.

Another possibility would be the violation of Dutch, Belgian, and Swiss neutrality. I have no doubt that all these States, as well as Scandinavia, will defend their neutrality with all available means. England and France will not violate the neutrality of these countries. Thus in actual fact England cannot help Poland. There still remains an attack on Italy. Military intervention is out of the question. No one is counting on a long war. If Herr von Brauchitsch had told me that I would need four years to conquer Poland I would have replied: "Then it cannot be done." It is nonsense to say that England wants to wage a long war.

We will hold our position in the West until we have conquered Poland. We must bear in mind our great production capacity. It is much greater than in 1914–1918.

The enemy had another hope, that Russia would become our enemy after the conquest of Poland. The enemy did not reckon with my great strength of purpose. Our enemies are small fry. I saw them in Munich.

I was convinced that Stalin would never accept the English offer. Russia has no interest in preserving Poland, and Stalin knows that it would mean the end of his régime, no matter whether his soldiers emerged from a war victorious or vanquished. Litvinov's replacement was decisive. I brought about the change toward Russia gradually. In connection with the commercial treaty we got into political conversations. Proposal for a nonaggression pact. Then came a comprehensive proposal from Russia. Four days ago I took a special step, which led to Russia replying yesterday that she is prepared to sign. Personal contact with Stalin is established. The day after tomorrow von Ribbentrop will conclude the treaty. Now Poland is in the position in which I wanted her.

We need not be afraid of a blockade. The East will supply us with grain, cattle, coal, lead and zinc. It is a mighty aim, which demands great efforts. I am only afraid that at the last moment some swine or other will yet submit to me a plan for mediation.

The political objective goes further. A start has been made on the destruction of England's hegemony. The way will be open for the soldiers after I have made the political preparations.

Today's announcement of the non-aggression pact with Russia came as a bombshell. The consequences cannot be foreseen. Stalin also said that this course will benefit both countries. The effect on Poland will be tremendous.

In reply, Göring thanked the Führer and assured him that the Wehrmacht would do their duty.

IX

The Emergence of the SS State, 1939–1945

MUCH THAT transpired in Germany after the Nazi seizure of power might have been predicted from reading *Mein Kampf* or subsequent Nazi declarations. The emergence of the SS state, however, was a result of forces, circumstances, and personalities interacting to produce an unanticipated thrust that by early 1945 gave Germany an appalling tone of life similar to that of Stalinist Russia in the 1930s. This startling comparison refers to the scope of social change the SS contemplated, its coercion of millions of individuals into "planned" agricultural and industrial enterprises, and the outright extermination of other millions as alleged opponents or undesirables. This emerging SS state within the Nazi state was most clearly evident in occupied Slavic eastern Europe. By 1944 its outlines were becoming apparent in the German homeland as well, psychologically illuminated by the mounting destructiveness of the Allied bombing of German urban centers.

The SS had an inauspicious beginning in the mid-twenties as a specially trained unit to guard the Führer and perform on ceremonial occasions. By 1930, however, Heinrich Himmler and Reinhardt Heydrich were giving the SS a new image as a biologically, intellectually, and ideologically superior elite corps. Rivalry developed between the SS and the Storm Troopers, between Himmler and other top Nazis. From 1933 onward the SS increased its scope of influence and visibility; in April 1934 Himmler took charge of the Gestapo and by that time the planning and management of the concentration camps were also passing to the SS. Himmler's great opportunity came during the bloody purge of June 1934, when the disciplined SS was turned on the unruly and discontented leadership of the Storm Troopers. Thereafter the Führer concentrated his confidence and favor upon the systematically selected and controlled black guards. Between 1936 and 1939 Hitler increasingly disdained the generals of the army for their reluctance to give all-out support to his military-political gambles in the reoccupation of the Rhineland, the seizure of Austria, and the dismemberment of Czechoslovakia. His distrust of the essentially conservative, professional, and nonideological stance of the officer corps deepened. When the war began in 1939, the SS leadership began to press for complete control of Germany's power structure, notably the armed forces.

33. The SS Takes over the Third Reich, 1939–1944

At the end of World War II a distinguished German dramatist, Carl Zuckmayer, wrote *The Devil's General,* a classic expression of the dilemma of a humane officer caught between duty and conscience in war *and* specifically under pressure to abandon his traditions and fellow officers by transferring to the SS. The following document gives a more succinct overview of the SS grasp for power. Its author, Erich Kordt, served with the German foreign office at home and abroad during the Nazi years.

SOURCE: Erich Kordt, *Wahn und Wirklichkeit* (Stuttgart: Union Verlag, 1947), pp. 344–350. Reprinted by permission of the publisher. Translation by the editor.

As the general condition of Germany grew more and more desperate, the role of the SS and of Himmler became more prominent. Now began that ghastly chapter of terror in the occupied territories, and no less in Germany itself, for which no parallel can be found in history.

Since the beginning of the war, the so-called *Waffen-SS* (Combat-SS) had increased enormously. Up to 1938 Hitler had let the military circles believe that the Army would remain the nation's prime defenders and that they, together with the Party, constituted the most important pillar of the state. Earlier, during the establishment of the National Socialist power structure, the toleration of the Army was bought by this formula. However, by the opening of the Polish campaign, Hitler had managed to establish three divisions of Combat-SS troops. Before and after the West European campaign of 1940, this number was rapidly increased, a trend which naturally caused grave concern in the Army. At the behest of Hitler, General von Brauchitsch issued a directive to the various Army commands in an attempt to justify this increase of heavily armed SS divisions and to dispel Army misgivings. He argued that after the war even police units would not be fully acceptable to the people unless they had had battle experience. Thus, the SS troops (which later were to be used only as police forces) were now to fight shoulder to shoulder with the Army divisions.

The SS infantry units were soon joined by SS armored divisions. Whenever the total strength of the Armed Forces was raised, Hitler ordered that a number of SS divisions be included. They were supposedly established as special elite units from selected volunteers. Their equipment exceeded considerably that of the Army. Only in a tactical sense were they under the control of the Army Corps to which they were assigned; in matters of discipline they were directly responsible to the organization of the SS Reichsführer Himmler. By 1942, the necessary quota of volunteers could no longer be found and the SS adopted progressively more energetic methods of recruitment, until they resorted finally to direct induction and transfer of men from the Army and the Air Force. By the end of the war the number of SS divisions rose to thirty-seven, more than fifteen percent of the total strength of the Army. Given its better equipment, the SS constituted an enormous power, which contributed in no small degree to the fact that no army leaders rebelled or revolted against Hitler's military orders. Only the admixture of SS troops to the regular Army enabled Hitler to continue the hopeless war. The so-called Supreme Office of Reich Security, the headquarters of the SS, was Hitler's main instrument for the control of Germany and the conquered territories.

Hitler had transferred all police functions to the SS in those areas of the Soviet Union not directly part of the war zone. Here, and in all other occupied areas, Himmler required that in every question of public security, the local police commander (the so-called Superior SS and Police Leader) be responsible directly to *him* and not to the Reichs-Commissar in question, not to the Minister for the Occupied Eastern Territories, Rosenberg; not to General-Governor Frank, in Cracow; not to the Reichs-Commissar in Holland, Seysz-Inquardt; nor to the Reichs-Protector in Bohemia and Moravia. Some of the Superior SS and Police Leaders achieved particularly notorious fame. Mostly they were also secretaries of state and deputies of the nominal chiefs of civil administration, whose power they greatly exceeded.

Himmler also continuously expanded his power in the economic field. His Department I, Administration and Economy (in the Supreme Office of Reich Security), supervised so many factories confiscated from Jews or other "undesirable" personalities, that it soon administered a greater industrial complex than even the gigantic organization of the "Herman-Goering Werke." In 1942 he also began to establish autonomous munitions factories. Since he had an abundance of workers from concentration camps, he was in a position of great independence. Only with the greatest difficulty did the Ministry of Armaments contain these efforts and prevent appreciable damage to the rest of industry. The SS played an essential role in recruiting workers from the occupied territories, and the terror evoked by its very name was ruthlessly exploited.

The consolidation of power by the SS had been decisively fostered by Reinhardt Heydrich. Indeed, it is no exaggeration to say that Heydrich, Chief of the Supreme Office of Reich Security and of the Security Police, deputy and close associate of Himmler, was the driving force of this burgeoning organization.

This man had also been selected by Hitler as executor of his program to murder as much of the entire Jewish population as he could. The order, unequalled in its monstrosity, was characterized by Hitler as a directive for the "Final Solution of the Jewish Question." Strictest secrecy was required. The systematic extermination of the Jewish population began as early as the summer of 1941 in many parts of the occupied Eastern regions. Although special Action Units were created, it was soon impossible to keep the necessary measures of secrecy. Since they feared the reaction of the population and of the troops, the criminals devised a more inconspicuous method of committing these atrocious mass murders with a bare minimum of collaborators. It is a horrifying fact that this plan, which defies description, could be realized only by the use of technology and new inventions, an expertism which became the curse and shame of humanity. To execute Hitler's orders on the "Final Solution of the Jewish Question," Himmler ordered mass gassing of Jews in the concentration camp at Auschwitz and several other remote locations. Less than one hundred persons were needed to form the SS Action Unit under SS Officer Eichmann and to commit the greatest mass murder in history. The pen resists describing the mechanical, almost dispassionate and terrifying inhumanity of those daily murders which went on for years.

The murders in Auschwitz continued until October, 1944. Then even Himmler must have felt gripping fear. He ordered the killing stopped and more careful treatment for the survivors. He hoped to use these and other prisoners in a final blackmail attempt, possibly to buy immunity for himself and his aides. Heydrich would surely have been intelligent enough to recognize the futility of such an attempt. Of all the dark and dubious characters in Hitler's entourage he, like Goebbels, would not have wavered from the principle of "all or nothing." Thus some courageous Czechs, in assassinating him on June 4, 1942, had a decisive role in foiling Hitler's plan for an apocalyptic finale in Central Europe.

With the growth of Himmler's power, the last remnants of an independent and "law-respecting" judiciary were eliminated. All who came into conflict with the regime, intentionally or not, were subjected to pure tyranny.

On April 26, 1942, Hitler convened the Reichstag. He tried to counteract the growing psychological repercussions of the great strategic errors committed in the winter campaign of 1941–42. In a unanimous declaration issued at his instigation, the Reichstag granted him broad discretion "in the present struggle for the existence of the German people, as Führer of the nation, Supreme Commander of the Armed Forces, Head of the Government and highest Member of the Executive, Supreme Judge and Führer of the Party." These powers permitted him to mete out punishment to all people, by his own judgment and regardless of lawful procedures or well established rights, thus coercing Germans to perform their duties. This act confirmed his absolute executive powers over all spheres of public life, although *de facto* he had already long been exercising them. The inescapable conclusion is that the new powers were aimed especially against those "advisors" who still reminded him too frequently of the proper form, if not the substance, of justice.

34. Heinrich Himmler on Germany's Future in the East, 1942

Of all the top Nazi hierarchy, Heinrich Himmler appeared to have the fewest administrative and leadership qualities. Yet, this erstwhile Bavarian poultry farmer developed the most lethal organization in the history of the Western world. His colorless external bearing concealed an amoral personality captivated by ruthless ideology that expressed itself in pedantic devotion to detail. Himmler delivered the following address on September 16, 1942, to members of an SS and police leadership conference convened by SS Police Führer of the Ukraine, Hans Prützmann, at Himmler's field headquarters in southwestern Russia. It is heavily excerpted, for Himmler was even more garrulous and repetitive than Hitler.

SOURCE: Himmler Files (Washington, D.C.); microfilm at Institut für Zeitgeschichte, Munich. Reprinted in H-A. Jacobsen and W. Jochmann, eds., *Zur Geschichte des Nationalsozialismus. Ausgewählte Dokumente* (Bielefeld, 1961). Translation by the editor.

My trusted SS Leaders,

Ten years ago we could hardly have dreamed that one day we would hold an SS leadership conference in a place now called Hegewald and near the once predominantly Jewish-Russian city of Shitomir. I am happy to be able to welcome you as guests, here in my quarters, to this conference convened by SS Obergruppenführer Prützmann, your Superior SS and Police Leader. I even suggested myself that you come here because it gives me the opportunity to meet you, talk to you, and tell you a few things.

We are still in the midst of a great strategic campaign in Russia. This struggle is very difficult. You who are now bogged down in this Russia know it best of all. This year we have again brought a considerable portion of the country under our control and we will conquer even more in the next few months. We have torn from this giant Slavic colossus another chunk of its military, manpower and armament capacity; and we can certainly completely demolish the rest of its remaining European segment during the next year. There is probably not a single soldier who has any doubts that the

Russian is the toughest opponent we have yet encountered and, I believe, the toughest we can possibly have in this World War. We also agree that this Russian will not capitulate. The conduct of this purely military struggle is truly severe; and we can expect some more difficult months, a more difficult quarter-year, half-year or year. But some time history will note, dispassionately as it does, that this war lasted three, four, or five years. This is what is said of the First World War; this is what it will say of the Second World War. All the sorrow, the blood, the responsibility, all the grief and worry of these months and years, which above all, rested on the shoulders of the Führer, will not be noted or mentioned. In the end, history will simply record the success that was achieved. After the war, it will state that a greater German Reich was established, particularly encompassing this eastern area. . . .

We must draw conclusions which I would like to summarize briefly: we are now conquering the approaches to Asia. We must round up whatever there is of good German blood anywhere in the world. We will bring the *Volksdeutsche* [ethnic Germans] home. Whether they want to or not, whether they understand or not, all people of Germanic origin will have to give their allegiance to this Reich by the obligation of their blood and the logic of historic destiny. Any desirable human material—and this is the first principle which you must note—that you find anywhere in the East, must be won over or annihilated. It would be a crime against ourselves to leave this physical resource with the other side so that tomorrow it might produce another leader of small, large or medium stature. Ultimately only our own blood can defeat us, or (to express it differently out here in Russia) the fruits, the conquests of our own blood. After all, the Russians did not invent the tank, the Stalin rockets, or any of these things; what they did invent was the most practical way to steal and imitate them. And then there are, of course, individual elements, Germanic remnants and products of our blood, who look like us and also have intelligence like us, and they are potentially dangerous. The really dim-witted little man is not dangerous without a leader. Therefore, let your maxim inexorably be: where you find good blood you must win it for Germany or you must be certain that it no longer persists. Under no circumstances should it survive on the side of our enemy. . . .

Our whole orientation is simply this: We have no need to bring our culture to these people. I can only repeat verbatim what the Führer wishes. This will suffice: (1) let the children learn traffic signs in school so they do not run into our cars; (2) let them learn their multiplication tables up to 25 so that they can count that far; and (3) let them learn to write their names—no more is necessary.

Our task is to sort out what is racially acceptable [among the Aryans we find here]. We will bring these youths back to Germany; they will go to German schools and those who are more highly qualified will go to boarding schools or to *Napolas* [National political educational institutions]. From the start, a boy will grow up as conscious representative of his blood, as a conscious citizen of the greater Germanic Reich; he will not be raised by us as a national Ukrainian. No one need worry that we of the SS, who have carried out this selection, will contaminate the blood of the German people [by taking these Ukrainians]. We will select only those who are truly racially acceptable. It is no betrayal of their national character if they comprehend the problem of the Slavic state for the very first time [indiscriminate racial mixture], and we explain to one of them: "You look like us, like a man from Schleswig-Holstein, and you think like us." We will show him another Russian who looks like a monkey and ask him: "Do you share Russian ideals with him or have you not a different set of ideals, namely those of one Reich of the same blood, regardless of your origins?" It will make him proud if we single him out as a worthy man and if we can tell him with conviction: "You are one of those we can select! . . ."

Our most immediate contact with people of this blood are the *Volksdeutsche*. . . . Look after them with infinite great love and effort. You must go into the country to these *Volksdeutsche* often. I do not again want to find that an SS and police officer is personally acquainted with hardly ten of his German villages. I demand that in the course of a year—despite weather and bad roads, in winter even with sleighs—the settlements of *Volksdeutsche* be visited repeatedly. They are grateful when a German general and SS Leader comes to them, spends the night at their house, and talks with them, converses with them about all their troubles; for they are indeed very suspicious and afraid this or that person might have informed against them. If they have a sick child, bring it with you in the sleigh or vehicle to your quarters or take it to the hospital. If a mother has a baby, be the godfather. Just imagine how grateful the people will be! That is the way to win their confidence! These people, who have remained Germans despite a generation of cruel persecution, have earned it. Aside from that, anyone who does not take care of his own blood is a fool anyway, for he is cutting his own throat.

I visualize the treatment of the *Volksdeutsche* as follows, and I have made an agreement with Gauleiter Koch on the matter. As Reichskommissar for the Strengthening of German heritage, I have issued a written directive to Germanize those of German descent who are registered in the *Volksliste* of Koch's Reich Commissariat. This Germanization will likely remain the business of the occupation administration, and we will work with them.

I have also directed that the 43,000 *Volksdeutsche* in the General Commissariat of Shitomir shall be settled in three areas. Some twelve to fifteen thousand people will be settled in a radius of about ten kilometers around each of the villages of Korosten, Hegewald (on the fringe of Shitomir with my headquarters area as the town center), and Winniza. I have further directed that the possessions of these Germans, as of January 1, 1914, are to be restored. In their new settlements they will receive at least the same amount of land which they had in 1914.

The resettlement is proceeding very well. It will occur in Hegewald during the next four to six weeks and by year's end these Germans will be stabilized. As a result of these changes the road from Korosten to Winniza will pass through German territory at three places, for a distance of twenty kilometers each. That is the best security! At the three points we will select approximately 800 to 1,000 men from these German people as home guards. Today they are doing us no good, for they live in 287 villages, in handfuls among a mass of Russians. We cannot help them, nor they us, and they signify no increase in our strength.

The farms will become presentable and large. We cannot build new structures during the war; we will have to improvise and first assist in combining several existing cottages. One will be lived in, the other used for storage. The planned farms are 15–25 hectares in size with the proviso that farms can grow up to 30 or 35 hectares, since that is the average size the Führer wants. Then these villages can also be somewhat improved architecturally.

When we leave here, SS regimental Commander Jungkunz will be the Area Commissar; at the same time he will be District Commander because after our withdrawal a replacement battalion of the SS will arrive. Thus we have both the government authority and the authorized SS Leader in one and the same person. A hospital, a school, a dispensary, etc. will be built so that German life can begin to function in no time at all. Within a year you will not even recognize this area. The German element will be as exemplary here as SS Oberführer Hofmeyer made it in Transnistria. He reported to me today that there, among those decimated Germans with many of their men gone, the birth rate is 45 per 1,000. He believes that in the next few years it will be 50 and more. Back in Germany we had 19 per 1,000, and when we hit 20 we saw even that as great progress. . . .

In summary, let me venture this forecast. You will sometimes groan under the tasks which you have been assigned, and which, I must say, your leadership and you have executed so well, notably the construction of Highway 4—so my worthy SS men, who formerly just marched on roads, now have become road builders! You will experience many another strange surprise. You will receive assignments—I do not know what yet—which neither you nor I can imagine.

When you sum up all this effort and all the work at the end of your career, you will be able to say that you have lived a very rich life, very rich because you could create and because you could prepare something of unique and decisive importance in the development of the German people—and I already view it totally as a Teutonic Empire of German nations—and of Nordic blood. We are preparing this soil to become land for German settlement.

In the next 20 years after peace is concluded, we of the present generation, especially we of the SS, must set ourselves the following tasks:

First and most important, we must do everything to affiliate and incorporate the Germanic people of this area with us. These people must be won over inwardly, not just superficially, so that our 83 million actually become 120 million conscious Germans.

Secondly, in the most important aspect of a nation's life, the continuity of its blood, we must dare to innovate, to give our own men the moral support to make certain that without discussion, without debate, without raising any problems, it becomes a matter of course that no family dies out and that there will always be sons and children. It does not suffice to say we will supply child support, tax relief, good housing, etc. Gentlemen, these subventions are as old as mankind! They were already available in Babylon, and in Rome before the empire collapsed, in Sparta and in Athens, in France, in England, and they are available in Germany. This is no innovation!

The only people to turn the tide of their drift to extinction were the Chinese. The Chinese people, of who 10 to 20 million drown annually in river floods (which is not evident because of the general population increase), was once so far along the path to extinction that it had to build a great wall. A reversal occurred only when this remarkable Confucius, almost two meters tall, revived the very ancient teaching of ancestor worship, which at one time was the universal creed of our Indo-Germanic peoples. We must venerate our ancestors and therefore need to have sons and grandsons. We of the SS must tackle this greatest of all problems, for no one else can do it.

Until now Christianity was worldwide morality; we must yet settle accounts with it and supersede it, in which cause we will be in the forefront of ideological struggle as the most faithful crusaders of the Führer and the Reich. It is no coincidence that more children are born in Catholic areas where Christianity is a stronger belief than in liberal Protestant ones. . . .

For centuries and especially in the very centuries when Christianity was active or when it was made especially active during the Counter Reformation, Germany was amazingly procreative. Even for our grandparents and great grandparents the question that one might not want a child did not even exist. . . . This orthodox attitude, which we acknowledge biologically and nationally, is no longer evident among the majority of so-called modern Christians. For them the Church is a convenient place for social gathering. They often go to Church just for political opposition, but not one of them would sacrifice himself for his Lord and Savior, not one would die a martyr. The moral stimulus for having German children and not preventing them has perished, as the Church itself is perishing.

If a people is not to die off, another stimulus must be found. Promotion limitations, salary increases, tax relief, child support, etc., are small measures which are never radically effective. If an inward spiritual conversion does not occur, then we die out as a people. Although we would then have conquered the outposts of

Asia because we had an Adolf Hitler, we would certainly not be able to survive later conflicts which may arise with re-invigorated Russians in Siberia or with any other peoples in the vast expanses of Asia.

This inward conversion can only emphasize—as I have already told you—veneration of ancestors. It is no new invention of ours; it is as ancient as the Aryan people.

I am responsible to my ancestors for what I do. If my ancestors have given me honor, prestige, renown, health, blood, strength of spirit and body, I have the obligation to pass on this inheritance and not to do with it as I please. Seen in another context, that means: If someone from a family fought in 1813 and if another soldier came from it in 1870/71, and again in 1914/18, and in this war, then the nation can require in 1950, 1960 or 1980 that this family supply yet another soldier. Any other action would be neglect of responsibility. . . .

Thirdly, we must develop land and soil for our people! In the next twenty years we must colonize the present eastern German provinces from East Prussia down to Upper Silesia and the whole of Polish territory under German rule. We must Germanize and colonize White Russia, Estonia, Latvia, Lithuania, Karelia and the Crimea. We will proceed in other areas as we have begun here, building small cities of fifteen to twenty thousand inhabitants, along lines of communication where our super-highways, railways and airports are protected by our garrisons, and surrounded by a ten-kilometer radius of villages, so that the people are always immersed in German life and related to an urban cultural center. These nuclei of settlements which we are extending forward from here to the Don and the Volga—and I hope to the Urals—will some day, some year, in the course of a generation have to accumulate more and more layers of an eternally young succession of Germanic blood. This Germanic East up to the Urals must be the seedbed of Germanic population. Thus in four or five hundred years, if the fate of Europe gives us that much time before some intercontinental conflict, instead of one hundred twenty million, there will be five or six hundred million people of Germanic race.

This is what we SS men are working for here in our thoughts, our living and teaching, as our comrades are fighting out there in the face of death. The greater German people can be born here, they can grow as farmers and become strong! Then we will have an agrarian nation in sensible relationship between city and country, and an expanse of land where a German man can develop without becoming a Philistine as he does in crowded Germany. Our beloved Nordic blood, our own German people from whom we descend and to whom we owe everything and who are truly the best on this earth, who have given this region context, content and culture, will become great through Adolf Hitler. As knights and yeomen of the Reich we SS men are able to lend a helping hand.

Fulfill your duties everywhere in matters large and small, and you will have acted as the law commanded.

35. A Memoir of Life in Concentration Camps

In September 1945 a young man eighteen years of age came to military government headquarters in Marburg, Germany. He said that he had a message which he wished to communicate to the American people. He was directed to the information control office where he talked with T/Sgt. Samson B. Knoll (in charge of intelligence for information control) about his experiences as a child who grew into young adulthood in a series of Nazi concentration camps.

Source: The document is the message of Walter Krämer, exactly as he wrote it for transmittal to the American people. Printed by permission of Professor Samson B. Knoll, Dean of Faculty, Monterey Institute of Foreign Studies. Translation by the editor.

My Life
Before concentration camp
after concentration camp, and into the
Light of
FREEDOM
by Walter Krämer

I was born on January 24, 1927, the son of the merchant Hermann Krämer and his wife Dina Krämer, née Stern, both of Jewish confession, in Niederklein, Marburg/Lahn district. The first three years I grew up with the other children of the village as if there were no difference between Jews and Aryans, which in fact there isn't; but the Nazis had a different version.

Widespread anti-Semitic agitation began in 1933. We were attacked in every possible way. Gradually even the schools began to indoctrinate the children with anti-Semitism. My two sisters, Ilse and Renate, both older than I, had to suffer even more than I because they were older and understood the situation better. But even though I was just six, I will never forget this period of grief and misery which I am now recording as I remember it.

Our family had lived in Germany for centuries. Now all of a sudden we were supposed to abandon everything we owned and which had cost us so much. My parents were preoccupied with all these thoughts night and day. My father was a great optimist and didn't believe everything Hitler and his vagrants were preaching: "We will not rest until the last Jew in Europe is wiped out." My father didn't take all of this seriously enough, which later became a great misfortune for our family. We had a small variety store that provided comfortable living for our family. But by and by the boycott of Jewish businesses by the Nazis became so severe that many were forced to sell their stores. We here in the village couldn't complain seriously until it suddenly began to intensify in 1938. "Buying from Jews will get you killed," wrote the weekly, *Der Stürmer*. The severity of anti-Jewish legislation constantly increased. How often my sisters and I would come home from school crying because the teacher had abused us so terribly. I will not forget one of his statements: "God created the whites, and the blacks too; but the Jew, that mongrel, comes from the devil." Although then we didn't understand the words as well as we would today, it was enough to excite the other children so that there was always violence after class. How often I came home bleeding. I was no coward, but they were in the majority. When I then went to bed in the evening, I hoped I wouldn't get hit in the head with a stone during the night. And if only school would end tomorrow! My parents tried their best, yet little could they do to change this suffering and misery. Jews were excluded from sports and all other amusements. Theaters and other places had signs: "No Jews allowed," or "Entry for Jews denied." I still remember the words of our mother: "You were born to suffer"; but in spite of everything we hoped for a different and better time, which yet would cost us a lot.

The end of 1938 was approaching, and with it the horror and terrible misery of all Jewish families living in Germany. November came. It seems as though it was just yesterday. I was sitting in the living room one morning. My mother came in quite upset, saying there was something mysterious afoot; but my father replied, "You're always worrying about something." By evening we learned that her fears were not in vain. We were sitting in a cosy family circle, when suddenly ten men burst into the room and attacked my father. They assaulted him barbarously, hitting him so hard that he was unconscious for almost an hour. My oldest sister ran to the local Sister of Mercy to get a nurse who could dress my father's injuries. This was soon done, but with the greatest difficulties, since an Aryan was not permitted to give first aid to a Jew. Later that night all the windows in the house were smashed. My mother's nerves were at the breaking point. I will never forget the moment when she said: "Forgive your parents for bringing you into the world at such a time." I can still hear it today. On the street they were shouting: "When Jewish blood from the knife blade spurts, the times will be twice as good!" The night of horror passed, but the next day brought nothing better. Toward the afternoon of November 9, 1938, two SS men came and took my father into protective custody, but no one told us where. My poor mother was distraught; my two sisters and I tried to comfort her, but our efforts were fruitless. Two weeks later, we heard that my father was in the concentration camp at Buchenwald. It was only a guess; other people had smuggled out postcards. A week later we did get a postcard and a letter from a fellow inmate of his who had since been released and gone home. He wrote to us that father was alive and hoped to come home very soon. A week later, one morning, a phone call which we had been anticipating came from Frankfurt where he had been released. I remember as if it were today. It was midmorning on Sunday; I was still in bed when the postman called my sister to the local telephone. We were too happy for words. Many others had already received death notices of their loved ones. Now our beloved father was coming home; but for how long?

All Jewish shops were expropriated and aryanized. We lost our store and had to pay an assessment on Jewish property that amounted to 25 percent of our total wealth. All our gold and silver was confiscated. From then on we were forbidden to attend Aryan schools. I was told to attend school in Frankfurt am Main. Finally my sister Ilse got her papers for emigration to the U. S., and in

April, 1939, she could leave this disreputable country on the liner
"Manhattan." She departed in sorrow, for her family had to stay
behind. My parents tried everything to get us all across, but it was
useless; this was our destiny and there was no other alternative.

One morning in July, it must have been about the 20th, a
Gestapo car drove up to our house. They questioned my father for
a while. Then they demanded that he accompany them to the bank
in Kirchhain to check if his statements were true. He went with
them. My mother was terribly depressed because she sensed that he
wouldn't be permitted to come home. We waited all afternoon, but
to no avail. I rode my bicycle to Kirchhain to get any information
as to the whereabouts of my father. I was told that my father
had been there with the Gestapo and had left again. I knew
then where I would have to turn. I got in touch with the Marburg
jail and asked the warden if a man by the name of Hermann
Krämer had been brought there that day. He answered that such a
man was imprisoned and awaiting investigation for smuggling
currency out of the country.

After two weeks of great agitation, I got a letter; I was to come
immediately to Frankfurt, where a place was reserved for me in the
home of the Flerscheim-Sichel Foundation. I packed my suitcase
and left for Frankfurt the next day. At first I got mail from my
mother and sister three times per week. But that didn't last long;
four, six, eight days without news drove me crazy. Finally on the
tenth day a letter came in my father's handwriting. At first I
thought it was from prison, but when I opened it I only read the
first few words: "am finally home again." I ran to the telephone
and just then received a call from home. They asked me not to
come and said they would visit me on Sunday. My sister got a
position in a household in Frankfurt soon after. I was very glad to
have one of my relatives near the home, where I felt quite comfortable by now. I went to the Jewish "Phylanthropin" School in a
very handsome building. Here I finally had friends burdened with
similar woes; it was much easier to bear such things in company.

The year 1941 came. It was April. I went home for the Easter
holidays, but to do so needed an extra travel permit because I was a
Jew. I spent the vacation as well as one could in those times, and
then traveled back to Frankfurt. On Monday morning when I
returned to school, I heard that there was supposed to have been a
"clean-up" in the Marburg district. I went to telephone my sister

first, but she didn't know anything yet. Then I got in touch with Niederklein, where the postmaster told me that my parents no longer lived there, that they had to clear out of their house for an SS man who had no place to live. The dowry and everything else that was held for my sister and myself were simply stolen from us. My father was taken to a labor camp in Breitenau near Kassel. I asked my mother whether I should come home, but she told me to stay. I could hardly wait for some news. Her letters were always very calm, but often I would read between the lines how she felt and how disturbed she was.

It was Sunday morning. I was still in bed when there was suddenly a great commotion in the home. The first transport of a thousand Jews left Frankfurt, destination unknown. Among them was the director of our home with whom fifty other children and I were to leave eight days later for Ecuador. Now that, too, had failed. Shortly thereafter I got a message from my mother that we were soon to be transported eastward. The next day I had a call from my father telling me that grandfather had died. My father had gotten two days leave from his camp commander. I went with my sister to Marburg to attend the burial of my grandfather. I saw my father here once again, but I never dreamed that it was to be the last time in my life. We went back to Frankfurt and he had to return to the camp. Some time later my mother told me that our transport was just about to leave and that I should come home immediately. I finished with all the formalities two days later and went to my mother in Mordorf; two days later my sister Reni arrived, too. We got mail a few times from my father when suddenly a letter came back stamped: addressee not here, await further address. Later a card came from Buchenwald, one of the most notorious concentration camps in Germany.

Then we were told that if we would voluntarily leave with the next transport from Kassel, our father would come with us. We registered, arrived in Kassel, and waited in vain. We left without him for Riga, in Latvia. We were permitted to take our baggage, but it was left en route in Posen and finally ended up in the coffers of the German Winter Relief Fund. We four, my mother's cousin, my mother, Reni and I, arrived on December 13 at the Shyratava station in Riga. It was a horrible day. Sheets of ice covered the streets, and it was much colder than in Germany. We stood at the station and were ordered to put down our hand luggage. I had trouble walking. I stumbled over a small suitcase and sprained my foot badly. I was put into a bus and driven to the camp, a so-called "Ghetto." It was horrible. I can hardly record what I saw there, it was too grim. There was only one transport there, which had arrived from Cologne some days before. We asked the people what the blood on the street and on the walls meant, but they couldn't answer, since they didn't know either. Yet we did find out, sooner than expected. We were now shown to living quarters which perhaps just one day earlier had been left by their rightful owners. There was food on the stove and plates were on the table. The sight was awful, worse than I can describe. I lay down on the ground and waited until my mother and sister came. They put my foot into a poultice, and the next day I was completely recovered. I was very lucky to have taken the first bus, for the occupants of the other three didn't even arrive in the camp, but were taken directly to be shot.

Six families were put up in the tiny house. With us lived my aunt and a Mrs. Hess with three small children, the youngest just eleven weeks old. Her husband was sent to the extermination camp at Salaspils, and now the wife was helpless and alone with three small children. We still didn't know precisely what actually had happened in this camp until a Latvian Jew, who had managed to escape the camp, told us. Thirty thousand Jews were living in this camp until just two weeks before we arrived. They were driven from the houses into the street, where they were massacred by the German and Latvian SS with machine guns and dumdum munition, the most horrible of all bullets. They threw little children up in the air like birds and shot them, or smashed their skulls on the nearest wall, to save ammunition, as these monsters explained to each other with mockery.

More transports arrived during the next few days. The first one was from Düsseldorf and Bielefeld. They arrived still halfway healthy and in good spirits since they were mostly young people, just as ours had been. Others came from Hannover, Leipzig, Prague, Berlin, and Dortmund; these arrived half frozen. It was the hardest winter the East had seen in a long time. It was minus 45° (centigrade) in Riga, which was terribly cold. Yet, only half of the Ghetto was filled. We went to work clearing up and burying the dead, who were piled on top of each other like cord wood. We often went out "requisitioning" in order to stay alive. Many of my fellow Jews lost their lives; they weren't careful enough. If one of us was home alone, it was so depressing; we could hardly wait until we were all together. My aunt Eina ran our household and worked like everybody else.

Then the first outside work detachments were called up. One evening I was told to appear the next morning on the Kassler Hof, as our area was called. Every area had its center square and its street. I rode with an SS man and 29 other inmates to a forest, supposedly to build bird traps. But we were soon otherwise instructed. We were to dig a ditch 20 meters long, 10 meters wide and two meters deep, which was to be ready by evening. The Latvian SS told us it was for an anti-aircraft position. It was ready at night and we drove back to the camp. I found my mother was terribly upset because twenty youths were shot that same day without reason. When we went back the next day, the ditch had been covered and in the bushes we found things which must have come from Jews of a Berlin transport, since there were identification cards, etc. They had taken the lives of these people during the night. A Russian prisoner whom we met a day later said that the night before his comrades had had to cover the ditch. What a feeling, digging the graves for your own coreligionists. During the next day, while we were digging the next grave, they kept telling us that if we didn't dig faster, we'd get it, too; we would get it sooner or later. They beat us with rifle butts and many of us were kicked unconscious. When I got home that evening, I went to our area office and told our camp superior my experiences, and he had me released from this murderous job.

Thanks to my uncle, who was a member of the Düsseldorf senior council, I got into the camp shoe repair shop. My mother got outside duty at the Daimler-Benz agency and my sister worked for the railroad. My mother had to work very hard, but she was glad to do it, since it was a relatively good job and she was given things occasionally by the Latvian workers. Though I was working in the shoe shop, I was often called off for other work. One day I had to unload and stack trunks from a transport which had been exterminated. A Latvian SS man came up to me and pointed his pistol at my temples. Just in the nick of time an SS officer, who was the camp commander, knocked his pistol upward; the shot went wild, and he said to him: "I'll do the shooting." Yet the same SS man killed twenty people from a Berlin transport that same hour. Why? It was pure lust and sadism. My life was spared once more. I was just fifteen years old.

People were slowly beginning to barter things in the camps. We couldn't have money; neither were we officially permitted to barter. Everywhere large posters read: "Death penalty for bartering." But there was only one solution: dead one way or the other. If we wanted to stay alive, there was nothing for us to do but to exchange whatever we had for food from the Latvian workers. Many lost their lives in the process. I will never forget one scene. One day, as happened so often, there was a search followed by executions. I saw the commander with his bloodhound go to the cemetery with a very young woman. Her children, two little girls, ran after their mother crying: "Mommy, Mommy, stay with us." But the SS man wasn't moved; the beast took the mother to the cemetery and killed her with a shot in the neck. Even today, and as long as I live, will I never forget this scene. Often I feared for my own mother's death whenever she was supposed to exchange something during the day, and when they checked the people at night at the entrance to the camp. Many people lost their lives this way. More severe regulations were established in order to prevent bartering once and for all. And so the ordinance was passed: Whoever barters will be hanged and his whole family shot. And still it did not stop because living conditions in the camp were so grim that no one could survive without barter with the Latvians. It was death one way or another.

In March, 1942, there was a roll call of the whole camp. All elderly people were selected out and went off to Dünamünde, supposedly to the fish net factory. Where did they end up?—that was the year 1942. Every Saturday about 10 o'clock, we witnessed executions. We lived right across from the cemetery. One day the streets were closed off again, but the cemetery was untouched. It was rumored that ten men were to be hanged for bartering. The gallows were built a day earlier, but we didn't know that by the next day they would already be soaked in blood. In the evening, the work detachments were led past it. The gallows were set up for only one man, so they hanged them one after the other. My mother and sister came home that evening completely shattered: such a scene for women to see.

Most of the year 1942 had passed. I remember it as if it were today; it was October 30 when at 10:00 A.M. the streets were closed off and machine guns fired through them. "What does that mean?" we asked at first. Everyone into the cellar, that was the first reaction. We had built a little shelter which no one but those living in the house knew of, in order to find refuge in case of an attack. We must have been down there about two hours when the shooting stopped. They had shot and killed the entire Latvian Jewish contingent of the camp that day, for the reason that they weren't dependable enough. Two hundred more young men were then selected out and shot as hostages in the Hochwald near Riga.

The year 1943 came. Several men had returned to the Ghetto from the extermination camp at Salspils. They were just skeletons. Now many women were receiving notices of their husbands' deaths. The men succumbed to hunger and misery there. Our worries increased. It was said that the Ghetto was to be dissolved. One night my sister gave a terrifying scream. I called for the camp doctor and he diagnosed appendicitis. She was taken to the infirmary immediately and three days later was back at home. Then I fell sick with infection of the spleen and liver due to bad nourishment. I had to stay in bed for four weeks. By now I had been working for two years as a shoemaker in the camp and had acquired enough experience so that the council of elders assigned me and another comrade to a group which had no shoemaker, the group from Prague. Yet, it was to be for only four weeks. At two in the morning on August 5, I received a call to come to the Central Concentration Camp for further work duty. Several transports had already gone ahead, but we received very depressing news about them. One can imagine the state my mother was in. My sister tried everything to keep me in the Ghetto, but to no avail. The next morning my mother had to go back to work and did not show me how deeply she was suffering. She wanted to make my departure easier. But she did say, "We won't see each other again." I couldn't believe it; no, I didn't want to believe it, but it was the truth. I followed her a few more steps and then turned and stood *alone*. My sister returned from her work in order to stay with me until I left the Ghetto. She faked sickness to be able to stay there. We were picked up by a car, and she waved to me until I had disappeared from her sight. Now began my life in one of the most notorious camps, the Main Concentration Camp at Riga—Kaiserwald.

We were unloaded at the camp square. Then we were ordered

to put down our baggage and form rows of five. We got a cross of oil paint on our backs and chests and a white stripe on the pants along the leg. Anything extra we wore was stripped off. Our hair was cropped and a cross was cut diagonally into the hair on the top of our heads; we later called it the louse track, which it actually was. The next day I was assigned to the labor group of the hardened criminal, Ise, who directed the landfill at Weidendamm 2. This was a veritable death squad. Every day we had at least two dead, either by drowning in the Düna or by execution. When we marched off in the morning, the question was: Whose turn will it be today? I can't describe how we felt going to work. After four weeks I got myself released by faking illness and then joined a comrade in the Spilve labor group. This was not so intimately related with death and it was also easier to make contact with the outside world. One evening when we came back to the camp, we had to get in line for delousing. We had to undress and were drenched with a shower of cold water. We then got old ragged clothes with the same identifications and went back to the compound. It must have been about 8:00 P.M. when the camp officer came into the barracks drunk as a pig and told us to turn over everything we had stolen that day. No one knew anything about it. Then it began: out of the compound; line up; back into the compound. There were about five hundred men in a compound and we had four of them in this section. The entrance served at the same time as the exit, and we had to be snappy going in and out. Hardened criminals stood at the windows and hit us over the heads with their rubber billy clubs. Many a man was killed with these blows. We jumped through windows, over chairs and benches; we didn't stop for anything. If anyone fell, others would fall; exactly what these gangsters were waiting for. Two men collided and tripped other comrades, as they were lying in the entrance. The billy clubs of the SS men and the hardened criminals were hitting our heads. And the SS leaders stood with their hands in the pockets and laughed maliciously. Luckily a transport arrived from Vilna that night; I don't know how many deaths there would have been beside the hundred already killed.

Conditions worsened day by day, so I seized the first opportunity to move into barracks of the main camp. Food was so miserable that no human being could subsist on it. Even here we tried to extend our lives by bartering, but it was only an attempt.

There was simply nothing to be done, and the lice just ate us up. Every time a transport came from the Ghetto, ten to twelve men slept on a bunk normally for four or five. I can't even remember how we could lie that way, five heads one way and five the other. One morning four weeks later, I heard the call: all shoemakers step forward. I stepped out of the ranks of my group, although my foreman told me it was nothing special and not to go. But I was glad to get out of this witch's cauldron.

On October 10, 1943, I entered the Combat-SS Quartermaster Camp. The camp elder was also a Jew and was a very capable fellow who had a good name with the SS and used it to our advantage. So, here I entered the SS shoe workshop which was manned by a hundred prisoners. At the time, I was the youngest worker there. After we closed in the evenings, we were often put in the food supply area where we had to work very hard. But I preferred working there than somewhere else, since one could scrounge a little better. In the shoeshop I pilfered half-soles and exchanged these for food. No one could survive on camp rations. In the meanwhile I picked up contact with the Ghetto again. I had gotten mail twice weekly from the Ghetto, which now was in a state of dissolution. One day I got a letter from my sister. On the front page my mother wrote she hoped to go to the A.B.A. (Army Clothing Office), but on the other side my sister wrote:

> Dear Walter, unfortunately I must inform you that yesterday our dear mother left the Ghetto with a transport of two and a half thousand people—destination unknown. There are lots of rumors but no one knows exactly. I came to the Ghetto in the evening and just imagine when we arrived, the place was a mess and no one was left. She wrote the letter the night before.

I was appalled; I knew it meant death.

Now, to try to forget everything a little, I took on a little girl friend. We lived with the women, but only in certain compounds. We lived for today and what tomorrow would bring we didn't worry about, since every day there were executions and thousands of people had to lose their lives. Every day I got news from my sister and usually even a little packet of bread, etc., which she had saved to send me. One day the Squad Leader entered the workshop, selected thirty men and said, "Get ready." We did not fear possible execution because he had selected the youngest and best workers. No one knew where he was taking us. We were loaded into a truck and taken to repair shoes for a Latvian SS division. We stayed there two days and rode back to camp. The Russian army was now advancing rapidly, so I was added to the Transport Department. It was fine and yet not; my girl friend always feared for me because I often overdid my scrounging. One day I had just opened a can of tinned fish. Earlier I had agreed with a friend that he would be on guard, but he was called away to another job, and so the Squad Leader caught me redhanded. I was stretched over a frame and got twenty-five blows with a steel-spined billy club. I couldn't stand or lie down for three days and nights. My friend, Erich Hirsch, who always worked with me here, had succumbed to beatings from the Staff Squad Leader three days before. He had also scrounged but had often been caught and was so badly flogged that he lost consciousness until the next day. They demanded that he betray all the comrades who had scrounged with him. This he did not do and ended his life by hanging himself in order to escape the further beatings of the SS. Every morning and evening there was roll call. One morning we were standing when a car, in fact a truck, from Kaiserwald Concentration Camp drove up. In our camp there were still about fifteen children who had escaped all the brutalities. They tore these children from their parents, put them onto the truck, and drove away. We all knew where they were going and yet didn't want to know, for in distress a person will grasp for even a blade of straw.

Quartermaster Camp established a branch on the other side of the Düna, in a former factory called Strassenhof. I was transferred to the shoe shop there. I didn't want to leave the main camp where my girl friend was, yet it had to be, for orders were orders. Here there was absolutely no connection with the outside world; we were completely cut off. Now the difficult task was how to live and augment our food supply. By chance I met a friend who had been with me in the Ghetto. He told me there was also a food storehouse here, but it was inaccessible. I went to check it out with him. After a half an hour, my friend and I were standing, unobserved, with a skeleton key at the entrance to the storehouse. A jerk and a jolt and the door was open. We dragged out what we could in all haste, shut the door the way we had opened it, and disappeared in the camp the way we had come. Our comrades in camp couldn't believe their eyes. Thenceforth the stomach question was no problem for us, but we still didn't have access to the basement where canned meat, fish, and vegetables were stored, along with all kinds of liquor. I often discussed it with my comrades, but without success until one day we got the idea of forcing an entrance by use of a glass cutter. We tried it from the outside under a recessed cellar behind which was the window, but we couldn't quite make it the first day. In the evening we looked for another way, which really gave us a fright. I went over the roof, opened a vent hole and saw six emaciated, frightened faces staring at me. They told me they had been living there for four weeks, had escaped the last set of executions, and hoped to be free soon. I could still feel the shock of that discovery in my arms and legs fourteen days later. Never had I seen such faces before. I asked them if they had enough to eat, and they said yes, the food supply was right beside them. The next day we got in. We just lived for each day; our lives were certainly not worth anything right then. The Russians were twenty kilometers from Riga and there was talk of shooting us all first; we heard every day from the SS: "Before the Russians come, we'll do you all in."

Before that happened we were shipped back to Germany. One day there was roll call. In an hour every one was ready to march. Several of my comrades had ducked out; I was too afraid to go with them since the lives of my sister and six other comrades were also involved. But they had put all their eggs in one basket and disappeared for good, including the camp elder. The atmosphere was terrible. Who would suffer for this action? But everything turned out well. In the evening we were taken to the ship in trucks and loaded on. The next morning we left for Danzig on this freighter without cargo, just a load of prisoners. The wind rose to gale force and caused much seasickness, especially among the women. Finally, after three days, we arrived in Danzig. I had hoped to meet my sister on the ship, but in vain; yet I did meet her friend Günther. From that day forward I was always together with him until he died a terrible death. In Danzig we were unloaded onto old barges in which the water was twenty centimeters deep. One tugboat drew the four barges up the Vistula to the notorious concentration camp of Stutthof.

The camp SS immediately took us into custody. They took everything from us; we didn't keep even a belt and had to fasten our pants with twine. They led us to Compound Three, designed for two hundred fifty men, but we filled it with nine hundred.

There were only three-level bunk beds—four men on the bottom, three in the middle and three more on the top. I always slept at top, for at least up there you don't get whipped so easily by the compound superior. The first two days we got nothing at all to eat, with the excuse that the camp was not prepared for us. In a camp such as Stutthof where there were forty-five thousand prisoners; nine hundred didn't matter very much. Everything to speed our deaths. The next day, there was already an outside work detail. I went to the A.B.A. (Army Clothing Office) where I filched some stuff on the very first day for resale in the camp. And so I made out for awhile. One evening, we had just lain down in our bunks when we had to line up for roll call. We simply stormed out of the barracks and the billy clubs did their work. Then right about face and to the gallows; forty-five thousand men were kicked out of bed to watch a prisoner being hanged for violation of camp ordinances.

I was only eight weeks in Stutthof; then I was put in the Schichau dockyards in Danzig as an electrician, together with my friend Günther. I worked the night shift and he, the day shift, so we only saw each other occasionally on Sunday afternoons. We filched potatoes and vegetables and somehow survived. When I had worked for four weeks as an electrician, the boss asked me what I had actually been trained for. I told him shoemaking, for I had learned this trade in the Ghetto and understood it. He asked me if I wouldn't be willing to work privately for him, and right away I answered yes. So I made satchels, shoes, and all kinds of things. He furnished a little room for me. I worked half the night and usually spent the other half sleeping. Now and then he would bring me a piece of bread which at that time was of very great importance to us. Günther would always cook something, and even if it were only potato skins, it was something that would satisfy your stomach.

One night I began to feel bad and noticed I was getting a fever. My comrades carried me back to camp. The next morning I went to the doctor with a raging fever. He gave me a pill and said: "Walter, pull yourself together. Which do you prefer, life or the crematorium?" That was quite enough said for me, for I had already seen enough of the crematorium in Stutthof, where even a good friend of mine (Benno Plappler of Kassel) had died. So I pulled myself together with all my strength and recovered quite well from this sickness. But the epidemic in the camp kept growing and affected everyone. Hundreds died daily of typhoid. After a while we heard that here, too, the Russians were not far away. And when the works were closed the next week, we knew that we would be on the march again.

So we set out on February 1, 1945, in wind and weather without so much as a piece of bread in our pockets. Nights we would camp in sheds, stalls, and churches. Yet many could not keep up with the march. The slow rows at the rear were simply mowed down with machine guns. I was at the end of my strength and couldn't keep up either. Günther grasped me by the arm and said, "We must make it; think of Reni and get ahold of yourself. Be strong and endure and don't get yourself shot like a dog at the last minute." With my last resources I followed Günther, for he was a friend one doesn't find very often. Finally, after a fifty-mile march, we came to a village; here we had to leave the other comrades. Three hundred fifty of us entered the National Labor Service Camp at Rieben; the other prisoners marched on. The camp was incredibly overcrowded with prisoners who hadn't eaten for six days. Typhoid was prevalent and starvation became worse and worse. I still had two frozen turnips in my pocket which they tore from my hand into pieces. No one can judge what starvation is, if he himself hasn't been in such a camp and hasn't experienced it with his own body. We now got a hundred grams of bread for four days, a watered-down soup in the afternoons, and sometimes nothing at all. Nevertheless, we had to work building tank traps. Every day twenty men died. At night we lay on bare cement floors, without blankets, between the dead and dying. I was among them. Someone who has never witnessed such a scene cannot even imagine it. Within four weeks our numbers had dropped from six hundred to thirty, and the way we looked was horrible. You can vividly imagine why. I had typhoid, dysentery, and hemorrhoids and was so badly undernourished that I weighed exactly thirty kilos when the Russian Army set me free.

It was in the afternoon on the 11th of March, 1945. I was lying in a semicoma and no longer listened to the speculations of my comrades. I had already resigned myself to death, when I suddenly heard the ecstatic cry of a comrade at about midnight: "Russian tanks!" We couldn't believe that we were to be freed at the last minute. It was incomprehensible. And yet there was already a Russian commanding officer coming to us with ten soldiers, even though they knew that we had typhoid. They cleaned the barracks, built beds, and laid us on straw mattresses. They gave us everything in the way of food and medication which we were able to take. We were nursed and nourished until our bodies had recovered to a certain extent from the dirt and filth of the last fourteen days. With rice and wheat cereal and all other possible means, we were coddled back to health like little children. Even then some of the men still died because of fatal internal injuries. In the camp there were piles of bodies which were now buried by the local German population. The Russians found the order of the Hauptsturmführer to execute us at midnight on March 11, but they had already arrived an hour before. The entire camp guard was taken prisoner and met their just punishment before our very eyes, ending up in the mass grave which they had dug for us the day before. Thanks to the Russian care and nursing, we had so far recovered within eight weeks that we could set out for home. We now rode back where we had been four years earlier, but I rode alone. My mother was gassed at Auschwitz; my father was murdered at Buchenwald. Of the four in my family I alone have returned to the family home and hope that soon my sister will also arrive.

But a force within me leaves me no peace: I MUST AVENGE MY PARENTS.

X

Collapse and Perspectives for Renewal, 1943–1945

THE COLLAPSE of the Third Reich began in the winter of 1942–1943. No matter what immense racial and spatial perspectives the planners of the SS state may have had, the area of Europe under Nazi control began to shrink. Anglo-American landings in French North Africa in November 1942 spelled the doom of Field Marshal Rommel's famed *Afrikakorps*. Dogged Russian resistance blossomed into the incredibly hard-fought campaign around Stalingrad which culminated on January 31, 1943, in the surrender of 140,000 men to victorious Soviet power. Allied bombing raids over Germany intensified. A week of determined bombing of Hamburg in late July caused destruction and casualties comparable to those of the first atomic blast over Hiroshima two years later.

Anglo-American forces moved into southern Italy and Mussolini fell from power. From the autumn of 1943 to the late spring of 1944, the struggle was bloody and destructive, up the "soft underbelly of Europe," in the Balkans, and all along the Russian front. Inside the Reich the SS accelerated its exterminations, commandeered millions of Europeans to work on farms and in factories, and shot anyone caught listening to enemy broadcasts. In early June the western Allies landed in France, hovered in peril at the invasion perimeter for ten days, then broke loose to free most of France by autumn.

Nazi Germany skipped a very long heartbeat on July 20, 1944. A bomb in Hitler's military headquarters killed several of his staff but only grazed the Führer. Hesitancy among the conspirators and bad luck gave the initiative to Goebbels and the SS; within hours the plot was compromised and crushed in Berlin and the western European armies. During the fall and winter, as his forces reeled back on every front, Hitler pursued the July conspirators in publicly staged purge trials. Five thousand men ultimately went to firing squads and gallows, while thousands more awaited an uncertain fate in prison.

Allied armies from the East and West cut the Third Reich to ribbons in the spring of 1945. With the Russians at his door in Berlin, Hitler loosed a final propaganda blast on the unworthiness of the German people to achieve historic greatness, then took his life. Goebbels followed his Führer in the battered Reichschancellery; Himmler was later captured and committed suicide. Most of the remaining Nazi leadership was seized and held for subsequent trial. The final surrender took place in the ruins of Berlin on May 8, 1945.

36. Soviet Russia Anticipates the Post-Nazi Era

Many German Communists fought a determined though losing battle against the Nazi seizure of power in 1933. By the end of that year most of their leadership was killed or imprisoned and subject to death. Relatively few of the German Communists escaped from Germany, but a key handful gravitated to Moscow to anticipate another round in the struggle—if they survived the Stalinist purges. When the western Allies seized Sicily in July 1943, Soviet Russia indicated its conception of Germany's future by announcing the formation of a Free Germany National Committee. It was no coincidence that this group included the major leaders of the post-Nazi German Democratic Republic: Wilhelm Pieck, its first president (1949–1960); Walter Ulbricht, its consistent "strong man" (1945–1971); and Johannes R. Becher, its cultural-intellectual authority (1945–1958). The following news story indicates how the world-at-large was first informed of these plans.

SOURCE: *New York Times*, July 22, 1943. Copyright © 1943 by The New York Times Company. Reprinted by permission.

GERMANS IN SOVIET BID REICH REVOLT

COMMITTEE FORMED IN MOSCOW CALLS ON TROOPS TO MUTINY AND
DESTROY HITLERISM
WAR PRISONERS IN GROUP
POLITICAL REFUGEES ALSO JOIN IN MOVE TO "SAVE" NATION
BY EMBRACING DEMOCRACY

Moscow, July 21 (U.P.)—An anti-Nazi German national committee, dedicated to the overthrow of Adolf Hitler and the establishment of a democratic regime in Germany, has been formed in Moscow, the Communist Party organ Pravda announced today.

Indicating official Soviet approval of the new committee, Pravda published a manifesto by that body calling upon German soldiers to mutiny, turned their backs on their leaders, and blast their way back home. It called upon German workers to lay down their tools, sabotage industry, and demand immediate peace.

The manifesto indicated the nature of the regime in Germany that the Soviet Union would favor after victory. It was consistent with Premier Joseph Stalin's declaration of Nov. 7, 1942, in which he said the Nazi state and army must and can be destroyed, but that the German state and people are indestructible. Mr. Stalin's program called for the defeat of the Wehrmacht, the annihilation of the Nazis and the punishment of Herr Hitler and other leaders responsible for the war.

"Germany Must Not Die"

"Anglo-American troops are at the gates of Europe," the manifesto said. "The day is approaching when Germany will collapse under the impact of simultaneous blows from all sides. The war is already lost, but Germany must not die."

It warned that unless the Germans overthrew their present rulers and sued for peace, Germany would be destroyed because the Anglo-Soviet-American coalition would not consider peace with Herr Hitler.

Pravda said the national committee, representing German war prisoners, political refugees, labor leaders, and intellectuals, held its first meetings in Moscow on July 12 and 13. It elected as its president Erich Weinert, famous anti-Nazi poet. Major Carl Hetz was named vice-president and Lieut. Count Heinrich von Einsiedel, second vice-president.

The manifesto, occupying a full page in Pravda, was signed by eleven officers and noncommissioned officers, four privates, four writers, and five former deputies of the Reichstag, including Wilhelm Pieck, former leader of the Communist bloc and secretary of the recently dissolved Comintern.

In addition to Herr Weinert and Herr Pieck, the signers included the former Reichstag deputies Martha Arendzee, Wilhelm Foren, Edwin Gernle and Walter Ulbricht; the writers Johannes

Becher and Willy Bredel; the playwright Dr. Friedrich Wolf and the trade union leaders Anton Ackerman and Hans Male. . . .

Immediate Decision Asked

The manifesto of the Free Germany National Committee . . . was broadcast to the Soviet Union by the Moscow radio. Addressed to the "German Army and the German People," . . . [it stated that] "formation of a real national German government is the urgent task of our people. It alone can bring peace. This government must be strong and have the necessary power to render harmless the enemies of the people—Hitler, his patrons, and accomplices—to put an end to terror.

"This government must be based on fighting groups who are united for the overthrow of Hitler. This government will at once stop military operations, recall German troops to the borders of the Reich, and open peace negotiations renouncing any conquests.

"Our aim is a free Germany. This means: A democracy that will mercilessly suppress any attempt of any new conspirators against the rights of free people or against European peace; full abolition of all laws based on national or racial hatred, of all institutions of the Hitlerite regime that are degrading our people, of all measures of Hitlerite power that are directed against liberty and human dignity; the rehabilitation and expansion of political rights and social achievements of the working people; freedom of speech, press, organization, conscience, and religion; freedom of economic life, of commerce, and of the trades; a guarantee of the right to work and the right to own acquired property lawfully; the restoration of property looted by the Fascists to the legal owners; confiscation of the property of those guilty of war crimes and of war profiteers; the exchange of goods with other countries in the interest of safeguarding a stable national prosperity; a just and merciless trial of those guilty of bringing about war and supporting it."

37. Objectives of the Anti-Nazi Conspiracy, July 20, 1944

The men who tried to kill Hitler and overthrow the Nazi regime on July 20, 1944, were neither radical nor desperate. They represented symbolically the troubled conscience of German nationalists and conservatives who had originally helped Hitler come to power. Three groups were represented: The Kreisau Circle, led by Count Helmuth von Moltke but speaking for a broad spectrum of opposition; a handful of military men including Field Marshal Rommel, General Ludwig Beck and Colonel Claus von Stauffenberg (who planted the bomb in Hitler's field headquarters); and a moderate bourgeois group led by Carl Goerdeler, former mayor of Leipzig. The following document is the third draft of a declaration drawn up by Goerdeler and Beck; it was intended to supplement and explain a briefer proclamation which the conspirators planned to broadcast as soon as their coup was successful.

SOURCE: "Entwurf einer Regierungserklärung" (Nr. 2, 3. Fassung) (Goerdeler-Beck). Kaltenbrunner Bericht vom 5.8.1944. Anlage. Reprinted in H-A. Jacobsen & W. Jochmann, eds., *Zur Geschichte des Nationalsozialismus. Ausgewählte Dokumente* (Bielefeld, 1961). Translation by the editor.

The principles of government and the goals for which we are working have already been proclaimed. We add the following detailed commentary:

1. The first task is to re-establish the complete sovereignty of law. The government itself must consciously seek to avoid all arbitrary power; it must subordinate itself to structured popular control. For the duration of the war this structure can only be arranged provisionally. For the immediate future, reliable and qualified men will be called to a National Council from all classes and provinces. We will be responsible to this National Council and seek its recommendations.

We were once proud of the rectitude and honesty of our people, of the security and quality of German justice. All the greater is our grief at seeing it virtually destroyed.

THE RESTORATION OF JUSTICE . . . .

The law will be enforced against everyone who has violated it. These violators will receive the punishment they deserve.

Security of person and property will again be protected against arbitrary power. Only a judge may intervene in the rights of the individual in accordance with laws which are indispensable for the existence of the state and for the happiness of the people.

The concentration camps will be abolished as soon as possible; the innocent will be released and the guilty will be subject to due process of law. In the same spirit, we expect that no one will participate in lynch justice. If we wish to restore the full sovereignty of the law, we must apply all our efforts to prevent acts of personal revenge, however humanly understandable they may be in light of injustice and mental anguish suffered. Persons with any complaints should report them to the public office of their choice. These complaints will be properly processed. The guilty will receive stern punishment. But such complaints must be valid; false accusations will be punished and anonymous complaints will be discarded.

An End to Corruption

2. We desire to reconstruct the foundations of morality in every aspect of private and public life.

High officials of the Nazi regime have fostered corruption in our once virtuous nation in hitherto unprecedented dimensions. While our soldiers fought, bled, and died far from home, men like Goering, Goebbels, Ley, and others led lives of luxury, filled their coffers with plunder and challenged the people to persevere, while they and their followers cravenly avoided service at the front. All criminals will be brought to justice with full severity of the law; their dishonestly acquired wealth will be confiscated and restored to the injured parties. But the chief culprits should suffer personal and material penalties. All their wealth and what they passed on to their relatives will be confiscated. Immunity gained by political pretext will be abolished. Every able-bodied man can prove his motives and endurance in war service. We will no longer tolerate braggarts.

Decent treatment for all must prevail in order to secure justice and propriety. The persecution of Jews, which was practiced in the most inhuman and unmerciful, deeply humiliating and irreparable ways, is forthwith prohibited. Whosoever sought to grow rich on Jewish wealth will discover that it is a disgrace for any German to aspire to such dishonest possession. The German people want no truck with despoilers or vultures.

We consider it deeply dishonoring to the German name that crimes of all kinds have been committed in the occupied territories and in the rear echelons of the war zones. These outrages defile the honor of our war dead. Here, too, we will press for atonement. Anyone who has used the war to fill his pockets or who has strayed from the line of honor will be brought firmly to justice. . . .

A Campaign against Falsehood

3. We declare war on the Big Lie. The sun of truth must dispel the dense fog of falsehood. Our people have been shamelessly deceived on economic, financial, and political issues, as well as to military events. The facts will be determined and made known so that every individual can verify them. It is a great error to assume that a government has the right to win the people for its own goals by deception. . . .

Freedom of Spirit and Thought

4. The shattered freedom of spirit, of conscience, of thought, and of opinion shall be restored.

The churches will again have the right to work freely for their beliefs. In the future they will function in complete separation from the state, for they can do justice to their task only in independence from all active political involvement. The processes of governing should be filled with Christian aspiration in word and deed, for to Christianity we owe the rise of the white peoples and the ability to combat our baser instincts. No national or political community can withdraw from the struggle against depravity. But true Christianity also demands toleration of non-Christians and free thinkers. The state will again give the church an opportunity to engage in the work of genuine Christianity, particularly in areas of social welfare and education.

The press shall again be free. During the war it must subject itself to limitations which are indispensable for any country engaged in hostilities. Anyone who reads a newspaper should know who stands behind it. The press will no longer be permitted consciously or negligently to publish untruths. A strict code of honor will give assurance that the editors will observe the laws of decency and respect for the well-being of the fatherland.

5. German youth especially is calling for the truth. . . . It was the greatest of crimes to disdain and misuse the spirit of truth and

with it the idealism of our youth. We will therefore protect and strengthen it.

Youth and education are one of our major concerns. Education should primarily be a responsibility of parents and the schools [not of political organizations]. In all schools elementary basic knowledge must be simply, cleanly, and surely implanted in the child. Education must again be broad and general, touching both the heart and mind. It must be rooted in the people and there must be no gulf between the educated and the uneducated.

Education must once more be consciously based on a Christian religious foundation, but without violating the Christian laws of the broadest toleration of non-Christians. On this basis the work of education and culture must once again proceed quietly and systematically, protected from continual changes and disturbances.

RENEWAL OF COURAGE TO TAKE RESPONSIBILITY

6. The administrative system of the nation must be re-organized. Nothing will be abolished which has proven its worth. But it is necessary promptly to re-establish clear lines of responsibility and freedom for independent decision making. Our once proud bureaucracy has become a mass of brainless robots and small machines. No one now dares to make an independent or appropriate decision. We will demand full responsibility from civil servants. They should do what is right with a minimum of paper work and a maximum of simplicity. . . .

In order to permit civil servants to conduct their duties with untarnished effectiveness, and to spare the people any exercise of public authority by incompetents, all appointments and promotions made after January 1, 1933, are hereby declared provisional. Every civil servant will soon be examined to ascertain whether he has transgressed the law, rules, or the morality expected of all civil servants. If such defects are ascertained, the appropriate consequences will follow in terms of punishment, dismissal, transfer, etc. Courts of inquiry composed of civil servants will assist in the process. Provisional civil servants whose accomplishments do not measure up to the requirements of their office will be tranferred to positions they can handle or, if this is not possible, they will be dismissed.

Luxury does not belong in the public offices, though comfort belongs in individual homes. Department heads have been directed to initiate the required measures immediately. Superfluous furnishings will be given to air raid victims.

THE CONSTITUTIONAL QUESTION

7. Orderly administration, just apportionment, and fulfillment of the community duties are possible only on the basis of a constitution. A permanent constitution can be established only after the end of the war, with the consent of the people; combat veterans have a right to exercise particular influence in this matter. Thus, we must all be temporarily satisfied with a provisional constitution which will be announced shortly. We are bound by it as well.

Prussia will be disbanded. The Prussian provinces, as well as the remaining German states, will be reorganized into national districts. Individual national districts will again be given autonomy within the Reich. They will be broadly self-governing. These autonomous national districts, with their counties and communities, will take over as much of public administration as is compatible with unity and purposeful leadership of the Reich. . . .

8. In war time the economy can only be maintained by some system of controlled structure and price management. An uncontrolled economy is not feasible as long as there is a shortage of essential goods. . . . For the time being, we can only simplify controls and rid them of obscurities, contradictory jurisdictions and irresponsibility. We will also repeal all measures which have encroached too deeply upon individual freedoms and which have arbitrarily destroyed enterprises in commerce, crafts, trades, industry, and agriculture. . . .

THE SOCIAL-ECONOMIC SYSTEM

It is the goal of our economic system that every worker, employee, and entrepreneur will have a share in our economic resources. This is not only a matter of freeing the initiative of the entrepreneur and forcing him into a competitive market. No, the German worker also must, and will, have the opportunity to contribute creatively in responsibility for the economy. The only thing even we cannot do, is to free him from the effects of the natural laws governing the economy.

Property is the foundation of all economic and cultural progress; without it man gradually becomes an animal. It will thus be protected, from large proprietors to the smallest owner who has only his household effects. Misuse of property will be opposed, as will unhealthy concentrations of capital that restrict the independence of human beings.

The structure of the economic system will be organized on the basis of self-government. The present system of manipulation from above must end. This means that independent decision making, and with it personal responsibility, must once more be brought to beneficial effectiveness. We must create the broadest possible confidence in the justice of the economic order, among the workers as well as all other groups.

THE SEARCH FOR SOCIAL EQUALITY

9. This is the process of seeking adjustment of differences by legislation of social policy. The weak and those innocently in distress must be protected, and insurance against the adversities of life must be provided. Social policy must also deal with conflicts like those of preservation of material savings (capital) versus guaranteed continuing employment. These conflicts arise in times of great political and economic distress. It would be highly irresponsible to resolve them by simply wiping out capital; nor would it please the small saver any more than it would serve the interest of the general public. On the other hand, capital goods alone are of no value if they cannot contribute more effectively to the support of the people now living. Therefore, a just, responsible, and conscientious balance must be found which will clarify for every individual from the very beginning that he, as everyone else, must make some sacrifices.

All productive citizens must participate in achieving a just economic balance, . . . and in an emergency the state must distribute the burden equally throughout the entire nation. Insofar as social institutions shall affect workers, they will have the right of full self-determination. . . .

PRESERVATION OF THE CURRENCY

10. A fundamental condition for a healthy economy lies in balanced public budgets. Expenditures must keep within the

framework of the actual revenue which the state, districts, counties, and communities receive from their citizens. It will require effort, character, sacrifice, and struggle to re-establish budgetary order, but it is the most important and indispensable basis for a secure currency and for all economic life. On it depends the value of all savings. Foreign trade, on which we have relied for more than a century, is impossible without a balanced budget.

Taxes will be sizeable, but we will be all the more careful in their economic use. It is more important for citizens to have the vital essentials than for bureaucrats to have sumptuous furnishings and initiate projects that conflict with the simple lives of individuals. . . .

We see an enormous danger in the accumulated debts that burden all belligerent and neutral states. They threaten all currencies. Every state will face an extremely difficult task after this war. We hope to be able to find solutions for repayment of these debts, if possible, to re-establish fiscal confidence and cooperation between nations.

11. Meanwhile the war continues. It demands our work, sacrifice, and devotion to the men who defend the fatherland at the front. We must give them all the psychological and material support that we can possibly muster. We stand in rank and file with them, with the knowledge that the sacrifices are necessary for the defense of the fatherland and the well-being of the people, but not in the service of a madman's thirst for conquest or his hunger for prestige. We know that until a just peace is achieved, we will wage this war with clean hands, in decency, with the honor that distinguishes all upright soldiers. Those who are already victimized by this war shall have all our care. . . .

The Voice of the True Germany

12. We gave warning against this war that has brought so much suffering to all of mankind, so we can speak candidly. Though national dignity presently demands that we dispense with bitter accusations, we are bringing those responsible to account. However necessary this is, it is more important to strive for an early peace. We know that we are not sole masters of war and peace; we depend on the other nations in this matter, we must stand our ground, but we want at last to raise the voice of the true Germany. . . .

In this hour, we must rally our people to the solemn task of bravely and patiently restoring lustre to the much-dishonored German name. We Germans alone can, and will, fulfill this task. Our future depends on our unrelenting, earnest, and proper pursuit of this goal no matter what the material consequences. For God is not to be called upon for His providence on any odd occasion; rather it is He who demands and watches that His order and His commands are not violated. It was a terrible misconception, rooted in the unfortunate Versailles Treaty, which assumed that the future could be built upon the misfortune of other peoples and upon the suppression and disdain of human dignity.

We do not want to violate the honor of other nations. We must desire to give others what we ask for ourselves. We believe that it is in the interest of all nations to make this peace a lasting one. This will require international confidence in the new Germany.

Confidence can neither be forced nor achieved with words. Whatever the future may bring, we abhor cowardly denunciation of the enemy and are convinced that all government leaders want not only the best for their peoples, but also a meaningful end of this struggle. We know they are ready, as we are, to lessen the inhuman hardships of total war, so irresponsibly unleashed, which ultimately affect all people of the world.

Let us once again walk the paths of justice, decency and mutual respect: In this spirit we all wish to fulfill our duty. . . .

38. A Journal of Defeat and Retribution, 1945

The collapse of the Third Reich was a crisis for many Germans. For those living east of the Oder and Neisse rivers (the present Polish-German boundary) it was a cataclysm of destruction and retribution. The advancing Russians were first preceded by the retreating German armies and the fleeing ethnic Germans and non-Communists of western Russia. In the winter of 1944–1945 millions of Germans in East Prussia and eastern Germany also took to flight with their families and possessions. By the spring of 1945 the swelling flood of refugees and disintegrating armies were overrun by the Russian forces and subjected to the pent-up vengeance of the suppressed Poles. When the military disruption and the great refugee trek were finally over, it was estimated that of some fifteen million German civilians who began to flee westward, roughly three-fourths survived the exodus. Records of this German calamity are plentiful, but few were written with the philosophical insight and humane judgement of Count Hans von Lehndorff. Descended from old Prussian nobility, he is a practicing surgeon and was one of a small number who professed the confessional Lutheran faith also held by Pastor Martin Niemöller.

SOURCE: Hans von Lehndorff, *East Prussian Diary. A Journal of Faith, 1945–1947* (London: Oswald Wolff Ltd., 1963), pp. 1–5, 10, 51–52, 54, 88–90, 96–97, 167–169, 249–252. Reprinted by permission of the publisher.

The first harbingers of the catastrophe made themselves felt at the end of June [1944]—faint shocks, hardly perceptible to the senses, which set the sun-drenched land quivering as if from some distant earthquake. And then all at once the roads were thronged with fugitives from Lithuania, and ownerless cattle went straggling across the harvest fields, following the irresistible urge towards the west.

It was difficult to grasp what had happened, no one dared give open expression to his fears. But by the time the storks were getting ready to leave a clearer notion of what lay before us could no longer be blinked. Everywhere in the villages one saw people standing, staring at the sky where the big, familiar birds were circling, as though this time it was to be the last goodbye. . . .

In the night, at this time, we saw the eastern frontier towns arrayed before us as if on a map. Memel, Tilsit, Schirwindt, Eydtkuhnen—those were the brightest points, flaring up again and again under the bombing attacks, on a line of fire that ran in a curve from north to south. And one day we heard that the frontier had been surrendered. The enemy had crossed it to a depth of twelve miles—eighteen miles; then the front came to a standstill again. What things looked like behind it, nobody knew. One could only hope that nobody had survived, for what was reported of a few advanced points which the enemy had abandoned after a brief occupation froze one's blood.

Another few days of immeasurable fugitive misery on all the roads—then a sudden quiet, an almost inconceivable quiet. The rumbling of the front died down, the fires went out, even the nightly disturbance flights had ceased. The deserted land, with its farms and villages, lay as if under a spell in the splendor of an incomparable autumn, offering an indefinable experience to the few who came back from places further west, to fetch something from their house or see to the livestock they had left behind.

It was uncannily quiet still after the November gales had swept the land bare and the frost had withered the last blades of grass in the meadows. Scattered for miles over the fields, along the roads and the railway lines, we saw the neglected cows standing, singly or in little groups, hardly able to move, with dried-up udders and prominent backbones, threatening and complaining. And when the first snow fell they collapsed, silently, one after another.

Christmas came, and could be celebrated almost as in peacetime by all those who had remained in their own homes. Shooting parties were actually organized, and people gathered to see the Old Year out in traditional fashion.

A fortnight later it was all over. The Russians had allowed themselves three months to prepare the final assault—now they broke in in full force. . . .

19th January

Our hospital is being evacuated. All the patients and most of the nurses are going to Pomerania, where they are to be given shelter in a private house. We are left without work. I packed a few things I value in one of the many thousand cases they've been turning out for months for transporting the whole inventory of the town to the west, and took it to the goods station on the toboggan. There it vanished among hundreds of others like it.

On the way back I noticed a lady standing by the roadside, surrounded by packages. As I passed her, hesitating, she said to me, "Oh, could you please tell me of a furniture remover? I want to send away the antique furniture from my flat. I've just got it out of Gumbinnen with the greatest difficulty, but the soldiers who helped me with it couldn't take it with them any further. They are all valuable pieces that I took from Wuppertal to some friends in Gumbinnen two years ago on account of the bombs. These things here are only the little ones, the big ones are over there in a court-yard." We went across the road to look at them. There were eight enormous pieces, including an oak dresser weighing at least half a ton. I can't think how she managed to get all that out of the burning town, surrounded on three sides by the enemy. We went back to the road again, and stood there to try and hold up one of the military vehicles that were rushing past at break-neck speed, for we were hardly likely to find a removal firm still working. Meanwhile I made a timid attempt to persuade the lady to leave without her furniture; but she wouldn't hear of it. Her husband had fallen in the war, she had no children, her house had been destroyed. These were the only things left to her and that she cared for.

While we were talking, heavy aircraft appeared at low altitude over the town. I couldn't believe my eyes when I saw every soldier within sight dive as quick as thought into the houses round. Only the civilians were left. But then a flashing and rattling started up overhead. Oh, so that was the explanation! It was the Russians! So near as that! We'd never yet seen them so near by day. They circled, and began firing on the station. Then at last our flak went into action. Like ships in a rough sea the heavy machines rose and fell, followed by our fighters, and turned away to the east. As though he had burnt them, the giant withdrew his fingers again. But he had broken open the door. I felt the icy draught as I returned to the hospital.

All was quiet in the afternoon. Only high up in the sky invisible aircraft went on tracing their bold condensation curves. I walked over the Tilting Square once more, and along the Angerapp, in sunshine and deep snow. The waxwings were there, pecking red berries off the bushes. Not a soul left on that side. They've all cleared out.

And in the evening, after dark, I went once again into our church. Ever since the bombing attack last summer we have gathered there daily for evensong. The doors are all smashed in, and through the main entrance the snow has drifted between the pews. I sat down under the pulpit and sang the hymn *"Mein schönste Zier"* by way of farewell. . . .

23rd January

Next morning I found the big square in front of Königsberg Main Station crowded with refugees. Farm wagons piled up with baggage were drawn up in serried rows, and more and more of them were coming out of the side streets, mostly driven by women. One dare not think where this is going to end. The trains are coming back from the west already, because the line is blocked. There is only the road to Pillau left. But that doesn't seem to be worrying people for the moment. They drive complacently along the street, eyes glued to the car in front, trying to find somewhere to put up. Pastor Müller of Haberberg, whom I called on on my way back, took me into a big room in which a number of these refugees had spent the night. There were a few sick people among them that he wanted me to have a look at. Everything was quiet and orderly here too, as at military maneuvers. I got the impression that nobody there had any clear idea of the situation. A woman stretched out a leg towards me, with a big varicose ulcer on it. It was a couple of years old, she said, but up to now she'd never had time to get it treated. Now I must do it. I tried to make it clear to her that in my opinion it was more important to get away from Königsberg first. She could then have it treated somewhere else, where she would have a better chance to rest. "Where are you supposed to be going?" I asked her. She didn't know; only that they were all to get into the Reich. And then she added astoundingly: "The Führer would never let us fall into the hands of the Russ; he'd gas us first." I stole a glance at the people round us, but nobody seemed to think there was anything extraordinary about this declaration. Dear God! I thought, if only we had as much faith in *You*! . . .

9th April 1945

Toward five in the morning I was awakened by a babel of voices and hurrying footsteps outside my door. I woke Doktora and told her to get dressed. "What's up?" she asked, drunk with sleep. "I think the Russians are here," I said, "I'm just going to see." "The Russians? Oh, have they actually come? I'd quite forgotten them." "Well, there you are," I said, "it was your own choice." She nodded. I put on my white jacket and went out into the passage. . . .

Outside the main building two Russians were rummaging in a trunk. There was something frightening in the sight. I felt like someone who'd gone bear-hunting, and forgotten his gun. As we approached them they left the trunk alone and transferred their interest to us. With tommy-guns pressed to our bodies we were honored by a thoroughgoing examination. An attempt by my companion to address them had no result. They made short, growling noises and carried on methodically with the work. Other Russians, meanwhile, came out of the main block, hung round like sleigh-horses with the most fantastic objects. They too ran their hands over us; my fountain pen vanished, money, and papers flew all over the place. My shoes were too bad for them. They hurried away with a short-legged gait over ruins and through bomb craters to the other blocks and disappeared in the doorways. Their mode of locomotion left us gaping: when the situation suggested it they dropped on their hands and ran on all fours.

In the main building they were already hard at work. As I was forever having to stop and let myself be felt all over, I advanced along our basement passages as if through dense undergrowth. Stifled sounds of protest came from all the wards. Patients were being rolled out of bed and their bandages removed; here and there masses of paper were being burnt to improve the lighting, and our people were desperately trying to extinguish the fires. We kept looking in vain for an officer, for if this sort of thing went on, there soon wouldn't be much of us left.

In the out-patients' department the young nurses were fending off some importunate fellows. I dare not think what it will be like when they've become more assured. For the moment they seem determinedly bent on looting, as we discovered when we reached the provision stores. I was struck dumb by the sight of the multitude of foodstuffs there, which we had been denied in the fortress days; it infuriated me to think I had let myself be hoodwinked into allowing both ourselves and our patients to go hungry all that time. Now a wild, howling mob was fighting over the finest tinned foods, and provisions that hundreds could have lived on for a whole year were being destroyed in a few hours. . . .

What, actually, is our situation now? Nothing has really changed, except that the process of attrition that began with the houses is now spreading to the people. The final decision concerning us has not yet been taken. I'm so exhausted that I can't even pray.

At the same time, to my horror, I feel a new sense awakening in me, a sort of cold curiosity. What is it really, I ask myself, that we are witnessing here? Is it simply an expression of natural savagery, or of revenge? Of revenge perhaps, but in a different sense. Isn't the animal revenging itself upon the human, in one and the same person—the flesh upon the spirit it has had forced upon it? Where do these types come from, human beings like ourselves, in the thrall of impulses in horrific contrast with their outward appearance? What a struggle to bring chaos to light! This dull, growling speech, from which words seem to have withdrawn themselves long ago, and these maddened children, fifteen-, sixteen-year-olds, flinging themselves like wolves on the women, without really knowing what they're supposed to be doing. All this has nothing to do with Russia, nothing to do with any particular nation or race—it is mankind without God, the apish mask of mankind. Otherwise all this could not affect me so painfully—like personal guilt. . . .

[From the end of April to mid-June of 1945, Lehndorff was sent, with thousands of other Germans, to a temporary relocation camp at Rothenstein, a preliminary step in expulsion further westward to Germany.]

Today everybody knows from hearsay what such a camp is like. It's a place where people are put away that one doesn't want to think about for a time, either because one has other concerns in mind, or because thinking about them proves too uncomfortable. In the camp they are automatically subjected to a process of attrition, which has no demonstrable connection with the intentions of whoever sent them there, but is to their advantage insofar as it dispenses them from any further trouble in the matter, or at any rate reduces the need for it to a minimum. The final result of the camp is in any case a condition that calls forth no more than a wrinkling of the nose; one can't be expected to feel any further responsibility for such people.

The feeling that one has been consigned to oblivion in this way is hard to describe; if one didn't know that God casts no one aside, one might fall into despair.

The barracks surrounding us were almost undamaged. We were led down the central roadway; on our left the yards between the garages were guarded by pickets; grey masses of humanity were creeping past them. We were pushed into Hall Number Eight. The floor couldn't be seen for people. Followed by feeble curses we went carefully feeling our way over a mass of legs, looking for an empty spot; but with the best will in the world no room could be made for us. Two thousand people were said to be collected here, all men. Some of them had been there for four weeks, the majority for a fortnight; they were literally living each on his eighteen inches of cement floor. Hardly any of them could lie down; most of them were squatting on their hunkers or standing upright.

I clambered on till a hand held me fast. An elderly man was looking at me as kindly as his stubbly face allowed, and said if I would sit back to back with him, and his neighbor could spare an inch, he could find room for me. With a sigh of relief I bent my knees and assumed the position he suggested. Mutual introductions were superfluous; here everybody was alike, and differentiation was apt to have a painful effect. In the course of conversation, however, I did learn his name, and that he was an engineer and a State Surveyor. He was sorry he had nothing to offer me in the way of eatables: once a day, with luck, they got a cup of gruel and a slice of bread. He had four coffee beans in his trouser pocket and gave me two.

The mood of the broken creatures round us varied from indignant to lachrymose. I gathered from their utterances that they had not yet realized their situation. They still believed they had fallen victims to some unpardonable error on the part of the Administration. As soon as the word got round, among those nearest me, that I was a doctor, I was besieged with questions as to what sense there was in all this, and when they would be let out again. It was really a crime to pack people together like this; it made one ill. And the food that was due to them they never got. I really ought to go to the Commandant and make a serious complaint about this abuse. There was no water at all, and no latrines. The whole thing was a filthy shame, which nobody "at the top" knew anything about, most likely.

I behaved as apathetically as possible, not wanting to implicate myself in these long orations. Tub-thumping was never in my line. An old man ventured on the ninety-first psalm, which he shouted out to the rest: "Who dwelleth under the defence of the Most High . . ." Nobody took any notice of him; maybe one or another among them was beginning to see clear.

Toward evening a woman put in appearance, who had evidently assumed a sort of medical service on her own responsibility. She was called over to us, and told to take me with her to the other German doctors. I was to get full information from them and then set things in order.

She went away, came back after a little while, and asked me to follow her. She took me past several patrols as far as Hall Number

Two, where we pushed through another dense crowd of people to a room that had been partitioned off. The door opened, and I saw several men in dirty white jackets bustling about. My escort went up to one of them and I followed diffidently. He looked at me, came quickly towards me and shut the door behind me. Without many words I was led to a wide wooden guard-bed and covered over with a big cape. I felt guilty, and moaned ashamedly to myself. One couldn't be better sheltered in Abraham's bosom.

From under the cape I took stock of my benefactors. All three of them had hats on, resting more on the nape of the neck than on the head, and civilian clothes under their jackets. What they were doing, I couldn't see. People kept coming in for treatment. When two Russians appeared the cape was drawn right over my head till they had gone again.

By and by a fourth man joined them, bringing a saucepan of porridge which was shared out among us. I came out of my corner and introduced myself to the others. They consisted of a young army doctor whom I will call Schreiner and two medical assistants, Holter and Klein. They had belonged to a unit posted on the outskirts of the town, and were brought here after Königsberg had fallen. Here in the camp, with the help of a hypodermic syringe and a few medicaments they had brought in their pockets, they had set up a surgery in which even the Russian custodians had begun to take some interest, coming occasionally to be treated in secret. In general, however, the Russians kept outside the patrols and left the restraint of the prisoners to the Poles. The latter made exaggerated use of their rubber truncheons to get good marks—i.e. better food—from the Russians.

As sickness increased among the internees, Dr. Schreiner had enlisted the energies of a few women to build up a volunteer medical service. With a Red-Cross badge on their upper arm they went through the camp halls, listened to complaints, made notes of them and told the doctor where he was wanted. The guards usually let them through without difficulty; they were free to carry on.

Except for the cold, I was feeling fairly fit again; I was merely quailing at the thought of meeting some connection of mine in this place. As there were no latrines, everybody, men and women alike, met in fantastical fashion between the halls, in a corridor some twelve feet wide. There was always a horrible crush there, for some of these people were already suffering badly from diarrhea.

Added to which it rained all day long. It was not unusual for someone to collapse from weakness. To have lived one's life only to end up in this place, literally "in the shit!" A hymn recurred to me involuntarily: "Thus far hath God brought me . . ." Was that blasphemy? But who else had done it? Well, if He had stood by one so far, He must surely continue to help one. . . .

The cellars under all the barrack blocks are crammed with people, some four thousand men and women, many of whom are examined every night by the NKWD official. The examination is not for the purpose of extracting from people what they know—which would be uninteresting anyway—but of forcing certain declarations out of them. The methods employed are very primitive; people are beaten up until they confess that they once belonged to the Nazi party. The result is more or less the opposite of what one would expect, namely that those that hadn't been of the Party would come off better. The authorities start from the assumption that everybody *must* have been in the Party. Many people die as a result of these interrogatories, while others, who confess their allegiance at the outset, hardly suffer at all. Only the lower classes are involved, anyway, for the higher officials got out of the affair earlier on, either by escaping in time or by suicide. A fairly large batch of these "partisans" is shipped off to Insterburg or Gumbinnen every day. The cellars left empty are filled up with men and women out of the halls in the following way. A Russian and a Pole appear with a list of German names in Russian script. These names are called out to the crowd by the two of them, one after the other, in a hoarse voice. Not one of them can be recognized; often they are not names at all, but designations of some kind, copied out of the collection of documents. A lot of people answer to them, nevertheless, in the hope of being released from the camp. All those on the list are removed and taken down to the cellars. There all interest in them ceases for the time being; some of them may be examined later up to three or four times, some not at all.

The first cellar the guard opened had just been refilled. Three men were staggering about in the passage and were driven in again with the butt of the guard's rifle, with difficulty, however, because the room was too small and the door could only be closed by force. People had been standing there for three days, waiting to be examined. At the sight of us a senseless hubbub broke out that left me helpless. It was impossible to deal with individual requests. As far as I could gather, the usual senseless questions were being reiterated: Why were they there, and for how long? There was no water, and hardly anything to eat. They wanted to be let out more than once a day, and so on. The guard was getting fed up with the outcry. I had just time to call out to them that they must think out their most urgent requests before the next visit and let a spokesman deliver them. Then the door was banged to on them. . . .

[Lehndorff's expulsion to Germany was delayed time and again because his skills were needed to aid Poles, Russians, and Germans alike. At times he lived a semi-independent life in areas where Germans had been expelled and Poles or Russians had moved in to take their place.]

I owed my good relations with the dreaded UB [Polish Committee of Public Safety] chiefly to the Doktourka. Right at the beginning she once gave three armed men who appeared to be about to search me such a dressing-down that they made off again, half stupefied. Moreover, she was zealously engaged in "polonizing" me. She kept asking me if a Polish name hadn't played a part at some time in my family. In the end I let myself be persuaded, and told her that before the Thirty Years War the name "Mgowski" had occasionally cropped up in connection with my own. She was delighted, and a few days later she handed me a sort of certificate, in which to my astonishment I found myself entered as "Jan Mgowski." Sad to say, this interesting document was lost on one of the later occasions when I was being searched.

I often had considerable booty to bring home. Once it was thirty pounds of wheat flour from the mill, where some Polish soldiers had called me in professionally, another time I was given a live fowl by some people whose entire family were down with typhus. The flour was particularly welcome in view of Christmas: with the fowl, whom we named Lorchen, we struck up an intimate friendship.

The Doktourka had long had a mind to introduce me to her friends in Allenstein and Osterode. She took me with her one day, greatly daring, to Allenstein. For fourteen zloty we were permitted to take advantage of the morning train, consisting of three goods trucks. When we got to Allenstein my first impression was one of intense dislike. The station, and all the immediate neighborhood, was swarming with Russian and Polish troops and the usual non-descript individuals among their hangers-on who had something to sell, or were merely loafing about. I felt again as if transported deep into Asia, and I saw that Doktourka herself was anxious to get away from the place as quickly as possible. Only a part of the town had been destroyed, the greater half appeared to be quite intact and densely occupied by Poles.

We went to St. Mary's Hospital and saw a doctor and several cigarette-smoking nurses. The Doktourka carried on an animated conversation with these, while I paid a visit to the seven German nurses who were leading a shadowy existence at the top of the house and were not being called upon to do any nursing.

Three days later the Doktourka took me with her to Osterode, to fetch the bottles of petrol, ether, and other liquids from the medical stores allotted to our dispensary. I didn't feel altogether happy about this expedition, as I had no desire to become better known among the Poles. On the other hand, I naturally welcomed an opportunity of seeing Osterode under feminine protection.

The town had been sadly devastated and was much less lively than Allenstein. I saw a good many people hanging about the sub-prefecture, and a few bicycles and horse-drawn vehicles. We called on the district doctor—the only doctor available at the time—did some bartering at the chemist's, and made various little purchases for our out-patients' department and for the Doktourka's house-keeping, which was beginning to flourish. We also went together to visit the five German Catholic Sisters who had remained behind in the parsonage, and to whom I was able to give greetings from St. Elizabeth's Hospital, their Königsberg training school. I was again given a great deal to carry, including a bag of bones for our kitchen.

The train service between Osterode and Allenstein was a some-what laborious affair, as the Russians had removed the second line over the whole stretch. There were only two passenger trains a day in either direction, one of which consisted of cattle trucks, and even these had some difficulty in getting through, as the line was constantly blocked by goods trains. These came fully laden from Berlin and travelled back empty. The Russians were using them to transport to the east everything they had taken to pieces in Ger-many, either packed in big crates or loose. Ten to fifteen of these trains were said to pass through every day, worked by German railwaymen as a rule, under Russian guard. I sometimes had a talk with these men when the trains stopped at Biessellen, and gave them letters to various addresses in Germany, in the hope that one or other of them might reach its destination. Getting away by one of these trains would prove almost impossible, since they were constantly searched on the journey, but I hoped none the less to seize some such opportunity one day, for of course I was longing to be with my own people again, and I didn't want to let myself be tied to this place.

The Russian railwaymen often took advantage of the stops at the stations to do a little private looting. I once saw one of them panting towards the line with a sofa on his back. As the engine had meanwhile run a long way out of the station with the railwaymen's staff wagon, he was forced to tramp some 400 yards along the embankment in deep snow; but he had hardly reached the wagon when the train slowly receded, and he had to carry his burden all the way back again. Even this was to no purpose, however, for just as he reached it, dripping with sweat, the train started off so suddenly that there was nothing for it but to throw the sofa away and jump on in a hurry. A tinge of malicious pleasure on our part when we witnessed such incidents was perhaps excusable in the circumstances.

The Polish signalmen have anything but an easy time with the Russians. When disasters occur, their only hope of salvation lies in total disappearance. One morning the regular train from Osterode ran into a Russian military transport in the dark, and there were many serious casualties. The furious Russians wanted to arrest the guilty pointsman, but he had bolted betimes, though not without dropping a hint to his brother in the village, who thereupon decided to decamp himself, since he had good reason to fear that the Russians would take it out of him instead. Escape didn't really present any very serious problem, for hardly anybody had anything left but what he stood up in, and the risk of being pursued in such unknown country was relatively small. . . .

On the 4th May [1947] I was sent for from Brausen for a confinement. It was freezing hard at sunrise. Just as I was leaving again the news came that motor vehicles would be coming about ten o'clock to take everybody there to the camp at Deutsch Eylau, whence they would be sent on to Germany, and I decided to wait for this. The cars actually came, and everything had to be done at top speed. One small package was the allowance per head. Frau Aust was smuggled in, although she was not officially included.

Once they had really started I went back to Rosenberg. I saw that the Germans in Faulen were being taken too, and I was much relieved, because they really had nothing left to live on. In the afternoon I was lying on my bed, wondering whether I ought to make myself another pair of shoes, when suddenly three militiamen came into my room saying, "Doktour, want to go home?" "Yes, very much," I said, "When?"—"Come with, at once!" "How much may I take with me?" "Forty pound." "I haven't got so much."

I quickly packed my things in the rucksack and took a hasty farewell of my somewhat bewildered feminine staff. . . .

I had to spend the night in the guardhouse. The Commandant sent for me to have supper at his house, and wanted me to sleep there in spite of the cramped quarters, but his new colleague wouldn't agree, so I was bowed back to the guardhouse. I found an almost naked Russian there, who had been arrested for kicking up a row, being interrogated—and thoroughly pummelled and pinched into the bargain.

In the morning I was taken to the station, along with a German militiaman who has been working here as a smith, followed by people waving to us in a friendly way. We went to Deutsch Eylau and were taken to the camp, where the people fetched the day before were already assembled.

We waited three days for the transport; we were to be coupled to a train coming from Allenstein. We were not really supposed to leave the camp, but the militia kept taking me to see their families, and as a result I succeeded in exchanging all my Polish money, which I must otherwise have given up, for articles of food. The militiamen are very skeptical about our destination, and above all they think it unlikely that as a doctor I shall be allowed to leave Poland; I must be prepared, they say, to be hauled out somewhere on the way, and appointed somewhere else.

To our surprise we were given soup twice a day in the camp, and the farewell rifling was not too drastic either. Fortunately the subprefect was present; I had come to know him on his friendly side. He prevented our clothes from being ripped up, though a few things that had been sewn in had to be given up all the same. I would have liked to save my three silver goblets, and asked the subprefect about them. State property must be given up, he replied, but as my name was on the goblets the affair seemed doubtful. He thought it over. In the end he gave the man in charge a hint, and the case was settled.

Before we were finally conducted to the station, a curious scene was enacted. We were drawn up more or less in battle array—some four hundred of us—and then the subprefect asked me to say a few words to the assembly on his behalf. Somewhat startled, I asked what he had in mind. He said he was anxious to emphasize that the way we were being treated here, as Germans, was not mere chicanery, but according to orders. The Germans had done the same to the Poles. We must therefore share in the atonement, even if as individuals we hadn't shared in the guilt. So I stepped in front of the company and spoke more or less to this effect: "Dear fellow countrymen, listen all of you! The Herr Subprefect here is sorry that we have to leave our home country under these conditions, but he can't help it, because our people did the same to the Poles earlier on, and unfortunately that is true. But we will thank him for the good soup we were given in the camp, and beg him to see to it that the next transport is as well treated. And now let us hope that we really do get to Germany."

By that evening we were trundling along in a goods train through the country, thirty people to a wagon, through Thorn, Bromberg, and Posen. The fields everywhere were as neglected as with us, but the towns seemed to be in much better condition. We were allowed to open the doors during the journey and hang our legs out.

At the end of two days we reached Kohlfurt; there we joined other transports and were detained for two days, dusted with louse powder and checked over once more. The two German doctors working there let me spend the night in their quarters; they would have liked to go with us if they had been able to, but in spite of the nearness to the frontier escape was as difficult here as with us. Wading by night through the closely guarded Neisse was the only chance.

Then we went on, as in a dream, very slowly over a little river; and at the next stop we were allowed to get out without being immediately shooed back again. We were in Germany.

We reached Wehrkirch towards evening. There we were greeted by a banner bearing a portrait of Thälmann. The sick were taken from us and kindly treated. At night the train rolled slowly on, and arrived in Hoyerswerda in the morning. The Elsterhorst camp, our last checking-up station, was close by. It consisted of a rectangular enclosure, surrounded by a great deal of barbed-wire fencing, and divided in two by a road with hutments on either side of it. We were led in. A few hundred yards away a similar complex had been fenced round for the sick. Doctors and nurses were at work there in sufficient number; they admitted me to their company, gave me a room and let me take part in their examinations. They even allotted me a ward. . . .

We spent Whitsuntide in the camp, and then our ways were sundered; that is, we evaded the imminent typhus quarantine by flight. After I had worked Frau Aust through the barbed wire, at dusk, into the arms of her nephew waiting outside, I couldn't hold out any longer. I flung my baggage over the fence, clambered after it and took the next train to Berlin.

And then the reunion! I was like a drunken man for days and weeks on end. So few people really knew what we had gone through in the East, and what a lot there was to tell! But one day a man to whom I was describing things took a piece of bread from his pocket while I was talking, broke it and handed me half of it—an accustomed gesture in the days of famine. Then I knew it was time to take the first steps along the road offering me a new existence. And I was faced with the question: What will this new existence be like, and who is to determine it? Will it be an indifferent one, one of the thousands that needn't have been lived at all? Or will God in his mercy ordain that I and all those that have gone through the same experience may be given grace to bear witness by our lives to the great things we have heard and seen?

39. German Confession, 1945

With the Third Reich in ruins, the victorious powers began to demilitarize and de-Nazify the Germans, while restoring essential public services to sustain their control. A much greater task of re-orientation and restoration remained for the Germans themselves. How would they come to grips with the moral issues and implications of their recent past? What course might they set for their future, particularly for the battered generation of youth straggling back from disaster at the front to destruction at home? What wisdom might they seek to convey to the next generation of youth now just entering adolescence? Two views are here presented, one from East Germany and one from West Germany, both interpreting the past, each already casting faint shadows of a future divided Germany.

Johannes R. Becher joined the German Communist party at age eighteen and sat in the Reichstag from 1919 to 1932. Novelist, poet, and literary commentator, he became one of the most prominent intellectuals of the German radical left. Living in Moscow between 1935 and 1945 and an original member of the Free Germany National Committee, he was made president of the Cultural Association for the Democratic Renewal of Germany, sponsored by the Russians in 1945. From 1954 until his death in 1958 he was Minister of Culture of the German Democratic Republic.

SOURCE: Johannes R. Becher, "Deutsches Bekenntnis," *Aufbau*, I (1945), Heft 1. Translation by the editor.

Our people still have not comprehended the extent of their defeat. We still have not achieved an awareness of our responsibility, or the dimension of our guilt. We are not yet aware of all that is needed to sense a new human and national existence, to give meaning to our life and, after all these frightful experiences, to make life worth living again. . . . We have fallen far from the heights of our German classicism to the degradation of purposeful falsehood and fraud characteristic of the Nazi ideology. We can measure the downfall by recalling the words of Goethe on truth and falsehood: "I prefer detrimental truth to useful falsehood. Detrimental truth is useful because it can be harmful only momentarily and then leads to other truths which must become more and more beneficial; by contrast, a useful falsehood is harmful because it can be only momentarily useful and leads to other falsehoods which grow more and more harmful."

A philosophy and way of life based on the objective search for truth was replaced by distorted propaganda and advertising: this decay of our moral fibre is conspicuously responsible for the fact that Germany has now suffered the worst defeat in its history. This defeat is also the worst moral catastrophe in the life of our nation; today we can barely begin to evaluate its devastating consequences. The catastrophe did not strike us overnight. It was preceded by conditions which prepared the way for a protracted spiritual crisis, a process of spiritual and moral dissolution and decay extending back over five decades that should be called: The Annihilation of

Reason. This process did not occur solely in the ideological-spiritual field. It was not as though philosophy, literature, and the arts alone were engulfed by surrealism and irrationalism, by agnosticism and relativism. All the thought and sensitivity of our people were influenced by views hostile to truth and reality, as reactionary as they were adventurous. The German political process was especially affected. Ever since the retirement of Bismarck [1890] it had abandoned all realistic modes of analysis, and from this renunciation of reason derived the failure which we already experienced in the First World War.

Perhaps some future historian will portray the period from 1914 to 1945 as a kind of second Thirty Years War, gathering impetus in the period between 1900 and 1914 as the beginning of the imperialistic age, with an intermediate phase from 1918 to 1939, flanked and held by the blood-drenched blocks of two world wars. In such a context this breathing spell, this centerpiece, will appear as the attempt of German imperialism to make all the economic and military preparations necessary to convert the defeat of the First World War into a victory in a Second World War. . . . Both wars were lost politically even before they had begun on the battlefield. German leadership had, from the very beginning in both wars, arrayed such political superiority against themselves that after some initial successes they were necessarily forced to capitulate economically and militarily. . . . Clausewitz taught us that war is a continuation of peacetime policy by other means and that it is the responsibility of political statesmanship to set up such conditions as will put the military leadership in a position to achieve material superiority in the course of the war. The "triumph of spirit" in politics consists of guaranteeing such material superiority before the war actually breaks out. Germany was not in a position to do this because it had generally misconceived its great historic task and because it pursued a policy, supported by the preponderant majority of our people, which was directed against Germany's true national interests. A nation which does not fulfill its historical obligations, but stubbornly and obstinately acts contrary to them, must pay a high price to finally learn what they are. . . .

Let us now briefly examine our past history in the light of truth so that in this light we may again achieve that firm measure and value necessary to construct an enduring frame of reference for our present and our future. . . . Our first great historical failure was the inability to centralize during the Reformation; our second great failure was the long delay in establishing a unified German nation; our third great failure was that in 1871 a unified empire was created without the active participation of the entire people. Henceforth the major challenge was to complement national unity by the creation of an inner democratic order. Our further subsequent failure to meet this historic challenge eventually led to the catastrophic final act of the German tragedy, which to this day burdens us with all its grave and oppressive weight.

In the wake of this unfortunate development, and because reactionary forces suppressed all efforts for liberalization, the Annihilation of Reason was able to make such deep inroads into our spiritual and moral life. Truthful thinking, the recognition of historic truth, is not in the interests of reaction; quite the contrary. The truth is that German imperialism, the monopoly of German capital, and all the reactionary forces connected with it, have always opposed the fulfillment of our most urgent national task, and continue to oppose it wherever they still survive. Just as the princes once made no secret of their hostility against the nation and directed every thought and aspiration towards perpetuating the fragmentation of Germany, so German monopoly capital has left nothing undone to prevent any and all further free development of the unified nation. These very same reactionary powers were the ones that opened the door for Hitler and made him the manager of their armaments business. It is nothing but the clear, unvarnished historic truth when we brand German imperialists, with a Hitler in the lead, as traitors and enemies of Germany, as the worst enemies ever in our history to spring from the midst of the German people themselves. . . .

It is only too logical that our German people, in this tragic misunderstanding of their national responsibility, should also reach a moral nadir not found in our entire previous history. The excess of loathsome bestiality, of which German people were guilty in this war, this excess of inhumanities and cruelties, shows us morally only too clearly what a fundamentally false direction our development has taken. Innumerable are the documents of inhumanity that reach us in letters, notebooks, photographs and memoirs of all kinds. . . . The material debris, wreckage, and ruins which we see today are only the outward expression of the inner, the spiritual life of our people; we can rightly speak of the ruins of our morality, of the wasteland of the German soul.

Just as in religion, there is a concept of rebirth in the life of a people. Even an active people can change and become different. We Germans are now again summoned to such a change, to such a transformation. This will also require an intellectual discussion, a philosophical analysis involving national clarification and self-understanding that will not let us conceal the issues which separate us but will make them fruitful in the interests of the greater community. That would already be a substantial realization of democracy. This is also what Pericles said in his famous funeral oration: "In our opinion action does not suffer from discussion but, rather, from the want of that instruction which is gained by discussion preparatory to the action required." Once again history has challenged us, has called us to account. Woe to us if we do not assume responsibility for ourselves and if, once again, we do not satisfy our national requirements and if we again try to deceive history.

A rebirth presupposes that the individual will look into himself and examine his heart and soul to see if he did not himself contribute his disruptive share towards the catastrophe. "We only wanted to do what was best," some will lament. A Latin proverb says "abusus optimi pessimus"—abuse of the best is the worst abuse. Are you therefore innocent? Most certainly not. With the best of will, with the best of faith, with your greatest strength did you serve the worst cause in the world? Anyone who permitted such an abuse of himself cannot claim to be free of guilt. But how is it with this "best of faith?" Did you fail to hear what kind of war aims Goebbels set for you as he toasted "your health" in his tavern oratory? Boisterous and cynical enough was the Nazi propaganda that blared out its barbaric amorality for all the world to hear. No one could have ignored the criminal game which was being played, with the possible exception of such criminal figures, such cases of "moral insanity," as saw their sole justification in the vocational practice of crime. . . .

The famous Periclean funeral oration reads, as every German student knows: "If a man takes no interest in public affairs, we alone do not commend him as quiet but condemn him as useless." It is precisely these, the nonpolitical individuals, who bear no little guilt for the awful downfall of our people. Only by their "silent toleration," by their nonparticipation could evil blossom so disastrously. But even we, [Communists] who so constantly attempted to combat evil, cannot absolve ourselves from guilt after carefully examining our consciences. We did not consistently serve our good cause as it best deserved. We made mistakes and demonstrated weaknesses; these mistakes and weaknesses become historic guilt in such tense times when even the best we do, or fail to do, can have a major impact. No, we will not stand before the German people in the overweening pretense that we are the chosen, that we are immaculate and free of guilt. But we do stand before the world with the unswerving will to change ourselves, to educate ourselves from robots and automatons into free German human beings. . . . Such a rebirth is meaningful only if the whole person is caught up by a new life, if thoughts and feelings are similarly incorporated in the new life, if truth is not only intellectually recognized, but also deeply experienced.

What shall we now do? We must at last bring our individual life and activity, our entire personal existence, into accord with the objective that the life of our people demands as a whole. We must do what is historically necessary. We must do what we have failed to do for one hundred years, since the year 1848. We must create the society which alone will endure as a free and democratic Germany. We must build a new, clean, respectable Germany that demonstrates to the world by voluntary achievement, without malice or deceit, without ulterior imperialistic and militaristic motives, that goodness is not extinct in the German character. . . .

The task of reformation we call for should constitute the spiritual and moral foundation from which the lasting edifice of a free nation can rise. When we dedicate ourselves to this high cause, we will be standing on the bright side of our history, united with the best of our people and allied with all the best that mankind has ever created. Truth is on our side. We stand in its light. In the spirit of freedom, in the spirit of valiant truth, we begin our task. Under this symbol we arise.

40. Our Most Urgent Task, 1945

Rudolf Pechel began his intellectual career in 1912 as editor of the *Literarisches Echo*. In 1919 he moved as editor to the prestigious *Deutsche Rundschau*, where he worked until 1960. Both the journal and its editor had a reputation for independence of judgment and courage that were reflected in the quality of their literary insight and political commentary. The Nazis closed down the journal, and Pechel was committed to the Sachsenhausen concentration camp from 1942 to 1945. A clearly identified personality in opposition to National Socialism, Pechel tried to speak to German youth about their future with firm credentials of integrity.

SOURCE: Rudolf Pechel, "Unsere vordringlichste Aufgabe," *Deutsche Rundschau* (1945–1946), Heft 1, LXIX: 45–49. Translation by the editor.

Show us a goal and a way; give us ideals again that are worth fighting for. We, the youth, appeal to your generation: do not put us off with superficial slogans. Although you knew the First World War, you led us into the Second by giving power to the Nazis. You sacrificed us on the battlefields of this war as youth has never been sacrificed before. Now at least show us a goal toward which we can work, for we are still willing, though perhaps not much longer.

From the letter of a son to his father.

No one with serious concern for the German people will deny that the most difficult problem we have to solve is the question of our youth. The fall of the Third Reich meant more than material destruction for the younger generation. Their minds and souls face a state of ruin comparable to that of our cities. They no longer have firm ground upon which they can confidently construct a new edifice. The ideals for which they risked their lives are revealed as perversions and frauds. It was not that the ideals themselves were necessarily false, but that they were proffered by stained hands and with such deceitful intent that no sober and rationally thinking person would have accepted even the Holy Grail from them.

It is senseless, and would be unjust, to blame the youth for their errors. The older generation must first ask itself what *they* did to protect youth from going astray. We all know that, once totalitarian terror lay upon the German land and waves of corruption had engulfed all true values or tarnished them with a layer of filthy lies, youth could be influenced only indirectly by individual example and individual bearing of decency and truth. We also know, and take into account, that any attempt to enlighten youth was fraught with a great personal risk, because the regime had raised denunciation to a patriotic duty, incited children against their parents, and brothers against brothers in order to destroy every basis of confidence and make even private conversation impossible. Youth was enveloped with self-satisfying political advertisement and obtrusive propaganda which, despite its arrogant self-praise, gave its victims much satisfaction.

Youth now completely lacks inward security and often faces the difficult contemporary realities with understandable stubbornness. They truly believed in those earlier ideals. When they were called to war, they sought only to fulfill their duty in defense of their fatherland, not to maintain Nazi sovereignty. Now they return home with shattered weapons after prodigious feats and are insulted by some groups as the "prolongers of the war." Everything they did in good faith and high spirit is now called a crime. In a world which still resounds with the rumble of weapons and is not yet rid of injustice and violence, despite the suppression of fascism, the youth are to be led [by the victors] on paths of justice and to renounce concepts of militarism that they hardly comprehend. They are supposed to become believers in democracy, yet they see much that is undemocratic. It is a curse that democracy is brought to Germany for the second time from abroad under conditions of total collapse, where it cannot be learned without hunger, chaos, and currency devaluation. Insecurity everywhere! And when youth raises questions, it is put off with the slogans [of the occupying powers].

We should say instead: all human affairs demonstrate weakness and perfection can never be reached. Yet, although others are also imperfect, we still are duty bound to aspire to perfection. In times of crisis the pendulum always swings too far, but it is also a law of life that it will return to a tolerable arc.

If it seems to you that militarism still rules the world and continues to employ force, you must first determine if extreme danger does not, for the time being, warrant the use of such means.

If you feel that justice is not yet sovereign in the world, sharpen your own sense of justice so that it will prevent you from doing wrong. Always recognize injustice, even when it affects only others. What did you do and feel when the Nazis committed horrendous crimes upon the Jews and other persons of opposing political views? Begin with yourselves and help build a part of the road towards establishment of the rule of law in the whole world!

Youth is now searching for truth and a new foundation. The Nazis said theirs would be the hardiest youth in the world: "tough as leather, hard as steel, fast as whippets." Today it is a lost horde of wounded cripples with broken spirits—tired, disillusioned, and embittered. What is to be their road? We, the older generation should avoid two mistakes. After 1918 and after 1933, the older generation succumbed to a kind of panic, deriving from a subconscious awareness of its own failure, and few dared to provide instruction and direction for youth. We should avoid this mistake, for in addition to parental *duty* there is also the parental *right*. We must also avoid the mistake of "straightening out" youth with preachments of dry morality instead of offering life-giving spiritual nourishment.

This youth, like none other at any other time, was irresponsibly sacrificed and driven into a hail of shells and bombs. Only one thing can help them: *the truth.*

They were carefully trained not to think forthrightly. As a result of this awful conditioning they should recognize that correct and clear thinking is a *moral* prerequisite. They should thoroughly scrutinize whatever programs and slogans come at them . . . with seriousness and respect for the truth. They should see if decency is not a suitable ideal and attractive to young people. . . . Youth should also analyze the substance of the Ten Commandments; they will soon recognize that these are the only preconditions by which man lives as man and not as a beast among beasts. Then they will understand that the ethics of the Sermon on the Mount must stand beside the Ten Commandments because human life worthy of the name is impossible in a world devoid of love and filled with hate. . . . Youth will begin to understand that they as well as other things must grow with patience. . . .

Youth should once more become accustomed to simple, intellectual nourishment and tune its ear for the delicate and quiet vibrations of the soul. Those who always eat peppers lose their taste, and those constantly exposed to fanfares, trumpets and drums lose the better part of their hearing.

Democracy is not yet a reality in Germany, just a slogan. It will be one of the tasks of youth to combine the concept of democracy with other concepts of idealism, courage, and patriotism—notably a patriotism free of nationalism and willingly acknowledging the nature and idiosyncrasies of other peoples. . . . Youth will then begin to understand the concept of freedom, the most holy of man's earthly possessions; no life worthy of man is possible without it. But freedom without limits does not exist, never did exist, and will not exist as long as people evolve as they hitherto have. . . . Respect for freedom requires a rejection of violence. Neither in the home community nor in the community of nations is boundless freedom possible. One must find and set the delicate line which divides responsibility to the society from private interests.

In face of the seemingly hopeless entanglement of our world in hatred and enmity, the awareness is growing that those old antagonisms which *cannot* be overcome by the Germans' recognition of their guilt, require a new and better [international] order for their accommodation. Hatred and enmity can lose their poisonous edge if they are moved to a new level where the essentials of life are guaranteed for even the smallest country and there is an atmosphere of cooperation for the future. Call it the United States of Europe, or whatever. As soon as German youth comprehends this fact and, despite their own suffering, approaches this task with courage, trust, and love, they will again find an ideal to cherish and offer to other nations. . . .

The sincere quest of youth, which gives us of the older generation deep satisfaction, demands relentless honesty. Youth will find this honesty first of all among those who remained true to themselves during the terror in the shadow of the gallows. It is they who have something to say and to give to youth, for they know the essence of things and will not conceal in trivialities the genuine reasons for our fall into the abyss. Despite all tribulations they work and keep their faith, even if they have forgotten how to laugh and know not if they will ever learn again. They will attempt to help so that our youth may in the future have uninhibited laughter.

Let us work with the youth of other nations in brotherly cooperation. Let us work as good Germans, but conscious of the fact that man is of a higher order than just being a German.

Chronological List

June 15, 1913	Twenty-fifth Jubilee of Kaiser William II
June 30	Extraordinary army and military budget bills
October 16–19	Federated Youth Movement conclave at Hohe Meissner
December	Zabern Affair: crisis of Prussian military intrusion into civilian rule
February, 1914	Statistics indicate 1913 as the greatest year of German industrial production and trade
June 28—August 4	Assassination of Archduke Franz Ferdinand (Austria-Hungary) leads to outbreak of First World War
September 12	German advance on Paris stopped in Battle of the Marne
August 29, 1916	Generals von Hindenburg and Ludendorff take over Supreme High Command: Kaiser overshadowed; totalitarian war economy launched
April 6, 1917	United States declares war on Germany
November 7	Soviet seizure of power in Russia
March 21—April 5, 1918	Final German offensive in France
September 29	General Ludendorff urges Kaiser to sue for peace
October 28—November 5	Mutinies in German navy and armies
November 9	Kaiser abdicates; Scheidemann proclaims German Republic
November 11	Armistice ends First World War
January 5–15, 1919	Ultra-left Spartacist revolt suppressed

February 6	Weimar Constituent Assembly opens
June 28	Germany signs Treaty of Versailles
July 31	New republican constitution adopted at Weimar
February 24, 1920	Hitler proclaims twenty-five points of National Socialist program in Munich
March 13–18	Abortive conservative Kapp *putsch* in Berlin
May 5	Germany receives reparations bill of 132 billion marks
June 6	German Communist party first enters Reichstag with 600,000 votes
April 16, 1922	Treaty of Rapallo normalizes relations between Germany and Russia
August 1922– November 1923	Frenzied climax of German monetary inflation
January 11, 1923	French occupation of Ruhr industrial basin
October	Communist disruption in Saxony, Hamburg, and Thuringia
November 8–9	Abortive Hitler-Ludendorff *putsch* in Munich
April 9, 1924	Dawes Plan gives new stability to German economy
February 28, 1925	Death of President Ebert
April 26	Von Hindenburg elected second president of Weimar republic
October 16	Conclusion of Locarno Treaties; triumph of Stresemann foreign policy
April 24, 1926	Treaty of Berlin: expanded Soviet-German economic relations
September 8	Germany enters League of Nations
August 1929	Visibility of German technology as liner "Bremen" recaptures Blue Riband of North Atlantic and "Graf Zeppelin" flies around the world
September 1929– May 1930	French forces evacuate demilitarized Rhineland
October 3	Death of Gustav Stresemann

October 24	Wall Street stock market crash signals onslaught of the Great Depression, 1929–1933
December 22	German referendum on Young Plan shows majority support for higher reparations payments
March 27, 1930	Republican coalition fails; beginning of rule by Brüning minority cabinet and presidential decree
September 14	Nazi election surge from 12 to 107 Reichstag seats
March 21, 1931	Abortive Austro-German treaty for customs union
May 11–July 15	Collapse of Austrian and German banking systems
July 6	Hoover moratorium on reparations and war debts
October 11	Harzburg Front: Hitler, Hugenberg, Schacht, and Seldte (head of "Stahlhelm") cooperate
1931–1932	Sporadic Nazi-Communist cooperation to destroy the Weimar Republic
January 27, 1932	Hitler address to the *Industrieklub*
April 10	Von Hindenburg re-elected president of Weimar Republic in contest with Hitler
May 30	Chancellor Brüning dismissed
June 16–November 17	Cabinet of Franz von Papen
July 9	Final agreement on reparations for 3 billion marks
July 20	Von Papen coup against Socialist state government of Prussia
November 6	Reichstag elections show major losses for Nazis
December 2–January 28, 1933	Cabinet of General von Schleicher
January 30	Hitler named chancellor
January–February	Expansion of Gestapo (secret political police)
February 27	Reichstag fire: suspension of Bill of Rights; Nazi terror

March 5	Last Reichstag elections of Weimar republic
March 21	Conservative-Nazi patriotic ceremonies at Potsdam
March 23	Reichstag votes suspension of Weimar constitution by giving Hitler dictatorial power till April 1, 1937
April 1	Nationwide anti-Jewish boycott and demonstrations
May 1	May Day taken over by Nazis; suppression of unions
July 14	Nazis force dissolution of all other political parties
July 20	Nazi concordat with Vatican
October 14	Germany leaves the League of Nations
January 26, 1934	Nazi-Polish nonaggression and friendship pact
February–September	Major reorientation of Soviet Russia towards Europe and against Nazi Germany
March–April	German concentration camps under SS control; Himmler to head of Gestapo
June 14–15	First Hitler-Mussolini meeting in Venice
June 30–July 1	Nazi "Blood Purge" of dissident stormtroopers and other enemies
July 25	Abortive Nazi *putsch* in Vienna
August 2	President von Hindenburg dies
August 19	Plebiscite supports Hitler as "Führer and Chancellor" instead of President
March 16, 1935	Germany denounces military clauses of Versailles Treaty
June 18	Anglo-German naval agreement
September 15	Nuremberg anti-Jewish legislation
October 3	Mussolini invades Ethiopia; growing dependence on Germany
March 7, 1936	Germany destroys Locarno Treaties by reoccupation of demilitarized Rhineland
July–August	Nazi propaganda exploits Olympic Games in Berlin
September 14	Proclamation of four year plan to make Germany economically self-sufficient

October 25	Italo-German treaty establishes Rome-Berlin Axis
November 5	Führer conference indicates "solution" of Germany's problems by 1943–1945 (Hossbach Memorandum)
November 25	German-Japanese anti-Comintern pact
February 4, 1938	Nazification of German military and diplomatic commands
March 12–13	Nazi seizure of Austria
September	Czechoslovak crisis culminating in Munich Pact
March 15, 1939	Destruction of Czechoslovakia; Hitler in Prague
April 28	Hitler abrogates pacts with Poland and Britain
May 23	Italo-German Pact of Steel; Führer's conference on imminence of war
June–August	Intensifying Polish-Danzig crisis
August 23	Nazi-Soviet nonaggression and neutrality pact
September 1–3	Second World War begins
September	Blitzkrieg against Poland; formation of SS combat divisions
April 9, 1940	Invasion of Denmark and Norway
May 10	Invasion of Belgium, Holland, and France
June 10	Italy enters the war
June 23	France surrenders at Compiègne
Winter–Spring 1941	Spectacular campaigns of General Rommel in North Africa
March–May	Nazi conquest of the Balkans
June 22	Opening of massive Nazi campaign against Russia
December 5	Leningrad under siege; farthest German penetration into suburbs of Moscow
December 11	Hitler declares war on the United States
January 20, 1942	Hitler authorizes "Final Solution" of German and European Jewish question
April 26	Reichstag confers absolute wartime powers on Hitler
November 7	Allied landings in North Africa

January 31, 1943	Massive German defeat and surrender at Stalingrad
May 7	Defeat of German armies in North Africa
July 21	Announcement of Soviet-sponsored Free Germany National Committee
July 24—August 3	Destruction of Hamburg by intensified air raids
July 25	Fall of Mussolini after Allied invasion of southern Italy
June 6, 1944	Allied landings in Normandy
July 20	Failure of German plot against Hitler
January 1945	Russian and Allied forces invade Germany from East and West
April 30	Suicide of Hitler in Berlin
May 7–8	German forces capitulate at Rheims (France) and Karlshorst (near Berlin)

Bibliography

General Works

Bruck, W. F. *Social and Economic History of Germany from William II to Hitler, 1888–1938*. Cardiff, 1938.

Crippen, H. R. *Germany: A Self-portrait. A Collection of German Writings from 1914 to 1943*. New York, 1944.

Holborn, H. *A History of Modern Germany*, vol. 3. New York, 1969.

Kohn, H., ed. *German History: Some New German Views*. Boston, 1954.

———. *The Mind of Germany: The Education of a Nation*. New York, 1960.

Mann, G. *The History of Germany since 1789*. New York, 1968.

Meinecke, F. *The German Catastrophe: Reflections and Recollections*. Cambridge, Mass., 1950.

Meyer, H. C. *Five Images of Germany: Half a Century of American Views on German History*, 2d ed. Washington, D.C., 1967.

Pinson, K. *Modern Germany: Its History and Civilization*. New York, 1954, 1966.

Rosenberg, A. *The Birth of the German Republic, 1871–1918*. New York, 1931.

Valentin, V. *The German People*. New York, 1946.

Vogt, H. *The Burden of Guilt. . . , 1914–1945*. New York, 1964.

Empire and World War I

Brandenburg, E. *From Bismarck to the World War. . . .* London, 1927.

Cowles, V. *The Kaiser*. New York, 1963.

Dehio, L. *Germany and World Politics in the Twentieth Century*. New York, 1959.

Fischer, F. *Germany's Aims in the First World War*. New York, 1967.

Gatzke, H. *Germany's Drive into the West*. Baltimore, 1950.

Lutz, R. H. *The Fall of the German Empire, 1914–1918*. Stanford, Calif., 1932.

————. *The Causes of German Collapse in 1918*. Stanford, Calif., 1934.

Mendelssohn-Bartholdy, A. *The War and German Society*. New Haven, Conn., 1937.

Meyer, H. C. *Mitteleuropa in German Thought and Action, 1815–1945*. The Hague, 1955.

Townshend, M. E. *The Rise and Fall of Germany's Colonial Empire, 1884–1918*. New York, 1930.

Veblen, T. *Imperial Germany and the Industrial Revolution*. New York, 1915.

Wolff, T. *The Eve of 1914*. London, 1936.

Woodward, E. L. *Great Britain and the German Navy*. London, 1935.

The Revolution and Weimar Republic

Angress, W. *Stillborn Revolution. The Communist Bid for Power in Germany, 1921–1923*. Princeton, N.J., 1963.

Bretton, H. L. *Stresemann and the Revision of Versailles*. Stanford, Calif., 1953.

Coper, R. *Failure of a Revolution: Germany 1918–1919*. Cambridge, 1955.

Deak, I. *Weimar Germany's Left-Wing Intellectuals. . . .* Berkeley, Calif., 1968.

Gay, P. *Weimar Culture: The Outsider as Insider*. New York, 1968.

Halperin, S. W. *Germany Tried Democracy, 1918–1933*. New York, 1946.

Kosok, P. *Modern Germany: A Study of Conflicting Loyalties*. Chicago, 1933.

Luehr, E. *The New German Republic*. New York, 1929.

Quigley, H., and Clark, R. T. *Republican Germany*. New York, 1928.

Ryder, A. J. *The German Revolution of 1918. . . .* Princeton, N.J., 1963.

Turner, H. *Stresemann and the Politics of the Weimar Republic*. Princeton, N.J., 1963.

Waldman, E. *The Spartacist Uprising of 1919.* . . . Milwaukee, Wisc., 1958.

Wheeler-Bennett, J. W. *Wooden Titan: Hindenburg in Twenty Years of German History 1914–1934.* New York, 1936.

The Emergence of National Socialism

Abel, T. *Why Hitler Came to Power.* . . . New York, 1938.

Bullock, A. *Hitler: A Study in Tyranny.* New York, 1952.

Butler, R. D. *The Roots of National Socialism, 1789–1933.* London, 1941.

Heiden, K. *A History of National Socialism.* London, 1934.

———. *Der Fuehrer: Hitler's Rise to Power.* New York, 1944.

Mosse, G. L. *The Crisis of German Ideology: Intellectual Origins of the Third Reich.* New York, 1964.

Orlow, D. *The History of the Nazi Party, 1919–1933.* Pittsburgh, 1969.

Snell, J. L. *The Nazi Revolution: Germany's Guilt or Germany's Fate?* Boston, 1959.

Tonsor, S. J. *National Socialism: Conservative Reaction or Nihilist Revolt?* New York, 1959.

Viereck, P. *Metapolitics: The Roots of the Nazi Mind.* New York, 1941.

National Socialism, 1933–1939

Allen, W. S. *The Nazi Seizure of Power: The Experience of a Single German Small Town, 1930–1935.* Chicago, 1965.

Brady, R. A. *The Spirit and Structure of German Fascism.* New York, 1937.

Fest, J. C. *The Face of the Third Reich: Portraits of the Nazi Leadership.* New York, 1970.

Hoover C. B. *Germany Enters the Third Reich.* New York, 1933.

Lehmann-Haupt, H. *Art under a Dictatorship.* London, 1954.

Lochner, L. *Tycoons and Tyrant: German Industry from Hitler to Adenauer.* Chicago, 1959.

Mayer, M., *They Thought They Were Free.* Chicago, 1955.

Mosse, G. L., ed. *Nazi Culture: Intellectual, Cultural and Social Life in the Third Reich.* New York, 1966.

Neumann, F. *Behemoth: The Structure and Practice of National Socialism.* New York, 1942.

Pollock, J. K. *The Government of Greater Germany*. New York, 1940.

Roberts, S. H. *The House That Hitler Built*. New York, 1938.

Roussy de Sales, R. de., ed. *Adolf Hitler: My New Order*. New York, 1941.

Schoenbaum, D. *Hitler's Social Revolution: Class and Status in Nazi Germany, 1933–1939*. New York, 1966.

Shirer, W. L. *Berlin Diary, 1934–1941*. New York, 1941.

Speer, A. *Inside the Third Reich: Memoirs*. New York, 1970.

Tolishus, O. *They Wanted War*. New York, 1940.

Wheaton, E. B. *Prelude to Calamity. The Nazi Revolution, 1933–1935*. New York, 1968.

The Emergence of the SS State

Höhne, H. *The Order of the Death's Head*. . . . New York, 1970.

Kersten, F. *The Kersten Memoirs*. London, 1956.

Kogon, E. *The Theory and Practice of Hell*. New York, 1951.

Krausnick, H. et al. *Anatomy of the SS State*. New York, 1968.

Reitlinger, G. *The Final Solution*. . . . London, 1953.

———. *The S.S., Alibi of a Nation, 1922–1945*. London, 1956.

Trevor-Roper, H. R. *Hitler's Secret Conversations, 1941–1944*. New York, 1953.

———. *The Last Days of Hitler*. New York, 1947.

———, ed. *The Borman Letters*. London, 1954.

Youth and Education

Becker, H. *German Youth: Bond or Free*. London, 1946.

Ebeling, H. *The German Youth Movement*. London, 1945.

Hartshorne, E. Y. *German Youth and the Nazi Dream of Victory*. New York, 1941.

Laqueur, W. Z. *Young Germany: A History of the German Youth Movement*. New York, 1962.

Lilge, F. *The Abuse of Learning: The Failure of the German Universities*. New York, 1948.

Ringer, F. K. *The Decline of the Mandarins: The German Academic Community, 1890–1933*. Cambridge, Mass., 1969.

Scholl, I. *Students against Tyranny*. Middletown, Conn., 1970.

Ziemer, G. *Education for Death*. . . . New York, 1941.

Women in Germany

Kirkpatrick, C. *Women in Nazi Germany*. Indianapolis, 1937.
Puckett, H. W. *Germany's Women Go Forward*. New York, 1929, 1967.

German Conservatism

Dorpalen, A. *Hindenburg and the Politics of the Weimar Republic*. Princeton, 1964.
Klemperer, K. von. *Germany's New Conservatism: Its History and Dilemma in the 20th Century*. Princeton, 1957.
Rauschning, H. *The Revolution of Nihilism*. New York, 1939.
———. *The Conservative Revolution*. New York, 1941.
Stern, F. *The Politics of Cultural Despair*. Berkeley, Calif., 1961.
Waite, R. G. L. *Vanguard of Nazism: The Free Corps Movement in Postwar Germany, 1918–1923*. Cambridge, Mass., 1952.

The German Working Classes

Anderson, E. *Hammer or Anvil: The Story of the German Working Class Movement*. London, 1945.
Berlau, A. J. *The German Social Democratic Party, 1914–1921*. New York, 1949.
Maehl, W. H. *German Militarism and Socialism*. Lincoln, Neb., 1968.
Roth, G. *The Social Democrats in Imperial Germany*. Totowa, N.J., 1963.
Schorske, C. *German Social Democracy, 1905–1917*. Cambridge, Mass., 1955.
Sturmthal, A. *The Tragedy of European Labor, 1918–1939*. London, 1944.
Valtin, J. *Out of the Night*. New York, 1941.

Germany and Russia

Carr, E. H. *German-Soviet Relations between Two World Wars*. Baltimore, 1951.
Dallin, A. *German Rule in Russia, 1941–1945*. New York, 1957.
Fischer, R. *Stalin and German Communism*. Cambridge, Mass., 1948.

Hilger, G., and Meyer, A. G. *The Incompatible Allies—A Memoir-History of German-Soviet Relations, 1918–1941.* New York, 1953.

Laqueur, W. Z. *Russia and Germany: A Century of Conflict.* London, 1965.

Weinberg, G. L. *Germany and the Soviet Union, 1939–1941.* London, 1944.

Nazi Foreign Policy

Deakin, F. W. *The Brutal Friendship: Mussolini, Hitler.* . . . London, 1962.

Presseisen, E. L. *Germany and Japan: A Study in Totalitarian Diplomacy.* New York, 1958.

Robertson, E. M. *Hitler's Prewar Policy and Military Plans, 1933–1939.* New York, 1963.

Seabury, P. *The Wilhelmstrasse: A Study of German Diplomats under the Nazi Regime.* Berkeley, Calif., 1954.

Wiskemann, E. *The Rome-Berlin Axis.* London, 1949.

German Military-Political Relationships

Craig, G. A. *The Politics of the Prussian Army, 1640–1945.* New York, 1955.

Goerlitz, W. *History of the German General Staff, 1657–1945.* New York, 1953.

O'Neill, R. J. *The German Army and the Nazi Party, 1933–1939.* London, 1966.

Taylor, T. *Sword and Swastika: Generals and Nazis in the Third Reich.* New York, 1952.

Wheeler-Bennett, J. W. *The Nemesis of Power: The German Army in Politics.* New York, 1954.

Church and State in Nazi Germany

Cochrane, A. C. *The Church's Confession under Hitler.* Philadelphia, 1962.

Frey, A. *Cross and Swastika: The Ordeal of the German Church.* London, 1938.

Mason, J. B. *Hitler's First Foes: A Study in Religion and Politics.* Minneapolis, Minn., 1936.

Micklem, N. *National Socialism and the Catholic Church*. London, 1939.

The German Resistance

Dulles, A. W. *Germany's Underground*. New York, 1947.
Manuel, R., and Fraenkel, H. *The Men Who Tried to Kill Hitler*. New York, 1964.
Prittie, T. *Germans against Hitler*. Boston, 1964.
Ritter, G. *The German Resistance: Carl Goerdeler's Struggle against Tyranny*. New York, 1958.

Population Transfers and Migration

Koehl, R. L. *RKFDV: German Resettlement and Population Policy, 1939–1945*. Cambridge, Mass., 1957.
Kulischer, E. M. *Europe on the Move: War and Population Changes, 1917–1947*. New York, 1948.
Proudfoot, M. J. *European Refugees, 1939–1952*. London, 1957.
Schechtmann, J. B. *European Population Transfers, 1939–1945*. New York, 1946.

Germany in Ruin

Bourke-White, M. *"Dear Fatherland, Rest Quietly."* . . . New York, 1946.
Gollancz, V. *In Darkest Germany*. London, 1947.
Knauth, P. *Germany in Defeat*. New York, 1946.
Spender, S. *European Witness*. New York, 1946.
Stolper, G. *German Realities*. New York, 1948.
White, W. L. *Report on the Germans*. New York, 1947.

Index

DOCUMENTARY HISTORY OF WESTERN CIVILIZATION
Edited by Eugene C. Black and Leonard W. Levy

ANCIENT AND MEDIEVAL HISTORY OF THE WEST

Morton Smith: ANCIENT GREECE *

A. H. M. Jones: A HISTORY OF ROME THROUGH THE FIFTH CENTURY
Vol. I: *The Republic*
Vol. II: *The Empire*

Deno Geanakoplos: BYZANTINE EMPIRE *

Marshall W. Baldwin: CHRISTIANITY THROUGH THE THIRTEENTH CENTURY

Bernard Lewis: ISLAM TO 1453 *

David Herlihy: HISTORY OF FEUDALISM

William M. Bowsky: RISE OF COMMERCE AND TOWNS *

David Herlihy: MEDIEVAL CULTURE AND SOCIETY

EARLY MODERN HISTORY

Hanna H. Gray: CULTURAL HISTORY OF THE RENAISSANCE *

Florence Edler de Roover: MONEY, BANKING,
AND COMMERCE, THIRTEENTH THROUGH SIXTEENTH CENTURIES *

V. J. Parry: THE OTTOMAN EMPIRE *

Ralph E. Giesey: EVOLUTION OF THE DYNASTIC STATE *

J. H. Parry: THE EUROPEAN RECONNAISSANCE: *Selected Documents*

Hans J. Hillerbrand: THE PROTESTANT REFORMATION

John C. Olin: THE CATHOLIC COUNTER REFORMATION *

Orest Ranum: THE CENTURY OF LOUIS XIV *

Thomas Hegarty: RUSSIAN HISTORY THROUGH PETER THE GREAT *

Marie Boas Hall: NATURE AND NATURE'S LAWS

Barry E. Supple: HISTORY OF MERCANTILISM *

Geoffrey Symcox: IMPERIALISM, WAR, AND DIPLOMACY, 1550-1763 *

Herbert H. Rowen: THE LOW COUNTRIES *

C. A. Macartney: THE HABSBURG AND HOHENZOLLERN DYNASTIES
IN THE SEVENTEENTH AND EIGHTEENTH CENTURIES

Lester G. Crocker: THE AGE OF ENLIGHTENMENT

Robert and Elborg Forster: EUROPEAN SOCIETY IN THE EIGHTEENTH CENTURY

* In preparation